TIN MEN
STEEL
SOLDIERS

True stories of the 82 men from a Pennsylvania mill town
who gave their lives for freedom
during and immediately after World War II.

TIN MEN

STEEL

SOLDIERS

John J. Turanin

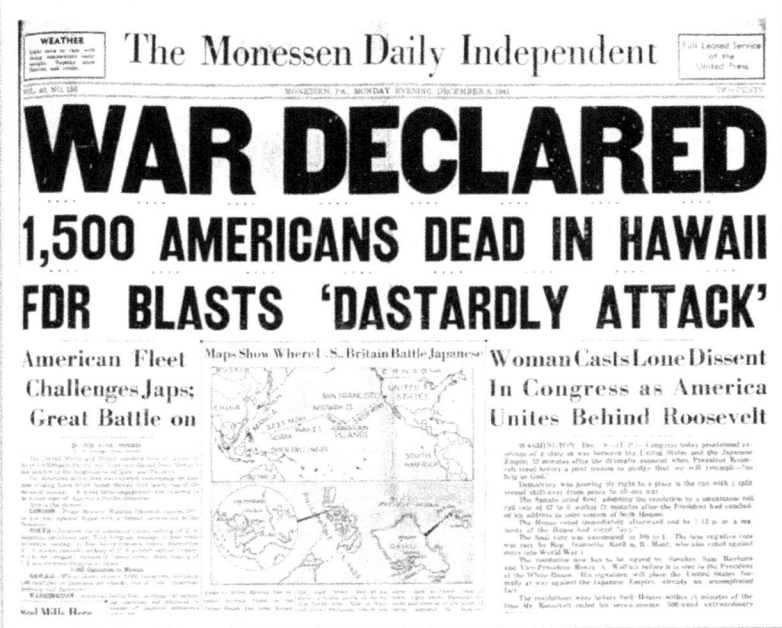

The Monessen Daily Independent

WAR DECLARED
1,500 AMERICANS DEAD IN HAWAII
FDR BLASTS 'DASTARDLY ATTACK'

American Fleet Challenges Japs; Great Battle on

Woman Casts Lone Dissent In Congress as America Unites Behind Roosevelt

ISBN: 979-8-218-68363-4

Library of Congress Control Number 2025909653

PUBLISHING HISTORY

Self-published paperback edition: June 2025, updated September 2025 El Dorado Hills, CA

PRINTED IN THE UNITED STATES OF AMERICA

Cover Art: Aerial view of the plant of the Pittsburgh Steel Company and Pennsylvania & Lake Erie Railroad Lines at Monessen, Pennsylvania, 1960, one of a series of paintings of the P&LE Railroad by Howard Fogg, reprinted with permission

To Mom and Dad,

This book is dedicated to the families of Monessen, Pennsylvania, who gave their sons in the fight against those who would deny freedom to others.

Although World War II ended in 1945, the freedom for all citizens of the world still remains elusive.

We remember all who lost their lives in WWII and strive to honor their sacrifices for freedom.

Contents
in Chronological Order of Loss

CONTENTS BY SURNAME IX

LOCATIONS OF LOSSES X

PREFACE 1

INTRODUCTION 5

1941-1942 10

    S2c LOUIS C. STEPHENS 14

    RM2c FRANK BARTOSIK 20

    PVT JACK E. JENNINGS 26

    FM/WT JACOVOS MONIOS 30

    SGT EDWARD R. CIPRIANI 35

    SGT JOHN W. WARGO 43

1943 46

    PVT CHARLES H. STONAGE 49

    PVT VICTOR A. TRILLI 56

    FM JOHN J. HOTOVCHIN 62

    PVT GEORGE SHOLTIS 67

    PVT MICHAEL GRAMATIKOS 70

    SGT JOSEPH O. SCRIP 73

    PVT JOHN KVAKA JR 76

    T/SGT AUGUST RESTAINO 80

    S2c JOHN E. ZAPORA 85

    CPL ALBERT S. WARGO 92

    CPL JOSEPH MALENA, JR. 98

    FL O THOMAS A. IRVINE 102

1944 107

    PVT ROSS J. NACCARATO 110

    PFC CHARLES W. LUCAS 117

    ENS WILLIAM E. NICODEN 122

PFC Andrew Desack, Jr. 125

T/Sgt Harry E. Boyer 128

Sgt Paul F. Newman 134

Pvt James Mazzer 139

S/Sgt Leonard A. Mihalich 142

Pvt Nicholas Kafkalas 148

Cpl Michael Leavor 153

PFC George Evanich 158

Sgt Patsy S. Columbus 162

S/Sgt John Komlos 166

Pvt Anthony Thiry 170

T/Sgt Ernest C. Renzetti 173

1Lt John Kalie 176

Pvt William H. Hagerty 181

1Lt William C. Caville 185

Sgt Wayne R. McVay 190

T/4 Paul Denitti 194

PFC Christopher S. Parnella 198

1Lt Bernard J. Rosenson 202

Pvt Joseph P. Leone 208

T/4 Joseph J. Skruber 212

Ens Arthur J. Stockus 219

PFC Joseph M. Fiorillo 224

T/5 Nicholas Ravenchak 229

PFC Anthony Saridakis 234

T/5 James Woods 237

PFC Pacifico Sacchini 241

Pvt Alexander Koszykowski 244

Pvt William K. Oliphant 248

PFC Michael Redish 251

SM2c John E. Varga 255

Cpl Cyril M. Liscik 262

Ens Elmer A. Harkema 267

PFC Walter Zajaczkowski 272

S/Sgt George T. Stanish 276

PFC Stephen Malinchak 281

S/Sgt Wallace Marcinkiewicz 284

Pvt Nicholas Beck 288

1945 292

    2LT Bernard F. Quinlan 295

    PVT Angelo L. Imburgia 301

    PVT Stanley Zazac 305

    PVT Michael Demko 312

    2LT Stephen G. Monick, Jr. 315

    T/4 Orlo Junk 322

    2LT John Matola, Jr. 326

    PFC Joseph P. Platko 333

    PFC Anthony F. Laszewski 336

    PFC Ernest J. Kachursky 341

    1LT Anthony R. Rizzuto 344

    SGT Carl Ramsey 349

    PFC Andrew Evanich, Jr. 355

    AOM3c Paul Grata 359

    PVT Andrew Zrenchak 365

    PFC Louis G. Katsuleris 370

    S/SGT Carl A. Kronander 373

    2LT Carl G. Cekola 376

    SGT Jack W. Swaney 382

    2LT Hugh B. Smyth 387

    PVT Hosey Dawkins 396

AFTER THE WAR 401

    PFC Walter L. Kujawa, Jr. 403

    CPL Matthew M. Comko 406

    Paying More Than Our Share 410

AFTERWORD 411

ACKNOWLEDGEMENTS 415

BIBLIOGRAPHY 416

ABOUT THE AUTHOR 439

CONTENTS BY SURNAME

Bartosik, Frank 20
Beck, Nicholas 288
Boyer, Harry E. 128
Caville, William C. 185
Cekola, Carl G. 376
Cipriani, Edward R. 35
Columbus, Patsy S. 162
Comko, Matthew M. 406
Dawkins, Hosey 396
Demko, Michael 312
Denitti, Paul 194
Desack, Andrew Jr. 125
Evanich, Andrew Jr. 355
Evanich, George 158
Fiorillo, Joseph M. 224
Gramatikos, Michael 70
Grata, Paul 359
Hagerty, William H. 181
Harkema, Elmer A. 267
Hotovchin, John J. 62
Imburgia, Angelo L. 301
Irvine, Thomas A. 102
Jennings, Jack E. 26
Junk, Orlo 322
Kachursky, Ernest J. 341
Kafkalas, Nicholas 148
Kalie, John 176
Katsuleris, Louis G. 370
Komlos, John 166
Koszykowski, Alexander 244
Kronander, Carl A. 373
Kujawa, Walter L. Jr. 403
Kvaka, John Jr. 76
Laszewski, Anthony F. 336
Leavor, Michael 153
Leone, Joseph P. 208
Liscik, Cyril M. 262
Lucas, Charles W. 117
Malena, Joseph Jr. 98
Malinchak, Stephen 281
Marcinkiewicz, Wallace 284

Matola, John Jr. 326
Mazzer, James 139
McVay, Wayne R. 190
Mihalich, Leonard A. 142
Monick, Stephen G. Jr. 315
Monios, Jacovos 30
Naccarato, Ross J. 110
Newman, Paul F. 134
Nicoden, William E. 122
Oliphant, William K. 248
Parnella, Christopher S. 198
Platko, Joseph P. 333
Quinlan, Bernard F. 295
Ramsey, Carl 349
Ravenchak, Nicholas 229
Redish, Michael 251
Renzetti, Ernest C. 173
Restaino, August. 80
Rizzuto, Anthony R. 344
Rosenson, Bernard J. 202
Sacchini, Pacifico 241
Saridakis, Anthony 234
Scrip, Joseph O. 73
Sholtis, George 67
Skruber, Joseph J. 212
Smyth, Hugh B. 387
Stanish, George T. 276
Stephens, Louis C. 14
Stockus, Arthur J. 219
Stonage, Charles H. 49
Swaney, Jack W. 382
Thiry, Anthony 170
Trilli, Victor A. 56
Varga, John E. 255
Wargo, Albert S. 92
Wargo, John W. 43
Woods, James 237
Zajaczkowski, Walter 272
Zapora, John E. 85
Zazac, Stanley 305
Zrenchak, Andrew 365

LOCATIONS OF LOSSES

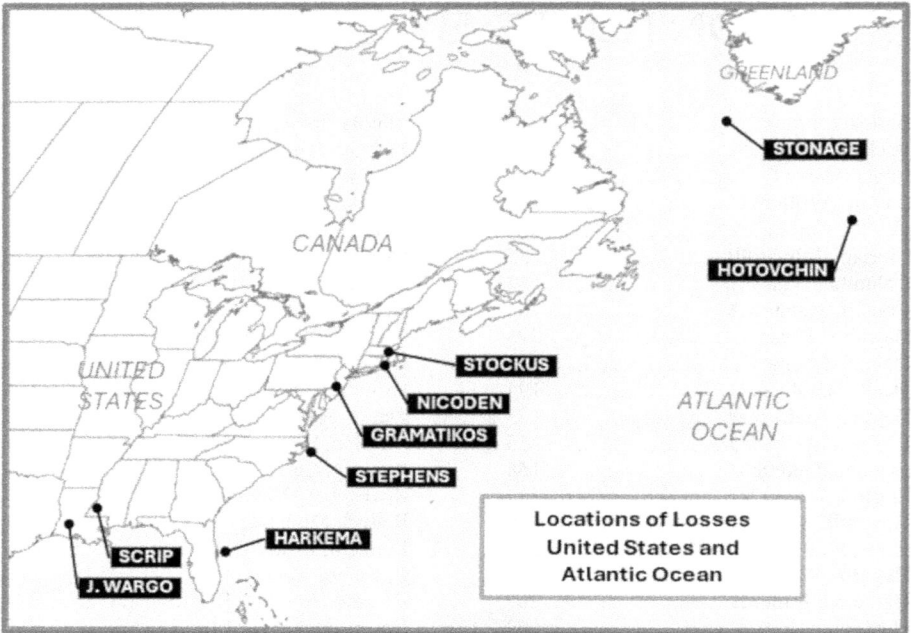

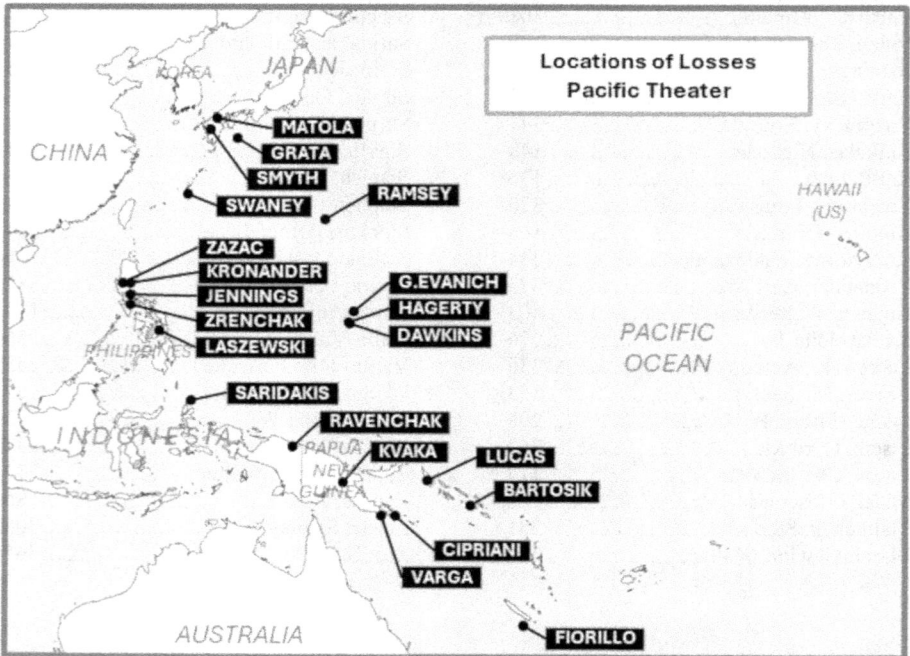

STONAGE

HOTOVCHIN

GREENLAND

CANADA

UNITED STATES

STOCKUS

NICODEN

GRAMATIKOS

STEPHENS

HARKEMA

SCRIP

J. WARGO

ATLANTIC OCEAN

**Locations of Losses
United States and
Atlantic Ocean**

**Locations of Losses
Pacific Theater**

KOREA

JAPAN

CHINA

MATOLA

GRATA

SMYTH

SWANEY

RAMSEY

HAWAII (US)

ZAZAC

KRONANDER

JENNINGS

ZRENCHAK

LASZEWSKI

PHILIPPINES

G.EVANICH

HAGERTY

DAWKINS

PACIFIC OCEAN

SARIDAKIS

INDONESIA

RAVENCHAK

PAPUA NEW GUINEA

KVAKA

LUCAS

BARTOSIK

CIPRIANI

VARGA

AUSTRALIA

FIORILLO

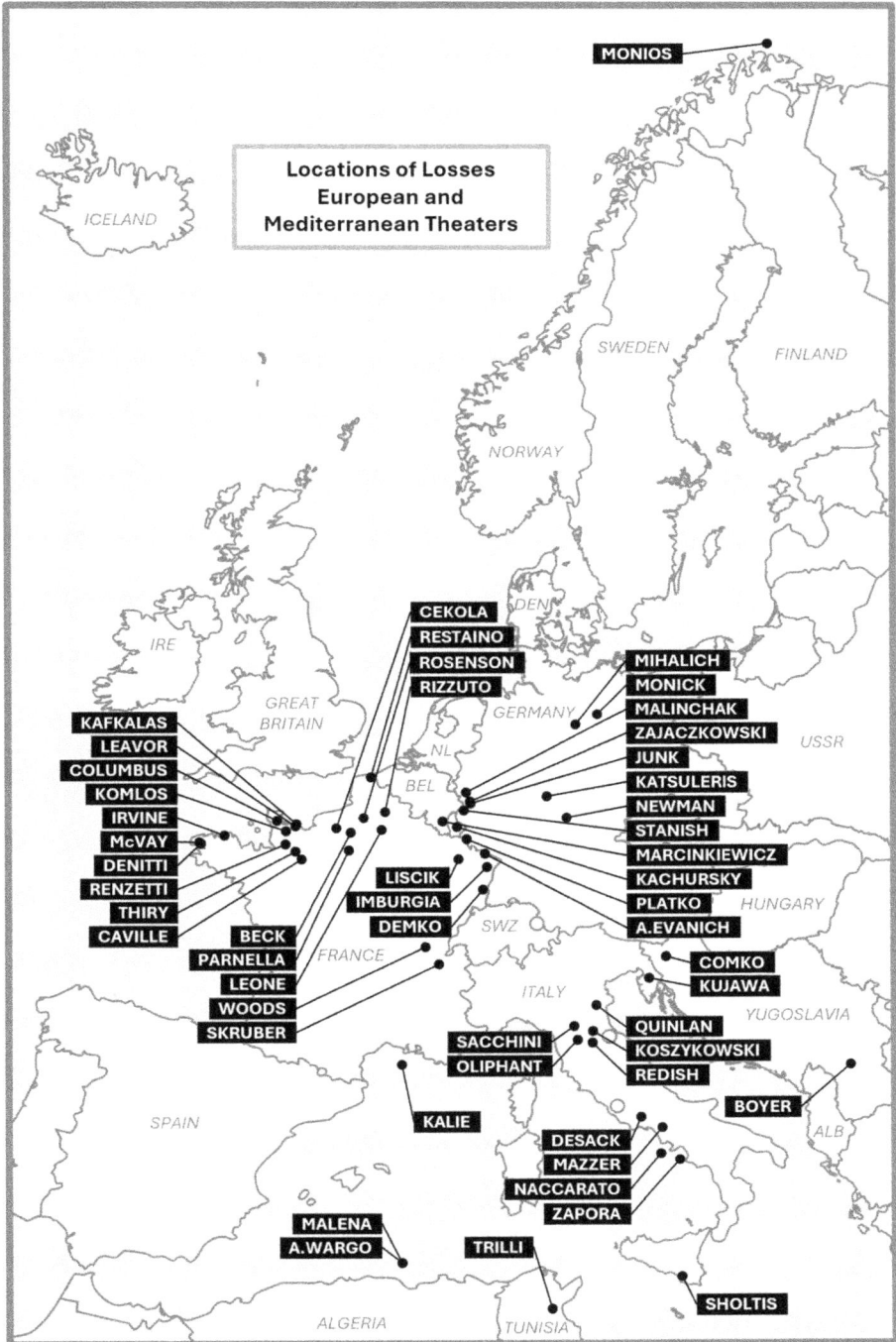

Locations of Losses
European and
Mediterranean Theaters

ICELAND

MONIOS

SWEDEN

FINLAND

NORWAY

IRE

GREAT
BRITAIN

DEN

USSR

CEKOLA
RESTAINO
ROSENSON
RIZZUTO

GERMANY

NL

BEL

MIHALICH
MONICK
MALINCHAK
ZAJACZKOWSKI
JUNK
KATSULERIS
NEWMAN
STANISH
MARCINKIEWICZ
KACHURSKY
PLATKO
A.EVANICH

HUNGARY

KAFKALAS
LEAVOR
COLUMBUS
KOMLOS
IRVINE
McVAY
DENITTI
RENZETTI
THIRY
CAVILLE

LISCIK
IMBURGIA
DEMKO

SWZ

BECK
PARNELLA
LEONE
WOODS
SKRUBER

FRANCE

COMKO
KUJAWA

ITALY

YUGOSLAVIA

SACCHINI
OLIPHANT

QUINLAN
KOSZYKOWSKI
REDISH

SPAIN

KALIE

BOYER

ALB

DESACK
MAZZER
NACCARATO
ZAPORA

MALENA
A.WARGO

TRILLI

SHOLTIS

ALGERIA

TUNISIA

PREFACE

Gold Star Mother of World War II

A Service Flag displayed in a window of a home (Evening Sentinel, Carlisle PA, Dec 15, 1941)

After retiring from a 45 year career, I learned about a team of volunteers who are writing memorial stories for every one of the 421,000 United States service members who lost their lives during World War II. As someone who grew up knowing many from my parents' generation who fought in the war, I was immediately intrigued.

The effort, under a global nonprofit organization founded by Don Milne, is called Stories Behind the Stars (SBTS). The name is in recognition of the gold stars on Service Flags displayed in the windows of homes during the war. A Service Flag contained a blue star for each family member in military service. If a service member lost their life, the blue star would be replaced with a gold one.

Blue stars were symbols of pride. Gold stars were symbols of painful sacrifice. No family wanted a Gold Star.

SBTS was (and still is) seeking volunteer researchers and writers to help compose memorial stories about all men and women US service members who paid the ultimate price in the global conflict. These stories are posted on-line and can be read at gravesite on internet-connected devices by visitors.

Author's Father
S/SGT John G. Turanin
of Monessen PA

My father and father-in-law served in the US Army Air Corps in WWII and were fortunate to return unharmed. I have always been intrigued by their experiences during the war and have been a voracious consumer of WWII history. Assisting non-profit warbird restoration projects and volunteering at aviation museums have kept me engaged with our WWII history. But I could not think of a more compelling way to apply my skills during retirement than to join the SBTS effort.

Author's Father-in-law
S/SGT Peter Findrick of
Duquesne PA,

Writing hundreds of memorial stories with SBTS has been a deeply affecting personal experience. But my most rewarding endeavor has been to write about those who grew up with my parents during the years leading up to WWII. Like most of the US service members in these stories, my parents were first generation Americans. My grandparents immigrated to the US from Central and Southern Europe before WWI (after arriving safely, their transport ships were later torpedoed and sunk by German U-boats in WWI). They raised large families, lost children to diseases, and suffered through the Great Depression.

My paternal grandparents immigrated to the US in the early 1900's from the Carpathian Mountain region in what is now western Ukraine. They lived hand-to-mouth yet gave birth to nine children, two dying before the age of 3 yrs. My grandfather told of the hazards working in "The Tin Mill", having once witnessed a co-worker accidentally step into a trough of molten metal, losing both legs. After my grandfather's emergency appendectomy, his doctor made daily home visits for months to clean and dress his open surgical wound without the benefit of pain drugs. Their four-room home on Monessen's Second Avenue had just two bedrooms for nine people, one toilet in the dirt-floor basement, and a wood and coal stove to heat the entire home. The children took their baths one after the other on Saturday night, with the rinse water from each child becoming the bath water for the next. A sheet hung from the ceiling provided their only privacy. They moved to a larger home on Donner Avenue in 1946 with the steel mill in their backyard.

The Donner Avenue home of the author's grandparents, to the right of the house with trees, 1946-1970. (Photo ca 1933, source unknown)

★ ★ ★

The citizens in these stories walked the same streets as my parents, attended the same schools, shopped the same markets, and shared the joys and hardships of their hometowns. I also walked these streets when visiting my grandparents during the 1960's and 1970's. Writing these stories was a personal debt that I owed to these communities and to these families.

If you think that you could write these stories, too, give it a try. I hope that you, like me, will find it to be immensely satisfying.

★ ★ ★

The information contained herein was uncovered during 2022-25 in records within in the public domain, and therefore not all sources are cited herein. Sources also include Individual Deceased Personnel Files obtained from the US Army Archives at Fort Knox and the National Archives, as well as unit histories from the Air Force Historical Research Agency. A public family tree and individual profile has been created on Ancestry.com for each fallen service member, which serves as a repository for their public documents and further reference.

Each of these stories was written as a stand-alone memorial and posted on the military website Fold3.com. Thus, readers may notice the intentional reuse of story structure and restatement of key historical facts in each subsequent story.

Any corrections are welcomed and may be brought to my attention at jjturanin@gmail.com.

The Author, far right, and his cousins enjoying watermelon in the backyard of their grandparents' home on Donner Avenue, Monessen, PA, 1964. Beyond the fence are rail cars hauling slag waste from the steel mill, just behind them.

★ ★ ★

INTRODUCTION

On December 7, 1941, most citizens of Monessen, Pennsylvania, were relaxing at home on the cloudy 40-degree Sunday afternoon. Many wage-earners were hard at work on the day shift at the local steel mills. The mills were operating around the clock, seven days a week to supply America's industrial base.

At 2:30 PM Eastern Time, the radios across the city interrupted their broadcasts with the news: The United States military bases at Pearl Harbor, Hawaii, the Philippines, and Guam were attacked by Japanese forces. Diplomacy between nations during 1941 had failed to sustain peace. The next day, the US declared war on Japan, bringing the nation into World War II. The citizens of Monessen stepped up to do their part.

✷ ✷ ✷

Forty-three years earlier, Monessen [mah-NES-sen] was founded by land speculators along the Monongahela [mah-NAHNG-gah-HEE-lah] River in Western Pennsylvania. The name of the town was a combination of the words "Monongahela" and "Essen", the German industrial city. Entrepreneurs and industrialists saw its geographic location as a perfect nexus of the region's natural resources of metal ores and coal and the river's natural transportation route to deliver to the mills their incoming materials and to ship their outputs downstream. Workers were needed to complete their economic formula.

Word quickly traveled to other states and to Europe that good jobs and new livelihoods were to be found in Monessen. People flocked to Monessen from within Pennsylvania, nearby states, and countries across the Atlantic.

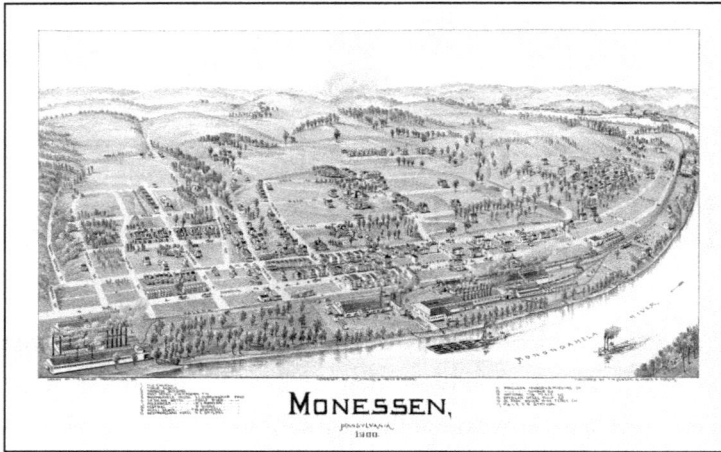

Monessen, PA ca 1900 (TM Fowler & JB Moyer)

People came to Monessen to work at the factories of Pittsburgh Steel, American Tin Plate (known as "The Tin Mill", acquired by Carnegie Steel), Page Steel and Wire, and other smaller operations. Within thirty years of its founding, Monessen had transformed into a city of more than 20,000 people. South of Pittsburgh, it had become one of the largest cities along the Monongahela River, a region known as "The Mon Valley". When Western Pennsylvanians heard talk about Monessen, they knew that tin and steel were the economic drivers of the city.

Monessen work was hard, gritty, and dangerous. Most laborers walked from their homes to the mills each day. Their spouses, parents, or siblings took care of the children while doing their best to put food on their tables. Families tended to their vegetable gardens and fruit trees, pickled and jarred the harvest, and cured meat at home. Some made their own clothes which were patched and handed

Pittsburgh Steel Mills, Monessen PA ca early 1900's (Postcard)

down when outgrown by the older children. Everyone contributed their sweat and ingenuity.

Many citizens of Monessen had immigrated during the 1900's, 1910's, and 1920's from the poorest countries of Eastern and Southern Europe: Slovakia, Poland, Hungary, Slovenia, Croatia, Italy, and Greece. Others migrated northward from the depressed agricultural regions in the southern United States. Families settled in neighborhoods where their languages and cultures of their homelands were shared. Neighbors formed churches, clubs, and friendships where they celebrated blessings and navigated hardships.

But most kids in Monessen who grew up to serve in WWII only experienced scarcity and difficulty. They witnessed parents and siblings ravaged by diseases such as

Downtown Monessen, ca late 1930's (City of Monessen Website)

influenza, tuberculosis, typhoid fever, and pneumonia. They learned to go without when the family breadwinners lost their jobs during the Great Depression. But these times did not feel unusual... it was just how life was. They made the best with what they had and were just as happy because they had never before experienced lives of abundance.

By 1940, the nation was emerging from the Great Depression and things were looking up. The mills were running around the clock. People were working. Those who sensed a patriotic duty volunteered for Monessen's Company D of the Pennsylvania National Guard. Company D left Monessen in February 1941 for a year of training at Indiantown Gap, Pennsylvania, which would be cut short before the end of the year.

Monessen's Company D of the Pennsylvania National Guard. Four lost their lives in WWII.
(Monessen Daily Independent, February 25, 1941)

But in December 1941, world events finally hit home. The US was going to war, and citizens from Monessen would join the fray. By the end of the war in August 1945, nearly 3,500 had left Monessen to serve in the armed forces. One of every six citizens had worn the uniform of the American military.

Eighty-two men did not return to Monessen alive. Some breathed their last in places that Monessen folks could recognize: Italy, France, Belgium, Germany, and even stateside. But many lost their lives in places unfamiliar to the Mon Valley locals: Tunisia, New Guinea, Iwo Jima, Luzon, Okinawa, and on the vast waters of the Atlantic, Pacific, and Mediterranean.

An idea attributed to several sources is this:

We die twice, once when we take our last breath, and the second time, when our name is last spoken.

By telling the stories of these men, their names can continue to be spoken by future generations, giving life to their spirits and their legacies.

* * *

There are many ways to present these stories... in alphabetical order, by branch of service, by date of enlistment, by geography, and by other organizing schemes. My goal was to convey an understanding of these losses within the historical progression of WWII. Thus, the book presents these stories in the chronological order of their losses as the war unfolds. The book is divided into periods during the war: 1941-1942, 1943, 1944, 1945, and After the War (1946). Each summarizes the period's major events which occurred, followed by the stories of each Monessen Fallen service member in order of their loss.

The names of all Monessen WWII Fallen service members are inscribed on the WWII Veterans Memorial Tablet, located at the intersection of Grand Boulevard and Euclid Drive in Monessen City Park.

***

Directly or indirectly, the families of these 82 men relied upon Monessen's tin and steel mills to sustain their livelihoods. One way or another, making tin and steel put food on their tables and coins in their pockets.

Many young Monessen men of the 1940's possessed tin's beneficial qualities. Like tin, they were adaptable and could withstand stress. They could be stretched without tearing and bent without breaking. These 82 Monessen men left home for war, and in the process, faced their ultimate fears. By placing themselves in harm's way, these "Tin Men" proved their bravery, and became Monessen's "Steel Soldiers".

***

1941-1942

"The war has really come home to us now"

Joseph Lescanac, Mayor of Monessen, April 22, 1942,
upon learning of the city's first loss in WWII

O n the eve of the United States' entry into World War II, the nation was ill-prepared to fight a global conflict. The military manpower of the US ranked just 17th in the world. Air forces around the world were still in their nascent stages, and the US had only 26,000 servicemen in its Army Air Force equipped mostly with obsolete aircraft. The Navy was in better shape with 380,000 personnel, but nowhere near the number of ships necessary to wage global warfare.

In the years leading up to 1941, global war had already erupted. For better or worse, the US had stayed isolated, trying to avoid involvement in far-flung conflicts.

Germany had long been executing the "Third Reich" political-military strategy of expansion of its Fuhrer Adolph Hitler. They entered alliances with the like-minded leaders of Italy and Japan. By the end of 1940, Germany had invaded Czechoslovakia, Austria, Poland, France, Denmark, Norway, Belgium, Luxembourg, and Netherlands. In 1941, Germany continued its aggression by invading Yugoslavia, Greece, and the Soviet Union. Pursuing its own empire-building aspirations, Italy had expanded into Ethiopia, Albania, and was invading France by 1940.

Japan had assumed control over Korea from the Soviets in 1905. By 1940, Japan had invaded China and French Indochina. Under the guise of their Greater East Asia Co-Prosperity Sphere, Japan rolled out an empire-building strategy to replace the influence of the Western powers of Great Britain, Netherlands, France, and the US over Asia with its own.

Even before the entry of the US into the war, the Battle of the Atlantic was being waged by German submarines against convoys of merchant ships hauling supplies from the US to Great Britain and the Soviet Union.

The US Congress, recognizing that the US might be drawn into war, passed the Selective Service and Training Act of September 1940, creating the first peacetime draft for men 21-35 yrs of age. Over 16 million men signed-up for the draft on its first day of registration, October 16, 1940. A month later, the first draftees headed off to training camps.

For the citizens of Monessen in 1941, the worries of war ranked far below the worries of earning a day's wage, putting food on the table, and raising families. Although some Monessenites were already serving in the US armed forces and merchant marines at far-flung outposts, concerns for their safety were mostly limited to their families.

The impact of the Japanese attack on the US military bases at Pearl Harbor, Hawaii and the Philippine Islands on December 7, 1941, is well known. The following day, the US declared war on the Japanese empire, followed by declaration of war

The Monessen Daily Independent

MONESSEN, PA., THURSDAY, EVENING, DECEMBER 11, 1941

U. S. AT WAR WITH GERMANY, ITALY

Yankee Planes Sink Jap Battleship Near Manila

'WE STRIKE FIRST', HITLER SHOUTS

Axis Joins Japan; British Battle to Hold Singapore

WAR DEPARTMENT REPORTS SINKING OF JAP WARSHIP

Chinese Not Japanese—Plea

Congress Acts Swiftly on Roosevelt Plea for War; Action Is Unanimous

Japan's allies Germany and Italy declare war on US. Misinformation was common during the war: Despite the headline, there were no Japanese warships sunk near Manila by Dec 11, 1941. The ship claimed to have been sunk, the battleship Haruna, was actually sunk in July 1945.

against the US by Japan's allies Germany and Italy. The men of Monessen already serving suddenly found themselves in harm's way on the islands of the Pacific and on the waters of the Atlantic Ocean. The invasion of the Philippine Islands by Japanese forces in December 1941 put a few Monessen men in immediate jeopardy.

***

The citizens of Monessen responded to the news of the US entry into war by lining up at their county enlistment offices. Men joined military service and left for boot camp and intensive military training. Their departures were announced almost weekly in the Monessen Daily Independent, and Monessen residents anxiously followed the news to find out which of their neighbors were heading to war.

The news of combat operations initiated by the US was sparse until April 18, 1942, when Major Jimmy Doolittle led a daring bombing raid upon Tokyo, Japan, from an aircraft carrier in the Pacific, boosting American morale. Reports of major naval engagements came with the Battle of the Coral Sea (May) and the Battle of Midway Island (June).

By August, the Guadalcanal Campaign was underway in the Solomon Islands. Operation Torch, the Allied invasion of North Africa against German occupiers, was launched in November 1942.

The year 1942 brought Monessen its first six casualties of the war. They occurred on the seas, in a prisoner-of-war camp, and stateside. The city had no way of knowing just how much more sacrifice was yet to come. The world had fallen from the precipice of peaceful coexistence into the abyss of brutal war.

✯ ✯ ✯

S2C LOUIS C. STEPHENS

Service Number 2506548
Scouting Squadron 9 (VS-9), US Navy
Lost off Cape Hatteras, North Carolina, April 21, 1942

By April 1942, German submarines (called "U-boats") had already sunk over 100 ships that year off the east coast of North America, in the Gulf of Mexico, and in the Caribbean Sea. The US had only been at war for four months, and tensions were high for every mariner sailing the eastern seaboard. Danger may be lurking just beneath the waves.

Monessen's Louis C. Stephens and the pilot of their submarine-hunting seaplane were carrying out the vigilance from the air for the US Navy. Little did they know that it would cost them their lives.

Seaman 2nd Class Louis Stephens was Monessen's first son lost during WWII.

The Stephens Family

Louis Clifton Stephens was born on August 21, 1920, to Robert Gilbert and Maude (née Luce) Stephens in Monessen, Pennsylvania. Robert and Maude had married eighteen years earlier in nearby Perryopolis. At the time, Robert was a carpenter while Maude managed the Stephens family household.

The Stephens family heritage traces back to the British colonies of Pennsylvania and Maryland prior to the American Revolutionary War, as well as to Germany and Wales. Maude's family traces to the colonies of Pennsylvania and New Jersey, and to Scotland and Germany. Both families settled in Fayette County in Western Pennsylvania by the mid 1800's.

Louis, named after his paternal grandfather, was the last of three children born into the family. Robert Eugene arrived in 1905, and a sister Eleanor Rachel was born in 1912. Their father spent a few years as a manager at the Fox Grocery Store in nearby Charleroi prior to becoming a carpenter. From 1910 through the 1940's, the family lived in their own home on McKee Avenue in Monessen. By 1930, their father returned to the grocery business as a wholesaler in the candy and tobacco business, and by 1940, he was the proprietor of his own grocery store. Theirs was a large house and they occasionally offered room and board for a few lodgers.

While a student, Louis and his brother Robert took great interest in radio equipment, which would later prove useful. After graduating from Monessen High School, Louis entered the grocery business with his father as a clerk. Louis soon went to work for the Charleroi division of Clover Farm Stores.

Off to the US Navy and to War

At the age of 20, Louis decided it was time for adventure. On July 8, 1941, he enlisted in Pittsburgh, Pennsylvania, with the US Navy.

Louis attended the US Navy's training school in Newport, Rhode Island, as an Apprentice Seaman, the Navy's entry rank for enlisted men. By September 23, 1941, Apprentice Seaman Stephens was in the Navy's Trade School at the Naval Air Station in Jacksonville, Florida. Louis' earlier interest in radios and the skills he developed as an amateur hobbyist elevated his candidacy as a radio operator within the Navy's aviation branch.

While Louis was in training, Japanese forces launched a surprise attack on the US military bases in Pearl Harbor, Hawaii, on December 7, 1941. The US declared war on Japan, and subsequently, as an ally of the Japanese Empire, Germany declared war on the US. Louis Stephens was about to learn what war was like as an active-duty member of the US Navy.

In light of the threat, the US Navy established a central command, Commander, Eastern Sea Frontier (COMEASTSEAFRON), responsible for anti-submarine warfare. The command was charged with protecting the sea lanes in the North Atlantic Ocean and along the country's Atlantic coast. They quickly organized Scouting Squadrons of aircraft to patrol the skies over the seas.

On February 3, 1942, Louis transferred to the US Naval Air Station in Norfolk, Virginia, on temporary duty awaiting further transfer to Scouting Squadron 9 (VS-9). He had graduated from radio operators' school, qualified as an aviation radioman, and was promoted to Seaman 2nd Class (S2c).

The radioman of a scouting aircraft was responsible for maintaining radio communications with the airbase, other aircraft, ships, as well as the intercom with the pilot. He was also responsible for the equipment that maintained contact with land or sea-based navigational transmitters. His role was crucial to the success of every mission.

Scouting for U-Boats in the Atlantic

Scouting Squadron 9 was formed on March 1, 1942, with six officers and 146 enlisted men, and attached to the Fleet Air Detachment at Norfolk. Between April 4-7, 1942, the squadron received eighteen OS2U-3 Vought Kingfisher observational float planes from New York.

Kingfishers were compact mid-wing monoplanes with a large central float and small stabilizing floats. They could take off and land from water and, for those equipped with landing gear, airfields. Kingfishers could carry 325 pounds of depth charges or 100 pounds of bombs for attacking ships or sub-marines.

On April 8, six Kingfishers were detached with six pilots and 50 enlisted men to the US Marine Air Station, Cherry Point, North Carolina. Their mission was to patrol their offshore Atlantic area. On April 12, the remainder of VS-9 transferred to Cherry Point. The squadron was now patrolling their assigned area from 0600 to 2100 hrs daily, from Cape Lookout to Cape Hatteras.

The squadron received orders to supply air coverage for its first convoy of ships on April 15 and dropped its first depth charges on a "suspicious object", later identified as something other than a submarine. This action would be re-peated not infrequently, as the patrolling pilots surely believed that it was bet-ter to be safe than sorry.

OS2U-3 Vought Kingfisher (World War Photos/US Navy)

Fate Intervenes

On Tuesday, April 21, 1942, S2C Louis Stephens and pilot Ensign Arnold W.P. LaGraff were assigned to fly Kingfisher OS2U-3 Bu.No.[1] 5852 in the squadron's North Sector Patrol. A report had been received of a submarine sighting, bearing 085 degrees "True" from Cape Hatteras Lighthouse at a distance of 35 miles. When Ensign LaGraff and the other Kingfishers arrived and thoroughly scanned the area, no submarines were spotted. They turned to head for their Cherry Point home base.

Before they could reach home, fate rudely and fatally interrupted.

At 1702 hrs, Ensign LaGraff's Kingfisher encountered trouble of an unknown origin, and the aircraft fell into the sea at a sharp angle and sank, bearing 175 degrees "True", 29 miles from Cape Hatteras Lighthouse. Rescue operations began at once, continued until darkness, and resumed the following morning for two days.

Ensign LaGraff and S2c Stephens were lost. Neither crewmen nor the aircraft would ever be recovered. At the Cherry Point base, a memorial service was held, and a Navy plane dropped a floral tribute into the sea at the scene of their loss.

Louis C. Stephens, Remembered

His family was informed the following day that their son had been lost. The local newspaper Monessen Daily Independent ran a front-page headline "Louis C. Stephens First Monessen War Casualty". The family of Ensign LaGraff were also informed of the loss of their son, who also was the first war casualty of his hometown of Potsdam, New York.

The following day, an editorial appeared in the Daily Independent headlining Louis Stephens' loss "They Must Not Die in Vain". It asserted "We must somehow see to it that the world becomes a better place because young

---

[1] The US military assigned a serial number to each aircraft. "Bu.No." is the US Navy's Bureau of Aeronautic abbreviation for "Bureau Number" and the aircraft is numbered according to the its order date by the Navy. The US Army assigned a prefix of the last two digits of the year that the aircraft was ordered, e.g., "41-", followed by the sequence of its order, e.g. "41-12345".

Louis Stephens has given the last full measure of devotion." Monessen's mayor was quoted, "The war has really come home to us now, and the sympathy of all our people extended to the family of Louis Stephens. His sacrifice will live long in the hearts of all of us". The mayor proclaimed an official period of mourning and ordered the city's flags flown at half-staff.

In July, a memorial service was held by the Veterans of Foreign Wars and American Legion at Monessen's First Presbyterian Church. A painted portrait of S2C Louis Stephens was presented to his family by David H. Woodward.

B&W version of color portrait of Louis Stephens by David H. Woodward (Greater Monessen Historical Society)

★ ★ ★

RM2C FRANK BARTOSIK

Service Number 4050037
USS Vincennes (CA-44), US Navy
Lost at Sea, Solomon Islands, August 9, 1942

Disaster was minutes away. In the dark early morning of August 9, 1942, Radioman 2nd Class (RM2c) Frank Bartosik was aboard the US Navy's battle cruiser USS Vincennes. He was either at his station in the radio room or asleep in his bunk.

The lookouts on the USS Vincennes had just observed explosions and flares south of their position east of the Southwest Pacific's Savo Island. The fires were initially thought to be coming from a land battle on the island of Guadalcanal twenty miles south. Ships were also spotted in the distance through the nighttime haze, but they had not yet been identified.

Then, at 0150 hrs (1:50 AM), the Vincennes was illuminated by spotlights from the unidentified ships. They were Japanese battle cruisers Kakao, Kinugasa, and Chokai, and they now had the Vincennes in her sights. The Japanese had the advantage of surprise, and they used it ruthlessly.

Over the next 15 minutes the Vincennes was struck by 74 shells and 3 torpedoes. She was fully engulfed in fire and had come to a halt. At 0216 hrs, the Vincennes' captain gave the order to abandon ship.

RM2c Frank Bartosik was never seen alive again.

The Bartosik Family

Frank Bartosik was born on December 18, 1917, to Joseph and Prokseda (née Ertman) Bartosik in Monessen, Pennsylvania. Joseph and Prokseda had married in 1913. Joseph was a machinist in an automobile shop while Prokseda managed the Bartosik family household.

Joseph, born Jozef Bartosik, in Wysocko Wielkie, Poland had immigrated to the United States in 1892 and became a naturalized US citizen in 1900. Prokseda, also born in Poland, had immigrated to the United States in 1913 and was naturalized the following year. Prokseda was Joseph's second wife. His first, Jadwiga (Hedwig or Hetty) Smolarek, died in 1911.

Frank was one of ten children born to Joseph Bartosik. Four children were born to Joseph and Hedwig: John (b1906), Frances (1908), and Florentyna (1909) were first to arrive, but Hedwig died in 1911 while giving birth to an unnamed daughter. After remarrying, Joseph and Prokseda had Stephen (1913), Edward (1915), Frank (1917), Helen (1919), Harry (1921), and Hattie (1923). Helen died in 1920 from measles and pneumonia. The family was living in their home on Aliquippa Avenue in Monessen in 1920, and by 1930, had purchased a new home on Monessen's Marion Avenue.

Frank attended Monessen High School where he graduated in 1937. While in high school, Frank was a member of the radio club Knights of the Kilocycles. His experience would serve him later in his military career.

By 1940, only Frank, Harry, and Hattie were still living in their parents' home. The older siblings had all married and moved to homes to start their own families. Their father had retired, and the family had moved into a rented home on Cross Street. Harry and Hattie were in high school while Frank worked as a laborer on road construction projects. However, Frank had just enlisted in the US Naval Reserve on December 11, 1939, in Pittsburgh, Pennsylvania, and was awaiting orders for deployment. He was soon sent off for US Navy training.

Aboard the USS Vincennes

USS Vincennes (CA-44), Panama Canal, 1938 (US Navy)

On July 15, 1940, Frank boarded his first navy combat ship, the battle cruiser USS Vincennes (CA-44), in Norfolk, Virginia, as Seaman 2nd Class (S2c). The ship was being overhauled in Norfolk and by the following January the Vincennes was ready for action. On January 21, 1941, S2c Bartosik successfully completed training in naval radio communications, and was promoted to Radioman 3rd Class (RM3c).

Radiomen were responsible for transmitting and receiving radio signals and processing all forms of telecommunications through various transmission media aboard ships, aircraft, and at shore facilities. The type of circuits maintained included voice and data circuits between the ships of a battle group and allied units. Their duties included message systems for generalized broadcasts and unit specific messages that were handled based on message priority and handling procedures. They were also responsible for the proper handling and destruction of classified material. Radiomen were responsible for periodic maintenance of the communications equipment, including transmitters, receivers and antennas.

The USS Vincennes, commissioned in February 1937, was one of seven heavily armed New Orleans Class cruisers built in the 1930's for the US Navy. All were to be front line battle cruisers in the Pacific theater and were destined to see the heaviest naval actions of the war.

Typical radio room of large 1940's US Navy ship (US Navy)

The Vincennes cruised the Caribbean Sea and the Atlantic Ocean on maneuvers and in support of convoys, included to and from South Africa. On December 7, 1941, Japanese forces attacked the US armed forces bases at Pearl Harbor, Hawaii, and the US declared war on Japan. On March 4, 1942, the USS Vincennes departed New York, headed for the Panama Canal and to the Pacific.

Into Harm's Way

RM3c Frank Bartosik had a ticket for a front row seat in the first strikes by US armed forces in WWII.

Their first stop, however, was San Francisco, California, where they joined Task Force 18 and departed on April 2, 1942, for a top-secret mission…. They were escorting the USS Hornet aircraft carrier and its deck load of B-25 Mitchell bombers. On April 18, 1942, these B-25 bombers carried out the famed and daring bombing of Tokyo, Japan, led by Major Jimmy Doolittle. The Japanese would learn much more about US military might in the months ahead.

After returning to Pearl Harbor, the Vincennes would again head to battle at the end of May 1942. This time their destination was Midway Island, where she participated in the island's surprise defense against a massive attack by the Japanese, a defense which would cripple the Japanese Imperial Navy for the remainder of the war.

Frank Bartosik had proven his muster aboard the Vincennes, and on July 1, 1942, RM3c Bartosik was promoted to Radioman 2nd Class (RM2c) after the Vincennes returned to Pearl Harbor. Six days later, the USS Vincennes departed Pearl again, this time for the South Pacific, with their final destination unknown by RM2c Bartosik and his peers.

Their destination was the Solomon Islands[2] where they would participate in Operation Watchtower, the US invasion of the island of Guadalcanal, launching in early August 1942. The Japanese were constructing a critical air-field that was a steppingstone for a potential invasion of Australasia. The US and its Allies were determined to stop them at Guadalcanal.

The Battle of Savo Island

On August 7, US Marines landed on Guadalcanal and began moving in-land. As transport craft continued arriving and unloading the following two nights, two groups of Allied cruisers and destroyers were positioned to defend the transports. Just north of Guadalcanal near Savo Island, the Allied groups were attacked by a Japanese naval force of seven cruisers and one destroyer. The engagement would become known as the Battle of Savo Island... and would be the last action by the USS Vincennes and RM2c Bartosik.

At 0150 hrs, in the dark of night on August 9, 1942, under sail with its fellow ships, the Vincennes was illuminated by searchlights from Japanese cruisers. The Vincennes opened fire at the attacking ships, but the Japanese had pinpointed their location first and within a minute had struck the Vin-

---

[2] Solomon Islands is an island country in the Southwest Pacific Ocean, consist-ing of six major islands and over 900 smaller islands northeast of Australia, north of New Zealand, and directly east of Papua New Guinea.

cennes with eight-inch armor-piercing shells. Despite valiant defensive actions, the ship continued taking deadly hits from the enemy cruiser. Within five minutes, Japanese torpedoes struck the ship. The engines and steering were knocked out. The Vincennes came to a halt, having been hit by at least 74 enemy shells. The order to abandon ship was given at 0216 hrs. By 0250 hrs, those who could jump into the sea had done so, and the USS Vincennes

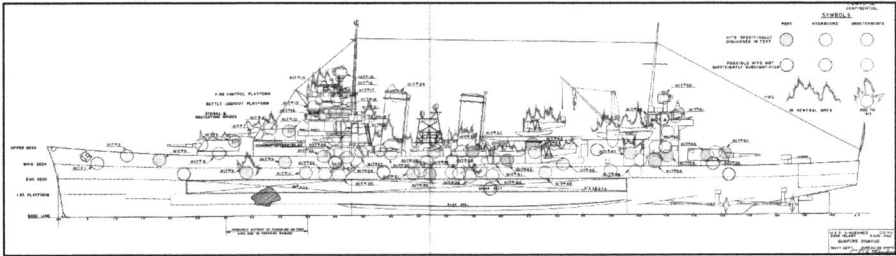

Diagram showing the gunfire damage to the USS Vincennes on Aug 9, 1942, (US Navy Dept of Ship). The radio room was in upper middle of the main superstructure and took direct gunfire hits..

would settle below the waves in what would become known as Iron Bottom Sound. One Australian and three American cruisers were sunk, and one American cruiser and two destroyers were damaged.

RM2c Frank Bartosik was among the 322 crew of the USS Vincennes lost in the Battle of Savo Island. US forces would eventually take Guadalcanal, and the Japanese would abandon their efforts to occupy the Solomon Islands. It was the first major land offensive by Allied forces against the Empire of Japan.

On September 16, 1942, his family was informed by the US War Department that their son was reported as missing in action.

RM2c Frank Bartosik was never recovered. He was officially declared dead a year later, on August 10, 1943. RM2c Bartosik is memorialized on the Tablets of the Missing at the Manila American Cemetery, Philippines. He was posthumously awarded the Purple Heart.

✯ ✯ ✯

PVT JACK E. JENNINGS

Service Number 20305266
93rd Bomb Squadron, 19th Bomb Group, US Army Air Corps
Died a POW, The Philippines, September 2, 1942

Jack Jennings wanted to be a soldier even before volunteering the Pennsylvania National Guard in February 1941. But it is very likely that he never wanted to become a prisoner of war in Cabanatuan, the most notorious Japanese POW camp in the Philippine Islands. Most certainly, he did not expect to die there.

The Jennings Family

Jack Ethridge Jennings was born on April 8, 1916, in Glassport, Pennsylvania to John Ethridge and Goldie Ava (née Essington) Jennings. John and Goldie had married in 1907. John was a switch man on the Pennsylvania & Lake Erie Railroad, while Goldie managed the Jennings household.

The heritage of the Jennings family traces back to the British colonies of Pennsylvania and Massachusetts, and to England. The Essington family traces back to the colonies of Pennsylvania and

Maryland, and to England as well. Both families eventually settled in south-western Pennsylvania where John and Goldie were born. Family ancestors fought in the American Revolutionary War.

Jack was the only child born to John and Goldie. By 1920, the family moved to Monessen, Pennsylvania, where John worked as a conductor on the railroad. That year the family was living in their home on 158 Oneida Street in Monessen. By 1935, the Jennings purchased and moved into a home at 44 Aliquippa Avenue in Monessen. John was now a yardmaster at the railroad. In 1936, Jack joined the Pennsylvania National Guard.

The family were members of the Methodist Episcopal Church in Monessen. Jack took vocal lessons while growing up and became a talented vocalist, singing baritone solo in the church choir and at other musical events in the town. In 1939, Jack wrecked his Pontiac into a utility pole but was uninjured. Jack graduated from Monessen High School in 1939. He was active in the Boy Scouts of America and earned Eagle Scout in 1940.

Jack Jennings Volunteers to Serve

In 1940 and after graduating high school, he went to work as a salesman for a wholesale firm and attended college for a year. Hearing the drumbeats of war in Europe and the Pacific, Jack decided to reenlist with the Pennsylvania National Guard in February 1941 and was assigned to Monessen's Company D of the 110th Infantry. Because aviation appealed to Jack, he requested and was granted a transfer to the US Army Air Corps on June 25, 1941. He reported for duty at Indiantown Gap, Pennsylvania, as a 5'10", 145 lb. single man. Private (PVT) Jennings was subsequently assigned to the 47th Bomb Group stationed at Hamilton Field, California, for training, and then to Fresno, California.

Four months later, on October 5, 1941, he was transferred to the 93rd Bomb Squadron of the 19th Bomb Group and shipped overseas to the Philippine Islands. The 19th Bomb Group was equipped with the Air Corps' new Boeing B-17 Flying Fortress heavy bombers. PVT Jennings was part of the "ground echelon", the group of men who supported the aircraft and flight crews but did not take to the air themselves.

To the Philippines and into War

Jack was one of the first boys from Monessen to leave before the outbreak of war. By November 1941, PVT Jennings was one of 8,500 men of the Far East Air Force stationed in the Philippines in anticipation of Japanese aggression. His 93rd Bomb Squadron was initially stationed at Clark Field near Manilla on the island of Luzon with the rest of the 19th Bomb Group. As a security measure in the event of attack, the 93rd Squadron was split from the other squadrons of the 19th Bomb Group and sent to Del Monte Field on the Philippine island of Mindanao on December 5.

The surprise attack by Japanese armed forces on the US military bases at Pearl Harbor, Hawaii, and the Philippines on December 7, 1941, changed the world for millions of Americans, as it did for Jack. PVT Jack Jennings was at Del Monte Field in December when the Japanese launched a major offensive on the islands.

The Japanese forces advanced through December, crushing the defending Filipino and American forces. By the end of December, the air echelon of the 19th Bomb Group retreated to the safety of Australia, but PVT Jack Jennings and much of the ground echelon remained behind and joined the infantry to fight the invaders. On January 13, 1942, Jack penned his last letter home, and in April 1942, he and thousands of other Allied troops were captured by the Japanese. PVT Jack Jennings was imprisoned at the POW camp at Cabanatuan on the main Philippine Island of Luzon.

But for the families of the POWs, no word was received of their capture until a year later, in April 1943. The Jennings family received a telegram from the War department informing them that he was a POW of the Japanese. However, PVT Jennings, while enduring the squalor of the camp and lack of sustaining nutrition, had succumbed to dysentery at 4:30 PM on September 2, 1942. He died as a POW in the makeshift prisoners' hospital in the Cabanatuan camp.

Cabanatuan Prisoner of War Camp (US Department of Defense)

On June 11, 1943, the family of PVT Jack Jennings was informed that he had died while being held by the Japanese as a prisoner of war.

PVT Jack E. Jennings was initially buried in a shared grave with three other soldiers in a temporary cemetery in the Cabanatuan POW camp. He was reinterred in 1947 at the US Military Cemetery #2 in Manila, Philippines. His remains were recovered under the Return of the War Dead program and returned to the US aboard the transport ship Private Joseph F. Merrill in September 1949. He was buried at the Grandview Cemetery in Monessen, Pennsylvania.

The name of PVT Jack E. Jennings is inscribed on the Cabanatuan American Memorial in Cabanatuan, Philippines.

★ ★ ★

FM/WT JACOVOS MONIOS

Service Number 56834
SS Mary Luckenbach, US Merchant Marine
Lost at Sea off Norway, September 13, 1942

D uring WWII, the highest rate of lives lost was not by the military. It was America's all-volunteer Merchant Marine. Volunteer sailors in the US Merchant Marine died at 3 times the rate of those in the US Navy. They were 90% more likely to lose their lives than those in the US Army, and 35% more likely than the US Marines. Over 700 US merchant ships were sunk by enemy submarines, surface ships, underwater mines, and aircraft. Nearly 10,000 Merchant Mariners never returned.

Everyone knew the criticality of their mission: To carry men, cargo, and fuel from the mighty US across the oceans into combat. Each soldier required 7-15 tons of supplies each year. Everyone knew... including the enemy.

After WWII, a few surviving Merchant Mariners would find fame: Actors Carroll O'Connor, James Garner, and Peter Falk. Playwright Eugene O'Neill. Pittsburgh Steelers' quarterback Bobby Layne.

Two of Monessen's Merchant Mariners, Jacovos Monios and John Hotovchin[3], would not be so lucky.

The Monios Family

Jacovos was born on April 17, 1882, on the island of Chios, Greece, to Constantine and Chrysoula (née Xydas) Monioudis. Jacovos later changed his surname to Monios. Jacovos was the first of nine children born to Constantine and Chrysoula. He was followed by Maria (b1890), Michael (1892), Odysseas (1897), Emmanuel "Manuel" (1897), Angelike (1901), John (1903), and George (1905).

Jacovos immigrated to the United States in 1913 aboard the SS Athinai with his brother Emmanuel. He was 5'2" 148 lbs with brown hair and brown eyes and had lost his pointer finger from his right hand. His brother Michael had arrived in the US in 1909 and settled in Monessen. Jacovos moved into an apartment at 215 Ninth Street in Monessen by 1917. Prior to immigrating, Jacovos had married Despina, who remained in Greece.

With the US Merchant Marine

Jacovos lived with Michael at 1553 Schoonmaker Avenue Monessen until 1929. Jacovos had been a seaman when he was in Greece, and he decided to resume the occupation in the US Merchant Marine. He moved to New York City to be close to port.

Through the 1930's, he worked on oil tankers and merchant vessels crossing the seas. In September 1941, he sailed aboard the oil tanker SS Oklahoma as Fireman (FM). A fireman's station was deep in the engine room, and he was responsible for operating the fuel oil burning system to generate steam in boilers and stand watch in the fire room.

---

[3] John Hotovchin was lost at sea March 17, 1943. His story appears later in this book.

As war began to emerge in Europe and the Pacific, the United States committed to support friendly nations around the world before being drawn into the war on December 7, 1941, when Japanese forces attacked Pearl Harbor, Hawaii. In February 1942, Jacovos had been at sea for over 15 years and was now a fireman on the SS Cities Service Toledo. Two months later his prior ship, the SS Oklahoma, was torpedoed by a German U-boat.

Transporting oil, vehicles, and other supplies became an essential service in support of the Allies who were fighting the war against Germany closer to the front lines. In the early 1940's the Battle of the Atlantic was now raging, pitting German U-boats against merchant vessels under sea escort by Allied destroyers and destroyer escorts, and patrol bombers from the air. For the merchant marine sailors, their jobs were to ensure that their ships maintained power and maneuverability day and night. Normally equipped with just a few defensive guns, merchant vessels depended heavily upon sea and air escorts to protect them from attack. The Allies began to group ships in convoys of multiple ship formations surrounded by escorts.

Aboard the SS Mary Luckenbach

Jacovos was now assigned to the SS Mary Luckenbach as a fireman/water tender (FM/WT). The ship was originally christened the USS Sac City (Iowa) in 1918 and mainly sailed the Atlantic Ocean in the 1920-30's. She was sold to the Luckenbach Steamship Company and renamed SS Mary Luckenbach in 1941.

Unfortunately for Jacovos, the SS Mary Luckenbach would only see one more year of service afloat. In September 1942, her luck would run out.

The SS Mary Luckenbach was put to work transporting desperately needed supplies and munitions to the Soviet Union. In September, the ship was assigned to Convoy PQ 18 consisting of 40 merchant ships. The previous Allied convoy, PQ 17 in June 1942, had been a disaster... Of the 35 merchant ships in PQ 17, 24 were sunk by German attackers. The Allies, having learned a lesson, would defend PQ 18 with 74 warships.

Several ships in PQ 18 originated in Reykjavik, Iceland, and sailed to Loch Ewe, Scotland where they formed into the full convoy complement. They sailed from Loch Ewe on September 2 heading northeast across the Barents Sea in route to Murmansk in the Soviet Union.

SS Mary Luckenbach (US Navy)

The SS Mary Luckenbach Meets her Fate

The SS Mary Luckenbach, with a crew of 41 and 24 US Navy Armed Guards, was carrying more than 1,000 tons of TNT explosives. She was a vulnerable ship.

The German Luftwaffe had established air bases at Banak and Bardufoss in northern Norway to attack northern shipping lanes supplying the Soviets. The convoy was detected by German reconnaissance aircraft as it traveled through stormy seas and was being shadowed by U-boats as well. As the convoy arrived just west of North Cape, Norway on September 13, 1942, it came under heavy aerial attack by German Junkers Ju-88 torpedo bombers.

A Ju-88 was zeroing in on the Mary Luckenbach as anti-aircraft gunners from the British cruiser HMS Scylla fired a barrage at the attacking bomber. The aircraft launched a torpedo, and it raced through the icy water toward Mary Luckenbach.

German Junkers Ju-88 Bomber

The torpedo found its mark and detonated. The ship's explosive cargo instantly erupted. The vessel vaporized before the eyes of the men in her escort ships as they watched in horror. A column of smoke rose thousands of feet into the air, topping in a mushroom where it met the clouds. The SS Mary Luckenbach and her crew were gone. There were no survivors.

Twelve other merchant ships were lost in Convoy PQ 18.

In December 1942, the family of Jacovos Monios learned that he had been lost at sea. Jacovos was 60 years old and was the oldest Monessen service member to lose his life during the war. He was posthumously awarded the Mariners Medal by the US Merchant Marine.

★ ★ ★

SGT EDWARD R. CIPRIANI

Service Number 13012501
30th Bomb Squadron, 19th Bomb Group, 5th Air Force, US Army Air Corps
Airman Missing Since November 1, 1942, Found in 1999

It was February 7, 1942. The B-17 Flying Fortress bomber had taken off from Florida weeks earlier and was now halfway around the world.

Monessen's Edward Cipriani was the bomber's radio operator. He and his crewmates were preparing to land on a jungle airfield on the island of Java in the Southwest Pacific Ocean. After dozens of stops along thousands of miles, they were relieved to be arriving at their final destination.

But the bomber was coming in to land way too fast. The crushed-coral runway was not long enough for the speeding aircraft. They were going to crash.

The crew braced themselves for impact. Many prayed. The bomber's wheels touched down, but the heavy aircraft could not stop before the runway ran out. The bomber careened off the landing strip and broke apart.

Incredibly, the crew were shaken but without major injuries... except to the confidence of the pilot. Their bomber, which had cost the US Government over $200,000, about $4 million in today's dollars, was a total loss.

It was Edward Cipriani's closest brush with death so far as a WWII airman. It would not be his last.

The Cipriani Family

Edward Ralph Cipriani was born on September 18, 1921, to Peter and Theresa (née Giordano) Cipriani in Monessen, Pennsylvania. Peter worked at Monessen's American Sheet and Tin Plate factory, while Theresa managed the Cipriani family household.

Peter was born Pietro Cipriani in the village of Pentima, L'Aquila in Abruzzo, Italy, and immigrated to the United States in 1905. By 1917, he settled in Monessen with two of his sisters. Theresa Giordano was born in Pittsburgh to parents from Sicily, Italy, who immigrated to the US in the late 1890's. At times her family went by the surname of Jordan. Peter and Theresa met and married in 1921 in Western Pennsylvania, settling in Monessen.

Edward was the first of five children born to the couple. His brother Eugene arrived in 1922, followed by Louise (1925), Ronald (1930), and Warren "Wayne" (1938). In 1930, the family was living in a rented home at 808 Second Street in Monessen, but the Great Depression forced the family into a crowded apartment at 263 Schoonmaker Avenue, where they still lived by 1940.

The Cipriani children attended St. Leonard's Catholic School, and Edward advanced to Monessen High School in the late 1930s. Although remembered as a shy teen, he was an exceptional speaker, debater, and honor student. In his senior year, Edward led his high school debate team to the state championship. By doing so, he earned a trip to compete in the national forensic competition in Beverly Hills, California. He graduated tenth in his class in 1939.

Cipriani joins the US Army Air Corps

Edward and his close cousin Nunzio Spalla had thought about joining the US Army Air Corps and finally decided to take the leap. They enlisted together on December 30, 1940. The next day, New Years Eve, the pair departed to Alabama for basic training.

After basic, Edward and Nunzio had to select a specialty. They wanted to train in aerial photography, but there was a waiting list. Instead, Edward decided to train as a radio operator in multi-engine aircraft. Edward transferred to Scott Field, Illinois, which contained the Army Air Corps' "Radio University", and graduated from there in November 1941. He left for Geiger Army Airfield, Spokane, Washington, for further assignment.

A radio operator was critical for the proper functioning of an air crew and for executing their mission. He had to be highly skilled in all of the radio equipment used for communicating within the aircraft as well as between aircraft and with ground stations. The radio operator had to memorize the ever-changing secret frequencies, codes, and signals in use by a bomb group on the day of a mission, and he needed to keep the flight crew informed as new information was received from other aircraft and the ground.

Upon demonstrating the required competencies, Edward was promoted to the rank of Corporal (CPL). He then trained with bomber crews through 1941 to gain the experience necessary to perform under combat conditions. CPL Cipriani was eventually assigned to train on the US Army Air Corps' Boeing B-17 Flying Fortress heavy bomber.

The B-17 Flying Fortress was designed in the mid-1930's as a modern, multi-engine bomber while leaders in the US Army Air Corps were still developing the doctrine for using bombers in warfare. By 1941, the B-17 was accepted as the primary bomber. Only 155 aircraft had been delivered to the Air Corps by November 1941, but production quickly ramped up with nearly 13,000 produced by the end of WWII. It carried a crew of nine, as many as 8,000 lbs of bombs, and up to thirteen 50 caliber machine guns.

Boeing B-17 Flying Fortress Bomber (US Air Force)

CPL Cipriani was assigned to the 30th Bomb Squadron (BS) of the 19th Bomb Group (BG) and trained for overseas deployment. Little did he know what was in store.

The 19th BG had been training in Albuquerque, New Mexico from June to September 1941 as the drums of war in Europe and the Pacific areas pounded loudly. So far, the US avoided direct participation, but the global situation was boiling over, particularly the relationship with Japan.

The 19th BG was put on alert for possible deployment to the Pacific. In October the unit was ordered to the main US airbase in the Philippine Islands: Clark Field on the island of Luzon. The 19th BG flew from California to Hawaii, then to Midway and Wake Islands, to Australia, and then to the Philippines. It was the largest mass flight of bombers over such a great distance to date. The first aircraft of the 19th BG arrived at Clark Field on November 1, 1941. The 19th BG, with 210 officers, 1300 enlisted men, and 33 B-17 bombers, now began preparing for the worst. It was soon to come.

But CPL Edward Cipriani had received a rare furlough and was visiting his family in their Monessen home during the first week of December. On December 7, 1941, his visit was suddenly interrupted with news from the Pacific. Japan had attacked the US. And his unit was in harm's way.

The US Enters WWII

On December 7-8, 1941, Japanese forces launched surprise attacks against seven targets: the US military bases at Pearl Harbor Hawaii and the Philippines, and on Malaya, Hong Kong, Wake Island, Midway Island, and Guam. The US declared war on Japan, whose ally, Germany, promptly declared war on the US. The war was now global.

CPL Cipriani ended his furlough early and began the long journey to join his unit at Clark Field. All men of the 19th BG were desperately needed, as were more bombers. The group's B-17s at Clark had been destroyed in the Japanese attack. The 19th BG only had 17 aircraft left, which had been relocated to Del Monte Airfield on Mindanao on December 5, out of range of Japanese bombers.

The group launched counter attacks against the Japanese, but staying in the Philippines had become untenable in the face of mounting Japanese aggression. In mid-December, the B-17s were flown to the safety of Batchelor Field near Darwin, Australia. Only a week later, the Allies decided to prioritize the defense of the island of Java in Indonesia and relocated the 19th BG there to an airfield at Singosari, Malang. They resumed their bombing attacks on Japanese ships, troops, and air bases.

Allied bombing strategy in the South Pacific was evolving. Later in the European war, the Allies launched strategic missions with hundreds of heavy bombers at industrial targets in Germany. However, in 1941-42, the missions of the 19th BG normally involved just four to six aircraft sent to tactical targets intending to stymie the progress of the rapidly advancing Japanese. The Allies would soon learn that bombing small enemy targets on islands or at sea using large slow-moving aircraft was not ideal.

Project X: Ed Cipriani's First Brush with Fate

Despite their limited effectiveness in the Pacific, Allied leaders called for more bomber aircraft to bolster the defenses of Australian and Java. "Project X" was initiated, which included flying 38 new B-17 E-model bombers with full crews from the US in January-February 1942. Bomber B-17E #41-2494 with radio operator CPL Cipriani joined Project X and set off for Java via the "African Route".

The African Route began in southern Florida and went south to Brazil. Aircraft then headed eastward across the Atlantic Ocean and Africa, continuing on to the Middle East, India, and Southeast Asia, making multiple stops for fuel, supplies, and rest.

Finally, at 1800 hrs on February 7, 1942, CPL Cipriani's B-17 approached their destination, Djogjakarta Airfield, Java. But the bomber overshot the runway and crashed. Fortunately, the crew survived.

Without a bomber to fly, the crew was split up and assigned to fly with other bomber crews. Four days after his harrowing arrival, CPL Cipriani was off on his first mission: a night raid on Japanese positions near Palembang, Java. He then joined two raids on Japanese shipping near Malang, Java, on February 15 and 18, and another bombing mission on February 26 to Bali.

Throughout February 1942, well-organized Japanese forces were rapidly overtaking Java against understrength Allied defenses. The 19th BG remained in Java until March, when, with Japanese troops only 20 miles from the airfield, they were ordered to retreat once more to Australia. They first settled at Melbourne but by April were repositioned to Longreach then Mareeba through October 1942. During that time, Cipriani (now a Sergeant) continued to fly in bombing raids against Japanese targets, including Guadalcanal and the stronghold of Rabaul on the island of New Britain.

After nearly a year of continuous combat operations, the 19th BG was deemed "punch drunk". It was time for the men and their aircraft to be withdrawn. In September 1942, the Army Air Corps ordered the 19th BG to return to the States by December. They were going home. Or so they thought.

"Whatever happens will happen"

The 19th BG was not leaving the Southwest Pacific just yet… there was more work to be done. The Japanese were not letting up.

On November 1, 1942, SGT Cipriani joined 1LT John S. Hancock and his crew for a night mission to bomb Japanese shipping in Tonolei Harbor at the island of Bougainville. The crew and their B-17 #41-2635 had stopped at the 7-Mile Drome airfield at Port Moresby on the southern coast of Papua New Guinea. Now armed with two 1,000 lb bombs, Hancock and five other B-17s climbed high across the mountains of eastern New Guinea towards their target 550 miles away.

When arriving over Bougainville, LT Hancock's B-17 was illuminated by Japanese searchlights and targeted by heavy anti-aircraft fire. The group had to turn back. But while the other B-17s returned to base, B-17 #41-2635 did not. They had disappeared without a trace.

Edward had written home many times, saying "whatever happens will happen". And so it did.

Seventeen days later, the doorbell rang at the Cipriani home in Monessen at 2:30 PM. Theresa Cipriani was handed a telegram which read "Your son SGT Edward Cipriani is reported missing in Australia". The family was devastated.

Three years went by without word of the whereabouts of Edward Cipriani and his crewmates. On December 7, 1945, they were officially declared dead.

Decades later, unexpected news arrives

Nothing more was learned about Edward… until 54 years later.

In 1999, a hunter traveling deep into the jungle on a New Guinea mountain range stumbled across the wreckage of an aircraft. US Army investigators were summoned to the site. In April 2001, they concluded that the aircraft wreckage was in fact LT Hancock's B-17 #41-2635. Edward's surviving brothers Eugene and Ronald were informed of the discovery the following month.

It is presumed that on the return flight in the dark of night, LT Hancock attempted to descend his B-17 below the clouds and collided with the eastern slope of a mountain overlooking Milne Bay, New Guinea. SGT Cipriani and the entire crew would have been killed upon impact.

Edward R. Cipriani, Remembered

The remains of SGT Edward R. Cipriani and the crew were returned to the US. SGT Cipriani was interred at Arlington National Cemetery, Virginia, next to a marker with the names of his crewmates. The name of Edward Cipriani is inscribed on the WWII Veterans Memorial Tablet, located at the intersection of Grand Boulevard and Euclid Drive in Monessen City Park.

SGT Cipriani was posthumously awarded the Air Medal and the Distinguished Flying Cross.

Unusual Coincidence Compounds the Family Grief

On November 17, 1942, the day that the Cipriani's were informed that Edward was missing, their grief was compounded when they learned more troubling news. Theresa Cipriani's cousin in nearby McKeesport had also just received an ominous telegram that day. Her son SGT William G. Kittiko was reported missing when his B-26 bomber failed to return from a training mission off the Gulf coast of Florida. Coincidentally, that telegram was also delivered at 2:30 PM that day. An unwelcome sense of dread came over the family.

Days later, Edward's cousin Bill Kittiko was presumed dead when the bodies of two of his crewmates were found off the Florida coast. In 1942, it was concluded that their bomber had crashed into the sea. Their B-26 was eventually discovered by divers in 1990.

★ ★ ★

SGT JOHN W. WARGO

Service Number 20305327
Company M, 110th Infantry Regiment, U.S. Army
Lost to Illness, Camp Polk Louisiana, November 12, 1942

M onths before the United States was thrust into WWII, John Woodrow Wargo decided that joining the military was the right thing to do.

Reading between the lines of the local newspaper, it became clear that the wars in Europe and East Asia were not going to stay there. The US had better be ready.

Little did John Wargo think that he would succumb to illness stateside. Nor did he think that his family's Service Banner might one day display two Gold Stars.

The Wargo Family

John Woodrow Wargo was born on November 14, 1918, to John "Jack" and Mary (née Paulo) Wargo in Monessen, Pennsylvania. Jack and Mary had married seven years earlier in 1914 in Stevensville, Virginia. Jack was a mail carrier, and Mary managed the Wargo household.

The Wargo and Paulo families trace back to the Austro-Hungarian Empire in the mid-1800's, and Jack and Mary's parents immigrated to the United States in the late 1800's. The Austro-Hungarian Empire spanned much of Eastern Europe, and the families were likely from villages located in modern Hungary and the Slovak Republic. Jack's father originally settled near Monessen where he was born, but the family relocated to Virginia as farmers, where the Paulo's were living and where Jack met Mary.

John was the third of five children born to Jack and Mary. First to be born was Willie (b1915), who died as an infant. Elsie Mae (1916) arrived next, followed by Albert Stanley (1921) and Mildred Agnes (1926). Elsie and John were born in Walkerton, Virginia, where the family was living at the time, and Albert and Mildred were born in Monessen after Jack relocated the family to his hometown in 1919 upon taking a job as a laborer in a steel mill. After a brief stint in the mill, Jack was hired as a mail carrier.

By 1930, the Wargo family was living in their home at 57 East Donner Avenue along with two boarders while the children attended school. By 1940, Mildred was in the seventh grade and Elsie, John, and Albert had graduated from Monessen High School. Elsie was working as a bookkeeper in a department store and John was a laborer at the Page Steel and Wire Company in Monessen. Their grandfather Andrew and grandmother Mary were living with them on Donner, as was their cousin Mary Staretz.

On October 16, 1940, John joined millions of other young American men and registered for the US armed forces draft on the first day it went into effect under the newly enacted Selective Service Act. He was a 5'11" 180 lb young single man with brown hair and brown eyes, living at the home of his parents. Hearing the growing drumbeat of war in Europe and the Pacific, John decided to enlist with the Pennsylvania National Guard, which he did on February 17, 1941, in Monessen.

After the surprise attack on Pearl Harbor, Hawaii, by Japanese forces in December 1941, John's Pennsylvania unit was activated. Before leaving for the service, John married Elizabeth Jones in Allegany County, Maryland, on December 25, 1941.

Off to Training, Succumbs to Illness

Private John Wargo was attached to Company M of the 110th Infantry Regiment and was soon promoted to Private First Class (PFC). Meanwhile, his brother Albert was drafted in August 1942 and left for the US Army Air Corps.

While in training, John demonstrated key leadership skills and was promoted to the rank of Sergeant. SGT John Wargo went to Camp Polk, Vernon, Louisiana, to participate in more extensive infantry training.

In September 1942, SGT Wargo became severely ill, was diagnosed with pneumonia, and was hospitalized at the Camp Polk Station Hospital. His condition remained grave, and he was kept in the Station Hospital until November 12, 1942, when he passed away.

The remains of SGT John W. Wargo were returned to Monessen and were buried at Saint Mary's Byzantine Cemetery. His name is inscribed on the WWII Veterans Memorial Tablet, located at the intersection of Grand Boulevard and Euclid Drive in Monessen City Park.

A year later, November 26, 1943, his brother CPL Albert Stanley Wargo lost his life when the transport ship HMT Rohna was sunk by a guided bomb in the Mediterranean Sea.

✯ ✯ ✯

1943

"Surge gently, tides of ocean deep,
Croon softly, wind on waves,
We know not where our sailors sleep –
No crosses mark their graves.
And though we grieve that they must be
So lost to all held dear,
God's arms hold fast our "lost at sea".
He will be near - - so very near"

The Family of FM John Hotovchin

B y 1943, the war was raging on several fronts around the world: Eastern Europe, North Africa, the North Atlantic, China, Southeast Asia, and the Southwest Pacific.

The Battle of the Atlantic continued as convoys of cargo ships plowed the icy waters of the North Atlantic Ocean. In the European theater, the air war was in full thrust as British and US aircraft launched attacks against German-occupied territories throughout Europe. Germany and its European allies had invaded the Soviet Union with over 3,700,000 troops.

Operation Torch, the Allied invasion of North Africa, had moved east across Morocco, Algeria, and Tunisia by the Spring of 1943. US and British troops were getting their noses bloodied as they took back territory from the enemy, but not without subjecting their German and Italian forces to devastating consequences with as many as 620,000 dead and wounded. Allied forces would jump to the invasion of Sicily by mid-year and to Italy by September.

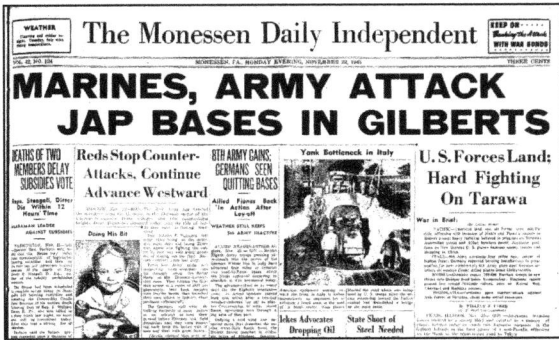

In the Pacific theater, the Allies' island-hopping offensive against Japanese-held territories continued in the Battles of the Solomon Islands and in New Guinea.

Attacks upon the islands of Bougainville, Tarawa, and Makin were costly for the combatants. US forces were gaining the advantage over the stubborn Japanese but losing men in difficult warfare.

During 1943, twelve Monessen service members sacrificed their lives. They were lost in faraway places such as the North Atlantic, North Africa, New Guinea, the Mediterranean, France, Italy, and once again, stateside.

As the citizens of Monessen read of lost service members, their boys continued enlisting in the armed forces. Everyone knew of families whose sons were already putting their lives on the line. Whether directly or socially, the war's impact was felt by citizens throughout the city.

Around the world guns, bombs, tanks, warplanes, warships, and even hand-to-hand combat were bringing devastation to soldiers and civilians alike. War had become a reality to most. But to many, it had already become a nightmare.

★ ★ ★

PVT CHARLES H. STONAGE

Service Number 33290177
SS Dorchester, Overseas Service Army, Casual Section, US Army
Lost at Sea Off Coast of Greenland, February 3, 1943

The torpedo exploded into the side of the SS Dorchester. It was 12:55 AM, 90 miles southwest of Greenland, and the sea was 34 degrees. A man could live no longer than 20 minutes in the icy waters.

SS Dorchester (US Coast Guard)

On that cold February night in 1943, Monessen's Private Charles Stonage and most of the 900 passengers and crew were asleep in their bunks. Three minutes after the explosion the Dorchester's captain ordered "Abandon Ship!"

Within 30 minutes the ship's mast was leaning into the water as the Dorchester tilted nearly 85 degrees. Suddenly, the ship plunged bow-first below the water. Only two of the ship's fourteen lifeboats had been launched. PVT Stonage and 674 others were gone. The sinking of the Dorchester was America's single largest loss of life during a ship convoy in WWII.

The Stonage Family of Monessen

Charles Henry Stonage was born into a family that would experience more than its fair share of hardship and tragedies. He arrived on November 18, 1902, son of John and Agnes (née Cresbar or Crebar) Stonage in Monessen, Pennsylvania. John and Agnes had immigrated from eastern Europe in the 1890's.

Because of the changing national borders during those years, conflicting records claim that they were born in Russia, Austria, and Germany.

John, a laborer, had some run-ins with the law and served time in the Allegheny County workhouse in 1895. In 1907, while living in the small Pennsylvania coal mining village of Dutch Town, police were summoned to his home on more than one occasion for "raising Cain" and brandishing a firearm.

Charles was the seventh of eight children born to John and Agnes. Andrew was born in 1888 in Austria and immigrated to the United States with his mother as an infant. Joseph arrived next (1891), followed by Josephine (1897), Frank (1898), Mary (1901), John Matthew (1902), Charles, then Emma (1906).

Charles' oldest brother Andrew was passionate about the emerging war (WWI) in Europe and was arrested in 1915 for disrupting proceedings at the University of Pittsburgh in the name of the war. He enlisted with the US Army and fought in France, only to return under the Army's care for his mental health. By 1930, Andrew was remanded to a Veterans Home in Ohio, where he lived out the remaining years of his life.

Joseph, Charles' second oldest brother, had left for Gary, Indiana, for a job in a Gary tin mill. When WWI began, Joseph and several friends enlisted with the US Army, and went to France where he was promoted to Corporal (CPL).

However, while serving in the 2nd Battalion of the 5th Infantry Division, CPL Joseph Stonage was killed in action just a month before Germany surrendered.

By 1920, the family was living at 176 Louis Avenue in Rostraver Township, Pennsylvania. All of the children but 14-yr-old Emma were employed as laborers.

Charles joined the US Navy by 1921, at the rank of Able Seaman. In February that year, he found himself in the Navy Hospital at Hampton

Charles' brother Joseph, killed in action WWI (Soldiers Of The Great War, Volume 3, 1920)

Roads, Virginia, with the German measles. Sometime between 1920 and 1930, his father John passed away. Charles decided against making a career in the US Navy and returned home to Pennsylvania. His brother John married in 1928 but would experience another Stonage family tragedy when his wife died in 1945 after falling from a window.

In 1924, Charles married Mary Lutes (Lutz) and they settled in Monessen. By 1930, they were renting an apartment at 17 East Schoonmaker Avenue, and Charles was working in a Monessen steel mill. A son, Charles Lutes Stonage, was born on November 25, 1925. In 1934, Charles' mother Agnes suffered a stroke, and passed away six months later at the age of 67. Four years later, Charles spent a night in jail for being drunk and disorderly at the Bank Tavern.

By 1940, Charles and Mary had separated and were living apart. Mary and their son, now in his first year at Monessen High School, were renting a home at 804 Donner Avenue in Monessen.

The US Enters WWII

Japanese forces launched a surprise attack on the US military bases in Pearl Harbor, Hawaii, on December 7, 1941. The US declared war on Japan, and as an ally of the Japanese Empire, Germany declared war on the US. Military service was now looming for any service-eligible American man, including 39-yr-old Charles.

Charles registered for the US military draft on February 16, 1942. He was unemployed and living with his sister Josephine and her husband Ferdinand Mankedick at 625 Rostraver Avenue in Monessen. At the time, Charles was a 5'8", 150 lb 39-yr-old with black hair and brown eyes. By July, he was hired by a beverage company.

Four months later, on July 30, 1942, Charles was drafted into the US Army. He entered active service at Fort George Meade, Maryland, on August 15, and three days later he arrived at Camp Croft, South Carolina, for training. Camp Croft was one of four Replacement Training Centers in the US, to prepare Army infantrymen for deployment wherever they were needed.

By mid-November, the Army was ready to put PVT Charles Stonage into service. He was sent to Fort Slocum, New York, where he staged with other units for deployment. PVT Stonage was temporarily placed in the Overseas Service Army, Casual Section, awaiting permanent assignment while continuing his training.

PVT Stonage remained at Fort Slocum until the third week in January, when he and 900 others boarded the transport ship SS Dorchester for a destination that would remain a secret until they departed the port. They left New York on January 22, 1943.

The Dorchester had been built in 1926 as a commercial passenger steamship. It was requisitioned by the War Shipping Administration in January 1942 as a troopship serving the transport needs of the US Army. It was nearly 400 ft long and over 50 ft wide, weighing over 5,600 tons.

The ship was loaded with 539 US Army officers and enlisted men, a 23-man US Navy gun crew, 35 Coast Guardsmen, 155 civilian employees of the War Department, 16 Danish citizens, and a crew of 132. The planned route would take them to St. John's Newfoundland, Canada, and on to its final destination. The secret was now revealed... They were heading to Narsarsuaq, Greenland.

Greenland! Greenland?

Certainly, PVT Stonage and the troops aboard the Dorchester wondered why they were heading to Greenland, a desolate Danish island possession at the top of the northwest Atlantic Ocean off the coast of Canada. Denmark was now in the hands of the invading Germany army, so what was the purpose for going to this remote destination?

The US could not allow Greenland to fall into the hands of the German enemy. They signed an agreement with Denmark's US ambassador to protect the territory in exchange for placing strategic military installations on the island. The US was sending aircraft and ships to Europe, and weather stations in Greenland would be critical for forecasting the weather moving across the North Atlantic. Importantly, the air route for ferrying military aircraft from the US to the United Kingdom required stops in Labrador, Greenland, and Iceland. Labrador was securely located in Canada, Iceland had just been occupied by the British, so airfields were necessary in Greenland to complete the ferry route.

The US Navy had established code names for places around the world, and the codename for Greenland was "Bluie". When the US Army Air Corps decided to build air bases on Greenland to support their ferrying route, the base at Narsarsuaq was called Bluie West One… the first based on Greenland, located on its west coast. Eventually, 14 "Bluie" bases with different functions were planned, from airfields to weather stations. Blue West One was the primary airfield in Greenland on the ferrying route to the UK.

The Dorchester departed New York as one of six ships in a lightly armed convoy SC-19 and traveled in its center. The others were two merchant ships (SS Lutz and SS Biscaya) and their three escorts (US Coast Guard cutters Comanche, Escanaba, and Tampa).

The captain of the Dorchester, fearing attack by German submarines, had ordered passengers and crew to their bunks fully dressed in their life vests. In the hot sleeping quarters of the ship, few followed the order.

Torpedo!

As the convoy approached its destination just before 1 a.m. on February 3, 1943, an explosion rocked the ship. German U-Boat U-223 had spotted the convoy and fired five torpedoes. Only one hit a ship, the Dorchester.

The Dorchester was hit amidships near the engine room. The explosion was muffled but there was considerable concussion felt throughout the ship. The engine room immediately flooded, bringing the ship to a halt as she swung to starboard and stopped. Within seconds the lights went out. As the men roused from their sleep and scrambled toward the exits in the dark, they began to cascade down the steep decks as the ship severely listed to starboard. Many never donned their life vests, and only two of the fourteen lifeboats were successfully launched.

During the 25 minutes after the explosion, men began to enter the frigid water. Four chaplains, George L. Fox, Clark V. Poling, John P. Washington, and Alexander B. Goode, assisted the men. Seeing that several men lacked life vests, the chaplains removed theirs and handed them to those without. The chaplains would go down with the Dorchester and would soon be memorialized as American heroes.

At about 1:20 a.m., the Dorchester sank beneath the surface of the sea. The water temperature was 34 degrees, and the air was 36 degrees. Survival in the water beyond 20 minutes was humanly impossible. The escorting ships rushed to the scene to rescue survivors, but there were too few ships and too many men in the frigid water to collect them all quickly. Six-hundred, seventy-four men lost their lives, including PVT Charles Henry Stonage.

Shortly after the disaster, his family was informed that he was missing. In late March, they were informed that he was now on an official casualty list. Information regarding the loss of the Dorchester remained unannounced until nearly 18 months later.

Charles H. Stonage, Remembered

PVT Charles Henry Stonage was never recovered. His name is inscribed on the East Coast Memorial in Manhattan, New York, and on the WWII Veterans Memorial Tablet, located at the intersection of Grand Boulevard and Euclid Drive in Monessen City Park. He was posthumously awarded the Purple Heart.

His son, Charles Lutes Stonage, joined the US Navy in November 1944 and served with the Navy for forty years, attaining the rank of Commander. He passed away in 2013, and his obituary noted that "He had a million-dollar smile". No doubt his father would have been proud.

★ ★ ★

PVT VICTOR A. TRILLI

Service Number 33078873
Battery D, 17th Field Artillery Regiment, US Army
Killed in action, Battle of Sidi Bou Zid, Tunisia, February 14, 2943

When Private Victor Trilli was assigned to the US Army's 17th Field Artillery Regiment in 1941, he was probably relieved. Their 155 mm howitzer guns could fire their shells at targets eight miles away, certainly a safe distance from front line combat.

But until February 1943, the US Army had yet to directly engage with German Panzer tanks. Their inexperience and inferior weapons would result in a dramatic defeat at the Battle of Sidi Bou Zid, Tunisia. The 17th Field Artillery was decimated.

Victor Trilli would never again embrace his family back home in Monessen, Pennsylvania.

The Trilli Family

Victor Albert Trilli was born on October 14, 1917, to Paul and Mary (née DiFlorio) Trilli in Monessen, Pennsylvania. Paul and Mary had married in

1901. Paul worked in a Monessen steel mill while Mary managed the large Trilli family household.

Paul, born Ippolito Trilli in the village of Roccaroso in the Italian region of Abruzzo, immigrated to the United States in 1901 aboard the SS Galia. Mary, born Maria in the city of Napoli, Campania, Italy, also immigrated to the US in 1901. They initially settled in the village of Derry, Pennsylvania.

Victor, the sixth of eight children born to Paul and Mary, was originally given the Italian first name of Vittorio upon his birth. First to be born was Rosario (1901), followed by Attilio (1903), and Guido (called William, 1907), while the family was living in Derry. After moving to Dunbar, Pennsylvania, where Paul had taken a job at a stone quarry, sons Gisberto (James, 1908) and Raffaele (Ralph, 1910) arrived. The family moved to Monessen where Paul opened the town's first shoe repair shop. After Victor, the family's only daughter arrived, Antonitta (Minnie or Antonette, 1918), followed by Arturo (Arthur, 1921). Paul went to work in the steel mill by 1920 and had purchased a home at 432 Knox Avenue. He eventually became very involved in the Monessen community and was a founding member of the Italian Mutual Aid Society.

By 1930, the five oldest sons were either working with their father in the steel mill or in the Monessen tin mill while living at home to support the large family. Victor and his youngest siblings were attending school. Their uncle Rudolph Trilli was living with them while working at the shoe repair shop. Victor graduated from high school in the mid 1930's, and he was the time-keeper and scorer for the local basketball team. Victor went to work for Page Steel and Wire in Monessen. In 1936, Victor attended Citizens' Military Training at Fort Meade, Maryland, for a month. In his spare time, avid sportsman Victor helped coordinate the community's "Cramer" basketball team in 1937 and a softball team in 1940.

By 1940, Rosario, William, and Victor were living at home with their parents while working in the Monessen mills. James had completed his education as a podiatrist and opened a practice in town. Antoinette had left high school after completing her sophomore year, and Arthur was now in his senior year.

With Uncle Rudolph retired and still living with them it was a full house of nine Trilli's.

With the rumblings of war heard in Europe and the Pacific, the US Congress passed the Selective Service and Training Act in September 1940, including the first peacetime draft for the US military. On October 16, 1940, Victor, Ralph, William, and James joined millions of fellow American young men and registered for the draft on its first day. According to his draft registration, Victor was a 23-yr-old young man standing 5' 6", 139 lb with brown hair and brown eyes.

It did not take long before Victor was drafted into the US Army. He enlisted on July 8, 1941, and reported for duty at New Cumberland, Pennsylvania. By August, PVT Victor Trilli was with the Field Artillery Replacement Training Center, assigned to Battery A, 7th Battalion, 3rd Regiment. PVT Trilli would train as a crew on the M114 155 mm howitzer artillery. The M114 was a towed howitzer used by the US Army as a medium artillery piece. It could fire a round over 8 miles and was used across all theaters of WWII.

Upon completion of his initial training, PVT Trilli was assigned to Battery D of the 17th Field Artillery (FA) Regiment.

Three of his brothers would eventually enter military service, and the Trilli's would become a 4-Blue-Star Family.

The US Enters WWII

Japanese forces launched a surprise attack on the US military bases in Pearl Harbor, Hawaii, on December 7, 1941. The US declared war on Japan, and as an ally of the Japanese Empire, Germany declared war on the US. The war that Victor Trilli had been training for had begun.

The 17th FA Regiment had been training at Fort Bragg, North Carolina. Late March 1942, the Regiment moved to Camp Blanding, Florida. Then in July 1942 the Regiment returned to Fort Bragg for final equipment and staging… it was time to head overseas, and to war.

FOUR TRILLI BROTHERS IN THE ARMY
Pvt. Victor Trilli   Pvt. G. L. Trilli
Pvt. Arthur Trilli   Pvt. William Trilli

These four sons of Mr. and Mrs. Paul Trilli, of Knox avenue, are all in the Army. Victor recently was reported missing in action in North Africa. G. L. "Doc" Trilli, president of the School Board, is in the medical corps at Camp Ritchie, Md. Arthur is in the Air Corps at Richmond, Va., and William is in a tank destroyer outfit at Camp Bowie, Tex.

Monessen Daily Independent, March 18, 1943

The Regiment sailed from New York City on August 5, 1942, and arrived in Liverpool, England on August 17, 1942. They moved to Perham Downs, England for further intensive training. In November, they proceeded to Liverpool to embark once again to an unknown destination.

Operation Torch, the Allied invasion of North Africa, had begun. It was the first mass involvement of US troops in the war in the European/North African theater of the war. Three task forces with more than 100,000 men landed in Morocco and Algeria on November 8, 1942. Allied forces experienced initial success and drove eastward across North Africa against French Vichy forces, who were aligned with the German occupiers of European France. The French eventually surrendered and joined the Allies, but reinforcements were needed to oppose the German troops in Tunisia and eastward.

North Africa and the Battle of Sidi Bou Zid

On November 27, 1942, the 17th FA Regiment sailed to Oran, Algeria where they joined the Army's II Corps upon landing on December 6, 1942. In February 1943 they began pushing over 600 miles east to Tebessa, Algeria, at the Tunisian border. On the other side were the amassed forces of the German 5th Panzer Army. The US Army drove into Tunisia . . . and into harm's way.

On February 14, the 17th FA Regiment, an element of Combat Command A, was in position near the small village of Sidi Bou Zid, located west of the Faid Pass in southern Tunisia. The 10th and 21st Panzer Divisions encircled and struck Combat Command A under cover of a sand-storm. The 3-day engagement would become known as the Battle of Sidi Bou Zid. The most sophisticated weaponry of both forces was employed in the battle. Unfortunately, German weaponry and their desert fighting know-how was vastly superior to the Allies. It would prove decisive.

The 10th Panzer Division descended upon the

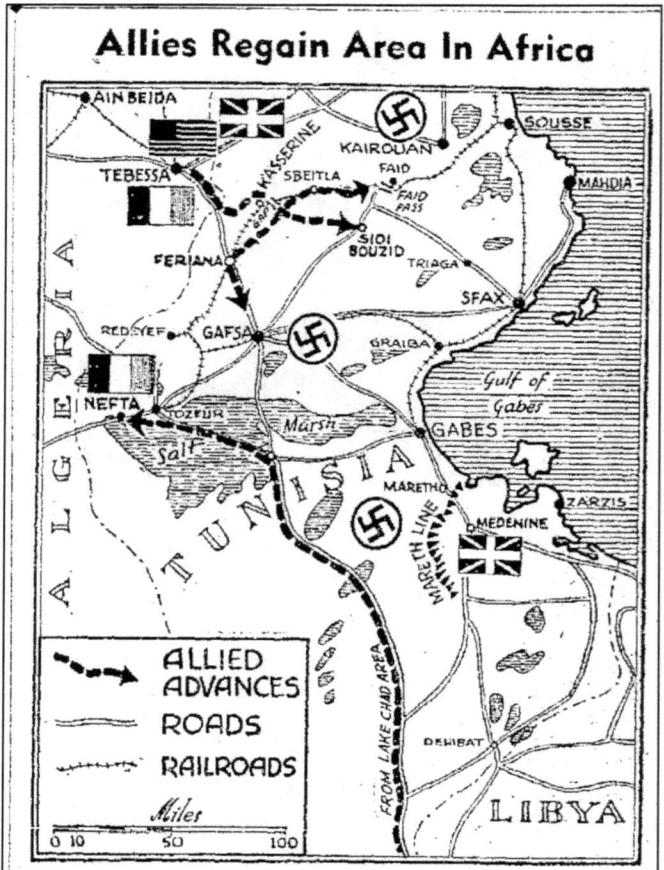

Map of Tunisia Campaign. Sidi Bou Zid is located upper center.
(Monessen Daily Independent March 6, 1943)

17th FA Regiment's 2nd Bn. Many of the artillerymen panicked and began to flee. They were ordered to displace to a safer position, but as they prepared to move, they were hit from the sky by German aircraft and were severely mauled. They lost one-half of their officers and enlisted men, and all twelve 155mm howitzers.

On the second day of the battle, February 15, 1943, PVT Victor Trilli was mortally wounded in combat. The Battle of Sidi Bou Zid had been the first action in which American soldiers were pitted against German panzers. It ended in disaster. PVT Trilli paid with his life.

Victor Trilli's family was notified by the War Department several weeks later that their son was missing in action. In September, they were informed that he had, in fact, been killed in combat.

Four men from Monessen were reported missing in the Tunisia Campaign, but only Trilli was ultimately reported killed in action. One Monessen man, PVT Howard May, had been captured and held as a POW in Germany until his escape in 1945.

Victor Trilli, Remembered

PVT Victor Trilli was initially buried at the American Military Cemetery in Gafsa, Tunisia. He was eventually returned to the US under the Return of the War Dead program and was buried at Grandview Cemetery in Monessen on March 12, 1949.

★ ★ ★

FM JOHN J. HOTOVCHIN

Service Number 271774
SS Harry Luckenbach, US Merchant Marine
Lost at Sea, North Atlantic Ocean, March 17, 1943

John Hotovchin was an adventuresome boy. Rules and scripted pathways were for others, not him. He tested those rules in the 1930's and learned that there were limits to what he could get away with.

So when the US entered WWII and his brothers considered military service, John decided to head for the high seas by joining the US Merchant Marine. He was going to see the world his own way.

Little did he know that the US Merchant Marine would incur a greater risk of death than any branch of the US military during WWII. He would contribute to that unfortunate statistic.

The Hotovchin Family

John Joseph Hotovchin was born on January 27, 1921, in Monessen, Pennsylvania, to Andrew and Anna (née Onda) Hotovchin. Andrew and Anna had married in 1914 in Butler, Pennsylvania. Andy was a laborer in the tin mill in Monessen while Anna managed the Hotovchin family household.

Andrew immigrated to the United States in 1911 from the village of Tusice in eastern Slovakia when it was within the Austro-Hungarian Empire. He sailed aboard the SS Prinz Adalbert under the name Andras Hotouszin. Anna immigrated to the US aboard the SS Kronprinzessin Cecilie in 1912 from the village of Celovce, also in eastern Slovakia. Celovce is only 24 miles from Andrew's home village of Tusice, but they traveled thousands of miles to America before they met. Andrew became a naturalized US citizen in 1938. Between 1911 and 1940, the family surname was also recorded in public documents as Hortorwiski, Hotochin, Hotochen, and Otovchin.

John was the fourth of nine children born to Andrew and Anna. The oldest brother Andrew John was born in 1915, followed by Annie (1917), and Mary (1918). John's younger siblings were Joseph Edward (1923), Mildred (1925), Emil Francis (1927), Irene (1928), and Helen (1930). Annie died from acute bronchitis at the age of two months.

For the first few years, the family lived in Monessen, then Brownsville, Lock Four, then back to Monessen by 1935, where they lived in a rented home at Rear 257 Linden Avenue. As a teenager, John ran afoul of the law more than once with a group of boys and was on a 5-year probation in the late 1930's. After a repeat infraction in 1939 during his second year at Monessen High School, he was placed at the Pennsylvania Industrial Training School at Morganza in Cecil Township.

The surprise attack by Japanese armed forces on the US military bases at Pearl Harbor, Hawaii, in December 1941 changed the world for John and his brothers Andy and Joseph. John was now home from Morganza, living on Linden Avenue with his parents, and working at the Page Steel and Wire Company in Monessen. On February 16, 1942, he registered in Monessen for the US armed forces draft as a 5' 4½ ", 140 lb 21-yr-old single man with brown hair and brown eyes. Brother Andy joined the US Army in August 1942 and Joseph joined the US Marines in September.

John Joins the Merchant Marine

John decided on a different path to the war and volunteered to serve with the US Merchant Marine. He joined on August 5, 1942, was assigned service number 271774, and left for training. The Hotovchin's were now a 3-Blue-Star family.

It is likely that John Hotovchin was trained at the US Maritime Service Training Station at Sheepshead Bay, Brooklyn, New York. The station was the largest maritime training station during World War II and was equipped to train 30,000 merchant seamen each year.

After training, John was assigned the entry-level position of Wiper. The Wiper position is the lowest-ranking unlicensed position in the engineering department, designated for apprentices to the engineering department where a basic working knowledge of plant layout is learned. Work to be performed by a wiper is typically of low-stakes nature and is meant to create a work-positive environment where sea time may be secured towards licensure. A wiper typically takes commands and directions from the 1st Assistant Engineer and works under the close supervision of the engineering department of his assigned vessel. He eventually rose to the rank of Fireman (FM). A fireman's station was deep in the engine room, and he was responsible for operating the fuel oil burning system to generate steam in boilers and stand watch in the fire room.

John was assigned to the American steam merchant ship SS Harry Luckenbach. The Luckenbach was originally ordered by the Luckenbach Steamship Company in 1919 and was converted into a troop ship (renamed USS Sol Navis) to bring US soldiers home from Europe after WWI. After returning to commercial operation as the SS Harry Luckenbach from 1920-1942, the company turned the ship over to the War Shipping Administration at Mobile, Alabama in April 1942 for use in transporting cargo across the Atlantic to the European theater of WWII. The Harry Luckenbach was armed with one 3 inch (i.e., diameter of ammunition) gun, one 4 inch gun, and eight 20 mm guns.

The Harry Luckenbach was scheduled to join Convoy HX 229 departing March 8, 1943, from New York City for Liverpool, England. Convoy HX 229,

SS Harry Luckenbach, formerly the USS Sol Navis (US Navy)

consisting of 40 ships, was to sail along the same route in proximity with Convoy SC 122, consisting of 60 ships. Little did the crews know that they were heading into the teeth of the German U-Boat fleet and largest convoy battle of WWII. Three U-Boat Wolfpacks totaling 37 torpedo-equipped submarines were lying in wait along three patrol lines in the middle of the North Atlantic Ocean 400 miles south/southeast of Greenland. The Harry Luckenbach was positioned at the vulnerable front corner of the convoy at station #111.

Disaster Strikes

At 2210 hrs the night of March 16, 1943, the first U-Boat torpedoed and sank the Norwegian ship Elin K, putting all ships on high alert. Over the next 1 1/2 hours, two more ships were struck and lost with four casualties, but the remaining crews rescued. The Harry Luckenbach had moved out of position, began to defensively and independently zig-zag its course, and had to be recalled back to station. But the luck of the SS Harry Luckenbach had run out.

Between 0337 and 0341 hours on March 17, German U-boat U-91 fired five torpedoes at Convoy HX 229 about 400 miles east-southeast of Greenland's Cape Farewell. The SS Harry Luckenbach was struck by two torpedoes on the starboard side amidships in the machinery spaces, causing her to sink within 3 minutes in the rough seas. Some of the nine officers, 45 crew members and 26 armed guards abandoned ship in three lifeboats, which were first spotted by the British destroyers HMS Beverley and HMS Volunteer. The British corvette HMS Pennywort came across them but could not pick them up because she already had 108 survivors of other ships on board. The British corvette HMS Anemone was ordered to locate the lifeboats but was unable to spot them. None of the men from the SS Harry Luckenbach were seen or heard from again.

The sea battle would continue for two more days. Twenty-two merchant ships and more than 300 merchant seamen were lost, 80 of which were from the SS Harry Luckenbach. FM John Hotovchin was among them.

The name of Merchant Seaman FM John Hotovchin is inscribed on the WWII Veterans Memorial Tablet, located at the intersection of Grand Boulevard and Euclid Drive in Monessen City Park. His name is also inscribed (as John Michael Hotochen) on the Fort Trumbull Merchant Marine Officers School World War II Memorial in New London, Connecticut. He was posthumously awarded the Merchant Marine Mariners Medal.

On April 9, 1954, a memorial tribute to John Hotovchin was printed in the Monessen Daily Independent newspaper by his family, which read:

> "Surge gently, tides of ocean deep,
> Croon softly, wind on waves,
> We know not where our sailors sleep –
> No crosses mark their graves.
> And though we grieve that they must be
> So lost to all held dear,
> God's arms hold fast our "lost at sea".
> He will be near - - so very near"

★ ★ ★

PVT GEORGE SHOLTIS

Service Number 33117171
Headquarter Company, 180th Infantry Regiment, 45th Infantry Division, US Army
Killed in Action near Pezzalistingo, Sicily, July 12, 1943

George Sholtis was drafted the same day that President Franklin Delano Roosevelt and the United States Congress declared war on Japan, December 8, 1941. He probably assumed that going into combat against the Japanese would be the first order of business.

But Japan's ally Germany declared war on the US, and Europe was now a possible destination for George. The Germans and their Italian allies were occupying the Mediterranean island of Sicily, and soon US forces would attempt to dislodge them on their way to the European continent.

After training stateside, Sicily was George's first stop. It was also his last.

The Sholtis Family

George Sholtis was born on November 14, 1919, to John and Susan "Susie" (née

TRANSFERRED TO FORT DEVENS

Pvt. George Sholtis, who recently transferred from Camp Croft, S. C., to Fort Devens, Mass. Private Sholtis is a son of Mr. and Mrs. John Sholtis of Graham avenue.

Monessen Daily Independent, June 3, 1942

Hamara) Sholtis in East Charleroi, Pennsylvania. John and Susie had married in Charleroi in 1906. John was a coal miner while Susie managed the Sholtis family household.

John, whose surname was originally Soltis, was born in Giraltovce in the Presov region of Slovakia and immigrated to the United States in 1902. Susie, whose native given name was Zuzanna, was born in Zelesnik, Slovakia, and also arrived in the US in 1902. They met and married in western Pennsylvania and settled in the industrial Monongahela River valley with opportunities for well-paying jobs.

George was the fifth of six children born to John and Susie. John (b1908) was first, followed by Anna (1911), Susan (1913), and Andrew (1916). His younger brother Michael arrived in 1924. In 1920 the family was living in a rented home in Rostraver Township, Pennsylvania, and by 1930, the family had purchased and moved into a home at 1029 Graham Avenue in Monessen. John was now working in a Monessen steel mill.

By 1940, George's sisters Anna and Susan had left home to start their own families. He was living with his parents and brothers in their home in Monessen. His father and older brothers were working in the steel mill. George completed his vocational education and was now working in the Civilian Conservation Corps. On July 1, 1941, he registered for the US armed forces draft in Monessen. George was a 5'9" 145 lb 21-yr-old with brown hair and blue eyes and was now working as a galvanizer at the local Pittsburgh Steel mill.

On December 7, 1941, the United States came under surprise attack at Pearl Harbor, Hawaii, and the US entered the war against Japan, Germany, and Italy. The very next day, on December 8, 1941, George enlisted in the US Army at New Cumberland, Pennsylvania.

PVT George Sholtis went off to US Army training at Camp Croft in South Carolina. In May 1942, he was assigned to the 45th Infantry Division and joined them in training at Fort Devens, Massachusetts. At Fort Devens, the 45th Infantry began training in amphibious landings in preparation for the invasion of Italy. It then moved to Pine Camp, New York for winter warfare training. In January 1943 the division moved to Fort Pickett, Virginia, for final training, and was sent to the Mediterranean Sea to join combat in the European theater of the war. PVT Sholtis was assigned to the Headquarters Company of the 45th's 180th Infantry Regiment.

Off to Sicily

The 45th Division was the only unit to ship straight from the US into the battle to take the island of Sicily from the German and Italian occupying forces in Operation Husky. They arrived in the Mediterranean in June 1943 and were assigned a lead role in the amphibious assault on Sicily. The 45th came ashore near Scoglitti on July 10 and began advancing north.

On July 12, 1943, about ten miles northwest of Scoglitti near the village of Pezzalistingo, an enemy artillery shell exploded near PVT George Sholtis' position. He was fatally struck by shrapnel and died that day.

The following month, his family was mistakenly informed that their son had been seriously wounded in combat. On September 16, they received a telegram from the War Department informing them that he had, in fact, been killed in action on July 12, 1943.

PVT George Sholtis was initially buried at the US Military Cemetery at Gela, Sicily. In 1947, all US servicemen buried in Sicily were relocated to Mt Soprano US Military Cemetery at Paestum, Italy. In 1948, he was finally interred at the Sicily-Rome American Cemetery at Nettuno, Italy. He was posthumously awarded the Purple Heart.

★ ★ ★

PVT MICHAEL GRAMATIKOS

Service Number 33292644
Medical Detachment, US Army
Killed in Auto Accident, New Jersey, July 5, 1943

Assigned to a Medical Detachment while in US Army training, Michael "Mike" Gramatikos thought that he was going to help his fellow soldiers recover from wounds suffered in combat. There was much to learn.

But even in training, men were exposed men to the same risks encountered by millions of Americans going about their daily lives.

Nearly a year into his training, Mike Gramatikos and four colleagues lost their lives to a reckless driver in New Jersey. They would never get the chance to save others as they had planned.

The Gramatikos Family

Mike Gramatikos was born on September 22, 1920, to Markos and Kiraniou "Anna" (née Koklanaris) Gramatikos in Monessen, Pennsylvania. Markos and Anna had married in

1912 in Greece before coming to the United States. Markos was a house painter, and Anna managed the family household as well as their boarding home where they also lived.

Markos and Anna were born in the town of Agios Kirykos on the Greek island of Ikaria in the Aegean Sea. Markos immigrated to the US in 1912 aboard the SS Argentina, and Anna followed in 1916 aboard the SS Themistocles with their first-born child. Markos had settled in Monessen and rented a home at 29 Sixth Street in Monessen's downtown. He became a naturalized US citizen in 1926.

Mike was the fourth of six children born to Markos and Anna. The first was Maria, who was born in 1913 in Greece. Stavroula "Stella" arrived next (1917) and was the couples' first child born in America. Nicholas (1918) arrived next, followed by Moschula "Molly" (1924) and Lillian (1928).

By 1930, Markos was employed as a painter at the Pittsburgh Steel mill in Monessen. The family was now living in a rented home at 1017 Highland Avenue, and they were no longer housing boarders. By 1940, the family had purchased the home on Highland. Maria had married and moved out to start her own family. Stella and Nick had graduated from Monessen High School and were working at the steel mill with their father. Mike and Molly were attending Monessen High and Lillian was still in grade school.

While in high school, Mike was in the academic curriculum. He was also in the school band and the school orchestra and was his homeroom secretary. Mike graduated from Monessen High in 1941 and went to work at Pittsburgh Steel.

The surprise attack by Japanese armed forces on the US military bases at Pearl Harbor, Hawaii, in December 1941 changed the world for Mike and his brother Nick. Mike registered for the US armed forces draft three months later on February 16, 1942, in Monessen. He was a tall (5'11½") skinny (140 lb) 21- yr-old single man with brown hair and brown eyes, living at home with his parents.

On August 28, 1942, Mike was drafted into the US Army. He enlisted in Greensburg, Pennsylvania, and reported for boot camp. Mike reported for duty at Fort George Meade, Maryland on August 30. His brother Nick was drafted into the Army three months later in November. The Gramatikos' were now a two-Blue-Star Family.

PVT Mike Gramatikos was eventually assigned to a medical detachment at Fort Dix, New Jersey, where he was serving through June 1943. However, fate would intervene, cutting short his military career and his life.

A Victim of Reckless Driving

While returning from the July 4th holiday weekend on July 5, 1943, PVT Michael Gramatikos was driving with four other servicemen between Camden and Berlin, New Jersey, when his car collided head-on with a public service bus near the intersection of Clementon Road and White Horse Pike near Hammonton shortly before 1 AM. The bus, heading for the bus garage, had made a sharp turn in the intersection, failed to stay on the right side of the highway and collided with the car traveling in the opposite direction. PVT Michael Gramatikos was pinned behind the steering wheel while his four colleagues were ejected from the vehicle. The five servicemen lost their lives in the accident. The driver of the bus was charged with reckless driving. [4]

PVT Michael Gramatikos was returned to Monessen where funeral services were held. He was laid to rest at Grandview Cemetery in Monessen.

★ ★ ★

---

[4] Others who lost their lives in the accident:
Private Anthony Meligritis, 23, 33379672, of Baltimore, MD, US Army
Private Herman Clark Tribolet, 29, 32764460, of Camden, NJ, US Army
Joseph Taylor Cornelius, 25, 6529975, of Dubois, PA, US Navy Reserve
AEM 3/C Orville Marion Norman, 20, of Galena, IL, 6210747, US Naval Air Station, Atlantic City

SGT JOSEPH O. SCRIP

Service Number 33402685
Headquarters & Supply Company, 324th Engineers Battalion, 99th Infantry Div, US Army
Died while training, Mississippi, July 20, 1943

US Army training is designed to build skills, discipline, and endurance. It's rigors expose human vulnerabilities with the expectation that further training will help recruits learn the techniques required to overcome them.

Through no fault of their own, sometimes the rigors of training can subject a soldier to circumstances that their physical condition is not prepared to withstand.

On July 20, 1943, in Camp Van Dorn in Southern Mississippi, daytime temperatures were in the 90's with high humidity. The combination of the day's weather and the strenuous training exercises were enough to take the life of SGT Joseph Scrip.

The Scrip Family

Joseph Oswald Scrip was born on March 2, 1922, to Mike and Mildred "Millie" (née Malanka) Scrip in Donora, Pennsylvania. Mike and Millie had married in 1912. Mike was a laborer on the railroad while Millie managed the Scrip family household.

Mike, whose surname was originally spelled Skrip or Skryp, immigrated to the United States from the Galicia region of Eastern Europe in 1904. Millie was also from Galicia, and she immigrated to the US in 1912. They met and married in western Pennsylvania and settled in the industrial Monongahela River valley with opportunities for well-paying jobs.

Joseph was the fifth of seven children born to Mike and Millie. John (b1913) was first, followed by Frank (1915), Mary (1917), Michael Jr. (1919), Peter Charles (1924), and Harry (1927). In 1920 the family was living in a rented home at 626 Second Street in Donora, and by 1924, the family had moved upriver into a rented home in Allenport. In 1936, their father Mike passed away from heart disease.

By 1940, Joseph's eldest siblings John, Frank, Mary, and Michael had moved out to begin their own families and careers. He was living with his widowed mother in Allenport with Peter and Harry. Joseph had left school after the eighth grade to support the family, and was now working as a truck driver in reforestation in the Civilian Conservation Corps.

On December 7, 1941, the United States came under surprise attack at Pearl Harbor, Hawaii, and the US entered the war against Japan, Germany, and Italy. Joseph registered for the US armed forces draft on June 30, 1942, as a 5'11", 185 lb 20-yr-old with brown hair and brown eyes. He was now employed at Pittsburgh Steel in Allenport.

On September 17, 1942, Joseph married his sweetheart, Margaret Kerestes, of nearby Monessen, and the couple moved there. However, the war interrupted their lives, and two months later Joseph was drafted into the US Army. He enlisted on November 25, 1942, and was off to Army boot camp on December 2. When he left, Margaret was pregnant with their child.

Four Scrip brothers, Michael Jr, Joseph, Peter, and Harry would all enter the US armed forces during WWII. The Scrips would eventually become a 4-Blue-Star family.

Private Joseph Scrip soon demonstrated strong leadership during training, and before too long he was promoted to the rank of Sergeant. SGT Scrip was assigned to the 324th Engineers Battalion of the 99th Infantry Division and was placed in the Headquarters and Supply Company.

Training in the Southern US

The 324th was training at Camp Van Dorn, Mississippi, with the 99th Division, when he arrived. Camp Van Dorn was in the far southwestern edge of Mississippi on the border with Louisiana. In 1943, there were over 30,000 troops in basic and advanced infantry training at the camp.

However, the hot and humid summer of 1943 took its toll on the troops. Then on July 20, 1943, SGT Scrip fell victim to sunstroke. He was transported to the nearby hospital, but SGT Scrip did not survive.

SGT Joseph Scrip was transported to Monessen where he was buried at Holy Name Cemetery on Sunday July 25. His son, Joseph O. Scrip, Jr., was born at 2 AM the following day, ten hours after his father's funeral service. He would only know his father from the memories shared by his mother and the Scrip family.

★ ★ ★

PVT JOHN KVAKA JR

Service Number 13057826
21st Troop Carrier Squadron, 374th Troop Carrier Group, US Army Air Corps
Lost in Combat, Tsili Tsili, New Guinea, August 15, 1943

The flight of unarmed Douglas C-47 Skytrains was coming in to land at Tsili Tsili airfield on New Guinea in the Southwest Pacific. They were in their landing pattern before they knew what was about to hit them.

Radio operator PVT John Kvaka, Jr, was maintaining radio contact with the airfield's control tower when his C-47, nicknamed "Liliane", was jumped by a group of Japanese Ki-43 "Oscar" fighters. Liliane was hit by the fighters' bullets and caught fire. PVT Kvaka and his crewmates did not stand a chance.

The Kvaka Family

John Kvaka, Jr. was born on April 26, 1919, in Polom, Czechoslovakia, to John Sr. and Mary (née Selcan) Kvaka. John and Mary were married in Polom in 1913. John was a farmer while Maria managed the Kvaka family household. John Jr's only sibling, his sister Pauline, was born in Polom in 1921.

John Sr, born Jan Kvakova in Polom, arrived in Halifax, Nova Scotia, Canada in March 1924 aboard the SS Cedric. He was heading to work on a farm in Winnipeg, Manitoba, but by October 1926, he was living in Montreal, Quebec. That month John immigrated to the United States, destined for his brother-in-law's home in Donora, Pennsylvania, but instead went to Cleveland, Ohio, where he applied for US citizenship the following month. John eventually made his way to Monessen, Pennsylvania, gained employment as a steelworker, and sent for his wife and children. Mary, John, and Pauline arrived in New York City in October 1929 aboard the SS Aquitania to travel to Monessen and live in the US permanently. John was ten years old, and Pauline was eight.

By 1930, John Sr. had saved enough of his earnings to buy a home at 1134 Rostraver Street in Monessen. John Jr. and Pauline were now in school, where they would continue their education until graduating from Monessen High School.

In 1940, after graduating from high school, John Jr. took respite at Torrance State Hospital in Pennsylvania for his mental well-being. While there, he registered for the first US armed forces draft on its first day, October 16, 1940, in accordance with the recently passed Selective Service Act. He registered as a 5'8" 150 lb 21-yr-old with brown hair and brown eyes. After treatment, John emerged from Torrance ready to serve his new country.

The surprise attack by Japanese armed forces on the US military base at Pearl Harbor, Hawaii, in December 1941 changed the world for John Jr. Instead of waiting to be drafted into military service, John volunteered and joined the US Army Air Corps. He enlisted on February 4, 1942, just two months after the US declared war.

John enlisted at the rank of Private and was sent to Air Corps training stateside. He was soon recognized for his competence in radio technology and communications, a specialty desperately needed in crews of long-range, multi-engine aircraft. PVT Kvaka was directed to specialize in aircraft radio communications and attended the Army Air Corp's "Radio University" at Scott Field, Illinois.

PVT John Kvaka was assigned to the 21st Troop Carrier Squadron, consisting of the twin-engine Douglas C-47 Skytrain transport aircraft. C-47s were military versions of the commercially proven Douglas DC-3 aircraft and would become the indispensable logistical workhorse of the Allied air forces around the world during the war.

Off to New Guinea

PVT Kvaka's stateside training was brief, and after six months, he was sent to the Southwest Pacific theater of the war. He departed the US on August 18, 1942, with the C-47s of the 21st Troop Carrier Squadron. Once established

Douglas C-47 Skytrain Transport Aircraft (US Air Force)

on its new base in Australia, the 21st Troop Carrier Squadron participated in paratroop drops at Nadzab, New Guinea in September 1942. It continued to fly combat resupply and casualty evacuation missions from Brisbane. In November 1942 the squadron was assigned to the 374th Troop Carrier Group. The 374th had recently arrived from the United States equipped with new C-47s.

PVT John Kvaka continued to fly transport operations with cargo and troops over the next year as US forces built their capabilities throughout the region. They were part of a critical supply chain that stretched thousands of miles over open seas to remote island bases. The C-47s faced the daily threat of Japanese fighter interceptors arising from their own island bases below. The number of missions logged by PVT Kvaka is not known… but his luck would run out in August 1943 in New Guinea.

On August 15, 1943, at Port Moresby, Papua New Guinea, PVT Kvaka joined the crew of 1LT Enoch P. Burley aboard C-47 #41-18682, nicknamed "Liliane", in a group of C-47s bound for Tsili Tsili Airfield. The C-47s were escorted by P-39 Airacobras from the 40th and 41st Fighter Squadrons.

Attacked by Japanese Fighter Aircraft

While in the traffic pattern to land at Tsili Tsili Airfield, a formation of Japanese bombers and fighters approached. The second flight of C-47s, which included Liliane, was intercepted by Japanese Ki-43 "Oscar" fighters from the 59th Flying Regiment.

During the first attack, Liliane was hit by gunfire and set ablaze.

Japanese Ki-43 Oscar Fighter

During a second attack, pilot Burley was killed, and the co-pilot LT James Miles tried to land between trees near Tsili Tsili. As the aircraft came to Earth, the fuel tanks exploded, and all but one of those aboard perished. The survivor would eventually die of his wounds.

PVT John Kvaka Jr. died in the crash of Liliane that day. Two weeks later, his family was informed by the War Department that their son had been killed in action in New Guinea. He was 24 years old.

PVT John Kvaka Jr. was initially buried at a temporary American cemetery in New Guinea. He was recovered under the Return of the war Dead Program and returned to the US in May 1948 aboard the Army's transport ship SS LT George W. G. Boyce. PVT John Kvaka Jr. was buried at Grandview Cemetery in Monessen on July 14, 1948, and was posthumously awarded the Purple Heart.

★★★

T/SGT August Restaino

Service Number 13010670
559th Bomb Squadron, 387th Bomb Group, Medium, US Army Air Corps
Killed in Action over France, September 2, 1943

For August Restaino, each decade since his birth brought another tragedy to his Monessen family. The 1940's were no different.

The Restaino Family

August was the son of Nicodemo "Nick" and Elvira (née Aterna) Restaino. He was born as "Agosto" in New Eagle, Pennsylvania on July 30, 1919. The family was living in Van Voorhis, Pennsylvania, where Nick was a farmer.

Nick was born in the town of L'Aquila in the Abruzzo region of Italy and immigrated to the United States in 1905. Elvira, also born in L'Aquila, arrived in the US in 1911. The couple gave birth to four children: Ladisca (b1914), twins Ida and Ada Clara (1915), and August.

Tragedy Strikes Twice

The family's first tragedy happened in January 1919, when Elvira came down with influenza, was urgently admitted to the hospital, and passed away from pneumonia seven days later at the age of 22. Despite their loss, the family pushed on.

By 1930, Nick worked in a Monessen steel mill and had purchased a home at 610 Third Street in Monessen. Three years later, tragedy struck once more when Nick was hit by a car. He died from the wounds received in the accident in May 1933.

Ladisca, Ada, and Ida each married in the mid 1930's, and August made his home with them. While at Monessen High School, August played guard on the football team and made his mark as a sophomore player. The local newspaper cited him as a "light but crack guard," and in 1936 he lettered for his role on the team. August graduated from Monessen High School in 1936. The school newspaper included him in their Senior Hall of Fame for his roles in football, senior council, and the class day play where he played "The Prophet" in "A Trip to Mars" and told of the prophecy for their senior class.

In January 1939, a near-tragedy visited August when, while driving a truck, he struck a sled-riding 10-year-old boy. Although the boy suffered a serious head injury, the boy survived much to August's relief. By 1940, August was working as a laborer in a Monessen steel mill.

August Heads to the Air Corps

August took great interest in aviation, and in September 1940, he volunteered to enlist with the US Army Air Corps. He was immediately sent off for training at the Air Corps Technical School at Chanute Field, Illinois, where he spent the following year.

August Restaino left Chanute Field to further his training at Hamilton Army Airfield, California, on the San Francisco Bay. He had just arrived at Hamilton Field when the Japanese made their surprise attack at the US military base at Pearl Harbor on December 7, 1941. August trained at Hamilton Field until transferring to Sarasota Army Airfield, Florida, in August 1942, and then to Fort Myers Army Airfield, Florida, that October.

August trained as a radio operator for bomber aircraft. The role of radio operator was critical for the proper functioning of the air crew and for accurately executing its mission. He had to be highly skilled in all of the technical communications equipment both within the aircraft as well as between aircraft and with ground stations. The radio operator had to familiarize himself with all of the frequencies, codes, and signals in use by a bomb group on the day of a mission, and he needed to keep the flight crew informed as new information was received from other aircraft and the ground. August was soon promoted to the rank of Technical Sergeant (T/SGT).

B-26 painted with unit markings of 387th Bomb Group, "Tiger Tails" (Commemorative Air Force)

The B-26 and the Tiger Tails

In January 1943, he again transferred, this time to McDill Field, Florida, where the 387th Bomb Group, Medium, (BG,M) had been formed. The 387th BG,M was equipped with B-26 Martin Marauder medium bombers. Although the B-26 could carry the same bomb load as a B-17 Flying Fortress heavy bomber, the B-26 carried less fuel, weight, and crew, and was intended for shorter range, tactical missions. The 387th BG,M would become known as the "Tiger-Striped Marauders" or "Tiger Tails" for their distinctive black and yellow stripes on their aircraft rudders.

T/SGT Restaino joined the crew of LT William F. Vosburgh and the 559th Bomb Squadron of the 387th BG,M. They continued their training as a unified crew at McDill Field before transferring to Drane Field in Lakeland, Florida in April 1943, and then to Godman Field, Ft. Knox, Kentucky in May. They trained at Godman in preparation for their overseas assignment and departed Godman in June for their US jumping off point at Presque Isle, Maine. The group departed Maine on June 19 for Labrador, then Greenland, Iceland, and Scotland before arriving at their new home in England: RAF Chipping Ongar in Essex in June 1943.

Their combat missions began in earnest at the end of July 1943. The group flew eight missions over German-occupied positions in France through August. Their primary targets were air bases of the German Luftwaffe, in conjunction with other bomb groups of the Army Air Corps' VIII Air Support Command.

Janet's Dream Becomes a Nightmare

On September 2, 1943, 216 B-26s were dispatched to five targets in France, with 36 aircraft per target. The missions were to bomb a power station at Rouen and Luftwaffe airfields at Poix/Nord and Lille/Nord Airfields.

The 6-man crew of LT Vosburgh and T/SGT Restaino was to attack the airdrome at Lille, France, at dusk. They would be flying their usual aircraft, B-26 #41-31629, nicknamed "Janet's Dream".

The 387th BG took off at 1730 hrs in a formation of 36 B-26 Marauders under escort by British RAF Spitfire fighters. They encountered no enemy fighters, but the German anti-aircraft artillery was quite heavy as they crossed the coast of France.

Due to heavy anti-aircraft artillery "flak", the B-26s of the 387th were forced to turn back before reaching their target. As the group flew over Dunkirk, France, the luck of Janet's Dream ran out. The aircraft was struck by flak in its right engine, catching fire. Janet's Dream was seen to fall, then level out, and then the wings folded, and the B-26 exploded as it fell to Earth. It crashed 1 km south of Mille Brugge and 6 km east of Bergues.

Four crewmen perished. Two parachuted to safety, were captured, and became prisoners of war.

But Monessen's T/SGT August Restaino was last seen by the crew of nearby aircraft, falling from his aircraft without a parachute. His body and those of his three comrades were found by German troops on the outskirts of Dunkirk.

Crew of B-26 Janet's Dream. Restaino is 2nd from right (American Air Museum)

August Restaino Remembered

In October, T/SGT Restaino's family received a telegram from the War Department that he was missing-in-action. In December, they were informed that he was, in fact, killed-in-action.

T/SGT August Restaino and his three crewmates were initially buried by French citizens under German supervision in a community cemetery in Dunkirk. They were subsequently relocated in October 1945 to the US Military Cemetery at St. Andre, France. His remains were finally interred at the Normandy American Cemetery at Colleville-sur-mer, Normandy, France.

★ ★ ★

S2C JOHN E. ZAPORA

Service Number 6531411
USS Savannah CL-42, US Navy
Lost aboard ship, Salerno Bay, September 11, 1943

John Edward Zapora was at battle stations as his warship USS Savannah fell under attack off the coast of Italy. In an instant, John was gone.

A radio-guided bomb had been dropped from an attacking German bomber. Its bombardier expertly steered the bomb toward the center of the Savannah. It penetrated 37 feet into the ship's hull before exploding. Seaman 2nd Class John Zapora and most of the 197 men who perished probably did not know what hit them.

The Zapora Family

John Edward Zapora was born on December 24, 1924, to John Stanley and Mary (née Frenchek) Zapora in Monessen, Pennsylvania. John and Mary had married in 1920 in Herminie, Pennsylvania, where John worked as a coal miner.

John Stanley, born Jan Zapara in the village of Nevtessiew or Nederuw, Poland, immigrated to the United States in 1912 aboard the SS Vaderland. Mary was born in Pila, Poland, and immigrated to the US in 1904 with her mother, following her father who arrived in 1902.

John Edward, called Edward within the family, was the fourth of nine children born to John Stanley and Mary. Sophie (b1919) was first to arrive, followed by Violet (1921), and Leon (1922). After Edward came Bernice (1926),

Mildred (1929), Constance (1933), Martin (1935), and Carey (1939). Sophie and Violet were born in Herminie before the family moved briefly to New Kensington, Pennsylvania, where Leon was born. By 1924, they had moved to Seneca Avenue in Monessen.

Tragedy befell the family in 1937 when four-year-old Constance succumbed to extensive burn injuries. Three days earlier, her clothing had caught fire when she came too close to their gas stove. The family was devastated.

By 1940, the Zapora's had moved into an eight-family apartment building at 328 Schoonmaker Avenue in Monessen. Sophie and Violet had completed their schooling and were helping their mother raise the youngest children, Martin and Carey. The rest of the children were attending school. Their father was now working at the Lober Coal Mine of the Hillman Coal Company in nearby Fayette City.

Even though it was 1940, the family still did not have a telephone. Every penny was going toward food, clothing, and rent.

The US Enters WWII

Japanese forces launched a surprise attack on the US military bases in Pearl Harbor, Hawaii, on December 7, 1941. The US declared war on Japan, and as an ally of the Japanese Empire, Germany declared war on the US. War was about to disrupt the Zapora family.

Young men all over the country were rushing to enlist and defend the US. John Edward decided to leave high school early and join the military. For him, the US Navy was the way to see the world. But at the age of 17, John needed the consent of his parents, which they gave with heavy hearts. So on October 16, 1942, John Edward enlisted with the US Naval Reserve in Pittsburgh. And by the end of the month, he was at the US Navy Training School in Newport, Rhode Island, as an Apprentice Seaman.

It did not take long for John to ship out. After just six weeks training at Newport, he was sent to New York City harbor to report to the USS Savannah. He stepped aboard the Savannah on December 3, 1942, at the rank of Seaman 2nd Class (S2c).

Aboard the Warship USS Savannah

Light Cruiser USS Savannah CL-42 ca 1943 (US Navy)

The USS Savannah, CL-42, was a Brooklyn-Class Light Cruiser launched in 1937. A light cruiser is an armored warship about two football fields long and one-tenth as wide. While lighter and smaller than heavy cruisers, they still had extended range and could act independently around the world.

The Savannah had five main turrets each housing three 6-inch diameter guns. Each gun could fire eight to ten 130 lb shells per minute at targets up to eleven miles away. She also had eight anti-aircraft guns, eight 50-caliber machine guns, and four catapult-launched scout planes. The ship was crewed with a total of 868 officers and enlisted men. Despite being a "Light Cruiser", the Savannah was a formidable ship indeed.

The Savannah had just returned from successful duty in November supporting Operation Torch, the Allied invasion of North Africa. After brief repairs in Norfolk, Virginia, and replenishment in New York, she departed to join the Navy's South Atlantic Patrol on December 25, 1942. It was a very special Christmas for S2c John Edward Zapora, his first cruise on the Atlantic.

The ship was on its way to the farthest eastern port of Recife, Brazil, where their primary mission was the destruction of any German blockade-running ships in the South Atlantic Ocean. These runners were attempting to transport desperately needed cargo from South America to German territory to support their war effort.

Pollywogs, Shellbacks, and the South Atlantic

En route, Savannah crossed the Equator, triggering the traditional "King Neptune" line-crossing initiation ceremony. Sailors who have never crossed the Equator, such as S2c Zapora, are "Pollywogs"… they were to be brutally hazed by the "Shellbacks", sailors who have crossed before. With an officer sitting as King Neptune in his court, humiliating treatment is doled out to the

Example of a Shellback Certificate, U.S. Navy / Robert Clovis Fay

Pollywogs by the Shellbacks. At the end of the ceremony, Shellback certificates were awarded to the bruised but relieved Pollywogs in recognition of their new status. S2c Zapora and his fellow Pollywogs would have paid a dear price to earn their Shellback status.

S2c Zapora and the Savannah arrived at Recife on January 7, 1943. After several days there, the Savannah put to sea with destroyers and an aircraft carrier. Throughout January and February, they searched for German blockade runners without success.

On March 11, 1943, a German blockade runner was finally spotted. The Savannah and her sister ships fired shots across her bow demanding them to stop. As a US boarding party pulled alongside, time bombs on the ship were intentionally exploded by the German crew, killing 11 of the boarding party. Savannah rescued and captured 72 German survivors, quartering them below decks as prisoners of war. It was S2c Zapora's first encounter with the enemy. It would not be his last.

Savannah and the Invasion of Sicily

Savannah returned to New York to deposit the prisoners, replenish supplies, and overhaul the ship. In May, Savannah headed back to North Africa to protect troop transport ships for the preparation of Operation "Husky", the Allied invasion of enemy-occupied Sicily.

As the invasion started on July 9, 1943, Savannah provided fire support for the troop landings and four spotter aircraft for reconnaissance. On July 12, Savannah fired over 500 shells at targets directed by Allied infantry. She also took aboard wounded infantrymen as the battle raged on the island. Before the Allied armies moved into the island's interior, they thanked Savannah for "crushing three infantry attacks and silencing four artillery batteries " and for demoralizing enemy troops with her bombardment.

Savannah continued to support the invasion of Sicily until it was taken on August 17. The humiliating collapse of Italian troops on Sicily led to the overthrow of the Italian Dictator Benito Mussolini. Savannah had done her part.

The Invasion of Italy… and Catastrophe

S2c John Zapora aboard Savannah returned to Algeria to prepare for the planned invasion of Italy with landings at Salerno. They set sail on September 5 and entered Salerno Bay three days later, ready for battle.

Savannah was the first US ship to open fire against the German shore defenses overlooking Salerno Bay. She launched nine fire support missions that day. Savannah continued her valuable support through September 10. S2c John Zapora did all that he was ordered to do, and he and his shipmates barely had time to rest. Little did they know that a catastrophe awaited them the next morning.

Before dawn on September 11, 1943, as Savannah was preparing to launch fire support for the Allies' invading troops, she was harassed several times by enemy aircraft. The men were on constant alert.

At 0930 hrs, Savannah was 5 miles from the beach when a red alert was broadcast from the Allied ships. Twelve German planes were entering the area from the south. Immediately, all hands went to battle stations, and the ship sped to 15 knots. S2c Zapora prepared as best he could for what might come next.

At 0944 hrs a twin-engine German Do-217 bomber was sighted overhead at a height of 18,700ft. Just then, a whooshing sound was heard and a bomb struck Savannah. A strong, sharp jolt was felt across the ship. The ship and her crew were in peril.

A "Fritz-X" radio-controlled glide-bomb had been released by the German bomber. Its bombardier aimed the bomb at the Savannah and scored a direct hit. It pierced through the armored roof of the number 3 Gun Turret, tearing through 37 ft of three decks into the lower handling room where it exploded and tore open the ship's port side. For the next 30 minutes, secondary explosions interrupted the firefighting and rescue crews.

USS Savannah, on fire after being hit by radio-guided bomb Sep 11, 1943 (US Navy)

The crew quickly put out the fires and sealed off flooding compartments. The damage had been severe, but their quick action kept the Savannah afloat. The ship was wounded, but not fatally. The same could not be said for its crew.

Savannah lost 197 men that day. S2c John Edward Zapora was one of them. Three weeks later, his family was informed by the War Department that John was missing in action and presumed dead.

John Edward Zapora, Remembered

S2c John Edward Zapora was never recovered, and he is presumed lost at sea at the moment of the bomb explosion. His name is inscribed on the Tablet of the Missing at the Sicily-Rome American Cemetery and Memorial, at Nettuno, Città Metropolitana di Roma Capitale, Lazio, Italy.

At the age of 18 years, 8 months, and eighteen days, John Zapora was the youngest US service member from Monessen to lose his life during WWII.

Hole in top of Savannah gun turret (center) after being hit by radio-guided bomb (US Navy)

★ ★ ★

CPL ALBERT S. WARGO

Service Number 33292627
322nd Fighter Control Squadron, U.S. Army Air Force
Lost at Sea aboard HMT Rohna, November 26, 1943

I t would become a decades-long secret.

In January 1944, Jack and Mary Wargo of Monessen were told that their son, CPL Albert Stanley Wargo, was missing. They were not told that he was in the single largest loss at sea of American fighting men. Those details would be kept from the public for nearly 50 years.

☆ ☆ ☆

World War II was raging on a wintry day in January 1944 in Monessen, Pennsylvania, when Jack and Mary (née Paulo) Wargo heard a knock on the door. They glanced at the red, white, and blue service banner hanging in their front window and shuddered. Their banner displayed one blue star and one gold star.

Every family with a son serving in the war proudly displayed a service banner. Each banner had an embroidered blue star stitched to a white rectangle against a red field. Some families had more than one son in the service, so their

banners displayed more than one blue star. If a son lost his life while in service to the country, the blue star was replaced with a gold one.

By January 1944, the Wargo's banner had already held one gold star. Was that not enough for one family?

When Jack and Mary Wargo opened the door, a telegram from the US War Department was gently placed in their hands.

A year earlier, they were handed a different telegram that was just as ominous. Their oldest son John Woodward Wargo was dead. He had enlisted with the Pennsylvania National Guard in February 1941, ten months before the US entered the war. John was promoted to Sergeant in Company M of the 110th Infantry Regiment and went to Camp Polk in Louisiana for training. He was stricken with pneumonia and hospitalized in September 1942. His health continued to deteriorate, and he lost his battle to survive on November 12, 1942. John was just 23 yrs old.

But fourteen months later, this newly arrived telegram was different: Their second son CPL Albert Stanley Wargo was reported as missing at sea. Was he lost, or could he still be alive?

Albert's whereabouts and the details regarding his loss would be shrouded in secrecy for years.

The Wargo Family

The Wargo ancestors had immigrated to the US to escape the Austro-Hungarian Empire in the late 1800's, eventually settling in Monessen. Jack became a mail carrier for the US Postal Service and by 1930 they bought a home at 57 Donner Avenue. Besides sons John (b 1918) and Albert, they had two daughters, Elsie Mae (1916) and Mildred Agnes (1926).

Albert had been a star basketball player for the Monessen High Greyhounds before graduating in 1939. He attended Waynesburg State College and was a standout freshman forward for the college basketball team. He left college after two years and went to work with his brother at Page Steel and Wire. In 1940, Albert was admitted to the hospital to have his appendix removed.

The surprise attack by Japanese forces at Pearl Harbor, Hawaii, brought the US into the war. Albert registered for the US armed forces draft three months later on February 16, 1942. He was a 6'1" 180 lb young single man with black hair and brown eyes. Six months later, Albert was drafted and entered military service in August 1942. Private Albert Wargo was assigned to the US Army Air Corps, and he immediately departed for army training. Three months later, he was grief-stricken upon learning of the death of his brother John.

By May 1943, he was promoted to the rank of Corporal (CPL) and had graduated from the US Army Air Corps' "Radio University" at Scott Field, Illinois. He then went to Boca Raton Field in Florida for advanced training.

Off to War

CPL Wargo was eventually assigned to the 322nd Fighter Control Squadron and joined his unit at Bradley Army Airfield, Connecticut. Coincidentally, another service member from Monessen had recently been assigned to the 322nd, Joseph Malena, Jr. It is unknown whether Wargo and Malena met during their tenure.

The 322nd Fighter Control Squadron was a little-known but critical unit of the US Army. Its duty was to provide ground-to-air communication infrastructure for Air Corps bases, including early warning, control of aircraft in flight, identification, homing and communications systems. The 322nd was a mobile unit with much of its equipment truck mounted.

While at Bradley, Albert met and fell in love with Elizabeth "Betty" Frances O'Brien. Betty, born in Massachusetts, was a machine operator at a local factory. On September 28, 1943, they married in Hartford, Connecticut.

But the war rudely interrupted their marriage. Six days after their wedding the 322nd was shipped out, and CPL Wargo kissed Betty goodbye for the last time. They would never have the chance to celebrate Christmas together.

The 322nd Fighter Control Squadron had been ordered to India to assist in the construction and operation of air bases for the Boeing B-29 Superfortress heavy bomber. On October 4, 1943, the 322nd boarded a troop train to Virginia, departing for Algeria several days later. On November 24, they traveled to El Kabir, Algeria where they boarded the ship HMT Rohna.

HMT Rohna (Wikipedia)

HMT Rohna and Disaster

The HMT Rohna was a 1926-British-built passenger and cargo liner that was requisitioned for transport service in the British Navy. It was an aging ship, crewed by British and Indian seamen, and was nearing the end of its serviceable life.

The Rohna departed port on November 26 and joined Convoy KMF-26 to traverse the Suez Canal destined for the Indian Ocean and India. The HMT Rohna would never make it to the Suez.

Aboard the HMT Rohna were 1,981 U.S. Army soldiers from the 853rd Engineer Battalion (Aviation), the 322nd Fighter Control Squadron, 31st Signal Construction Battalion, the 44th Portable Surgical Hospital, and several other units. The HMT Rohna was carrying 2,193 American and British military personnel and 195 crew members, roughly twenty times its design capacity. The ship was headed through Suicide Alley, a stretch of the Mediterranean

Sea that was vulnerable to attack by enemy aircraft. The troops continuously drilled on the procedures for abandoning ship.

While sailing off the coast of Bougie, Algeria, the convoy was attacked by two waves of about thirty Luftwaffe Heinkel He-177A "Greif" ("Grif-fin") long-range bomb-

Heinkel He-177 "Greif" Bomber carrying Hs-293 Bomb

ers escorted by Junkers Ju 88 fighters and torpedo bombers.

At 4 PM an alert sounded, and all troops were ordered below decks while the gun crews were ordered to their stations. The escort ships opened fire.

The German bombers launched forty-two Hs-293 radio-controlled rocket-boosted glide bombs. Forty-one of the German guided bombs failed to score a direct hit on their targets. The forty-second glide bomb hit the HMT Rohna directly above the water line at 5:15 PM, penetrating the port side and blowing holes in the star-board side.

Hs-293 Radio-Guided Bomb (US Navy)

All power was lost, and the crew of the Rohna began emer-gency procedures in earnest as the ship began to list. The weather had become difficult, and the sea was producing 15-foot swells. Of the 16 lifeboats, only 5 were successfully launched. At 5:30 PM, the order to abandon ship was given. Hundreds landed in the cold water, leading to hypo-thermia which took the lives of many that had escaped the sinking ship. The minesweeper USS Pioneer (AM-105) jumped into action and collected 606 survivors despite the heavy seas.

The rescue went into the night. Eventually 1,149 lives were lost. Of those, 1,051 were Americans, including CPL Albert S. Wargo.

The attack upon the HMT Rohna resulted in the single largest loss of US troops at sea due to enemy action. But the public was not to be told anytime soon.

Two months later, in January 1944, the telegram was delivered to Jack and Mary Wargo: Albert was missing. Six months later they were informed that he lost his life when his troop ship was sunk during enemy action in the Mediterranean Sea.

No details were shared.

Hidden from the Public

To prevent the Germans from learning how effective the guided bomb had been against HMT Rohna, the entire matter was classified by the War Department. Wartime censors delayed any public revelation of the number of casualties to prevent specific details from becoming public knowledge. Secrecy prevailed until the 1960s, and only those who were involved in the incident knew anything about it. The details were officially declassified in 1990.

The body of CPL Albert Stanley Wargo was never found. He was posthumously awarded the Purple Heart, and his name was listed on the Tablets of Missing in Action or Buried at Sea in The North African American Cemetery in Carthage, Tunisia. A memorial marker was placed at St. Mary's Byzantine Catholic Church Cemetery in Monessen. His brother SGT John Woodward Wargo was buried at the same cemetery.

The Wargo family had made the ultimate sacrifice of two sons in service to their country.

Their banner displayed two gold stars for the remainder of the war.

★ ★ ★

CPL JOSEPH MALENA, JR.

Service Number 33290189
322nd Fighter Control Squadron, U.S. Army Air Force
Lost at Sea aboard HMT Rohna, November 26, 1943

By Chris Moyer and John Turanin

The HMT Rohna disaster claimed more than one Monessen soldier. CPL Joseph Malena, Jr. was also aboard the ship with CPL Albert S. Wargo when it was sunk by a radio-guided bomb from a German Luftwaffe bomber.

Joseph Malena, Jr. was born on February 20, 1914, in Cokeburg, Pennsylvania to Joseph Sr. and Sarah (née Pasquarella) Malena. Joseph Sr. was a blacksmith for a coal mining company while Sarah managed the Malena family household.

Joseph Sr., born Giuseppe Luigi Malena in Verzino, Calabria, Italy, immigrated to the United States in 1909. Sarah was named Raffaela at birth in Bridgeville, Pennsylvania, by parents who immigrated from Arvino, Italy. Joseph Sr. and Sarah met in Western Pennsylvania and married by 1914.

Joseph Jr. was the first of three children born to Joseph Sr. and Sarah. Christina followed in 1915. In 1916, a sister Theresa was stillborn. Their mother Sarah contracted pneumonia and passed away in 1918 when she was 22. Joseph Sr. remarried in 1922 to Alice Edna May Behenna. Alice had two children from a previous marriage, Louis (1919) and James (1921) Commons. Louis remained with his birth father and James accompanied Alice into the Malena family. Alice gave birth to Joseph Jr.'s half-siblings, Mary Matilda

(1924), Louise (1925), Angelina (1927), Rose Ellen (1928), Dolores Jean (1930), Viola Lorraine (1933), and Shirley (1940).

By 1930, Joseph Jr. ended his formal education with the completion of eighth grade and was performing odd jobs to earn his way. In March 1934, the Malena's and four other families lost their homes to fire in the village of Bunola on the Monongahela River. The Malena's relocated to Hickory Street in Forward, Pennsylvania, where Joseph Jr. met Sophie Sowa living on the same street. They wed that October. The marriage lasted until December 1938 when Sophie was granted a divorce.

In 1939, he married Anna Marie Campus of Monessen. The couple welcomed the birth of their daughter Saraella in October of that year but endured the heartbreak of a stillborn son the following January. By 1940, the family was renting an apartment at 328 Schoonmaker Avenue in Monessen, Pennsylvania where Joseph Jr. worked for the Federal Government's Works Progress Administration.

The US Congress passed the Selective Service and Training Act in September 1940, establishing the first peace-time draft for the armed forces. On October 16, 1940, Malena registered for the draft on its first day. He stood over 5' 7" tall, weighed 160 pounds, with blue eyes and brown hair. Malena was now working at the Page Mill of the American Chain and Cable Company.

The US entered WWII in December 1941 following the attack by Japanese forces upon the US military bases at Pearl Harbor, Hawaii.

In February 1942, the couple welcomed their second child, a son Joseph Armand Malena. But the boy's father was drafted in the summer of 1942, and he enlisted in the US Army Air Corps in Greensburg, Pennsylvania on July 30, 1942.

Private Malena was immediately sent for training, leaving his young family behind. In early April 1943, he was stationed at Grenier Field, New Hampshire where he was in charge of all recruits assigned to his unit. While there, he was selected to instruct the Women's Defense Corps of Manchester, New Hampshire in close order drill.

Malena was eventually assigned to train with the 322nd Fighter Control Squadron where he was promoted to the rank of Corporal (CPL). The 322nd Fighter Control Squadron was activated in April 1943 at Bradley Field, Connecticut. Its mission was to provide early warning, control of aircraft in flight, identification, homing and communications using high frequency (HF) and very high frequency (VHF) radio systems. The 322nd was to be a mobile unit with much of its equipment truck-mounted. For training, they set up control stations around Bradley Field at Mesamasic, Groton, Putnam, Bridgeport, and Winsted, Connecticut, and controlled this airspace. Another service member from Monessen, CPL Albert S. Wargo, had also been assigned to the 322nd.

While serving, Joseph and Anna formally separated. Little did they know that Joseph would never see his family again.

The 322nd Fighter Control Squadron had been ordered to India where they would assist in the construction and operation of air bases for the Boeing B-29 Superfortress heavy bomber. On October 4, 1943, the 322nd boarded a troop train to Camp Patrick Henry, Virginia, arriving the next morning. During the next week, troops completed preparation for overseas deployment. The group departed on October 12 by train to Hampton Roads, Virginia, where they boarded the Liberty ship SS Nicholas Gilman, which departed the next morning and joined a convoy to cross the Atlantic Ocean. The Gilman docked at Argew, near Oran, Algeria, and the 322nd was trucked to a staging camp. On November 24, they were transported to El Kabir, Algeria where they boarded the HMT Rohna, an Indian troop ship under the control of the British Royal Navy. The Rohna departed November 26 and joined convoy KMF-26 to traverse the Suez Canal destined for the Indian Ocean and India.

The HMT Rohna suffered an attack by German bombers late that afternoon, sinking the ship. Eventually 1,149 lives were lost. Of those, 1,051 were Americans, including CPL Joseph Malena.[5]

---

[5] Further details of the HMT Rohna disaster are described in the story of CPL Albert S. Wargo immediately preceding this story.

His wife was informed that he was missing in action on December 23, 1943. The following March, Anna Malena was notified by the US War Department that her husband's life was lost in the sinking of an Allied troopship.

CPL Joseph Malena, Jr. is memorialized on the Tablets of the Missing, North Africa American Cemetery and Memorial, Carthage, Tunis, Tunisia. Malena was posthumously awarded the Purple Heart.

★★★

FL O THOMAS A. IRVINE

Service Numbers 13061373 / T-001616
511th Bomb Squadron, 351st Bomb Group, US Army Air Corps
Killed in action, France, December 31, 1943

T he B-17 Flying Fortress bomber had already absorbed several hits from German anti-aircraft guns. And now, as they struggled to make it from France to its home base in England, the German fighters pounced.

The aluminum skin of the B-17 was pierced by bullets from the attackers. The bomber began to burn.

Co-pilot Flight Officer (FL O) Thomas Irvine struggled to maintain level flight as the crew parachuted from the crippled aircraft.

Thomas Irvine never made it home.

The Irvine Family

Thomas Alexander Irvine was born on May 11, 1922, in Monessen, Pennsylvania to Alexander and Elizabeth Ann Trengrove (née Harvey) Irvine. Alexander and Elizabeth had married a year earlier, in 1921. Alexander was a machine operator in a Monessen steel mill while Elizabeth managed the Irvine family household.

Alexander was born in Renfrew, Scotland to parents of Irish descent, and immigrated to Canada in 1911. He served in the Canadian Navy during WWI and immigrated to the United States in 1920 through Buffalo, New York. Elizabeth was born in Pennsylvania to parents of Scottish, English, and Welsh descent who immigrated to the US in the 1880's. Alexander came to Monessen for work, where he met and married Elizabeth.

Thomas was the first of three children born to Alexander and Elizabeth. His sister Mary Elizabeth was born in 1925, and brother William Elton arrived in 1930. William passed away from anemia at the age of two. The Irvine family traveled to visit relatives in Canada and Scotland in the 1920-30's. Thomas had the usual childhood illnesses, measles in 1924, mumps in 1937, and had a tonsillectomy in 1936. In 1930, the family was living in a rented home at 1065 Leeds Avenue in Monessen and were members of the Trinity Episcopal Church. Five years later, Alexander had been promoted from the factory floor to a clerk position in the steel mill, and the family moved to a rented home at 62 Rostraver Street. In 1936, Thomas starred as Jack Sprat in his church operetta Children of Old Mother Goose. During high school, Thomas played various roles in school plays, was a skilled orator and participated in a forensic competition, winning third place in the district Dramatic Declamation competition. He was also a member of the Stone House Players of Roscoe. Thomas graduated from Monessen High School in 1941.

The surprise attack by Japanese armed forces on the US military bases at Pearl Harbor, Hawaii, in December 1941 changed the world for Thomas. On May 6, 1942, he enlisted in the US Army Air Corps in Pittsburgh, Pennsylvania, as a 6'1", 145 lb young single man. At the time, he was a skilled worker in the field of photographic processes. Thomas was assigned the rank of Private with service number 13061373 and was off for training.

Joins the US Army Air Corps

During training in Miami Beach, Florida, PVT Irvine received a transfer to the Army Air Corps base at Scotts Field, Illinois, in June 1942. While there, he met famed actress/singer Jeannette MacDonald who was giving a concert at the camp that evening. After discussing their shared interest in acting, Mac-Donald dedicated a song to him during the show, "Smilin' Through."

PVT Irvine learned about the opportunity to become a pilot as a Flight Officer in the Army Air Corps, a newly created position as of September 1942. Enlisted and aviation cadet trainees who successfully passed air qualification training were appointed as Flight Officers and served as rated pilots, navigators, flight engineers, bombardiers and glider pilots. PVT Irvine applied for admittance into the program and was accepted. He was diverted for specialized training as a Flight Officer.

Thomas Irvine received his pre-flight training at Santa Ana, California, his primary flight training at Cal-Aero at Chino, California, and graduated as a pilot at Stockton Army Airfield, California on Aug 31, 1943. He completed the necessary requirements for becoming a pilot of a multi-engine heavy bomber and graduated as Flight Officer (FL O) Thomas A. Irvine. He was assigned a new service number T-001616. FL O Irvine was qualified to pilot the Boeing B-17 Flying Fortress heavy bomber.

By October 1943, FL O Thomas Irvine was assigned to the 511th Bomb Squadron (BS) of the 351st Bomb Group (BG). The 351st BG had been established at Geiger Field in Washington in November 1942 where the group was assembled for initial training, with the second phase of training at Biggs Field, Texas, December 1942 - March 1943. The unit then moved to Pueblo Army Air Base, Colorado for preparation for overseas movement. In April–May 1943, the unit moved overseas to RAF Polebrook, England (Station 110) to serve in combat with the Eighth Air Force. FL O Irvine joined the 351st BG as a replacement crew. When he arrived on November 8, 1943, the BG had already flown 40 combat missions.

FL O Irvine in England

FL O Irvine was assigned to the crew of 2LT Warren Putnam as his co-pilot. They flew their first mission, the BG's 56th mission, on November 29, 1943, to Bremen Germany, but had to abort. Their next mission, on December 1 to bomb an industrial sector of Solingen, Germany, was their first to see combat. Through December, FL O Irvine took to the skies six more times to attack targets in Germany and France, aborting two of those missions. They flew seven different B-17 Flying Fortresses during those missions.

On December 31, 1943, FL O Thomas Irvine was again to join 2LT Putnam and his crew for another mission. This time, they were flying B-17G #42-31179 nicknamed "Stinky Weather". Stinky Weather had just arrived from stateside on December 23. The target was a German aircraft assembly plant near Bordeaux, France, with a secondary target as the Luftwaffe airdrome in Cognac, France. They would be joining 34 other B-17s of the 351st BG on the mission. Putnam's B-17 would be flying in the left element of 6 aircraft in the low box formation of 16 aircraft at about 17,000 ft altitude. Fighter escorts of P-38 Lightnings and P-51 Mustangs were arranged. Enemy Me-110 and Me-210 fighters were anticipated.

When the group arrived over Bordeaux, the target was obscured by cloud cover, and the formation turned to deliver their load on the airdrome at Cognac. Over Cognac at 1253, flak was intense and extremely accurate.

Stinky Weather in Trouble

Stinky Weather absorbed several flak hits while over the target. After dropping their bomb load, the crippled aircraft turned and headed for home. Between Pleubian and Kerbors France at about 1315 hrs, Stinky Weather was struck by gunfire from enemy Bf 109 and FW 190 fighters,

German Bf-109 Fighters (German Federal Archive)

and the aircraft started to burn. LT Putnam gave the order to the crew to bail out.

Six of the crew bailed out, and of the six, five became prisoners of war and the sixth was rescued by French resistance and returned to England. Four crew

German FW-190 Fighter (US Air Force)

members, including, FL O Thomas A. Irvine perished when their B-17 fell to Earth near Kerbors, France.

The family of FL O Thomas Irvine was informed that he was missing in action mid-January 1944, and in February that he was killed in action. He was 21 yrs old.

FL O Thomas Irvine and his three crew mates were initially buried in the French Garrison Cemetery at Lannion, France, and then reinterred at the US Military Cemetery St. James at Rennes, France. In 1948, his remains were recovered under the Return of the War Dead program, transported to the US aboard the USAT Greenville Victory, and buried at the Belle Vernon Cemetery in North Belle Vernon, Pennsylvania, on July 17..

FL O Thomas Irvine was posthumously awarded the Air Medal.

★ ★ ★

1944

"He little thought when leaving home,
He would no more return,
That he in death so soon would sleep,
And leave us here to mourn.
We do not know what pain he bore,
We did not see him die,
We only know he passed away,
And never said goodbye,
But God is good; he gave us strength
To bear our heavy cross;
He is the only one who knows
How bitter is our loss".

The Family of S2c John E. Varga

The year 1944 was especially brutal. In Europe, the Italian Campaign was in full swing as Allied troops marched northward up the boot of the Italian peninsula against stiff German resistance. Rome was liberated by June, but the fighting in Italy continued for the rest of the year. The massive Allied invasion of Normandy, France, was launched in June, followed by their invasion of southern France in August. By year's end, Allied forces had pushed across France and were knocking on the door of the German border, culminating in the start of the difficult Battle of the Bulge in December. The defeat of Germany was in sight, but the looming defense of The Fatherland would threaten to be costly for the Allies.

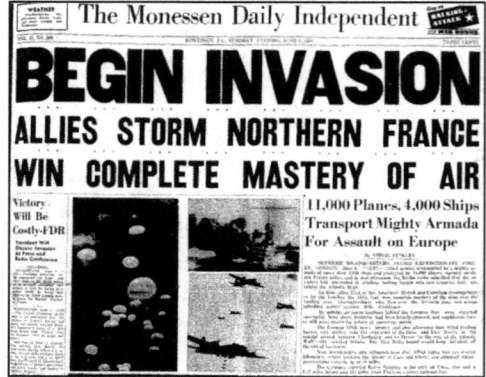

The war against the Japanese continued its island-hopping across the Pacific as US forces advanced across the Gilbert and Marshall Islands. Folks at home read about battles in unheard of places such as Kwajalein and Eniwetok. The aggressive Mariana Campaign took Guam, Saipan, and Tinian to establish air bases from which long range American bombers could finally bring the war to the Japanese home islands. The year ended with the American invasion of the Philippine Islands, fulfilling General Douglas MacArthur's promise to return after his retreat in 1942.

Nineteen-forty-four proved to be the most costly for the families of Monessen. Forty-one sons lost their lives during the year in locations as disparate as was the presence of US forces around the world. As the Allies advanced against the retreating forces of Germany and Japan, the end of the war was finally coming into sight. But the families of Monessen could not yet breathe easily.

★ ★ ★

PVT ROSS J. NACCARATO

Service Number 33413390
Company C, 83rd Chemical Battalion, US Army
Lost aboard LST-422 off coast of Italy, January 26, 1944

Private Ross Naccarato and his colleagues probably did not know what hit them on the morning of January 26, 1944.

Operation Shingle, the Allied amphibious landings at Anzio, had begun four days earlier. More than 36,000 troops had already made it ashore. Their objective was to outflank the German Army from the west and enable an Allied attack northward to Rome.

Private Naccarato was with the 83rd Chemical Battalion aboard their amphibious ship, the HMS LST-422, waiting to land. An LST, or "Landing Ship, Tank", was a shallow-draft, ocean-going ship designed to land onto a beach, swing open its large front doors, and deliver tanks, vehicles, cargo, and troops for battle. LSTs were 30% longer than a football field and about one third its width.

LST-422 was an American ship built in 1942. It was transferred to the British Royal Navy in 1943 and designated HMS ("His Majesty's Ship") LST-422. It was crewed by 38 British sailors.

On the night of January 25, 1944, HMS LST-422 departed the Allied-held port of Naples, Italy, in a convoy with 12 other LSTs heading to Anzio and into the thick of battle. LST-422 was carrying two companies of the US Army's 83rd Chemical Battalion, its headquarters staff, and the 68th Coast Guard Artillery Battalion. The ship was loaded to capacity with 2½-ton trucks, Jeeps, M3 half-tracks, ambulances, and other vehicles. Fifty-gallon steel drums of gasoline were strapped to her deck, along with mortar shells containing smoke, gas, and high explosives, including highly volatile white phosphorus.

LST-422 was a floating tinderbox, awaiting a spark. It was not going to take long.

The Naccarato Family

Rosario "Ross" Joseph Naccarato was born on October 10, 1916, in Monessen, Pennsylvania, to Joseph and Michelina (née Garofalo) Naccarato. Joseph, born Giuseppe in Mangone, Calabria, Italy, had immigrated to the United States in 1902. Michelina, born in Marzi, Italy, also from the province of Calabria, had arrived in the US in 1907. They met in Monessen, discovered their shared Calabrian roots, and fell in love. They married in 1908, and Joseph went to work in the Monessen tin mill.

Ross was the sixth of nine children born to Joseph and Michelina. The oldest brother Anthony (b1910) was the first to arrive, followed by Albert John (1911), Emilia Viola (1912), Rose Josephine (1914), Louis John (1915), Mary (1918), Virginia (1924), and Stella (1927). By 1930, the family had purchased a home at 419 Motheral Avenue in Monessen. Like his brothers, Ross left school before graduating and went to work at the tin mill.

The son of Ross' sister Mary, Santo Bocchinfuso, recalls his mother's fond memories of Ross, "She talked about him all the time. Her favorite story was about a quarter he used to let her borrow and need it back. Then loan it to her again and again .... He was a musician, and he had his own band he played on the radio." Ross played several instrument, most notably the guitar.

Three Naccarato Brothers Off to War

As 1940 approached, the threat of war in Europe and the Pacific became imminent. That September, the US Congress passed the Selective Service and Training Act of 1940, creating the first peacetime military draft. On October 16, 1940, Ross joined his three brothers and millions of other American men and signed up for the draft on the first day of registration. According to his registration card, Ross was a 5'5½", 160 lb 24-yr-old with black hair and brown eyes. He was now employed at the Belle Vernon Restaurant on Main Street in Belle Vernon.

The surprise attack by Japanese armed forces on the US military base at Pearl Harbor, Hawaii, in December 1941 changed the world for Ross and his brothers. Ross was drafted into the US Army, and he enlisted on December 22, 1942. His brother Anthony was drafted into the Army the following June, and Albert joined the US Navy in December 1943. The Naccarato's were now a Three-Blue-Star family. Only their brother Louis did not enter the service.

PVT Ross Naccarato reported for US Army boot camp. He was eventually assigned to Company C of the 83rd Chemical Mortar Battalion sometime between January and April 1943 at Camp Gordon, Georgia.

Chemical mortar battalions were originally formed to respond in the event chemical warfare was initiated by the enemy. The battalions' mission was to answer such attacks with munitions containing toxic chemicals. Otherwise, they were called upon to fire shells containing high explosives in support of ground infantry. According to the US Army: "The battalion was designed to carry thirty-six 4.2 inch mortars, with each shell weighing about 25 pounds, for a total firepower effect equivalent to three 105mm howitzers. The 4.2 inch mortar brought a lethal, mid-to-close range fire support capability to the infantry units the 83d supported."

In April, the 83rd left for the European theater of the war, arriving in North Africa. They trained intensively in Algeria for amphibious beach landings.

Mortars were their primary weapon, and they were to provide close fire support behind advancing riflemen.

PVT Naccarato Fights for his Family's Homeland

PVT Naccarato's entry into combat was when the 83rd Chemical Mortar Battalion landed in Sicily for its first major campaign. They arrived in July 1943 and fought successfully against entrenched German and Italian troops, ending the Sicilian campaign the fol-

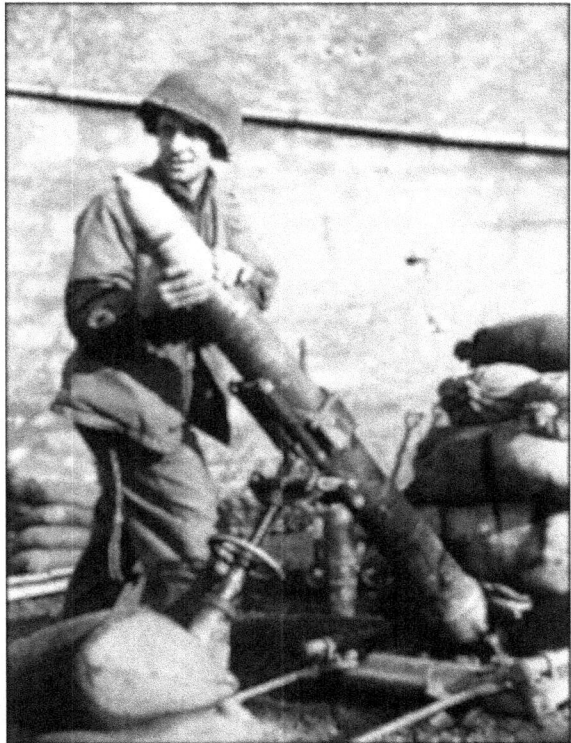

4.2 inch Mortar being loaded (National Archives)

lowing month. In September, the Italians surrendered to the Allies, but the German forces occupying the Italian peninsula would not give it up. More fighting lay ahead.

Elements of the 83rd landed at Maiori, Italy, with the US Army Rangers on September 9, 1943. PVT Naccarato found himself in the homeland of his parents, about 170 miles from their hometowns in Calabria. They fought their way northward, eventually taking the city of Naples. The 83rd was relieved for rest at Amalfi in October.

The 83rd reentered combat with the Rangers in November and continued the advance north toward San Pietro and Cassino. PVT Naccarato received a minor wound in November and was awarded the Purple Heart, which he shipped home to his family. After very heavy fighting and difficult winter

weather through December, they were again relieved. The 83rd camped at Poz-
zuoli and trained again for another upcoming amphibious landing: Anzio.

Heading to the Battle of Anzio

Companies A and B of the 83rd Chemical Battalion landed with the first
wave of troops at Anzio on January 22, 1944. PVT Naccarato and the rest of
the Battalion were to follow four days later.

At 1 a.m. on January 26, 1944, HMS LST-422 arrived about 12 miles from
Anzio and dropped anchor. A backlog of ships was unloading at Anzio, and
they had to wait their turn. PVT Naccarato and most men of Companies C and
D of the 83rd Chemical Battalion were sleeping as best they could in the
crowded berths lining the tank deck. Surrounding and above them were vehicles and containers holding flammable, volatile, and explosive materials.

Soldiers rest before boarding LST-422 in Sicily (NavSource)

In the early morning hours, a storm with gale force winds blew over their
position, whipping up 20–30-foot waves. The winds sent the ship into a field
of underwater explosive mines.

LST-422 was in peril.

Disaster Strikes

At 5:20 a.m., the ship collided with a submerged mine, blowing a 50-foot hole in the bottom and starboard side. The ship's fuel oil supply immediately ignited. The vehicles in the tank deck began to explode in succession. It was a fireworks display that no one ever wanted to see.

The men of the 83rd Chemical Battalion aboard LST-422 did not stand a chance.

LST-422 explodes off Anzio (NavSource)

Those who could escape the fiery blaze landed in the frigid waters, many succumbing to hypothermia. Another ship, LCI-32, came to the rescue but hit a mine and sank with a loss of 30. One hundred-fifty survivors of LST-422 and LCI-32 were ultimately rescued by nearby ships amid stormy seas. Rescue attempts ended by 9 AM. What remained of LST-422 eventually broke in two and sank at 2:30 PM.

PVT Ross Naccarato and 482 others aboard HMS LST-422 lost their lives that morning.

Buried at Sea

The US minesweeper YMS-34 had joined the rescue effort. Their crew recovered the body of Ross Naccarato on the water near Torre Astura, Italy, and subsequently buried him at sea in a solemn ceremony that morning.

Two months later, the family of PVT Naccarato was informed by the War Department that he was missing in action in the Mediterranean Area. A month later, they learned that he had been killed.

LST-422 and LCI-32 on fire in Anzio Bay (NavSource)

PVT Ross Naccarato was posthumously awarded an Oak Leaf Cluster for his Purple Heart medal. His name is engraved on the Tablets of the Missing at the Sicily-Rome American Cemetery and Memorial at Nettuno, Italy. His brothers Anthony and Albert returned to the Mon Valley after the war, without their brother Ross. He would forever be missed.

On the first year anniversary, the Monessen Daily Independent newspaper printed an In Memorium on behalf of his family:

> *"A precious one from us has gone*
> *A voice we loved is stilled;*
> *A place is vacant in our home,*
> *Which never can be filled.*
> *God in his wisdom has recalled,*
> *The boon his love had given,*
> *And though the body slumbers here,*
> *The soul is safe in Heaven".*

★ ★ ★

PFC CHARLES W. LUCAS

Service Number 463133
Seacoast Artillery Group, Third Defensive Battalion, Fleet Marine Force, US Marine Corps
Lost to friendly-fire, Bougainville, February 19, 1944

A micicide is a term for the killing of a friend. In the military, the word is sometimes used to formally document a loss due to "friendly fire."

During WWII, it was not un-common for anxious ground troops to fire upon aircraft before its iden-tification was confirmed. Under the stress of combat and the haze of fa-tigue, soldiers sometimes learned to fire first and ask questions later.

On February 19, 1944, above the Southwest Pacific island of Bougainville, artillery-spotter PFC Charles Lucas and his pilot were returning from a reconnaissance mission in their SBD Dauntless scout/bomber. They were about to find out just how dangerous friendly-fire could be.

The Lucas Family

Charles William Lucas was born on July 16, 1922, to Peter and Katherine "Katie" (née Sikula) Lucas in Monessen, Pennsylvania. Peter and Katie were married in 1921. Peter was a laborer at the Pittsburgh Steel mill while Katie managed the Lucas family household.

Peter Lucas was born with the surname Lukach in the village of Nove Davydkovo in the Austro-Hungarian Empire, now within present-day western Ukraine. He immigrated to the United States in 1912 at the age of 18 aboard the SS Amerika from Hamburg Germany to New York City, settling in Pennsylvania. Katie was born in the village of Turja Poljame, also within the empire of Austria-Hungary. She immigrated to the US in 1920 aboard the SS Aquitania to New York City at the age of 20. They met and married in Monessen. Members of the family would eventually use either or both Lukach and Lucas as their surnames in public records.

Charles was the first of eight children born to Peter and Katie. Sisters Helen (b1923) and Mary (1924) died as infants before their first birthdays. They were followed in birth by George (1928), John (1933), Peter Jr.(1934) and Catherine (1938). John passed away at the age of eight from appendicitis.

By 1930, the family was living in a rented home at 1244 Maple Avenue in Monessen. By 1940, the family had purchased a home at 1208 Knox Avenue in Monessen, and Charles was in his last year at Monessen High School.

The surprise attack by Japanese armed forces on the US military base at Pearl Harbor, Hawaii, in December 1941 changed the world for Charles. On June 30, 1942, Charles registered for the first US armed forces draft as a 5'11" 170 lb 19-yr-old with brown hair and brown eyes. After graduating high school, he took a job at Pittsburgh Steel where both his father and his brother Michael worked.

Charles Volunteers for the Marines

Charles decided to volunteer for US military service and enlisted with the US Marine Corps Reserves. He reported for training on September 21, 1942, in Pittsburgh, Pennsylvania.

Private Charles Lucas trained stateside in the Seventh Recruit Battalion at USMC boot camp at Parris Island, South Carolina. The following month, he was sent to the Tenth Separate Recruit Battalion to train with the Fleet Marine Force at New River, North Carolina. PVT Lucas was sent overseas on February 19, 1943, assigned to the Special Weapons Group, Seacoast Artillery Group of the Third Defensive Battalion.

Marine defensive battalions were charged with coastal defense of various naval bases in the Pacific during World War II. They maintained large anti-ship guns, anti-aircraft guns, searchlights, and small arms to repel landing forces. Unlike the mobile Marine forces involved in offensive actions, defense battalions were detached to key outposts and remained at the station they defended.

The 3rd Defensive Battalion had been in Guadalcanal in the Solomon Islands in the South Pacific since August 1942. In February 1943 the unit was relieved and spent the next six months in New Zealand for additional training where PVT Charles Lucas joined them. That October the 3rd Defensive Battalion returned to American-held Guadalcanal in preparation for an invasion of the island of Bougainville.

The Marines at Bougainville

Bougainville had been in the hands of the Japanese Empire since early 1942. The Allies had identified the need for an airfield on Bougainville in order to conduct sustained air operations against the central Japanese base at Rabaul.

In November 1943, the US Marines landed on the beach at Torokina, the area chosen for the airfield. PFC Charles Lucas and his artillery unit arrived at Torokina and were under daily pressure to support the advancing and defending Marine troops and to ensure vigilance against air attack from Japanese aircraft. All the while, US Navy Construction Battalions (CBs or Seabees) were constructing three airstrips. Through December, the 3rd Defensive Battalion tenuously secured the area despite being surrounded by occupying Japanese troops. It was a busy time and a very dangerous situation.

Defending Torokina and supporting the Marines on the ground required knowledge of enemy positions and movement, thus scouting their locations was critical to both defensive and offensive success. On February 19, 1944, PFC Charles Lucas was chosen to embark on an aerial spotter mission for the artillery. He was to board a scouting aircraft that would fly over enemy positions, identify artillery targets, and communicate their coordinates to US gun crews for firing actions. This was a dangerous assignment indeed.

Douglas SBD Dive Bomber (US Marine Corps)

On the morning of that day, PFC Lucas boarded US Marine Air Douglas SBD-4 Dauntless Dive Bomber Bureau Number 10350 of Squadron VMSB-244 (nicknamed the Bombing Banshees), piloted by 1LT Hobart Kemp. They took off from Piva North, one of the first operational airstrips at Torokina.

After completing their spotting mission, LT Kemp returned to Piva. At 1010 hours LT Kemp's aircraft entered the traffic circle at an altitude of 500 ft when it was accidentally struck by friendly fire from a US Army anti-aircraft crew. Unfortunately, in war, danger was not limited to actions conducted by the enemy.

Their Dauntless caught fire and fell to Earth. PFC Charles Lucas and his pilot 1LT Hobart Kemp did not survive the accident. The family of PFC Lucas were informed of his death three weeks later.

Charles Lucas, Remembered

PFC Charles W. Lucas was initially buried in a temporary cemetery in Bougainville. The cemetery was subsequently closed, and his remains were reinterred at a US military cemetery at Munda on the island of New Georgia on April 10, 1945. In December 1945, the cemetery at Munda was closed and his remains reinterred at Finschhafen, New Guinea. In 1948, US military cemeteries in the South Pacific were consolidated at the Manila American Cemetery in the Philippines, where PFC Charles William Lucas was finally laid to rest.

★ ★ ★

ENS WILLIAM E. NICODEN

Service Number 0-331467
Quonset Point Naval Air Station, Rhode Island, United States Naval Reserve
Killed in auto accident, Rhode Island, February 20, 1944

O ver 25% of American service members lost during WWII was not from
to combat. Illnesses and accidents killed US service members across all
theaters of the war, including those who were stateside. Serving in the military was a dangerous business, indeed.

Ensign William Nicoden was a bright young Naval Aviator who had just graduated with his wings. One month later, at the age of 20, he was gone.

The Nicoden Family

William Ernest Nicoden was born on June 27, 1923, to Thomas John and Anna Margaret (née Heinrich) Nicoden in Monessen, Pennsylvania. Thomas and Anna had married in 1905 in Pittsburgh. Thomas was a foreman in a Monessen steel mill while Anna managed the Nicoden family household.

Thomas was born in Stahlen, Germany, and immigrated to the United States with his parents in the 1880's. Anna's parents were also born in Germany and immigrated to Western Pennsylvania where Anna was born in the early 1880's.

William was the seventh and last child born to Thomas and Anna. His oldest brother Paul Thomas was born in 1906, after which the family moved to Monessen. A second son, Harold John, was born in 1908 but died as an infant. Next to be born were Walter John (1909), Charles Henry (1913), Marie (1915), and Jeanne Kathryn (1919). His brother Charles died in 1924 at the age of eleven from a ruptured appendix.

William was a member of the Boy Scouts, and he excelled at public speaking while a student at Monessen High School. As a sophomore, he took first place in original oration in the Westmoreland County Forensic League competition for his speech "Time Marches on with the Boy Scouts". He went on to the semi-finals at the California State Teachers College where he competed in humorous declamation and placed second, becoming eligible for the national forensics' competition in Beverly Hills, California in 1939. The team traveled there in June 1939, but the competition was stiff, and they returned with memories but no awards. William took first place in dramatic declamation among 200 participants in a March 1940 regional forensics competition.

He was an honor student and graduated fourth in his senior class from Monessen High in May 1940. For the commencement program, William presented "Pioneering in World Understanding" at the Faculty-Graduate Night. That August William and his fellow Boy Scouts placed third in a first aid competition. In September 1940 William followed in the footsteps of his brothers Paul and Walter and entered Pennsylvania State University.

The surprise attack by Japanese armed forces upon the US military base at Pearl Harbor on December 7, 1941, changed the world for William. On June 30, 1942, he registered for the US military draft as a 6' 150 lb 19-yr-old with brown hair and brown eyes. He was halfway done with his studies as a metallurgy major and was a member of the Alpha Chi Rho fraternity where he lived in State College, Pennsylvania.

William graduated with a Bachelor of Science degree in metallurgy from Penn State October 1943. That month, he learned that his brother's 11-yr-old son, Richard, died after suffering a head injury while playing football. His sister Jeanne enlisted with the US Marine Corps and left to serve at Camp LeJeune, North Carolina.

William Joins the Navy

In September, William enlisted with the US Navy and entered the United States Naval Reserve Midshipmen's School at Notre Dame University. William had ambitions to become a naval aviator. He graduated from the program on January 20, 1944, with the rank of Ensign, and was now ready to do his part in the war.

Unfortunately, ENS Nicoden's life was cut short before he had the chance to do his part.

A month after graduating from Notre Dame, ENS Nicoden was in training at Quonset Naval Air Station, Rhode Island. In the early morning of Sunday, February 20, 1944, he and two colleagues were walking along the road returning to their quarters when they were struck by a car. While his companions came through the accident cut and bruised, ENS William Nicoden had suffered a serious head injury. He did not survive.

ENS William Ernest Nicoden was buried at Belle Vernon Cemetery, North Belle Vernon, Pennsylvania.

★ ★ ★

PFC ANDREW DESACK, JR.

Service Number 33690344
Company F, 30th Infantry Regiment, 3rd Infantry Division, US Army
Killed in Action in Italy, April 25, 1944

The Desack family sent four sons to fight in WWII, making them one of the rare 4-Blue-Star families in Monessen. Unfortunately, before war's end, one Blue Star would turn Gold.

The Desack Family

Andrew Desack, Jr., was born on March 13, 1925, to Andrew "Andy" Sr., and Helen (née Kaliszewska) in Monessen, Pennsylvania. Andy and Helen had married between 1920-22 in Pennsylvania. Andy was a laborer in a Monessen steel mill while Helen managed the Desack family household.

Andy was born in a region in eastern Europe that was part of the Austrian-Hungarian Empire and immigrated to the United States in 1907. Helen was born in Poland and immigrated to the US in 1911. Helen was previously married to John Wisniewski in New London, Connecticut, and they moved to Monessen in 1919. The Desack surname was occasionally

30th Infantry Regiment Coat of Arms (US Army)

spelled Descak. The Wisniewski surname was often spelled Wisniski or Visniski.

Andrew Jr. was the second of five children born to Andy and Helen. His brother Joseph "Babe" arrived first (b1923), followed by Edward (1926), Eugene Walter (1929), and Walter Stanley (1933). Helen's five children from her first marriage joined the Desack family household. Andrew's half-siblings were Zygmundt "Ziggy" (1913), Walter William (1914), John (1915), Jennie Jane (1918), and Sophia (1919). Sophia was born in Monessen, and her older siblings were born in New London, Connecticut. In 1930, the Desack family of eleven was living in their rented Monessen home at 1041 Highland Avenue.

By 1940, the family had moved to another rented home up the street at 1240 Highland Avenue. Ziggy, Walter, Jennie, and Sophia had moved out to start their own adult lives. Andy was still working at the steel mill, where his stepson John was also now employed and still living with his parents. Son Andrew Jr, now 15 yrs old, had left school after the third grade.

The US Enters the War

The surprise attack by Japanese armed forces on the US military bases at Pearl Harbor, Hawaii, in December 1941 changed the world for Andrew. By 1943, he was working at the Corning Glass Works in Belle Vernon, up the Monongahela River from Monessen. On March 13, 1943, Andrew registered for the US armed forces draft as a 5'9" 175 lb young single man with brown hair and brown eyes. Three months later, Andrew was drafted into the US Army, and he enlisted at Greensburg, Pennsylvania on June 29, 1943. Private Andrew Desack reported to US Army boot camp at Fort George G. Meade, Maryland, on July 14, 1943. His brothers Ziggy, John, and Edward would also enter the military during WWII.

PVT Desack trained stateside until January 15, 1944. He was deployed to the 30th Infantry Regiment of the 3rd Infantry Division as a replacement in Company F and was promoted to Private First Class (PFC). The 3rd Infantry Division was nicknamed "Rock of the Marne" for its heroic defensive efforts during WWI. The 3rd Division is the only division of the U.S. Army during

World War II that fought the Axis on all European fronts and was among the first American combat units to engage in offensive ground combat operations. The Division had been fighting in the European theater since landing with the Allied invasion of North Africa in November 1942 during Operation Torch. The unit saw combat in North Africa, Sicily, Italy, France, Germany and Austria for 531 consecutive days. During the war, the 3rd Division consisted of the 7th, 15th, and 30th Infantry Regiments, together with supporting units.

Andrew and the 30th Infantry Regiment

PFC Andrew Desack arrived with the 30th Regiment in time for the beginning of the Battle of Anzio of the Italian Campaign, January 22, 1944. The Regiment participated in the Battle of Cisterna di Littoria, advancing inland from the Anzio beachhead. After constant engagement with German defensive forces, the 3rd Division was relieved of command on March 28 for a two day respite. After its rest, the Division moved into the Torre Astura area where it trained intensively for the next two weeks on defense and limited-objective attacks. By April 16, the Division was in place to attack the enemy and repel any offensive maneuvers at its new front line along the Spaccasassi Creek near Padiglione, Italy.

An attack against German forces codenamed "Mr. Black" was planned for the 30th Regiment, beginning the night of April 23. It was to be fast and aggressive. The attack went forward, but the German's counterattacked on April 24. The assault by the 30th Regiment continued through April 25, but PFC Andrew Desack fortunes had run out. During the fight on April 25, 1944, PFC Andrew Desack was fatally struck in the back by shell fragments from an artillery round and died in battle that day. His family would be informed in early June that he had been killed in action.

PFC Andrew Desack, Jr. was buried at the Sicily-Rome American Cemetery and Memorial at Nettuno, Città Metropolitana di Roma Capitale, Lazio, Italy, along with 7,844 other American military dead. He was posthumously awarded The Purple Heart.

★★★

T/SGT HARRY E. BOYER

Service Number 13087444
454th Bomb Group, 736th Bomb Squadron, 15th Air Force, US Army Air Force
Killed in action near Nis, Yugoslavia, May 7, 1944

F ew folks of Monessen had ever seen a B-24 Liberator bomber before. Sure, they saw photos of the heavy four-engine aircraft in the newspapers and magazines. But never did they see one flying overhead.

GUNNERY SERGEANT

T/SGT Harry Boyer, flight engineer / aerial gunner and a son from Monessen was determined to give them a real treat.

Boyer and his crewmates were flying their B-24 Liberator from their western US training base to their east coast point of departure for Europe. Their route was taking them over Western Pennsylvania, and Boyer asked his pilot for a favor: Fly over Monessen and buzz the city!

On a chilly day in February 1944, people in Monessen heard a sound from overhead that they had never heard: the loud, low-rumble of four large radial aircraft engines. As they gazed skyward, many could not believe their eyes as the bomber flew

A recent graduate of the aerial gunnery school at Harlingen Tex., who was promoted to sergeant and received the silver Gunners' Wings, is Harry E. Boyer, above, son of Mrs. M. Karlosky, of 208 Seneca street.

low and circled the city along the Monongahela River. No one knew who it was or why the aircraft was circling.

A week later the mystery was solved. Harry Boyer called home and came clean: he was in the bomber and had asked the pilot to buzz his home town. Harry's parents informed the local newspaper who reported the news.

Three months later, Harry was missing in action.

The Boyer Family

Harry Edward Boyer was born on July 20, 1920, to Marietta Elizabeth Boyer and an unrecorded father in Pittsburgh, Pennsylvania. Two years later, in Wheeling, West Virginia, Marietta married August Frederick Karlosky, an employee of the Page Steel and Wire Company in Monessen, who raised Harry as his son. Marietta managed the family household in their rented home in Rostraver Township, Pennsylvania.

Marietta's family heritage traces back to the British colonies of Pennsylvania, New Jersey, and Virginia prior to the American Revolutionary War, and to England, Ireland, and Germany. August, Harry's stepfather, had immigrated to the United States from Germany in 1899 as August Karlofski with his parents on the SS Munchen and would become a naturalized citizen of the US in 1943.

Harry was joined by a sister Shirley Rae in 1924, and by a brother Frederick Albert in 1927. The family was living together in a rented home at 208 Seneca Street in Monessen in 1040. Harry used the last name of Karlosky for most of his school years.

Growing up, Harry enjoyed little league baseball, where he played left field and was a recruiter for local players. At Monessen High School, he was involved with the Hi-Y Club, an extension of the YMCA. After graduating from Monessen High School, he went to work at the Page Steel and Wire Company with his father.

The surprise attack by Japanese forces upon the US military bases at Pearl Harbor, Hawaii on December 7, 1941, would intervene in the lives of millions of American youth. Three months later, on February 16, 1942, Harry heard the call and registered for the US armed forces draft in Monessen. He was a 5'6" 170 lb 21-yr-old single man with brown hair and hazel eyes. He registered using his legal surname Boyer.

Five months later, on July 2, 1942, Harry enlisted with the US Army. In urgent need of personnel, the US Army transferred him into the Air Corps, and he went off to training. Harry found himself at the Harlingen Aerial Gunnery School at the southernmost tip of Texas, where he learned the skills of flexible gunnery for assignment to bomber aircraft. He was to be assigned to a crew of the US Army Air Corps' Consolidated B-24 Liberator heavy bomber.

The B-24 Liberator was designed in 1939 as a potential replacement for the B-17 Flying Fortress. It was eventually approved as a second heavy bomber for the US Army Air Corps and went into production in 1940. With a crew up to ten, it could carry an 8,000 lb bombload and was equipped with as many as ten 50 caliber machine guns. The B-24 eventually became the most produced bomber in history with nearly 18,500 made.

Harry Qualifies as Flight Engineer

Harry was soon recognized for his strong technical competencies and was directed to train as a flight engineer. A flight engineer is responsible for knowing all technical aspects of his assigned aircraft type, including how to fly it should the pilot and co-pilot become incapacitated. He is responsible, along with the ground crew chief and the pilot, to ensure that the aircraft is ready for its mission, and to maintain the technical performance of the aircraft in-flight and for addressing any technical issues during missions. Upon graduation, PVT Harry Boyer was promoted to the rank of Technical Sergeant (T/SGT).

T/SGT Harry Boyer was assigned to the 454th Bomb Group (BG) and placed in the 736th Bomb Squadron (BS). In February 1944, he was sent overseas to join the group in the Mediterranean Theater of Operations. On his way east from their base, Harry asked the pilot to fly low over Monessen. A week later Harry called home to let them know it was his aircraft that had "buzzed" the city, which made the local newspaper.

A Consolidated B-24H Liberator of the 454th BG 736th BS (US Air Force)

The 454th BG had been activated in June 1943 at Davis-Monthan Field near Tucson, Arizona. They subsequently transferred for additional training to Pinecastle Field in Florida, McCook Airfield in Nebraska, Charleston, South Carolina, and Mitchel Field, New York, before heading to Morrison Field, Florida, the stateside jumping-off point for the southern route to the Mediterranean Theater of the war in Europe. The group was headed to its base of operations at San Giovanni Airfield, west of Cerignola, Italy. The 454th eventually flew 243 missions to more than 150 targets in Italy, Yugoslavia, Austria, Bulgaria, Hungary, Rumania, France, Germany, Czechoslovakia, Greece, and Poland. The group delivered more than 13,389 tons of bombs during 7,091 sorties upon enemy marshaling yards, oil refineries, bridges, installations, and airdromes.

T/SGT Harry Boyer was assigned to B-24H #41-29436, playfully nicknamed "Umbriago", an Italian slang word for drunkard or village idiot. He arrived in time for the group's twelfth mission, his first, a bombing run on the German Luftwaffe Aerodrome at Klagenfurt, Austria, on March 19, 1944. Reflecting upon the mission, he was quoted in the local newspapers back home:

"We were 20 miles beyond Klagenfurt when from my position in the top gun turret, I looked past the tail of the ship at the sea of black smoke and flames that had been our target. You can be darn sure though, that they didn't like the idea of having us in their neighborhood. Their ack-ack guns really let loose to tell us so. That bursting flack was paving a highway in the heavens, and Umbriago had to follow it all the way. When you've never gone to church you don't know too much about praying, yet up there it just came to me natural-like."

On May 7, 1944, T/SGT Harry Boyer was assigned to take his usual position aboard Umbriago with pilot 1LT LeRoy H. Beck for the group's 39th mission. The target for the day was the railroad marshaling yard at Bucharest, Romania. At 0755 hrs, 43 B-24s took off, escorted by P-38 Lightning and P-47 Thunderbolt fighters. It was to be the last mission for Umbriago and T/SGT Harry Boyer.

SGT Harry Boyer's Final Mission

After successfully dropping its bomb load on and near the target from 24,000 ft., Umbriago turned for home, the San Giovanni Airfield. The flak over the target had been intense, accurate, and heavy, and was both the barrage and tracking types. As the aircraft passed over Nis and Pristina, Yugoslavia, the intense flak continued. Umbriago was now attacked by German fighters, and three crewmen stationed in the mid-section of the aircraft were struck by bullets and fatally wounded. At about 1245 hrs, the aircraft was hit by enemy anti-aircraft artillery fire and was quickly losing altitude. LT Beck gave the order to bail out while attempting to maintain control to allow the safe escape of his crew. As the aircraft went into a flat spin, the bomb bay caught fire, and after those who could do so bailed out, the aircraft exploded in the air. Umbriago fell to Earth, crashing on Jastrebac mountain near Nis, Yugoslavia (now Serbia).

The pilot and nose gunner remained with the spiraling aircraft and perished in the crash. Three crew members survived the jump, and of those, the bombardier and navigator evaded capture for eleven weeks while being protected by Yugoslavian partisans; the third, the tail gunner, died from his wounds.

T/SGT Harry Boyer bailed out, but according to an eyewitness report, he was shot and killed by the Germans before he hit the ground.

T/SGT Harry Boyer and his four crewmates were initially buried near the church in Barbatovac by local citizens and overseen by their priest. They were subsequently reburied at the US Military Cemetery in Belgrade, Yugoslavia in April 1946. T/SGT Boyer's remains were brought to the US under the Return of the WWII Dead program and interred at the Belle Vernon Cemetery in North Belle Vernon, Pennsylvania on July 2, 1949.

T/SGT Harry Boyer was posthumously awarded the Purple Heart as well as the Air Medal and Oak Leaf Cluster, citing "…meritorious action in aerial flight in participating in sustained operations against the enemy from May 17 to April 30 [1944]".

★ ★ ★

TECHNICAL SERGEANT HARRY E. BOYER, son of Mrs. Marietta Kurlosky, 208 Seneca street, has been officially listed dead by the War Department. Sergeant Boyer was first reported missing in action May 7, 1944 over Yugoslavia, and after full consideration was given to all available information bearing on his absence, the War Department has informed his mother of a presumptive finding of death. His mother holds his Air Medal and Oak Leaf Cluster, and Purple Heart Awards.

Officially declared dead, Monessen Daily Independent, May 19, 1945

SGT PAUL F. NEWMAN

Service Number 13111854
95th Bomb Group, 336th Bomb Squadron, 8th Air Force
Killed in action over Germany, May 12, 1944

L ike many who joined the US Army Air Corps, Paul Francis Newman hoped to become a pilot. Their aspirations were fueled while growing up in the 1920's and 1930's, known as "The Golden Age of Aviation".

During these years, aircraft rapidly developed from fabric-covered wooden biplanes to sleek metal monoplanes that both looked and flew fast. Most of the parents of these boys were born before the age of manned flight, and were as intrigued by these marvelous inventions as were their children. Everyone was in awe of the pilots of these otherworldly machines.

But piloting required keen intellect, level-headedness, and quick thinking. It required sharp eyesight, stamina, and fast reflexes. Pilots

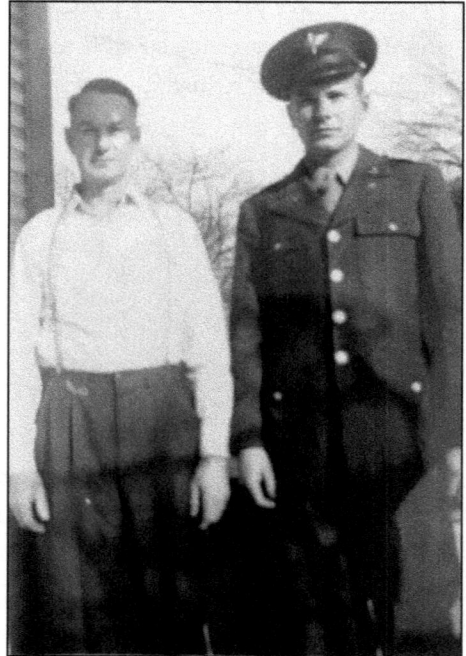

Glen Newman and son Sgt Paul Newman

had to withstand moments of disorientation and strong forces that could cause most to lose consciousness. The majority of those aspiring would-be pilots would wash-out of training. In fact, in 1941 the Air Corps determined that graduating 30,000 pilots required 60,000 candidates and 300,000 applicants.[6]

Although Paul Newman was accepted into Aviation Cadet training, he was disappointed not to advance in the flight training curriculum. Like many of his peers, he was transferred to train as an aerial gunner in bomber aircraft. He would still fly, just not as a pilot.

However, once in combat, Paul would only complete two missions. The third would be his last.

The Newman Family

Paul Francis Newman was born on September 3, 1920, to Glen Herbert and Mary Elizabeth (née Westfall) Newman in Clarksburg, West Virginia. Glen and Mary had married in 1915. Glen was a machinist at an oil well supply company, while Mary managed the Newman family household.

The Newman family heritage traces to the British colonies of Maryland, Pennsylvania, and Virginia prior to the American Revolutionary war as well as to Germany, Ireland, and Canada. The Westfall family traces to the pre-war British colonies of Virginia, Massachusetts, Rhode Island, and New York. The families settled in West Virginia and Western Pennsylvania, where Glen and Mary met and married.

Paul was the second of four children born to Glen and Mary. Glenn Herbert Jr. arrived first (b1918), followed by Sarah Josephine (1924), and David Joseph (1931). The family lived in Clarksburg and Bridgeport, West Virginia, before moving to Monessen, Pennsylvania by 1935. Glen had been hired as a machinist in a wire mill in Monessen. They first moved into a rented home on Meadow Avenue, then to 1502 Leeds Avenue in Monessen. In 1937, Paul was stricken with the mumps. By 1940, Paul had graduated from Monessen Vocational High School and was working as an auto mechanic.

---

[6] https://www.airandspaceforces.com/article/0209wings/

The surprise attack by Japanese armed forces upon the US military base at Pearl Harbor on December 7, 1941, changed the world for millions of Americans as it did for Paul. On February 16, 1942, Paul registered for the US military draft as a 5'8" 140 lb 21-yr-old with brown hair and brown eyes. He had changed jobs and was now working at Page Steel and Wire Company in Monessen.

Paul Joins the US Army Air Corps

Paul had set his eyes skyward, and decided to volunteer for the US Army Air Corps. He enlisted on July 20, 1942, in Pittsburgh. While in basic training, he applied for the Air Cadet program in hopes of becoming a pilot. Paul was accepted and left for the Aviation Cadet Classification Center in Nashville, Tennessee, in January 1943.

Aviation Cadet Paul Newman was immediately sent to Maxwell Field, Alabama, for primary flying training. He was not selected to continue to train as a pilot and instead was designated to train for other crew positions of multi-engine aircraft.

In June 1943, he transferred to Keesler Field, Mississippi, for several weeks before heading to Sioux Falls, South Dakota, from June to October, where radio operators were being trained. After training in Sioux Falls, Paul was sent to Harlingen Army Air Base in Texas where he trained in aerial gunnery. He spent the month of March 1944 training at Avon Park Army Airfield, Florida, where he was assigned to the Boeing B-17 Flying Fortress bomber crew of fellow

B-17 Bomber Waist Gunner (US Air Force)

Pennsylvanian 2LT Edwin Yablonowski. They reported for assignment at Hunter Field, Georgia, before being deployed overseas that month. Paul had been promoted to the rank of Sergeant (SGT) and was now a trained aerial gunner on B-17 bombers.

SGT Paul F. Newman was destined for England where he joined the 95th Bomb Group (BG), 336th Bomb Squadron, of the 8th Air Force stationed at Horham Field, Suffolk, in East Anglia. The 95th BG had settled at Horham in June 1943 and would eventually conduct 320 bombing missions over Occupied Europe and receive 3 Distinguished Unit Citations.

While on his way overseas, SGT Newman's father became seriously ill with double pneumonia and died on April 23rd. Unfortunately, he was unable to take leave to attend the funeral.

SGT Newman flew his first and second combat missions on May 7 and 8, 1944, both against Berlin, Germany. His third mission, however, would be his last.

SGT Newman's Third and Final Mission

On May 12, SGT Newman's pilot, 2LT Yablonowski, led his crew of ten aboard B-17G #42-39884 on a mission to bomb the oil refineries in Brux, Czechoslovakia. This was part of a large-scale bombing operation against German synthetic oil refineries and aircraft component manufacturing plants consisting of 886 B-17 and B-24 bombers and 576 P-38, P-47, and P-51 fighters. The 95th BG dispatched 40 B-17s in two groups. At 0824 hrs, LT Yablonowski's B-17 took off from Horham in the second group.

After their aircraft crossed over the English Channel and past the Belgian coast, but before arriving over their target, they were attacked by fighters of the German Luftwaffe. The right wing was hit by one or more rounds from a fighter and caught fire, and the aircraft dropped out of formation. Two crew members bailed out before B-17 #42-39884 was seen to explode in the air and fall to Earth near Rod En Weil, 20 miles northwest of Frankfurt, Germany.

Two days later, Russian prisoners of war under German guard recovered the remains of the crew and buried them in a common grave.

On May 24, 1944, SGT Paul F. Newman's family received word that he was missing. A year later, in May 1945, the War Department concluded that he had been killed in action.

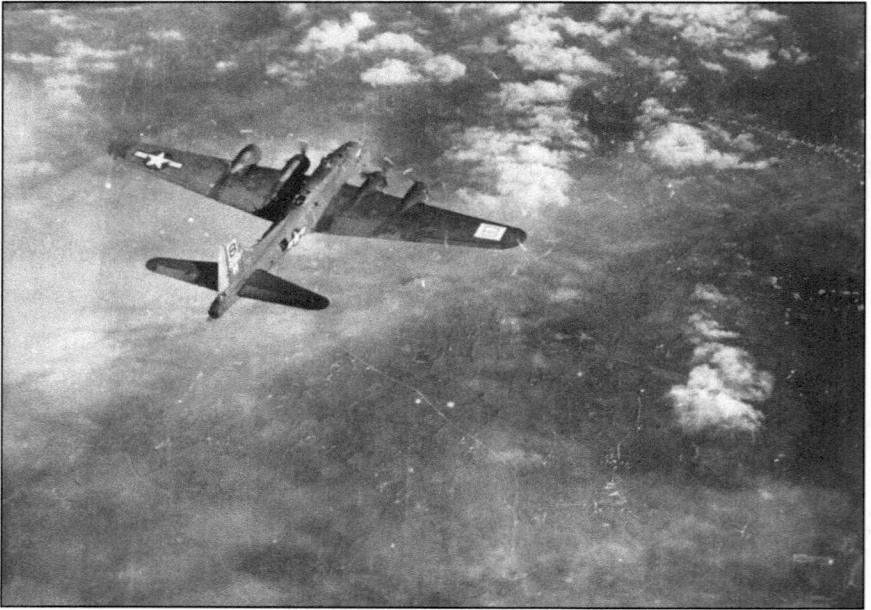

Boeing B-17G Flying Fortress #42-39884 (US Air Force / American Air Museum Archives)

Two crew members survived, were captured, and became POWs for the duration of the war. After the war in 1946, SGT Newman's remains and those of his crewmates who perished in the crash were found and identified. SGT Newman reinterred at the Ardennes American Cemetery at Neuville-en-Condroz, Belgium, on April 2, 1946, at the request of his mother. A memorial marker was placed at the West Newton Cemetery in West Newton, Pennsylvania.

He was posthumously awarded the Purple Heart.

★ ★ ★

PVT JAMES MAZZER

Service Number 33691850
Company I, 337th Infantry Regiment, 85th Division, Fifth Army, US Army
Killed in action in Italy, May 13, 1944

James Mazzer and his parents were born in a small village in northern Italy. They escaped the poverty of the early 1900's with hopes of building a more prosperous life in Monessen, Pennsylvania.

Little did they know that James would return to Italy 17 years later wearing the uniform of a US Army soldier.

Nor could they imagine that he would return to them six years later, to be buried.

The Mazzer Family

James Mazzer was born on August 7, 1911, to Antonio and Angela (née Santarossa) Mazzer in the village of Tiezzo in the province of Pordenone in the Friuli-Venezia Giulia region of northern Italy. He was born with the given name Algime but was fondly called Gimme (or Jimmy). Antonio and Angela had married in Italy in 1909. Antonio was a laborer while Angela managed the Mazzer family household.

Antonio had immigrated to Canada via New York City in 1912 aboard the SS La Savoie, and made a living in Hamilton, Ontario, until coming to Monessen, Pennsylvania in 1919 to work as a laborer at the Page Steel and Wire mill. His wife Angela and their two sons immigrated to the United States in November 1926 aboard the SS Dante Alighieri from Genoa, Italy. Their father became a naturalized US citizen that year and rented a home at 111 Third Street in Monessen.

James had one sibling, a brother Giovanni, or John, born in 1909. Both sons ended their schooling in Italy after the sixth grade. After arriving in Pennsylvania, they were hired as laborers in Monessen factories.

By 1940, James was working at the American Chain and Cable Company in Monessen. The 29-yr-old James met and fell in love with 23-yr-old Adelia Desua, also born of Italian parents and living in Monessen. They married on September 15, 1940. His brother John was James' best man, and Adelia's sister Yolanda served as her maid of honor. They set up home in their parents' house.

On October 16, 1940, James and John joined millions of other American men and registered for the first peacetime US armed forces draft under the newly enacted Selective Service Act. At the time of registration James was 5'8.5", 180 lbs with brown hair and brown eyes.

The surprise attack by Japanese armed forces on the US military base at Pearl Harbor, Hawaii, in December 1941 changed the world for James and John. The following year, in December 1942, John was drafted into the US Army. James soon followed when he was drafted in July 1943.

James reported for his enlistment on July 28, 1943, in Greensburg, Pennsylvania, and left for boot camp the following month. Now a Private, he trained stateside with the US Army.

PVT James Mazzer was assigned to Company I of the 337th Infantry Regiment in the 85th Infantry Division. The 337th Infantry Regiment had reformed from its WWI heritage in May 1942 at Camp Shelby, Mississippi, and participated in the "Louisiana Maneuvers" in April 1943, and the California "Desert Maneuvers" in June 1943. By July, it consisted of 3,256 officers and enlisted men. It was already a sizable group when PVT James Mazzer joined them for the rest of their stateside training. PVT Mazzer and the 337th Regiment left the states on December 24, 1943, for Casablanca, North Africa, and arrived there in January 1944. While there, they trained in amphibious warfare in preparation for the Allied invasion of Italy.

Six months prior to PVT Mazzer's departure, his wife Adelia had relocated from Monessen to live near him while he was in training. It would be the last they would ever spend time together.

PVT Mazzer Into Harm's Way

PVT Mazzer and the 337th Regiment landed at Naples, Italy in March 1944, and entered the fray against the entrenched German occupiers in the Rome-Arno, North Apennines, and the Po Valley campaigns. The regiment saw heavy combat attacking the German's Gustav and Gothic Lines as they moved north up the Italian Peninsula. The regiment initially held defensive positions north of the Garigliano River until it attacked and seized Castellonorato in May 1944.

In the heated battle for Castellonorato, PVT James Mazzer was struck by shrapnel when a German artillery shell exploded near his position on May 13, 1944. He lost his life that day, fighting in the country of his birth while serving the Army of his new home, the United States of America. His wife and family were informed by the War Department of his death three weeks later.

PVT James Mazzer was initially buried locally in Italy. In February 1949, his remains were transported from Europe with those of 5,200 other American soldiers aboard the US Army Transport Corporal Eric G. Gibson under the Return of the War Dead program. He was reinterred in a grave in his American hometown of Monessen at Grandview Cemetery.

★★★

S/SGT LEONARD A. MIHALICH

Service Number 13156472
613th Bomb Squadron, 401st Bomb Group, 8th Air Force, US Army Air Force
Killed in action over Germany, May 28, 1944

Twenty-year-old Leonard Mihalich was stuffed into his bomber's ball turret, a 48-inch-diameter glass and aluminum sphere dangling from the bottom of the aircraft by a single metal bracket. In the round window between his feet, he had a perfect view of the Earth's surface 24,000 feet below.

Staff Sergeant Mihalich may have also spotted the attacking enemy fighters. But bullets from his twin-50-caliber machine guns could not stop the onslaught that would bring down his bomber.

The Mihalich Family

Leonard August Mihalich was born on October 23, 1923, to Matt and Kathryn (née Yursich) Mihalich in

Portsmouth, Ohio. Matt and Kathryn had married in 1911 in Pittsburgh, Pennsylvania. Matt was working as a laborer in Portsmouth when Leonard was born. The family soon moved to Monessen, Pennsylvania where Matt had been hired as a laborer at Pittsburgh Steel, and Kathryn managed the Mihalich family household.

Matt had immigrated to the United States from the village of Cerovac, Croatia under the name of Matto or Mato Mihalic aboard the SS Kronprinz Wilhelm in 1907. Kathryn, also from Croatia, immigrated to the US in 1911 under the name of Kata Jursich. Matt became a naturalized US citizen in 1920.

Leonard was the first child born to Matt and Kathryn. Two brothers arrived next: Gilfert Matthew (b1926) and Herman (1930), both born in Monessen, Pennsylvania.

By 1930, the Mihalich family had purchased and were living in a home at 1134 Knox Avenue in Monessen. In 1933, the family opened a tavern in Monessen called Mihalich's Beer Garden, while the family lived in the apartment above it. Matt was a big fan of rye whiskey, and, perhaps not coincidentally, Herman's son would later open a rye whiskey distillery.

The surprise attack by Japanese armed forces on the US military base at Pearl Harbor, Hawaii, in December 1941 changed the world for millions of Americans, as it would for Leonard and Gilfert.

Leonard graduated from Monessen High School in 1942 where he was studying bookkeeping. He registered for the US armed forces draft immediately upon graduation on June 30, 1942, in Monessen. He was a 5'10" 165 lb 18-yr-old with blonde hair and blue eyes.

Leonard entered Duquesne University in Pittsburgh to further his studies. However, before completing his freshman year, he decided to join his peers and volunteer to serve with the US Army Air Corps. Leonard enlisted on March 4, 1943, in New Cumberland, Pennsylvania.

Leonard Enters the US Army Air Corps

Leonard, now Private Mihalich, was off to train in the Army Air Corps. He spent the next year learning the skills of his new trade and eventually became an aerial gunner on the Air Corp's Boeing B-17 Flying Fortress heavy bomber. Leonard was promoted to the rank of Sergeant (SGT) and assigned to the 613th Bomb Squadron (BS) of the 401st Bomb Group (BG).

The 401st BG had already been formed in April 1943 at Ephrata, Washington, and then sent to Geiger Field, Spokane, Washington for training in June. In November 1943, the group left the states for Europe, arriving at Deenethorpe Air Base in Northamptonshire, England. The 401st was attached to the 8th Air Force and flew its first combat mission later that month.

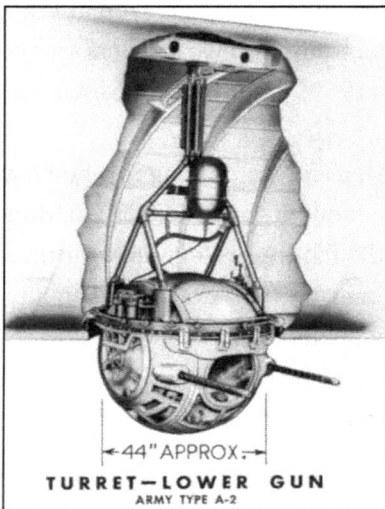

TURRET—LOWER GUN
ARMY TYPE A-2

US Air Force

SGT Mihalich specialized as a B-17 ball turret gunner. It was not a job for the faint of heart.

Once a B-17 is airborne, the ball turret gunner in his electrically-heated flight suit and oxygen mask would open the turret's hatch, step into the ball turret and crouch into the fetal position. A waist gunner would close the hatch. There was no room inside for a parachute. The ball turret gunner was now strapped into an unpressurized, unheated 4-foot-diameter metal and glass sphere. His only means of communication with his crewmates was via interphone radio. Alone, suspended tens of thousands of feet in the air

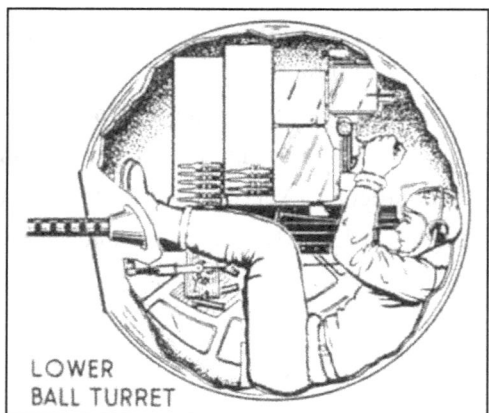

LOWER
BALL TURRET

US Air Force

for hours, the gunner and his turret were held in place by a bracket while traveling hundreds of miles-per-hour. With his head inches between twin .50 caliber machine guns, the gunner takes aim by looking down between his feet out of a small round window. His job was to search for enemy fighters approaching from below, notify the crew, and defend the aircraft with his weapons.

SGT Mihalich was eventually promoted to the rank of Staff Sergeant (S/SGT) and assigned to the B-17 crew of 2LT Frederick H. Windham, and they trained together in January 1944 at Rapid City Army Air Base, South Dakota. In March, they arrived at Deenethorpe as a replacement crew after the 401st had already flown 30 combat missions. The Windham crew was slotted into the 613th BS and they prepared in March and April for combat operations .

The crew's entry into combat was on the 401st's 68th mission against the IG Farben industrial plants in Merseburg, Germany on May 12, 1944. Their second mission was to the shipbuilding yard at Kiel, Germany on May 19, then to Bayon, France on May 23.

So far, Windham's crew had only encountered light to moderate enemy anti-aircraft fire and little to no enemy fighters. Their luck, however, was about to change…dramatically and for the worse.

The Final Mission

On May 28, 1944, S/SGT Leonard Mihalich joined LT Windham aboard B-17G #42-102647 nicknamed *BTO in the ETO* (abbreviating "Bombing Through Overcast in the European Theater of Operations"). The crew's fourth mission was part of the 8th Air Force's infamous Mission 376: a single-day, concerted attack on seven high priority targets to disrupt the supplies of oil and aircraft components.

Mission 376 was a complicated operation. It consisted of five "Forces" with nearly 40 bomb groups of B-17 Flying Fortress and B-24 Liberator bombers escorted by 31 fighter groups of P-38 Lightnings, P-47 Thunderbolts, and Royal Air Force P-51 Mustangs. In addition, over 600 B-26 Marauder medium bombers and A-20 Havoc light bombers, and fighters P-47s and RAF Spitfires and Typhoons were to attack logistical targets and V-weapon[7] sites in France and Belgium. The skies over continental Europe would be filled with attacking aircraft of the Allies and defending aircraft of the German Luftwaffe.

LT Windham's target was one of the largest aircraft engine manufacturing plants of the Junkers Aircraft and Motor Works, located in Dessau, Germany. Junkers engines powered many aircraft of the Luftwaffe, and disrupting their manufacture could cripple the ability of the Third Reich to launch its aircraft in the sky.

LT Windham's B-17 was one of seven aircraft of the 613th BS in the planned attack. The 401st was to fly in the low box position of the formation, and the 613th BS would fly in the high squadron position of their box.[8]

The forces departed England between 1200-1242 hrs on May 28. As LT Windham's B-17 approached the initial point (IP) over Dessau, at about 1440 hrs flying at 24,000 ft, a flak burst alongside the right side of the aircraft, knocking out the number 3 engine, and killing the co-pilot instantly. As the aircraft slipped out of formation

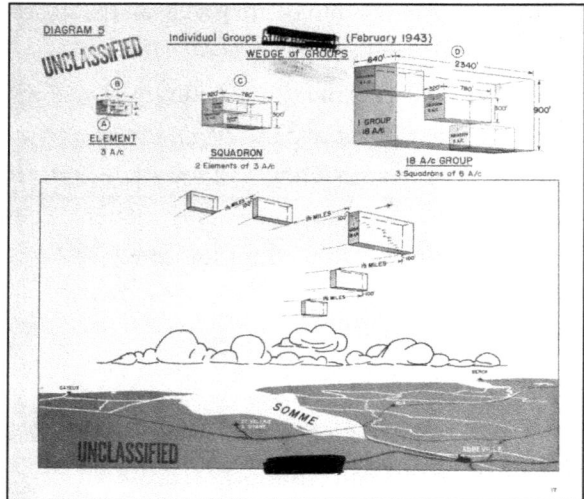

A bomber formation with "boxes" of aircraft (US Air Force)

about 5 minutes past Dessau, it lost 2-3000 feet of altitude. German Me-109

---

[7] German V-(Vergeltungswaffen) weapons were flying, unmanned, guided explosives. The V-1 was a cruise missile, and the V-2 was a ballistic missile. They were launched from sites in continental Europe to targets in England.

[8] US bombers often flew bombing missions in large formations of multiple aircraft. The purpose was to concentrate bombs on targets and to provide grouped aerial gunnery defense against enemy fighter attack. A "box" typically contained the aircraft of a specific squadron or bomb group. Boxes were often staggered in a specific configuration of the formation.

and FW-190 fighters pounced, riddling the aircraft with machine gun fire, knocking out the interphone system and part of the oxygen supply.

Windham's B-17 was in deep trouble, and he gave the order to bail out about 10-15 minutes past Dessau. With the interphone system knocked out, he ordered the flight engineer to walk to the rear and then the nose of the aircraft and verbally inform the crew to bail out. Five crew members received the order and escaped with their parachutes as the aircraft fell to Earth. Five, however, could not follow them.

S/SGT Mihalich was last heard on the interphone system after reaching the IP. He had been fatally struck by fighter gunfire while in his turret. A waist gunner tried to pull him from the turret but could only extract the unresponsive gunner halfway before realizing that SGT Mihalich showed no sign of life, so he left him to bail out and save his own life.

The B-17 crashed near Niemegk, Germany, 13 KM southwest of Treuen-brietzen. Five crew members of Windham's B-17 died that day. The five others who parachuted were captured by German troops and remained prisoners for the duration of the war. The 8th Air Force lost 32 bombers with over 300 airmen missing in action that day.

The family of SGT Mihalich was informed that he was missing in action in July 1944, and he was declared killed in action a year later.

S/SGT Leonard A. Mihalich and his fallen crewmates were buried locally in a community cemetery in Niemegk. His remains were eventually removed from Germany and reinterred at the Ardennes American Cemetery in Neuville-en-Condroz, Belgium. He was posthumously awarded the Purple Heart.

His brother Gilfert, who also served in the US Army Air Corps, returned from the war, graduated from law school, and would become a well-respected judge in Westmoreland County, Pennsylvania. His brother Herman would serve as a representative in the Pennsylvania State Legislature for seven years.

✵ ✵ ✵

PVT Nicholas Kafkalas

Service Number 33690296
116th Regiment, 29th Infantry Division, US Army
Killed in action, Normandy, France, June 6, 1944

Co-written with Gary Smith

W hen his ship departed the coast of England for France on June 6, 1944, Nick Kafkalas was likely overwhelmed by the conflicting emotions of excitement and dread. His regiment had been selected to be the first to land on Omaha Beach and spearhead World War II's Allied invasion.

For Nick Kafkalas, this would be his first taste of battle. It would also be his last. Private Kafkalas would never see his family and the Mon Valley again.

The Kafkalas Family

Nicholas "Nick" Stefanos Kafkalas was born on January 5, 1925, in Monessen, to Stefanos "Steve" Nicholas and Angeliki "Angeline" (neé Gianiodis) Kafkalas. Steve and Angeline had

married two years earlier and settled in Monessen. At the time, Steve was working as a baker while Angeline managed the Kafkalas family household.

Steve and Angeline Kaflakas were both born on the Greek island of Chios. Steve immigrated to the United States in 1916 aboard the SS King Constantine, following his brother Pantelis "Peter" to Monessen who arrived in 1911. Angeline came to the US in 1920, and the couple met in Monessen. Learning that they shared a birthplace made them at ease as young immigrants in a strange country, which led them to the altar.

The first child born into the family was Nick's sister Kaliope "Kally" (b1923). After Nick arrived, his brothers Democrates "Demo" (1927) and Mihalia "Mike" (1929) came along. By 1930, the family of six was living in a rented home at 1205 Summit Avenue in Monessen. Their father was now working as a truck driver for a local bookstore.

By 1940, the family had earned enough money to purchase a home at 800 Schoonmaker Avenue in Monessen. Their father had taken a job for the local sanitation company, and the children were now all attending public school.

Drumbeats of War

In anticipation of possible global hostilities, the US Congress passed the Selective Service and Training Act in September 1940. That October millions of men and boys registered for the first peacetime draft. Just over a year later, their preparation appeared prescient.

A peaceful holiday season for Mon Valley families was rudely interrupted on December 7, 1941, when Japanese forces launched a surprise attack on the US military bases at Pearl Harbor, Hawaii, bringing the country into war with Japan, Germany, and Italy. It would not take long for millions of young Americans to sign up to defend the country and fight for democracy worldwide.

Nick attended Monessen High School while watching WWII unfold. He was active in intramural sports. The Monessen Greyhound Yearbook described Nick as "...a chap of few words except when food is mentioned, especially steaks. He doesn't like dances and cold weather. Uncle Sam has Nick's future laid out for him." He had registered for the draft while a high school senior in January 1943. Nick graduated high school in June, and on June 28, 1943, he was drafted into the US Army.

After High School, Uncle Sam Beckons

PVT Nicholas Kafkalas reported for duty in Pittsburgh on July 12, 1943, and was off to Army boot camp. He trained stateside as an infantryman for the next six months, and in January 1944, PVT Kafkalas was sent overseas to join his new unit, the 116th Regiment of the 29th Infantry Division.

The 116th Regiment, a Virginia-based unit, had been called into active Federal service in February 1941. Upon entry of the US into the war, the 29th Division guarded the Eastern shore of the country and began training in amphibious exercises in the possibility of landing on foreign shores. It was not going to be long.

In September 1942, the 116th shipped overseas to England, where they began lengthy training for the eventual possibility of joining a ground war in England or on the European continent. Tensions were high and the training was serious business.

PVT Kafkalas Arrives in England

When PVT Nick Kaflakas arrived in January 1944, the 116th was now over 3,200 men strong. They had been training in England for nearly a year and a half. More troops, vehicles, weapons, and other supplies were arriving from the US as the build-up for an eventual invasion mounted. Nick was assigned to the Regiment's Company B where he made a home with new colleagues.

As preparations were underway for Operation Overlord, the codename for the upcoming invasion, plans were being made for the 116th Regiment. The regiment was to be part of "Force O", the initial assault force at Omaha Beach. PVT Kafkalas, in Company B, would take part in the second wave of that assault. It was an ominous assignment indeed.

From May 3-8, 1944, the regiment participated in "Exercise Fabius" at Slapton Sands, England, the final rehearsal before D-Day, the planned invasion of Normandy, France. On May 15, 1944, the regiment relocated to Bland-ford Camp where it was confined behind barbed wire to preserve secrecy. Anticipation was certainly high.

Invasion!

On June 3, the 116th boarded ships at Weymouth, England, and remained in the invasion queue for departure for Normandy. The 1st Battalion, which included Companies A, B, C and D, boarded the SS Empire Javelin for its journey. Inclement weather, however, delayed the start of Operation Overlord, much to the dismay of the shipbound infantrymen.

The order to sail for Normandy was given, and during the early morning hours of June 6, 1944, the infantrymen transferred from the safety of their ships to their amphibious landing craft, called LCVP's (Landing Craft, Vehicle Personnel).

The first wave of LCVP's left their ships by 0430 hrs and chugged towards Omaha Beach over the unending waves of the English Channel. By 0636 hrs, the landing craft had arrived at the beach. The second wave began moving towards Omaha Beach at 0700 hrs and landed by 0740 hrs.

D-Day Invasion at Normandy, France (Imperial War Museum)

Early morning bombardment of the German defensive installations by the Allied navies and air forces were intended to soften and if possible, break the resistance of the enemy. The heavily constructed German gun emplacements and troop bunkers, however, survived the aerial onslaught. The arriving American, British, and Canadian infantrymen were about to learn how effective the German defenses could be.

German Defenses Unleash Hell

As soon as the front door ramps of the landing craft were lowered into the water, the soldiers were faced with heavy fire from entrenched enemy machine guns, mortars, and small arms. Some of the landing craft became stranded on sand bars, and their soldiers had to wade through, at-times, neck-high water to reach the beach. Many were killed or drowned as they advanced. Bad weather and rough seas forced many landing craft out of position and deposited their troops at wrong locations, causing additional confusion. To be on the beach was to witness mayhem.

During the chaos of the 116th's second wave assault, PVT Kafkalas lost his life, the precise circumstances still unknown. It was a devastating day for Company B: Out of 220 men, only 28 survived D-Day.

The family of PVT Nick Kafkalas was informed in July that he was missing in action. Their worst fears came true when they were finally notified in September that their son had been killed in action on D-Day, June 6, 1944.

Nicholas Kafkalas, Remembered

PVT Nicholas Kafkalas was initially buried at a temporary cemetery at Saint Laurent, Baveux, France. He was eventually and finally reinterred at the Normandy American Cemetery, Colleville-sur-Mer, France. PVT Kafkalas was posthumously awarded the Purple Heart.

His older cousin, Nicholas Peter Kafkalas, also from Monessen, would serve as an officer in the US Army during WWII where he was wounded during the Battle of the Bulge. He went on to serve as a 37-year career Pennsylvania National Guardsman where he retired in 1980 as Major General.

★ ★ ★

CPL MICHAEL LEAVOR

Service Number 13009567
29th Field Artillery Battalion, 4th Infantry Division, US Army
Killed in action, Normandy, France, June 6, 1944

During land-based Army artillery training, Michael Leavor might not have expected that he would be firing canons from a boat. On June 6, 1944, that is exactly what his unit was called upon to do. They needed to protect Allied troops during the largest amphibious landing during World War II: The D-Day Invasion on the beaches of Normandy, France.

Corporal Michael Leavor would become one of two Monessen men to lose their lives on the first day of the invasion.

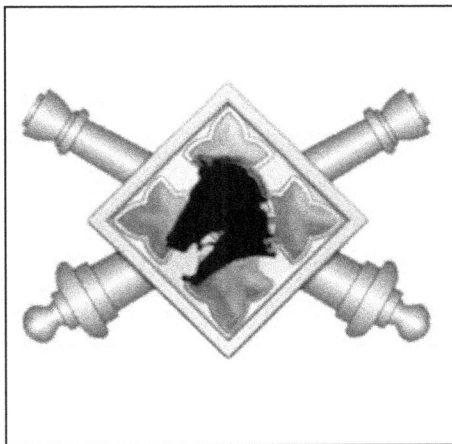

4th Infantry Division Artillery Insignia (US Army)

The Leavor Family

Michael Leavor was born on March 17, 1918, to Peter and Mary (née Ostoffie) Leavor in Vestaburg, Pennsylvania. Peter and Mary had married in 1908. Peter was a coal miner for the Vesta Coal Company, while Mary managed the Leavor family household.

Peter, of Ruthenian[9] descent, was born with the surname Hliva or Hlyva in an area of Poland under the Austro-Hungarian Empire before immigrating to the United States in 1904. Mary was also of Ruthenian descent and immigrated from Eastern Europe to the US in 1906. They eventually adapted their surname to Leavor in the early 1900's, and initially settled in the small community of Bessemer, Pennsylvania, where their first child, Anna, was born in 1908.

A daughter Dorothy was the next child born to the couple, arriving in 1910. The young family moved to Vestaburg where sons John (1913), Steve (1916), and Michael were born, followed by Helen (1920), Julia (1922), and Frank (1925).

Starting in 1927, a string of tragedies befell the family when a son arrived stillborn. In 1929, their mother Mary lost her life to cardio-renal disease at the age of 45. Two years later, son Steve was working as a coal miner at the age of 15 when he died of typhoid fever in 1931. Then, in 1934, their father Peter died of tubercular peritonitis after unsuccessful surgery. There were seven surviving children. Anna had married and moved away to start her own family. Dorothy married and took in her younger siblings, becoming their guardian.

By 1940, Dorothy's family were living at 1245 McMahon Street in Monessen, Pennsylvania, and boarding her brothers Michael and John. Michael, now 21, had left school after completing eighth grade and was working in a Monessen steel mill. That year, he decided to enlist in the US Army, and signed up on July 29, 1940, in Pittsburgh, as a 5'9", 147 lb young adult. He immediately left for training. During 1941, he trained at Fort Benning, Georgian.

Michael Leavor in the US Army

On December 7, 1941, military bases of the US at Pearl Harbor, the Philippines, and Guam were attacked by Japanese forces, bringing the country into

---

[9] Ruthenians (or Rusyns) are an ethnic group primarily from Central Europe in the area of the Carpathian Mountains, comprising parts of Hungary, Poland, Ukraine, and Slovakia, with a distinct Slavic language or dialect.

World War II. The US armed forces mobilized for war in the Pacific and in Europe against Japan's ally, Germany.

By January 1942, Private Michael Leavor was stationed at Camp Gordon, Georgia, where he was designated to field artillery training with the 4th Infantry Division. PVT Leavor was eventually assigned to the 29th Field Artillery Battalion (FA Bn) of the 4th Division Artillery.

The 29th was one of four Field Artillery Battalions in the 4th Infantry Division, and one of three responsible for manning the 105 mm howitzer artillery gun. The 105 was the standard US light field howitzer and was deployed throughout the war by the US military. It could deliver a devastating punch to enemy combatants by firing 33 lb shells at a rate of 10 per minute at targets up to 7 miles away.

According to its battalion commander Colonel Joel F. Thomason, "While at Camp Gordon, GA, the battalion became the "show" unit of the 4th Infantry Division, hosting all

105 mm Howitzer Artillery Gun (US Department of Defense)

inspectors and many visitors from the War Department, among others. The battalion excelled in firing artillery in all tests, had the best mess halls, best motor maintenance, and was the best all-around unit of the division." PVT Leavor and his colleagues certainly had a reason to be proud.

PVT Leavor was eventually promoted to the rank of Corporal (CPL). He continued his training stateside including at Fort Dix, New Jersey, in 1943. On January 10, 1944, the 4th Division departed the US for England. The time was approaching for the US, Canada, and Great Britain to invade the German-occupied territory of mainland Europe, and to push German forces back to their homeland.

Col. Thomason recalls, "The 29th Field Artillery arrived in Axminster, Devon, England in January 1944, and began extensive training. The amphibious training received in the United States was repeated in England at Slapton Sands, during February- May 1944, culminating in the VII Corps Exercise TIGER."

By May's end, the unit was ready to commence the invasion. CPL Michael Leavor and the 700 men of the 29th FA Bn were assigned as the supporting artillery battalion for the 8th Infantry Regiment of the 4th Division. They made up the 8th Combat Team of the 4th Infantry Division, whose mission was to make the H-Hour landing on Utah Beach. A, B, and C Batteries had been equipped with M7 "Priest" self-propelled armored 105 mm howitzers, instead of conventional truck-drawn (i.e., towed) artillery pieces. Each gun battery was equipped with 4 guns. On June 5, 1944, they boarded their LCT[10] landing crafts and headed for the beaches of Normandy, France.

D-Day!

On D-Day, June 6, 1944, the invasion began. The 29th FA Battalion was the first artillery unit to land in Normandy, at Utah Beach.

According to the 29th's PFC Irving Smolens, "During the Invasion of Normandy, at Utah Beach, the batteries would fire from the deck of the LCT's, with the Battery Commander issuing the "fire order". He received his orders from the Battalion Fire Direction Center, which was located on another ship, along with the men of the Headquarters Battery. Our M7s were loaded on the LCT's two in front, and two in back, each with their "active" crew. The "reserve" crews were located on other boats. As the front guns performed firing

---

[10] LCT, or "Landing Craft, Tank", is an open-air, shallow-draft sea-going vessel with a large front door that served as a ramp upon landing upon a beach. They were designed specifically to transport armored vehicles such as tanks onto a combat zone.

missions, the back guns also performed firing missions, actually firing high trajectory "over" the front guns".

In the melee of the fighting that day, CPL Michael Leavor was struck by fragments of an enemy artillery shell. His wounds proved fatal, and he lost his life that day.

The following month, Michael Leavor's family was informed by the War Department that he was missing in action. It was not until November of 1944 that they were informed that he was, in fact, killed in action.

CPL Michael Leavor was initially buried in at Sainte Mere-Eglise Cemetery #2, Carentan, France. He was eventually reburied at the Normandy American Cemetery, Colleville-sur-Mer, France. CPL Leavor was posthumously awarded the Purple Heart.

★ ★ ★

PFC George Evanich

Service Number 492091
Company I, 3rd Battalion, 24th Marine Regiment, 4th Marine Division, USMC
Killed in action, Saipan, June 18, 1944

The Evanich family sent two of their sons, George and Andy, to fight during World War II. Their Blue Stars, once a symbol of pride for the Evanich family, would turn Gold with grief.

The Evanich Family

George Evanich was born on February 15, 1923, to Andrew, Sr. and Anna "Annie" (née Marin) Evanich in Monessen, Pennsylvania. Andrew and Annie met in Glassport, Pennsylvania, down the Monongahela River from Monessen, and they married in Glassport in 1921. Andrew was a laborer in a Monessen steel mill while Annie managed the Evanich family household.

Insignia of the 24th Marine Regiment (USMC)

Andrew Sr. was born Andraj Ivanis II in Zavosyna, Hungary, and immigrated with his father to the United States in 1912 aboard the SS Bremen. Annie was born in Velke Berezne, a village 6 miles away from Zavosyna, and immigrated to the US in 1920 aboard the SS Rochambeau. Both villages are in the region of Carpathian Ruthenia, in the present-day area of far western Ukraine. Little did they realize that they would travel more than 4,500 miles to meet their future spouse who once lived but 6 miles away from where they grew up.

George was the first of three children born to Andrew Sr. and Annie. His brother Andrew Jr., "Andy," arrived next (1924), followed by his brother John (1927). By 1930, the family was living in their home at 929 Grant Street in Monessen. They continued living there through 1940 while the boys attended school. The family were members of St John the Divine Church. George was in the church choir.

George attended Monessen High School where he played on the football team. In May 1941, his mother Annie was stricken with myocarditis associated with hepatitis, and she passed away at the age of 37 yrs.

George graduated from high school in 1940-41 and went to work at the Pittsburgh Steel Company in Monessen while living at home with his father and brothers. George joined the Federated Russian Orthodox Club (the Monessen "R" Club) in May 1942.

George Evanich Joins the Marines

The surprise attack by Japanese armed forces on the US military bases at Pearl Harbor, Hawaii, in December 1941 changed the world for George. On June 30, 1942, George registered for the US armed forces draft in Monessen. He was a 5'8" 178 lb young single man with brown hair and brown eyes.

Six months later, on December 7, 1942, George enlisted in the US Marine Corps in Pittsburgh, Pennsylvania. Private George Evanich was off to Marine boot camp on January 1, 1944. Three months later, his brother Andy was drafted into the US Army. With George in the Marines and Andy in the Army, the Evanich's were now a two-Blue-Star family.

PVT Evanich was assigned to Company I, 3rd Battalion, which was formed in February 1943. The 1st and 2nd Battalions had been formed in October 1942 and January 1943, respectively. The three battalions were organized under 24th Regimental Headquarters at Camp Lejeune, North Carolina in March 1943, and proceeded to Camp Pendleton, San Diego, California, by April. In August, the regiment was attached to the newly created 4th Marine Division, which was raised specifically for deployment in the Pacific theater of the war.

By July 1943, PVT George Evanich had been promoted to Private First Class (PFC). Their unit continued its training in preparation for deployment, amphibious landings, and jungle warfare.

PFC George Evanich to the Pacific

The 4th Division deployed to the Pacific in January 1944, heading for the Japanese-held Marshall Islands. The first combat assignment was to capture Roi-Namur, twin islands in the Kwajalein Atoll. The 24th Regiment began the assault on February 1, with the 2nd and 3rd Battalions leading the attack. Despite strong resistance, the island was taken from the Japanese by the following day. The 24th Marines returned to Hawaii to prepare for its next assault, the Mariana Islands.

The Mariana Islands of Saipan, Guam, and Tinian were strategically important to the war effort for two reasons: 1) They were large enough to hold the monstrous air bases necessary to support the US Army Air Force's new Boeing B-29 Superfortress bomber, and 2) they were within the B-29's range of flight to the Japanese home islands. With the Mariana's in the possession of the US Army Air Force, they could bring the war to the Japanese homeland.

The first objective of the Mariana Island Campaign for the regiment was the capture of Saipan, yet to be learned by PFC Evanich and his peers until embarking from Hawaii. The plan was for the 4th Division's 24th Marines to be in reserve at the time of initial troop landing on Saipan on June 15.

On June 13, capital ships of the US Navy began two days of relentless bombardment of Japanese positions on Saipan. The Marine landings on the western shore of Saipan began on the morning of June 15. The 4th Division's 24th Regiment went ashore that afternoon to join the initial Marine units in pushing inland. Over the next two days, the Marines advanced about 2 miles inland, facing counterattacks by the entrenched Japanese units.

Marines Arrive on Saipan June 15, 1944 (USMC Archives)

On the morning of June 18, the 4th Division resumed a concerted attack toward the east coast of Saipan to split the Japanese forces in two. The entire Division, with its three rifle regiments abreast, launched its assault at 1040 hrs.

Fate Intervenes

During the advance, PFC George Evanich was fatally wounded. He died in battle that day. His family would be informed by the War Department in July that he had been killed in action.

PFC George Evanich was initially buried at the 4th Marine Division Cemetery on Saipan. On February 21, 1949, his remains were reinterred at the National Memorial Cemetery of the Pacific, at Honolulu, Hawaii, along with more than 10,000 other American military dead.

Nine months after George's loss, his brother PFC Andrew Evanich, Jr, was killed in action in Germany. The family's second blue star had turned gold.

★ ★ ★

SGT PATSY S. COLUMBUS

Service Number 13086836
313th Regiment, 79th Infantry Division, US Army
Killed in action, France, June 22, 1944

S ergeant Patsy Columbus and his combat unit arrived on the beaches at Normandy, France, six days after the initial D-Day landings. Their job was to overwhelm the entrenched German defenders and clear a path for Allies forces to drive deep into France.

However, on D-Day + 16 (days), SGT Columbus met his fate when he was struck by fragments from an enemy artillery shell.

The Columbus Family

Pasquale "Patsy" Salvatore Columbus was born on October 19, 1921, to Sebastian and Lillian Felice (née Letizia) Columbus in Monessen, Pennsylvania. Sebastian and Lillian had married four years earlier in 1917 in Chicago, Illinois. Sebastian was a laborer in the steel mill in Monessen while Lillian managed the Columbus family household.

Sebastian Columbus was born Sebastiano Santacolombo on the island of Sicily, Italy, and immigrated to the United States aboard the SS Neckar in 1907. Lillian was born in Chicago to parents who had immigrated to the US from the Campania region of Italy in 1883. After marrying, Sebastian and Lillian settled in Monessen where local employers were fervently seeking laborers for their churning factories.

Patsy was the second of four children born to Sebastian and Lillian. Ernesto Nuncio was the couple's first-born child (b1920), followed by Filippo "Phillip" (1925) and Michele "Michael" (1930). By 1930, the family was living in a rented home at 399 Third Street in Monessen along with Sebastian's widowed mother, Concetta "Jennie", while the children attended school.

By 1940, Sebastian had changed employers and was now working at the Monessen tin mill. The family had moved into a rented home at 252 Park Way. That year Sebastian had completed his US citizenship requirements and had become a US citizen. Patsy participated in the annual "Minstrel and Follies" show at the Monessen Vocational School in 1940, playing the role of "Snooks". In 1941, Patsy's brother Ernesto enlisted in the Pennsylvania National Guard, and would eventually be deployed overseas.

Patsy graduated from Monessen Vocational High School in 1941. He had been studying in the Machine Shop curriculum and had taken an active interest in sports. Patsy was on the cheerleading squad his senior year but had also served as a manager for the football, basketball, and wrestling teams during his junior and senior high school years. After graduation, Patsy went to work as a machinist for the Lee-Norse Company in nearby Charleroi, a manufacturer of mining equipment. He was living at 646 Third Street in Monessen.

On November 2, 1941, Patsy's mother was admitted to Charleroi-Monessen Hospital for heart surgery. She succumbed to complications of the surgery and cardiac illness four days later.

US Enters the War

The surprise attack by Japanese armed forces on the US military bases at Pearl Harbor, Hawaii, in December 1941 changed the world for Patsy. He registered for the US armed forces draft on February 16, 1942, in Monessen as a 5'6" 135 lb young single man with black hair and brown eyes. Four months later, on June 20, 1942, he joined his fellow patriotic volunteers and enlisted with the US Army, ready to serve the nation. Private Patsy Columbus was off to boot camp.

While in training, Patsy's brother Phillip enlisted with the US Navy in August 1943. With Patsy, Ernesto, and Phillip in the US armed forces, the Columbus' were now a three Blue-Star family.

During training, PVT Columbus was assigned to the 313th Regiment of the 79th Infantry Division. The 79th was activated at Camp Pickett, Virginia in June 1942. It participated in the Tennessee Maneuver Area, after which it moved to Camp Laguna near Yuma, Arizona, where it trained in the desert. The 79th was then ordered to Camp Phillips, Kansas for training in winter conditions. At the beginning of April 1944, the division reported to the port of embarkation at Camp Myles Standish, Massachusetts, in preparation for deployment to the European theater of the war.

PVT Patsy Columbus was recognized for his leadership and was promoted to Sergeant (SGT). SGT Columbus was prepared to lead his troops into battle.

The 79th Division arrived in Liverpool, England on April 17, 1944 and began training in amphibious operations in preparation for the Allied invasion of the European continent on D-Day June 6, 1944. After the initial landings secured the Normandy beachheads, the 79th landed unopposed at Utah Beach, France, on June 12-14. But soon the troops of the 79th would enter combat, and on June 19 they began with an attack on the high ground west and northwest of Valognes along the main highway to Cherbourg, and on the high ground south of Cherbourg.

As the 79th's 313th Regiment fought its way toward Cherbourg on June 22, SGT Columbus' team found itself under enemy attack. They were encountering considerably more resistance than was anticipated. On the night of June

21-22, surrender demands were sent to the defending German troops, followed by their reply - a few well-placed salvos of artillery that landed in the immediate vicinity of the 313th. A joint air-land operation against German forces in Cherbourg was ordered for June 22. The assault began, and SGT Patsy Columbus was leading his squad.

SGT Columbus Loses his Life

But fate would intervene that day, and on June 22, SGT Patsy Columbus was fatally struck by shrapnel from an artillery shell near the town of La Haye-du-Puits, France. He was 22 yrs old. His family was informed in September that he had been killed in action in France.

SGT Patsy S. Columbus was initially buried at the temporary American-St. Laurent Cemetery, France. His remains are now memorialized at the nearby permanent Normandy American Cemetery with 9,387 of his brothers-in-arms.

✷ ✷ ✷

S/SGT JOHN KOMLOS

Service Number 33391678
Company G, 330th Infantry Regiment, 83rd Infantry Division, US Army
Killed in action, France, July 4, 1944

John Komlos was born on September 6, 1911, in Monessen, Pennsylvania, to Andrew "Andy" and Helen Alice (née Garber) Komlos. Andy and Helen had married a year earlier. Andy was a laborer at the Page Woven Wire Fence Company in Monessen while Helen managed the Komlos family household.

The Komlos Family

Andy, born Andras in the village of Jesztreb in Soros, Austria-Hungary, immigrated to the United States in 1906 aboard the SS Bremen. Helen was born in Punxsutawney, Pennsylvania, to parents born in Saros, Hungary, who immigrated to the US in the 1880's. Their Hungarian surname was Gabor.

John was the first of six children born to Andy and Helen, followed by George (b1913), Andrew Jr.(1916), Emil Vincent (1920), Michael (1920), and their sister Olga (1924). In 1920 the family was living in a rented home at 239

Oneida Street, and they would soon buy their own home at 1215 Morgan Avenue in Monessen.

Their mother Helen became gravely ill with Addison's disease, and she succumbed to her illness in January 1927. Their father Andy passed away between 1930-1932. In 1930, John was in an automobile accident and charged with reckless driving, and several months later was in another accident which injured two passengers.

John Komlos Joins the National Guard

In 1932, John joined the Pennsylvania National Guard where he served as a Private in Company D, Machine Gun Unit, 110th Infantry. He participated in training maneuvers annually.

After their father's passing, John became head of the Komlos household, and they continued to live in the home on Morgan Avenue. He had left Monessen High School after his second year and went to work as a laborer at the Pittsburgh Steel mill in Monessen. John met and fell in love with Margaret Esther Marsden, and they married in November 1932. But the marriage did not last, and they separated in November 1938, with John granted a divorce from Margaret a year later on the grounds of "cruelty and indignities".

In 1940, John was still the head of the household and living at home with his four brothers. John was working at the steel mill as a pipefitter. Their sister Olga, at 15 yrs old, was living at a home for orphans on Oneida Street in Monessen.

On October 16, 1940, John Komlos joined millions of his fellow American men and registered for the US armed forces draft on its first day after the recent passing of the Selective Service Act. His draft card reveals that he was a 5'8", 185 lb 29-yr-old man with black hair and brown eyes and working at Pittsburgh Steel. Meanwhile, John met Evelyn "Effie" Smith of North Belle Vernon, Pennsylvania, and they began their courtship.

The surprise attack by Japanese armed forces on the US military bases at Pearl Harbor, Hawaii, in December 1941 changed the world for John and his brothers. John and Effie announced their engagement in April 1942. On September 29, 1942, John was drafted into the US Army, but before reporting for duty, John and Effie tied the knot, and married on October 5, 1942, in Oakland, Maryland. John said his goodbyes to Effie, and reported for duty on October 14 in Greensburg, Pennsylvania.

PVT John Komlos trained stateside with the 330th Infantry Regiment of the 83rd Infantry Division. He demonstrated key leadership traits and was eventually promoted to the rank of Staff Sergeant (S/SGT).

Off to Europe

The 83rd Infantry Division had been ordered into active service in August 1942 at Camp Atterbury, Indiana. After extensive training, the Division shipped overseas on April 6, 1944, in confidential preparation for Operation Overlord, the Allied invasion of continental Europe. They continued their training in Wales.

Operation Overlord began on D-Day, June 6, 1944, with troop landings at Normandy, France. The 83rd Division landed in Normandy on June 18 at the secured Omaha Beach, entering the struggle with German enemy troops in the hedgerows of the Carentan Peninsula.

The 330th Regiment was situated 1.8 miles southeast of Carentan when it made its thrust against the enemy on Independence Day, July 4. According to the Regiment's After-Action Report for that day:

"The Regiment...launched an attack at 0500... The attack met stiff resistance, especially mortar and arty [artillery] fire which was zeroed in on hedgerows over which the attack had to pass. At 0800 the 2nd Bn [Battalion] was pinned down by mortar and arty fire and were unable to advance. The attack was halted. 1st Bn resumed the attack at 0855. The 2nd Bn received a counterattack and was forced to withdraw to their original O.P.L. The 3rd Bn was committed at 1907 across the 2nd Bn front and were held up at 1937. Very little progress was made during the day."

On July 4, 1944, S/SGT John Komlos met his fate in battle. While engaged in combat, John Komlos was killed in action. A month later, the War Department informed his wife Effie that he had died in combat in France.

S/SGT John Komlos was buried at the Normandy American Cemetery at Colleville-sur-Mer, Département du Calvados, Basse-Normandie, France. He was posthumously awarded the Purple Heart.

★ ★ ★

PVT ANTHONY THIRY

Service Number 33290200
Company A, 115th Infantry Regiment, 29th Infantry Division, US Army
Killed in action, France, July 11, 1944

Whe Private Anthony Thiry landed on Omaha Beach at Normandy, France, on D-Day, June 6, 1944, late in the day, he was likely astounded by the destruction from the morning's battle. Hulking wreckages of landing craft, destroyed tanks, abandoned weapons, and most vividly, the remains of his fellow infantrymen.

Anthony Thiry survived combat for another 35 days.

The Thiry Family

Anthony Thiry was born on February 19, 1919, to Joseph and Barbara Thiry (née Flesch) in Youngstown, Ohio. Joseph and Barbara had married in 1913. Joseph worked in a Youngstown steel mill while Barbara managed the Thiry family household.

Joseph, born in the village of Wekeakfalva in the Austro-Hungarian empire, immigrated to the United States in 1914 and became a naturalized citizen

in 1919. Barbara, born in the same region as Joseph, immigrated to the US in 1913 and was also naturalized in 1919.

Anthony was the first of five children born to Joseph and Barbara. Eva Barbara arrived next (1920), followed by Frank Joseph (1922), Marie (1925), and Albert John (1940). The family moved to Monessen, Pennsylvania, in the early 1920's, then back to Youngstown where Eva and Frank were born. Family members of both Joseph and Barbara were living in Youngstown. They returned to Monessen by 1925 where Marie and Albert were born. By 1940, the family was living at 1061 Graham Avenue in Monessen where Joseph was employed by Pittsburgh Steel. Anthony had ended his formal education after completing grammar school.

With the rumblings of war heard in Europe and the Pacific, the US Congress passed the Selective Service and Training Act in September 1940, including the first peacetime draft for the US military. On October 16, 1940, Anthony joined millions of his fellow American young men and registered for the draft on its first day. According to his draft registration, Anthony, a 6 ft, 162 lb brown-hair and gray-eyed 21-yr-old, was working at Pittsburgh Steel and living at the home of his parents.

The US Enters WWII

Japanese forces launched a surprise attack on the US military bases in Pearl Harbor, Hawaii, on December 7, 1941. The US declared war on Japan, and as an ally of the Japanese Empire, Germany declared war on the US. Anthony and other young Monessen men would soon be called to duty.

It did not take long. Anthony was drafted into the US Army, and he enlisted on July 30, 1942. He reported for duty at Camp George Meade, Maryland in August. He trained stateside for the next six months.

In February 1943, Private Thiry left the shores of the US for England. There, he joined Company A of the 115th Infantry Regiment, known as the "Blue and Gray". The 115th Infantry Regiment, a unit of the Maryland National Guard, had been reactivated prior to the entry of the US into WWII. They were shipped to England in October 1942 and were attached to the 29th

Division to prepare for the eventual Operation Overlord, the Allied invasion of the European continent.

When PVT Thiry arrived, the 115th was stationed in Cornwall in the southwestern corner of England. By November 1943, the group had been in the area so long that they became known as "England's Own". Here they trained in many types of combat, primarily amphibious landings.

PVT Thiry Lands at Normandy

On D-Day, June 6, 1944, the 115th came ashore on Normandy, France, at Omaha Beach at 9:30 AM after the Army's Rangers had landed. The Rangers had taken heavy casualties but eventually secured the beachhead for the arrival of reinforcing Allied troops.

Throughout the month of June, the 115th fought aggressively against the German defenders. They were to drive southward, inland, and advance to take the enemy stronghold of St. Lô, France. The town was at a key crossroads, and Allied advancement was contingent upon taking control of St. Lô.

The 115th was to join a coordinated attack on St. Lô. On the morning of July 11, 1944, the 115th Infantry launched during which some bitter fighting took place. At about 0100 hrs, they were heavily counter-attacked by the enemy, causing heavy casualties.

It was during this combat that a bullet struck PVT Anthony Thiry in the jaw. The wound proved to be fatal. He died that day. Anthony Thiry's family was notified by the War Department several weeks later that their son had been killed in action in France.

Anthony Thiry, Remembered

PVT Anthony Thiry was initially buried at the American Cemetery in La Cambe, France. He was eventually reinterred at the Normandy American Cemetery and Memorial, Colleville-sur-Mer, Basse-Normandie, France. PVT Thiry was posthumously awarded the Purple Heart medal.

★ ★ ★

T/SGT Ernest C. Renzetti

Service Number 33391632
Company K, 331st Infantry Regiment, 83rd Infantry Division, US Army
Killed in action, France, July 14, 1944

Marksman Ernest Renzetti arrived on Omaha Beach at Normandy, France, twelve days after the initial landings of Allied forces on D-Day, June 6, 1944.

As his unit moved inland into France the following month, he was struck in the back by shrapnel from an exploding artillery shell. Days later, his body relented to the severity of his wound. His family would not learn his fate for four more months.

The Renzetti Family

Ernest Charles Renzetti was born on April 6, 1922, to Ernesto and Concetta (née Clausi) Renzetti in Monessen, Pennsylvania. His father Ernesto, a coal miner, died from pneumonia and influenza at the age of 33, exactly one month before his son's birth. Ernesto had immigrated to the United States from Italy in 1909 and was drafted into the US Army in 1917. He served during World War I with Company I of the 326th Infantry Regiment as a Private First Class and fought overseas from April 1918 through May 1919. Concetta immigrated from Italy in 1919, and married Ernesto shortly thereafter.

After the death of her husband and birth of her son, Concetta met and married Amato Tineri. Amato was born in Aquila, Italy, immigrated to the US in 1917, and worked in the blast furnace department at a Monessen steel mill. The couple had four children together, Laura (b1923), Susan Rose (1924), James (1926), and Nello Anthony (1927). Although Ernest never met his birth father, he kept the Renzetti surname.

The Tineri family rented a home at 514 Knox Avenue in Monessen in 1930 while the children attended school. At one point Ernest became ill and had his appendix removed. By 1940, they moved into another rented home in Monessen at 1240 Maple Avenue and Ernest and Laura were now attending Monessen High School. Ernest was in the high school Glee Club and Intramural Champions and was the president of his class homeroom in 1941.

The surprise attack by Japanese armed forces upon the US military base at Pearl Harbor on December 7, 1941, changed the world for millions of Americans as it did for Ernest. On June 30, 1942, Ernest registered for the US military draft as a 5'11" 148 lb 20-yr-old with black hair and brown eyes. He had taken a job with Pittsburgh Steel in Monessen. The family had moved once more, and they were now living at 915 Marguerite Avenue.

Three months later, Ernest was drafted, and he enlisted on September 29, 1942, in Greensburg, Pennsylvania. He was assigned to the US Army, and he reported for Army boot camp on October 13, 1942.

Ernest Renzetti in the US Army

PVT Renzetti was assigned to the 331st Regiment of the 83rd Infantry Division, and during training, he qualified as a marksman and was promoted to Technical Sergeant (T/SGT). The 331st was activated in August 1942 at Camp Atterbury, Indiana. By the end of 1943, the Regiment totaled nearly 3,000 personnel. The Regiment moved to Breckenridge, Kentucky for advanced training in September 1943 for five months before heading to Camp Shanks, New York in preparation for deployment to the European theater of the war. The entire 83rd Infantry Division shipped overseas to England in April 1944 in preparation for the Allied invasion of the European continent. Upon arriving, the 331st transferred to northern Wales where they underwent intensive training for the invasion.

The 331st landed at Omaha Beach in Normandy, France, at D-Day plus 12, June 17-18, after the initial landings of the attacking Allied forces. The unit's first taste of combat occurred on June 26 southwest of Carentan, Normandy. The Regiment was charged with moving toward and overtaking the French town of Sainteny. The fighting over the next week was described as vicious and bloody.

A Life Cut Short

On July 9, as the 331st was finally overcoming tough German resistance at Sainteny, T/SGT Renzetti was struck in the back by shrapnel from an exploding German artillery round. Although he survived the day and was transported to the field hospital, he succumbed to his wounds 7 days later. He died on July 14, 1944. His family was informed of his loss by November that year.

T/SGT Ernest C. Renzetti was initially buried in the American military cemetery at St. Mere Eglise, France. He was eventually reinterred at the Normandy American Cemetery and Memorial at Colleville-sur-Mer, Département du Calvados, Basse-Normandie, France. T/SGT Ernest Renzetti was posthumously awarded the Purple Heart.

✶ ✶ ✶

1LT JOHN KALIE

Service Numbers 13087537 / O-696376
758th Bomb Squadron, 459th Bomb Group, 15th Air Force, US Army Air Corps
Killed in action, Mediterranean Sea, July 24, 1944

Forty-four bombing missions. Asking the pilot of a B-24 Liberator bomber to fly that many missions and return safely was asking a lot in 1944.

When 1st Lieutenant John Kalie was asked to fly a 45th mission, he did not question the order. He had a job to do and a crew of eight depending upon him.

It was his last mission.

The Kalie Family

John Kalie was born on July 6, 1921, in Monessen to Wasil and Barbara (née Luckas) Kalie. Wasil and Barbara were married in 1914 in Strabisova, Czechoslovakia[11]. Wasil was a laborer at a Monessen steel mill while Barbara managed the Kalie family household.

---

[11] Czechoslovakia was formed in 1918 then split into the Czech and Slovak Republics in 1992. Kalie public family records were created after 1918, but none state the precise countries of their home towns.

Wasil was born Vazelj Kali in the village of Barboa, Czechoslovakia, and immigrated to the United States under the name Laszlo aboard the SS George Washington. Barbara was born in the village of Strabisova, Czechoslovakia, and came to the US fifteen days after Wasil. Both of their home villages were within the borders of the Austro-Hungarian Empire when they were born, which became part of Czechoslovakia after WWI. They settled in Monessen after arriving in the US in 1920.

John was the second of eight children born to Wasil and Barbara. His older brother Charles was born in Czechoslovakia in 1915 and came to the US with his mother in 1920. His sister Mary was third to be born (1923), followed by George (1925), Anna (1929), Michael (1932), Andrew Paul (1934), and Emerick James (1935). In 1930, the family was living in their home at 167 Indiana Avenue, and Wasil was working as a laborer in the Monessen tin mill.

By 1940, the family had purchased and moved into another home at 425 Indiana Avenue. John had graduated from Monessen High School and was living with his parents while working as a laborer at the Page Steel and Wire Company in Monessen. His brother Charles had enlisted in the US Army Air Corps and was stationed at the Panama Canal Zone.

The surprise attack by Japanese armed forces on the US military bases at Pearl Harbor, Hawaii, in December 1941 changed the world for John. John registered for the US armed forces draft on February 16, 1942, in Monessen as a 6' 175 lb single 20-yr-old with brown hair and blue eyes.

John Kalie Joins the US Army Air Corps

John volunteered to serve in the US Army and enlisted in Pittsburgh on July 4, 1942. But Private Kalie aspired to become a pilot, so he applied to train as an Aviation Cadet in the US Army Air Corps and was accepted. On January 11, 1943, Cadet John Kalie left for the Air Forces Classification Center in San Antonio, Texas, where he would be assigned to train either as a pilot, navigator, or bombardier. His brothers Charles and George also entered the service, and the Kalie's were now a three-blue-star family.

In April 1943, Cadet Kalie was selected for pilot training, and advanced from pre-flight training in San Antonio to begin primary, basic, and then advanced flying training. In January 1944, Cadet Kalie surpassed all Army Air Corps requirements and received his pilot's wings at Ellington Field, Texas. He was commissioned as Second Lieutenant (2LT) John Kalie and was off to train in the multi-engine heavy bomber Consolidated B-24 Liberator. 2LT John Kalie completed his training and was assigned to join the 459th Bomb Group (BG) and its 758th Bomb Squadron (BS).

The 459th BG was first activated at Alamogordo Army Airfield, New Mexico in July 1943 and trained on B-24s thru October. By February 1944, the group had moved overseas to its new base in Giulia, Italy and began flying combat missions in March. The 459th BG engaged in very long-range strategic bombing missions to enemy military, industrial and transportation targets in Italy, France, Germany, Austria, Hungary, Romania, and Yugoslavia, bombing railroad marshaling yards, oil refineries, airfields, heavy industry, and other strategic objectives.

LT Kalie Arrives in Italy

2LT John Kalie and his crew arrived with the 459th BG on May 14, 1944, as replacements. By July 24, 1944, he had flown 44 combat missions with the 459th BG. He had earned a promotion to 1st Lieutenant (1LT) and had earned the Air Medal for flying more than 25 missions. To that, he added his first and second Oak Leaf Cluster.

On July 24, 1944, 1LT John Kalie took off in B-24H #42-94935 with his crew of eight on their 45th mission. They joined their squadron in formation position nine of "A" Flight on a combat mission to bomb the Luftwaffe fighter aerodrome at Les Chapoine Airfield near Marseilles, France. Both the 459th and 454th BGs were assigned to the mission and escorted by P-51 Mustangs of the 325th Fighter Group.

Enemy Fighters!

At midday over St. Martin, France, the bombers were met by fourteen Bf 109 fighters. An estimated three aggressive German fighters attacked stragglers between Toulon and the target while the main group "made aggressive double passes just prior to IP, from 12 o'clock high and 6 o' clock level." LT Kalie's B-24 was under attack.

LT Kalie's B-24H released his bomb load before reaching the target, presumably as a result of the fighter attack. They were twenty miles from the target at 21,500 feet when the formation encountered heavy and accurate anti-aircraft fire from the ground. At 1208 hours, LT Kalie's B-24 took a direct hit in its bomb bay by an 88mm anti-aircraft round. The aircraft's fuel lines and control cables were immediately cut, leaving it out of control and the plane's interior in flames. LT Kalie gave the order to bail out as his B-24 fell to Earth.

A B-24 on fire falls from the sky after attack (US Air Force)

1LT John Kalie and five crew members remained in the aircraft as it came apart in the air and fell into the Mediterranean Sea near Fos-sur-Mer, France. Three of the crew bailed out and were taken prisoner.

In early August, the family of 1LT John Kalie were informed that he was missing in action. They were later informed that he was presumed dead. His remains and those of his five crewmates were never found.

In May 1945, his family received an Air Medal with two Oak Clusters which were awarded to their son. The citation accompanying the medal stated, "For meritorious achievement in aerial flight while participating in sustained operational activities against the enemy from 19 May to 26 May 1944, 27 May to June 1944, and from 13 June to 12 July 1944."

1LT John Kalie is memorialized the St. Mary's Byzantine Cemetery in Monessen, Pennsylvania, and at the Normandy American Cemetery and Memorial in Normandy, France.

★ ★ ★

PVT WILLIAM H. HAGERTY

Service Number 33166826
Company A, 306th Infantry Regiment, 77th Infantry Division, US Army
Killed in action, Guam, July 28, 1944

E xpelling Japanese forces from the Mariana Islands in the central Pacific Ocean would allow the US Army Air Force to construct air bases close enough to bring the war to the Japanese homeland. From the Marianas, Japan was within the range of the new Boeing B-29 Superfortress heavy bomber.

The US Armed Forces paid a heavy price to take the islands from their stubborn occupiers. Private William H. Hagerty paid with his life.

The Hagerty Family

William Herman Hagerty was born on October 19, 1906, in Waynesburg, Pennsylvania, to Irvin and Minne Martha (née Weise) Hagerty. Irvin and Minnie had married in 1905 in Westmoreland County. Irvin was a stonemason while Minnie managed the Hagerty family household.

The Hagerty family heritage traces back to Northern Ireland and the British colony of Maryland prior to the American Revolutionary War. The Weise family was from the Saxony region of Germany and immigrated to the United States in about 1880. The Weise's eventually had a large extended family in the US and would hold well-attended family reunions regularly. Both Irvin's and Minnie's families had settled in Western Pennsylvania, where they met.

William was the first of three children born to Irvin and Minnie. His brother Lewis Weise Hagerty arrived in 1909 and his sister Marion Adelia Hagerty was born in 1912. In 1910, the family was living in the home of Minnie's parents on Monongahela Road in Rostraver Township, Pennsylvania. By 1920, the family was living in a rented home on Monessen-Pricedale Road in Rostraver, with Minnie's parents still residing with them, while the children attended school. Their father Irvin was now working as a clerk in the post office. In 1936, William played tennis in a Monessen city tournament.

By 1940, the family was now living in their purchased home on Monessen-Pricedale Road in Rostraver Township. The children had all graduated from high school. William was working as a wire inspector at Pittsburgh Steel in Monessen, Pennsylvania, and Marion had completed her four-year college degree and worked as a stenographer. Lewis had moved to Alabama for work, where he married. Irvin had retired from the postal service.

On October 16, 1940, William joined millions of other young American men and registered for the US armed forces draft in Monessen on the first day it went into effect under the newly enacted Selective Service Act. William was a 5'10", 140 lb 33-yr-old adult with black hair and brown eyes.

William met Loretta Edna DeLozier from Monessen, they fell in love, and married on February 2, 1942, when William was 35 yrs old. Loretta, 23 yrs old, was a graduate of Monessen High School.

The surprise attack by Japanese armed forces on the US military bases at Pearl Harbor, Hawaii, in December 1941 changed the world for William. Four months later, William was drafted into the US Army, and enlisted on March 27,1942 in New Cumberland, Pennsylvania. Private William Herman Hagerty was off to boot camp. He trained at Fort Jackson, South Carolina during 1942.

Private Hagerty trained stateside with the US Army's 77th Infantry Division. The 77th, activated in March 1942 was known as the "Statue of Liberty" division, which was embroidered on their shoulder patches. PVT Hagerty was assigned to Company A of the 77th.

PVT Hagerty to the Pacific

The 77th Infantry Division was deployed to the Pacific theater of the war on March 25, 1944, landing in Hawaii on March 31, 1944. They continued training in amphibious and jungle warfare for the next three months. On July 1, 1944, elements of the 77th began to leave Hawaii to join Operation Forager in the amphibious assault on the island of Guam. Guam which was expected to be vigorously defended by nearly 19,000 entrenched Japanese troops.

The Marianas island chain of Guam, Saipan, and Tinian were crucial strategic targets for the US armed forces. The islands had enough flat land to support multiple large air bases for the US Army Air Force's new Boeing B-29 Superfortress heavy bomber. From the Marianas, the B-29 had sufficient range to bring the war to the Japanese homeland.

Before landing, US forces sought to ensure both air and naval superiority. A total of 274 US Navy ships supported the landings by the Army and Marines by hitting the island with nearly 45,000 explosive shells. In addition, aircraft from thirteen US Navy air-

Boeing B-29 Superfortress Bomber (US Air Force)

craft carriers attacked Japanese emplacements with over 4,000 bombs dropped July 18-20, the days before the landings. The heavy bombardment burned all the palm trees on the beach and destroyed every building that could be seen.

Attached to III Amphibious Force, the 77th made an assault landing on Guam, July 21, 1944, south of the town of Agai. Lacking amphibious vehicles, they had to wade ashore from the edge of the reef where the landing craft dropped them off. The men stationed in the two beachheads were pinned down by heavy Japanese fire despite the preceding US air and naval strikes, making initial progress inland quite slow.

After taking over the beachhead, the 77th drove north

First American Flag planted on Guam (National Archives)

to seize Mount Tenjo and joined with the 3rd Marine Division west of the town of Agana, linking the northern and southern beachheads on July 28.

During combat on July 28, 1944, PVT William H. Hagerty was mortally wounded by an enemy hand grenade. PVT Hagerty's wife Loretta and the Hagerty family would not learn of his death until October of that year.

PVT William Herman Hagerty was initially buried locally at the American cemetery on the island of Guam. His remains were brought to the US under the Return of the War Dead program, and he was interred at West Newton Cemetery, West Newton, Pennsylvania, on January 17, 1949.

★★★

1LT WILLIAM C. CAVILLE

Service Numbers 20305255 / O-425461
Company D, 110th Infantry Regiment, 28th Infantry Division, US Army
Killed in action, France, August 4, 1944

"Moonbeam Memories" was the last song written by Monessen's aspiring songwriter William Caville. World War II would forever interrupt his ambitions in the field of music. .

Before he could return to his two young children, the life of 1st Lieutenant William Clarence Caville was cut short. They would never again see their father.

The Caville Family

William Clarence Caville was born on April 11, 1917, to Arthur Maurice and Elizabeth (née Armbruster) Caville in Charleroi, Pennsylvania. Arthur and Elizabeth had married a year earlier in West Virginia. Arthur was a laborer at the American Sheet and Tin Plate Company in Monessen, while Elizabeth managed the family household.

Arthur, born on the French island of Corsica, had immigrated to the United States in 1904 aboard the SS Touraine. Elizabeth's family had immigrated to the US in the late 1800's from Germany. Both families had settled in western Pennsylvania where mining and industrial work opportunities were plentiful.

William was their first child. His sister Hazel Mae arrived next (b1918), followed by Marjorie Elaine (1923), Arthur John (1929), and Marie Estelle (1934).

In 1930 the Caville family lived in a rented home on Fallowfield Avenue, Charleroi. Hazel was musically-inclined and sang at various venues around the community. William also enjoyed music and was in the chorus of his junior high school. After being promoted to Charleroi High School, the family moved to a rented home on 646 Third Street in Monessen after their father, at the age of 50, had taken a job as a janitor at a bank. William completed his studies at Monessen High School, where he was elected senior class president in 1934. He graduated in 1935, but not before playing the role of Don Diego in the school operetta "Don Alonzo's Treasure". William was hired at Page Steel and Wire Company mill in Monessen, a major employer in the town.

Brief Songwriting Success, then Marriage

William had an interest in composing music, and along with his friend George Junda, they wrote two songs, "Dust on my Romance" and "Moonbeam Memories", the latter being copyrighted in June 1939. To everyone's pleasant surprise, the songs were performed at dance halls by Mon Valley's number one band, Frank Lombardo and his Orchestra.

William met and fell in love with Dorothy Mae Grant of Fairhope, a town upriver from Monessen. They married on September 4, 1939, in Belle Vernon, Pennsylvania. A month later, William was driving his car alone around midnight when it was struck head-on by another vehicle that had just collided with two other cars. Fortunately, he only incurred minor injuries.

In 1941, Dorothy gave birth to their first child, daughter Karen Lee Caville. Weeks later, she would be photographed in the arms of William Hite, her neighbor and Civil War veteran, celebrating his 102nd birthday. The image was often captioned "Over 100 years apart" and ran in papers across the US.

"Happy Birthday, Neighbor—"

—Karen Lee Caville would say (if she had reached the talking stage) as she greets her neighbor, William Hite, on his one hundred and second birthday yesterday. Mr. Hite who lives with his daughter, Mrs. John Fritz, in Monessen, had his home in McKeesport until two years ago, and was known as the town's last surviving Civil war veteran.

LT Caville's daughter with neighbor Civil War veteran William Hite, Pittsburgh Post Gazette, February 3, 1941

William Caville Joins the Army

Recognizing his patriotic duty, William joined the Pennsylvania National Guard. By August 1940, he had been promoted to Sergeant and was participating in National Guard maneuvers where he was charged with instructing his battalion on machine gun handling in attack and defense. His unit was the 110th Infantry Regiment of the 28th Infantry Division, and he was assigned to Company D.

On February 17, 1941, the 28th Division was called into federal service, and on that date, SGT William C. Caville was formally "enlisted" in the US Army. Starting at Camp Livingston, Louisiana, the 28th Division would subsequently train in the Carolinas, Virginia, Louisiana, Texas, and Florida, under the command of Major General Omar Nelson Bradley. He was promoted to 2nd Lieutenant (2LT) in March 1941.

In May 1941, the 110th Regiment participated in war games at Indiantown Gap, Pennsylvania, where 2LT Caville played a leadership role in his battalion. By August, he had just completed extensive training in chemical warfare.

In November, he was ordered to infantry school at Fort Benning, Georgia. He was sent to Camp Livingston and back to Fort Benning for officers training school in June 1942. He was eventually promoted to 1st Lieutenant (1LT).

On April 12, 1943, Dorothy gave birth to the couple's second child, a son Dennis Lane, while again stationed at Camp Livingston, Louisiana. The family would not be there for long, as LT Caville was transferred to Camp Gordon, Johnston, Florida, only weeks later.

The Allies Advance at Normandy

On October 8, 1943, LT Caville and the 28th Infantry Division were deployed overseas, landing in South Wales in the British Isles. There, they began training in earnest for the planned invasion of the European continent. The invasion began with the Allied landings on D-Day, June 6, 1944, and the 28th landed in Normandy, France, on July 22. The 28th was to spearhead Operation Cobra, distracting and confusing German forces through the end of July. The earlier landings had secured northern France, and the 28th Division pushed east through the bocage, a terrain of woodland and pastures, toward the eventual liberation of Paris. Now, the "breakout" from northern France was underway. LT Caville's 110th Regiment assumed the front line of the Division's offense.

In early August, the Division was suffering substantial losses. According to the 28th Division history, the German *defenders "fought excellent delaying action, skillfully using mobile weapons and taking every advantage of the terrain. The Germans had every advantage while fighting in the hedgerows and sunken roads with observation posts concealed in commanding points in trees and buildings....the intensive fire brought to bear on our leading elements by the enemy, made advancing a very slow process......Consequently, many officers became casualties due to their pushing forward, trying to speed up the advance."*

LT Caville Struck Down

On August 4, 1944, as the 110th Regiment was advancing, LT Caville was killed in action. The tragic news was sadly received by friends and family in the Mon Valley.

1LT William Clarence Caville was initially buried in France. His remains were recovered under the Return of the War Dead program and returned to the US. LT Caville was buried at Grandview Cemetery in Monessen on September 11, 1948. He was posthumously awarded the Purple Heart.

★ ★ ★

SGT WAYNE R. MCVAY

Service Number 33167271
Sixth Armored Division, US Army
Killed in action, France, August 8, 1944

W ayne Reed McVay was born on June 1, 1920, to Charles Benjamin and Bertha Elizabeth (née Kraft) McVay in Monessen, Pennsylvania.
Charles and Bertha had married in July 1918 in Washington, Pennsylvania. Charles was an electrician in a Monessen wire mill while Bertha managed the McVay family household.

The McVay Family

The heritage of the McVay family traces back to the British colonies of Pennsylvania and Vir-

Insignia of the 6th Armored Division (US Army)

ginia and to Ireland prior to the American Revolutionary War. The Kraft family traces to western Pennsylvania in the early 1800's. Charles' first wife, Eva Jane Daugherty, died in 1914 from typhoid fever and tuberculosis.

Wayne had four half-siblings from his father's first marriage: Mary Margaret (b1900), Lois (1902), Amelia Eva (1907), and Joseph Charles (1911). Wayne and an older brother John Lee (1918) were the only children born during Charles' marriage to Bertha.

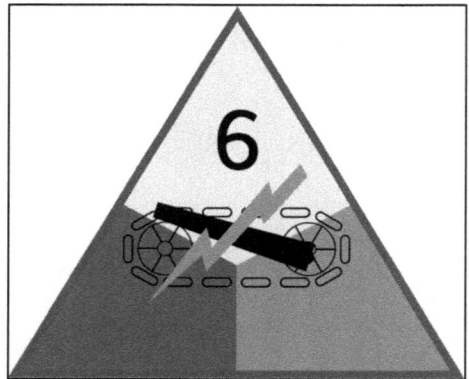

By 1930 the family was living in their home at 11 Knox Avenue in Monessen. By then the daughters had married and moved out to begin their own families. At the age of 11, Wayne earned honorable mention in Monessen's Yard and Garden Contest. He was also active in the Boy Scouts. In 1936, he was a finalist in a local typewriting design contest. While at Monessen High School, he played trombone in the school band. In the annual commencement play in 1938, Wayne played the lead role in the comedy farce "Adventure, Incorporated". Wayne graduated from Monessen High School and went to work selling and installing furnaces for the Holland Furnace Company in nearby Charleroi. The family was active in the First Presbyterian Church and in 1941 Wayne presented a talk there entitled "The Christian Answer in Action".

On July 1, 1941, Wayne registered for the US armed forces draft in Monessen. He was a 6'1" 175 lb 21-yr-old with brown hair and brown eyes.

The surprise attack by Japanese armed forces on the US military base at Pearl Harbor, Hawaii, in December 1941 changed the world for millions of Americans, as it would for Wayne and his brother John. The following year, on March 28, 1942, Wayne was drafted into the US Army. John was drafted in December of that year. The brothers were both off to war, and the McVay's were now a 2-Blue-Star family.

Private Wayne McVay left for boot camp. By August 1942, he was stationed at Camp Chafee, Arkansas, in the Service Company of the 50th Armored Infantry when he received a promotion to Technician 5th Grade (T/5). He was soon assigned to the 6th Armored Division within the US Army to train on armored infantry vehicles such as battle tanks.

PVT McVay in the Super Sixth

The 6th Armored Division would become known as the "Super Sixth". The division was activated at Fort Knox, Kentucky, in February 1942, began training at Camp Chafee, Arkansas where T/5 McVay joined the unit. The division eventually made its way to Camp Cooke, California for more extensive training.

By December, T/5 Wayne McVay was promoted to the rank of Sergeant (SGT) and was training at Camp Cooke. That month, his brother John arrived home to Monessen on Christmas furlough and, upon seeing his mother, hugged her so hard he broke her ribs, according to the local newspaper.

By January 1944, the Super Sixth was ready for combat operations and shipped to Camp Shanks in New York in preparation for deployment to the European theater of operations. They arrived in Great Britain in February and began extensive training for what would become Operation Overlord, the Allied invasion of the European continent. The invasion began on D-Day, June 6, 1944.

SGT Wayne McVay and the Super Sixth landed on Utah Beach at Normandy, France, after the initial D-Day invasion, disembarking on July 18, 1944. The division was attached to VIII Corps of the First Army and was ordered into battle. Its first encounter with enemy German troops was ten days

Tanks of the Super Sixth on the march (US Army Sixth Armored Division)

later near Coutances, France. The Sixth was then ordered up the center of France's Brittany peninsula to capture the city of Brest from the Germans.

As the division was battling during the advance upon Brest, fate intervened in the life of SGT McVay. The German 266th Infantry Division attacked the Sixth from the rear on the night of August 8, 1944. SGT McVay was mortally wounded when struck in the chest by enemy fire, and he died that day. His family was informed of his death the following month.

SGT Wayne R. McVay was initially buried locally in France. In June 1949, his remains were transported from Europe with those of 3,700 other American soldiers aboard the US Army Transport Greenville Victory under the Return of the War Dead program. He was reinterred in a grave at Belle Vernon Cemetery, Belle Vernon, Pennsylvania during a solemn ceremony on July 16, 1948.

★ ★ ★

T/4 PAUL DENITTI

Service Number 33167228
Company D, 15th Tank Battalion, 6th Armored Division, US Army
Killed in action, France, August 10, 1944

Paul Denitti was born on June 21, 1920, to Matteo "Patsy" and Antonia (née Abatantuono) Denitti in Monessen, Pennsylvania. Patsy and Antonia had married in May 1918 in Worcester, Massachusetts. They moved to Pennsylvania in November where Patsy obtained work in a Monessen steel mill.

The Denitti Family

Patsy, born Matteo Giglietti, had immigrated to the United States from Mattinata, Foggia, Italy, in 1911 aboard the SS Duca D'Aosta at the age of 10. Antonia had immigrated to the US from Viesta, Foggia, Italy, with her parents in 1911 aboard the SS Canopic at the age of 14. Patsy changed his name to that of his second father, Denitti, in 1928, when he became a naturalized US citizen.

Paul, born Paolo, was the second of thirteen children born to Patsy and Antonia. His older sister Theresa was born in 1918 in Worcester before the

family moved to Pennsylvania. Filomena (Phyllis) arrived after Paul (1921), then came Peter (1928), Luciano (1929), Claudia Gloria (1931), Josephine (1933), Marie Jane (1935), Matthew "Doundie" (1937), Joan (1938), Michael Paul (1940), Laura Mae (1941), and Madeline (1944). Luciano had died as an infant.

The Denitti family lived at several different homes in Monessen. In the 1920's they lived on one of the main streets in Monessen at 349 Schoonmaker Avenue. In 1927, Antonia took the three oldest children with her to visit family in Italy. During the 1930's the family moved to Smithton, Pennsylvania, but returned to Monessen by 1937. In 1940, they were living in Monessen at 1051 Alexander Street. Patsy had learned new skills and was now a crane operator in the steel mill.

Paul left high school after a year and went to work at Pittsburgh Steel in Monessen while living at the home of his parents at 948 Lookout Avenue. With war drums beating in Europe and Japan, the US armed forces draft was instituted in October 1940. Paul registered for the draft on July 1, 1941, as a 5'9" 160 lb 21-yr-old with brown hair and brown eyes.

The surprise attack by Japanese armed forces on the US military bases at Pearl Harbor, Hawaii, in December 1941 changed the world for Paul. Four months later, on March 28, 1942, Paul was drafted into the US Army, and he enlisted at New Cumberland, Pennsylvania. Private Paul Denitti was off to US Army boot camp.

PVT Denitti trained stateside for two years and was routed to train in armored forces, namely battle tanks. During training, he became a skilled tanker and was promoted to the rank of Technician 4 (T/4). T/4 was equivalent to the rank of Sergeant (SGT), and he was addressed as SGT Paul Denitti. SGT Denitti was eventually assigned to the 15th Tank Battalion of the 6th Armored Division, known as the "Super Sixth". The 6th Armored Division was composed almost entirely of drafted citizen soldiers.

SGT Denitti becomes a Tanker

The Super Sixth was activated in February 1942 in Kentucky. The division participated in the VIII Corps Louisiana Maneuvers in August 1942 and then returned to Camp Chaffee Arkansas in September 1942. The 6th then moved to Camp Young at the Desert Training Center in October 1942 and participated in California Maneuvers.

While on leave, SGT Paul Denitti married the girl of his dreams, Rose Marie Erdely, of Pennsylvania, on July 28, 1942, in Cumberland, Maryland. But he could not stay home for long.

SGT Denitti immediately returned to training. In September 1943, he was enrolled in a special course of instruction in the Gunnery Department of the Armored School at Fort Knox, Kentucky. Upon graduation later that month, he and his classmates were deemed "expert armorers and gunnery mechanics for the lightning-fast, accurate-shooting divisions that make up the Armored Command". While with the 6th Armored Division at Camp Cooke California, he was assigned to the Division's Company B of

AT FORT KNOX

Sgt. Paul Denitti, above, son of Mr. and Mrs. Matthew Dennitti, of Lockout avenue, and a brother of Mrs. Fred Steck, of Schoonmaker avenue, was recently enrolled in a special course of instruction in the Gunnery Department of the Armored School at Fort Knox, Ky. Sergeant Denitti has been in the Army for the past 18 months, and prior to induction was employed at Pittsburgh Steel Company.

Monessen Daily Independent, September 15, 1943

the 69 Armored Regiment. The 6th then staged at Camp Shanks, New York, in preparation for deployment to combat. The division departed New York for the European theater of the war and arrived in England at the end of February 1944. SGT Paul Denitti was with them.

After continuing training in England, the 6th landed on Utah Beach in Normandy, France, on July 18, 1944, as a follow-on unit to the D-Day invasion. The Super Sixth went on the offensive as separate combat commands in the Cotentin Peninsula in support of the Normandy Campaign.

During the push by the Super Sixth across the Brittany region of France during August, the 15th Battalion encountered heavy resistance by the defending German occupation forces. On August 10, SGT Paul Denitti lost his life during battle, at the age of 24. His family would not learn of his death until October, when they were informed by the War Department.

SGT Paul Denitti was buried at the Brittany American Cemetery, at the Saint-James, Département de la Manche, Basse-Normandie, France, along with 4,403 other American military dead. A memorial marker was placed near his hometown at the Belle Vernon Cemetery, North Belle Vernon, PA.

His wife Rose Marie would go on to serve in the Pentagon in Washington, DC, in 1945 at the Casualty Branch of the Armed Service Forces to assist in the administration of the war effort.

✯ ✯ ✯

PFC CHRISTOPHER S. PARNELLA

Service Number 33702960
Company C, 137th Infantry Regiment, 35th Infantry Division, US Army
Killed in action, France, August 16, 1944

Christopher Salvatore Parnella was born on June 29, 1915, to Salvatore and Caterina "Catherine" (neé Filardi) Parnella in Monessen, Pennsyl-

vania. Salvatore owned a produce wholesale company while Catherine managed the Parnella family household.

The Parnella Family

Salvatore and Catherine were from the town of Trabia on the Italian island of Sicily, where they married in 1900. The couple immigrated to the United States and settled in Monessen where Salvatore's brother Joseph was living. Monessen was a burgeoning industrial town with work opportunities that drew immigrants from southern, central, and eastern Europe. By 1910, the Parnella's were living in an apartment building at 249 Schoonmaker Avenue in the same building with three other Parnella families and three more Parnella families

next door. Public records show various spellings of the family name over time, such as Parinella and Parnelli.

Christopher, affectionately called "Kizzie", was the sixth of seven children born to Salvatore and Caterina. Salvadore Joseph "Tom" was first to be born (1902), followed by Domenica "Mammie" (1905), Giuseppe "Joseph" James (1907), Antonio "Tony" (1909), and Antonina Marie "Lena" (1920). The fifth child, born 1912 and also named Christopher, succumbed to tuberculosis at the age of 11 months.

Salvatore had entered the wholesale fruit/produce and ice cream business, the Parnella Brothers, with his siblings. In 1920, the business was successful and expanding, so the company built a new modern facility at the corner of Oneida and Donner Streets with state-of-the-art refrigeration. By 1930, the family had purchased the building in which they were living. Tom had married and moved out, Mammie had married and was living with her husband and granddaughter with her parents, Joseph and Tony were working in the family business, and Kizzie and Lena were attending school. The family was working hard and doing well.

In 1936, Kizzie's father had a heart attack and died at the age of 60. Kizzie left school after the seventh grade and joined the family business. In 1940, Kizzie was still working in the family business as were Joseph, Tony, and Lena, and they were living with their widowed mother in her home on Schoonmaker.

On October 16, 1940, Kizzie joined millions of his fellow countrymen and registered for the US armed forces draft on its first day under the recently passed Selective Service Act. He was now working for himself as a chauffeur as a 5'3" 132 lb single man with black hair and brown eyes. Christopher chauffeured and managed the affairs for the widow of a Civil War veteran, Kate Derickson.

Kizzie Marries

In January 1941, the family announced Kizzie's engagement to Catherine Adeline Bartolotta of nearby Monongahela, Pennsylvania. Her parents were also born in Italy and had immigrated to the US in 1905. Catherine and Kizzie married on September 29, 1941. The couple drove to Florida on their honeymoon and returned via Baltimore, Maryland by boat.

September Bride

Louis Studio

Mrs. Christopher Parnella

Mrs. Parnella before her recent marriage was Miss Catherine Bartolotta, of Monongahela.

Monessen Daily Independent, Oct 15, 1941

The surprise attack by Japanese armed forces on the US military base at Pearl Harbor, Hawaii, in December 1941 changed the world for Kizzie. Although he had returned to working in the family business, Kizzie was well-aware of the war raging overseas and his compatriots heading off to fight. In late 1943, he was drafted into the US Army and enlisted on August 28, 1943. He was off for training on September 18 at Camp Van Dorn, Mississippi.

A minor scandal arose when Mrs. Derickson filed charges against Christopher for embezzlement in December 1943, which made the local newspaper. The situation was cleared up the following month, with Christopher quoted as saying "Everything remained as it was before."

By May 1944, Christopher was promoted to Private First Class (PFC), and had been transferred to Ft. George Meade, Maryland, for further training. PFC Parnella was assigned to Company C, 137th Infantry Regiment, 35th Infantry Division. On May 11, 1944, the 137th Regiment departed New York City, arriving in England on May 24. They camped in Cornwall where they continued their training. PFC Parnella was about to participate in the Allied invasion of France. The first wave of Allied troops arrived in Normandy, France, on D-Day June 6, 1944, and the 35th Division would soon follow.

On July 5, the 35th Division landed at Omaha Beach, Normandy, France, which had been secured from the German occupiers during the D-Day invasion a month earlier. In its first combat attack, July 11 at St. Lo, the green recruits met stiff resistance and the 137th Regiment suffered 126 casualties. The 35th Division continued to press into France, and on August 13, it was attached to the 12th Corps and tasked with securing the right flank of General Patton's 3rd Army.

PVT Parnella Killed in Action

The 35th Division advanced quickly, reaching Chateaudun on August 16. Enemy resistance was encountered in the woods between Coulmieres and Ormes, and the 137th Regiment suffered 2 casualties. One of them was PFC Parnella. An enemy artillery shell had exploded near his position. PFC Parnella suffered mortal shrapnel wounds to his chest, and he died that day.

Three weeks later, his wife Catherine was informed by the War Department that her husband had been killed in action in France. Earlier in the year during their last time together, Catherine became pregnant. Kizzie would never meet his child, Christopher Parnella, Jr., who was born on December 11, 1944.

PFC Christopher Parnella was buried at the Brittany American Cemetery at Saint-James, Département de la Manche, Basse-Normandie, France. He was posthumously awarded the Purple Heart.

A year later, an In Memoriam appeared in the local newspaper:

"A precious one from me has gone

A voice I loved is stilled

A place is vacant in my heart

That never can be filled".

✻ ✻ ✻

1LT BERNARD J. ROSENSON

Service Numbers 33078862 / O-661804
335th Fighter Squadron, 4th Fighter Group, US Army Air Corps
Killed in action, France, August 18, 1944

A pilot of the fast and highly maneuverable P-51 Mustang fighter was believed to have every advantage in combat against their enemy counterparts.

But the advantage of surprise could be enjoyed by any combatant. Surprise often depended upon timing and luck. Unfortunately for 1st Lieutenant Bernard Rosenson on August 19, 1944, he was on the wrong side of that equation.

The Rosenson Family

Bernard James Rosenson was born on October 12, 1919, to Charles Rubin and Nettie (née Lefkovits) Rosenson in Steubenville, Ohio. Charles and Nettie were living in nearby Mingo Junction, Ohio, where Charles owned a clothing store. Charles and Nettie had married in 1914.

Charles was born in Smolin, Subalk, Russia (now Lithuania), and immigrated to the United States aboard the SS Zeeland in 1905. Nettie was born in

Philadelphia, Pennsylvania, to parents from Russia who immigrated to the US in 1885. Both families were of the Jewish faith.

Bernard was the second of two children born to Charles and Nettie. His older brother, Saul Milton, was born in 1915. By 1930, the family had purchased a home at 417 Maxwell Street in Steubenville. Charles was now working as an insurance agent while Nettie managed the Rosenson family household.

While attending high school in Steubenville, Bernard became a talented writer and orator. In 1936, he and another senior started the school newspaper, The Big Red Beacon. In 1937, he was one of 12 winners in the state of the Ohio American Legion essay contest on the topic "Our Constitution and What It Means". After graduation, he entered Ohio State University in Columbus, Ohio, in the Arts and Sciences curriculum where he joined the freshman editorial staff of the Makio, the university yearbook. In his sophomore year, Bernard was appointed as the editor of the Makio. He was also a member of the Alpha Epsilon Pi fraternity, and the Hillel Foundation. Bernard was selected for the Bucket and Dipper Honorary organization for his display of leadership, scholarship, and service.

The Rosenson's moved to Monessen, Pennsylvania, by 1940, where Charles and his son Saul obtained work as salesmen in a furniture store. Charles would eventually open Rosenson's New and Used Furniture Store in Monessen. In June, when Bernard was visiting from college, his Dodge automobile collided head-on with a truck. He sustained a head injury and lacerations but recuperated.

October 16, 1940, was the first day of the US armed forces draft under the newly passed Selective Service and Training Act. Bernard joined millions of other young men that day and registered for the draft, listing his parents' new home at 470 Donner Avenue in Monessen as his residence. He registered as a 5' 8.5" 135 lb 21-yr-old with black hair and blue eyes.

By his senior year at Ohio State, Bernard was elected president of his fraternity and sat on the university's Council of Fraternity Presidents. He was also involved in student government and was a justice on the university's Student

Court. Bernard came up with the idea to produce a film for orienting new freshmen to the university for the first time, which was done in May 1941. By the end of his senior year, he had been editor of the Fraternity Booklet and the Football Programs, and was on the Ohio Union Board of Overseers, Vice President of The Ohio Staters, Inc., Chairman of the Hillel Refugee Committee, a member of the Board of Student Publications, and in the Student Senate.

Drafted and Transfers to Air Corps

Bernard graduated from Ohio State in June 1941 with a bachelor's degree in journalism. He was immediately drafted into the US Army, and he enlisted at New Cumberland, Pennsylvania, on July 8, 1941. But Bernard had his sights set skyward and applied to become an Aviation Cadet (AC) in hopes of becoming a pilot. He was accepted into the program and set off for US Army Air Corps training. By the end of 1941, the Japanese had attacked the US military installation at Pearl Harbor, Hawaii, and the world was at war.

AC Rosenson successfully trained through primary flying training at Bruce Field, Texas, where he also served as editor for their yearbook The Cadet. He completed basic flying training at Kelly Field, San Antonio, Texas, by December 1941. He transferred to advanced flying training on AT-6 Texan aircraft at Moore Field, Mission, Texas in Class 42-F, where he also served as editor for their yearbook. In Spring of 1942 while flying solo on a training mission, he ran low on fuel over Mexico and made an emergency landing at

B.Rosenson (center seated), Editor of Moore Field Yearbook (Moore Field Yearbook)

the town of La Rosita. The mayor of the town personally escorted AC Rosenson around the town and fed and quartered him overnight. The next day another pilot landed with fuel and accompanied him back to Moore Field. AC Rosenson's glowing remarks about La Rosita prompted his training comrades to call it "La Rosenson". In May, he earned his pilot's wings and was commissioned Second Lieutenant (2LT).

By October 1943, he had been promoted to First Lieutenant (1LT) and was training with the 85th Fighter Bomber Group in the 500th Squadron at Waycross Army Airfield, Georgia. The 85th was operating as a Replacement Training Unit, and they were training on North American A-36 Apache dive bombers, the precursor to the P-51 Mustang fighter. In early 1944, the group converted to Curtiss P-40 Warhawk fighters and then added Republic P-47 Thunderbolt fighters to the group.

In May 1944 the 85th was disbanded and the trainees deployed to other assignments, including overseas. 1LT Bernard Rosenson was assigned to join the 4th Fighter Group, 335th Squadron, based in Debden, England, and he departed the US on May 11.

It is likely that LT Rosenson's first stop in England was with the 496th Fighter Training Group in Goxhill, Lincolnshire. Here he would

LT Rosenson (far left) with fellow pilots, England
(National Archives)

receive orientation training on the North American P-51 Mustang fighter in the 555th Squadron. Upon completion, he arrived at Debden on July 13th with six other replacement pilots.

Operation Overlord, the Allied invasion of the European continent, began on June 6, 1944. Allied aircraft were continuously striking German defensive positions and any counterattacking efforts in support of the Allied advance into France.

P-51 Mustang Fighters of the 335th Fighter Squadron (American Air Museum)

LT Rosenson's first mission was flown three days after arriving with the 4th FG, on July 17, 1944, on an escort mission of "penetration-target-with-drawal support, Type 16 control for 96 2nd ATF B-24"[12]. Through August, he flew twelve more missions escorting bombers or for strafing and dive-bombing attacks.

---

[12] Fighters were ordered to escort the bombers to, over, and back from their target. Type 16 control means that fighters may pursue any detected enemy fighters along the way. This mission was to escort 96 B-24 bombers of the 2nd Air Task Force.

A Fateful Mission

On August 18, 1944, LT Bernard Rosenson climbed aboard P-51 # 44-13567 for a dive-, or skip-, bombing and strafing mission in the French Beauvais-Chantilly-Pontoise area north of Paris. He was flying in #4 position behind 2LT Brack Diamond leading Caboose Red Section.

However, his luck was about to run out.

Caboose Red Section had just bombed the railroad marshaling yard and was about to attack a truck north of La Ferte when, at about 1930 hrs, they were jumped by 50 or more German Me-109 and FW-190 fighters.

LT Rosenson's P-51 was last seen just as the enemy fighter attacked. He did not return to Debden and was reported as missing-in-action. His family was notified that he was missing on August 31, 1944.

In January 1945, after the Allied forces had overtaken nearly all of France, the remains of 1LT Bernard Rosenson were found buried in a village cemetery in Cauffry, France. French citizens had recovered his remains and performed the solemn burial, as explained by the town's mayor. The town's people reported that his aircraft had been shot down and landed and burned in a nearby field. The town held a memorial service for LT Rosenson on September 17, 1944.

LT Rosenson's remains were reinterred at Solers Cemetery, Département de Seine-et-Marne, Île-de-France, France, on March 5, 1945. A month later, the War Department formally declared that LT Rosenson had been killed in action and informed the Rosenson family.

1LT Bernard J. Rosenson was relocated to the Epinal American Cemetery in Dinozé, France in January 1949. He was posthumously awarded the Purple Heart and the Air Medal.

★★★

PVT JOSEPH P. LEONE

Service Number 20305296
Company D, 110th Infantry Regiment, 28th Infantry Division, US Army
Killed in action, France, September 2, 1944

Joseph Patrick Leone was born on March 17, 1913, to Joseph Martin and Mary Cecelia (née Etzel) Leone in Monessen, Pennsylvania. Joseph Sr. and Mary had married in 1912. Joseph was a barber while Mary managed the Leone family household.

The Leone Family

Joseph Sr. was born Giuseppe Martino Leone in Palermo, Sicily and immigrated to the United States in 1906 aboard the SS Luisiana. Mary's parents were born in Germany and immigrated to the US in the 1880's, settling in Ohio where Mary was born before their family moved to western Pennsylvania. Joseph became a naturalized US citizen in 1917.

Insignia of the 110th Infantry Regiment (US Army)

Joseph Patrick was the first of two children born into the family. His sister Carolline Catherine was born in 1915. By 1920, the family was living in their own home on Dutch Town Road in the LaGrange district of Rostraver Township, Pennsylvania. In 1926, their father, who was a hotel keeper by then, passed away unexpectedly at the age of 36 yrs due to "super-induced burns of an unknown origin". Mary later purchased a home at 962 Donner Avenue in Monessen where she and her children lived while she helped keep house at a boarding home.

By 1940, Joseph graduated from Monessen High School and went to work at the local steel mill in Monessen. Carolline had married and moved to a home with her new husband to start their family. Mary had sold their home and she and Joseph were living in an apartment at 440 Schoonmaker Avenue Monessen. Mary was now working as a laundress at the local hospital. In February 1941, Joseph was a passenger in a car when it collided with another, and he suffered painful bruises and cuts to his face and knees.

Joseph Volunteers for the National Guard

Joseph joined the Pennsylvania National Guard in March 1940, and rose to the rank of Sergeant. He joined millions of their fellow American young men and registered for the first US armed forces draft on its first day, October 16, 1940, in accordance with the recently passed Selective Service Act. Joseph registered as a 5'11" 165 lb 23-yr-old with black hair and brown eyes.

The surprise attack by Japanese armed forces on the US military base at Pearl Harbor, Hawaii, in December 1941 changed the world for Joseph. He immediately entered into federal service with his unit, Company D of the 110th Infantry Regiment and the 28th Infantry Division, which had been called into federal service earlier in February 1941. His rank would resume as a Private in the regular Army.

Starting at Camp Livingston, Louisiana, the 28th Division would subsequently train in the Carolinas, Virginia, Louisiana, Texas, and Florida, under the command of Major General Omar Nelson Bradley.

While passing through Greensboro, North Carolina, on weekend maneuvers, the community welcomed the soldiers into their homes to eat and sleep. PVT Joe Leone became friends with the JK Isley Family, who were so impressed "with his good nature and amiable disposition" they began a correspondence with his parents.

PVT Leone Goes Overseas

On October 8, 1943, PVT Joseph Leone and the 28th Infantry Division were deployed overseas, landing in South Wales in the British Isles. There, they began training in earnest for the planned invasion of the European continent.

The invasion began with the Allied landings on D-Day, June 6, 1944, and the 28th landed in Normandy, France, on July 22. The 28th was to spearhead Operation Cobra, distracting and confusing German forces through the end of July. The earlier landings had secured northern France, and the 28th Division pushed east through the bocage, a terrain of woodland and pastures, to the eventual liberation of Paris. Now, the "breakout" from northern France was underway.

But PVT Leone's luck ran out. On September 2, 1944, he was driving a jeep in a convoy in northern France near the town of Saint-Quentin, Aisne. when it came across an enemy half-track. Spontaneous combat ensured, and PVT Leone was killed in action when he was fatally struck in the neck by a bullet. His mother was informed by the War Department of his death in November 1944.

PVT Joseph Patrick Leone was initially buried at a temporary American cemetery in France. He was eventually recovered under the Return of the war Dead Program and returned to the US. On October 25, 1948, PVT Joseph Patrick Leone was buried at Grandview Cemetery in Monessen next to his father. His mother Mary would join them there in 1980.

PVT Joseph Leone was posthumously awarded the Purple Heart medal.

Upon the time of his burial in Monessen, the local newspapers cited the memories of Joseph as shared with Joseph's mother by the Isley's of Greensboro, NC.:

"Joe typifies … the good, solid, friendly boys who fought the battle even though it meant giving all they had to give."

***

SOUTHERN FRIENDS OF SOLDIER HERO HONOR HIS MEMORY

MONESSEN, Pa. — The friendly, companionable qualities of a Monessen soldier, who was later to give his life in the great war, has won him a permanent place in the hearts of friends he met along the way and today bring new comfort and a quiet satisfaction to his mother.

Sgt. Joseph Leone was one of the boys of Monessen's Company D when the unit was called to active service in February, 1941. The following year his outfit passed through Greensboro, N. C., one week-end on maneuvers. The people of the community, in a gesture of spontaneous hospitality, opened their homes to the infantrymen, let them sleep in deep, soft beds and filled them full of good fried chicken.

Joe spent his time with Mr. and Mrs. J. K. Isley, of 1207 Grayland street, Greensboro, and so impressed them with his good nature and amiable disposition that they remembered him through many months and several years of war. An Army base unit was later established at Greensboro, and the Isleys entertained scores of soldiers, but they never forgot Joe, and they kept up a correspondence with his mother in Monessen to let her know what they thought of her boy.

On Sept. 2, 1944, Joe was driving a jeep in a convoy making a quick trust against the enemy near St. Quentin, France. An enemy half-track was engaged, and Joe was killed.

Today his mother, Mrs. Mary Leone, 443 Schoonmaker avenue, awaits patiently the arrangements which will return Joe's body to Monessen for burial. But while she waits she treasures a letter from the Isleys in Greensboro. It tells of why they have contributed to the new million-dollar Greensboro Memorial Coliseum in the name of Joe Leone—because of all the soldiers they met and entertained during the war, Joe typifies to them the good, solid, friendly boys who fought the battle even though it meant giving all they had to give.

Charleroi Mail, April 30, 1948

T/4 JOSEPH J. SKRUBER

Service Number 33167252
Headquarter Battery, 59th Armored Field Artillery Battalion, US Army
Killed in aircraft accident, France, September 3, 1944

When Monessen's Joe Skruber entered the US Army in 1942, little did he realize that he would be flying over enemy territory as an observer in the US Army's smallest aircraft. His assignment as his artillery battalion's "eye in the sky" brought a danger that his fellow artillerymen never faced... one that would cost him his life.

The Skruber Family

Joseph "Joe" John Skruber was born on September 28, 1913, to Jakob "Jack" and Maria "Mary" (neé Berkes) Skruber in Weirton, West Virginia. Jack and Mary had married in Hungary in the early 1900's.

Joe's father immigrated to the United States in 1903 to find work, which he found in McKeesport, Pennsylvania. He sent for Mary, and she arrived in 1910 aboard the SS Carpathia, with their first child, Andraz.

Joe was the third of seven children born to Jack and Mary. After Andraz (called Andrew), Kathryn was born in 1911. His sisters Barbara (b1916) and Ann Regina (1917) came next, followed by Jacob "Jack" William in 1920. Their last child was stillborn in 1925.

By 1920, Jack purchased a home at 156 Donner Avenue in Monessen, Pennsylvania where the family now lived. He had been hired at the tin mill in Monessen where he now worked. The family later purchased and moved into a home at 337 Schoonmaker Avenue in Monessen by 1930. In 1931, their father Jack died of cancer.

Joe left high school after his junior year and was working as a shipper in a Monessen steel mill in 1940. He was living at home with his widowed mother and his brother Jack. Joe was an avid bowler in the Monessen Ravens Bowling Club.

In September 1940, the United States Congress passed the Selective Service and Training Act that included mandatory registration by young men for the first US peacetime armed forces draft. On October 16, 1940, Joe joined millions of others and registered for the draft on its first day. He was a 5'11" 160 lb 27-yr-old with brown hair and blue eyes. By that time, he had been hired by Carnegie-Illinois Steel and was working at their Irvin plant in Dravosburg, Pennsylvania, downstream on the Monongahela River from Monessen. In April 1941, Joe was involved in a brawl with three other men outside of the Monessen Italian Hall. They were arrested and fined.

Drafted!

On December 7, 1941, the United States came under surprise attack at Pearl Harbor, Hawaii, and the US entered the war against Japan, Germany, and Italy. Four months later, Joe was drafted with 80 other Monessen men into the US Army. On March 28, 1942, he enlisted at New Cumberland, Pennsylvania. Private Joe Skruber was off to training.

A month later, PVT Skruber was training at Camp Chafee, Arkansas, with the 59th Armored Field Artillery Battalion (59th AFA Bn). Camp Chaffee specialized as an armored training base. The 59th had been formed at Fort Knox,

Kentucky, in February of that year. Its personnel were assigned from Fort Knox, Camp Chafee, Fort Sill (Oklahoma), and several Reception Centers.

The "Priest" at War

The concept of Armored Field Artillery units was formed during the early stages of WWII. These were specialized armored units equipped with self-propelled guns: artillery pieces mounted upon a motorized platform. At least ten types of self-propelled guns were designed and deployed in combat by the US. They differed from battle tanks which were typically used in close quarter combat. Self-propelled guns were developed for specific purposes, such as long-range field artillery, anti-aircraft defense, and tank destroyers.

One such weapon was the M-7 "Priest". It looked like a battle tank formed by committee, but it packed a punch. The M-7, with a 105-mm howitzer on a motor carriage, was a variant of the M-3 tank chassis. It was nicknamed the

M-7 Motorized Artillery "Priest" (Library of Congress)

"Priest" because of its pulpit-like 50 caliber machine gun ring mount and was one of the most popular weapons of the War. It threw a 33-pound shell 12,000 yards and provided mobility for the artillery equal to that of the forces it supported. It also deployed in a hexagonal or circular firing formation, rather than a linear one. This allowed the battery to go into action faster and defend itself better (like settlers circling their wagons). One of the most important aspects of the armored artillery forces was its fighting spirit. Even in the written doctrine you will find the statement, "In the defense, Armored Artillery is best used in an offensive posture." Armored Artillery traveled with the maneuver forces, many times finding itself in the direct-assault role-taking out enemy bunkers and strong points.[13]

By May 1943, PVT Skruber had been promoted to Staff Sergeant and had earned a 1st Class Gunner's Badge and an Expert Gunner's Badge. In 1942, the US Army created the rank of Technician for non-commissioned, enlisted officers with special technical skills who were not trained as combat leaders. SGT Skruber's rank was changed to Technician Fourth Grade, or T/4, but he was still called "Sergeant".

By September 1943, the 59th AFA and T/4 Joe Skruber had arrived overseas in the Mediterranean Theater of WWII, where they were briefly stationed for additional training in Fleurus, Algeria before marching to Algiers. Two weeks later, they were in Naples, Italy, and were moving up the Italian peninsula through November and December with the 6th Field Artillery Group. The 59th was a highly valued and useful unit that was shared among the Allies and was attached to the British 46th and 56th Divisions to provide mobile and forward artillery for the advancing British forces. Their introduction to combat was both welcome and impactful. Their success would result in their being reassigned to whatever unit of ground troops required their expertise and their "wallop".

By March 1944, the 59th had marched northward and was supporting New Zealand's 4th Field Regiment in the brutal Battle for Monte Cassino. During

---

[13] https://www.fieldartillery.org/field-artillery-history

this time the 59th's own "air arm", forward air observers flying small liaison aircraft such as L-4 Grasshoppers and L-5 Sentinels, began to make their mark.

Grasshoppers in Italy

The ubiquitous civilian J-3 Piper Cubs of the early 1940's had been repurposed for the US military for training, transport, and combat reconnaissance, and were called L-4 Grasshoppers. The 59th AFA deployed both Grasshoppers and Sentinels to locate enemy targets and direct their artillery fire to hit them.

T/4 Skruber had demonstrated strong mapping, communication, and leadership skills, so he was assigned to the 59th's air section as a forward aerial observer/scout on Grasshoppers. His new role was to accompany a Grasshopper pilot, scout enemy positions, and radio-in artillery firing coordinates and instructions. They would remain in the vicinity of the target, observe the incoming artillery fire, and call in corrections as necessary. Flying at low altitude, they were vulnerable indeed.

L-4 Grasshopper flying over towed 105 mm Howitzers (National Archives)

The 59th AFA fought with the Allies further up the Italian peninsula as Allied forces engaged in the fourth Battle of Monte Cassino in May 1944. That month, T/4 Skruber was wounded by shrapnel when an artillery shell exploded near his position. He survived and returned to duty and was awarded the Purple Heart.

In June, the Allies took Rome and the 59th AFA was the first artillery unit to enter the city. They departed Rome attached to the 85th Infantry Division and fought their way north toward Viterbo. The commanding officer commented about the success of the unit and "The air observers also did a very fine job". By July, the 59th was reassigned to the 34th Infantry Division. From May through July, the unit had fired 56,000 artillery rounds. At the end of July, the 59th was sent to Naples and informed that they were reassigned to the 45th Infantry Division for an impending operation: the Allied invasion of southern France, Operation Dragoon.

France and The Final Departure

On August 15, 1944, the 59th AFA landed with the 45th on the Mediterranean coast near St. Tropez, France. They fought their way northward, and by September, were near the French town of Montelimar. The 45th was rapidly advancing northward east of Lyon, France.

On September 3, 1944, T/4 Skruber joined 2nd Lieutenant Robert R. Freeman (Service number O-1183288), for an aerial reconnaissance mission in their L-4 Grasshopper. It was their last flight.

While taking off over a small stream, the plane hit a high ferry cable which snapped, crashing the plane into a bank where it burned near the village of Marcilleux, Isère, France. According to the 59th AFA Historical Report for September 1944:

2LT Robert R. Freeman

"At 1015 hours, LT Robert Freeman, our liaison pilot, and Tec 4 Joseph Skruber, his observer, were killed when their plane crashed and burned after hitting a cable near Cremieu. LT Freeman had flown very gallantly at Montelimar from dawn until dusk and was responsible for breaking up numerous counter-attacks during that battle in August 1944. Almost every time that he had taken to the air he had been fired upon by every weapon that the enemy could turn on him. Despite these dangers, he had remained in the air constantly and played a considerable part in the success of

the battle at Montelimar. SGT Skruber had been his observer on many occa-sions there. Their loss is felt greatly by members of this battalion."

In November 1944, Joe Skruber's family was informed that their son had been killed in action.

Joe Skruber Arrives Home

T/4 Joseph Skruber and 2LT Robert Freeman were initially placed in cas-kets by French citizens near the location of the crash. T/4 Skruber was subse-quently buried at the US Military Cemetery at Montelimar, France. In 1945, he was reburied at the US Military Cemetery at Luynes, France. In October 1948, his remains were transported aboard the US Army transport ship Carroll Victory to the United States. He was finally interred on November 19, 1948, at Grandview Cemetery in Monessen.

On the fifth anniversary of his death, the Monessen Daily Independent published an In Memorium in his honor by the Skruber Family:

"Deep down in our hearts there's a picture
More precious than silver or gold.
It's a picture of you, our dear one
Whose memory will never grow old.
Often bring a silent tear,
Thoughts return to scenes long past,
Time goes on, but memory lasts".

✶ ✶ ✶

ENS ARTHUR J. STOCKUS

Service Numbers 4471527 (Cadet) / 363531 (Officer)
Night Fighter Squadron VF(N)-43, Carrier Aircraft Service Unit 27, US Naval Reserve
Killed while training, Massachusetts, September 12, 1944

As Ensign Arthur Stockus climbed toward 30,000 feet in his US Navy F6F-3 Hellcat fighter during a training exercise, something went wrong.

His squadron of fellow pilots watched as Stockus' fighter began to fall from their formation and into a roll.

Attempts to raise him over the radio failed to receive a response. They watched in anguish as their colleague fell from the sky. It was the last time anyone would see Arthur Stockus alive.

The Stockus Family

Arthur Joseph Stockus was born on September 10, 1921, to Joseph Anton and Eva Barbara (née Gruodis) Stockus in Monessen, Pennsylvania. Joseph and Eva married in 1911. Joseph was a laborer in the barbed wire department of Pittsburgh Steel in Monessen, while Eva managed the Stockus family household.

Joseph, born Josef Stoczkus in the village of Zverblauskis, Lithuania (part of the Russian Empire at the time), immigrated to the United States in 1907

aboard the SS Gera. He initially settled in Pittsburgh with his cousin. Eva was from Grigaluniski, Lithuania, and came to the US in 1905. By 1917, they had settled in a home at 1133 McMahon Avenue in Monessen where they would live through 1950.

Arthur was the second of two sons born to Joseph and Eva. Robert Louis was born in 1913. During the 1920's, their father opened a side business of painting and wallpaper hanging, which he advertised in the local newspaper. By 1930, Arthur was attending school while his older brother worked as a draftsman and attended college. In 1936 at the age of 14, Arthur and two other boys were arrested for "hopping" (riding without paying) the Hilltop bus and were fortunate to be released with a stern warning. Arthur graduated from Monessen High School before 1940 where he was a regular on the academic honor roll and played clarinet in the high school band.

The US Enters WWII

Japanese forces launched a surprise attack on the US military bases in Pearl Harbor, Hawaii, on December 7, 1941. The US declared war on Japan, and subsequently, as an ally of the Japanese Empire, Germany declared war on the US. Arnold's friends soon were off to serve their country in the military.

Arthur took an opportunity to work with the US Army Signal Corps and traveled to Philadelphia to work on communications equipment by February 1942. On February 16, 1942, Arthur registered for the US armed forces draft in Philadelphia where he was living at 1421 Arch Street. He was a 5'10.5", 160 lb young single man with brown hair and blue eyes. By August, he had been transferred within the Signal Corps and was working at the Delco Radio Division plant in Kokomo, Indiana.

Becoming a Naval Aviator

Arthur decided that he wanted to be a pilot, and the US Navy offered a pathway. So, on October 15, 1942, in Washington, DC., he enlisted with the US Naval Reserve as an Aviation Cadet, with a four-year commitment. The Naval Aviation Cadet Act had set up a volunteer naval reserve class known as

"V-5 Naval Aviation Cadet (NavCad)" program to send civilian and enlisted candidates to train as aviation cadets. Candidates had to be between the ages of 19 and 25, have an associate degree or at least two years of college, and had to complete a bachelor's degree within six years after graduation to keep their commission. Training was for 18 months and candidates had to agree not to marry during training and to serve for at least three more years of active-duty service. Arthur applied as a V-5 Cadet and was selected by the Naval Aviation Cadet Selection Board in the Naval District of Washington, DC.

On February 10, 1943, Aviation Cadet Stockus transferred to the Civil Aeronautics Authority (CAA) War Training Service at the Southwest Louisiana Institute in Lafayette, Louisiana, where the V-5 Officer Training Program was underway. After completing his training there, he transferred to Pre-Flight School at the University of Georgia in Athens, Georgia on April 21, 1943. On July 13, 1943, Cadet Stockus was transferred to the Naval Air Station in Hutchinson, Kansas, for continued flight training. He completed training in Kansas and was transferred to the Naval Air Training Center in Pensacola, Florida, on October 18, 1943.

A year later, Arthur Stockus had completed his training as a US Naval Aviator and was commissioned as an officer at the rank of Ensign. ENS Stockus had become qualified on the US Navy's newest fighter, the Grumman F6F-3 Hellcat. In particular, he was recognized for his special skills that would be required to become a night fighter.

ENS Stockus, Night Fighter

The US Navy had become acutely aware of the need to deploy fighters at night against nocturnal enemy aggressors. But taking off and landing from an aircraft carrier at night presented unique challenges. In addition, pilots had to be experts in flying by instruments and using the newly developed radar to locate and pursue enemy aircraft. The Navy began developing its night fighting doctrine and technologies at its base at Quonset Point, Rhode Island in April 1943. Pilot training was organized under the Night Fighter Training Unit at nearby Naval Auxiliary Air Facility (NAAF) Charleston, RI.

By August 1944, ENS Stockus was assigned to the US Navy's Night Fighting Squadron VF(N)-43. The squadron was formed that month at the Naval Air Auxiliary Facility in Westerly, Rhode Island, near NAAF Charleston. It consisted of 35 officers and 30 enlisted men. They were temporarily assigned stateside to Carrier Aircraft Service Unit (CASU) 27.

A Grumman F6F Hellcat Fighter of CASU-27 (US Navy / World War Photos)

CASU's were formed to support air operations of aircraft carriers, including receiving new aircraft and preparing them for delivery aboard carriers. VF(N)-43 worked with CASU-27 to prepare their F6F Hellcats for combat operations at sea.

Fate Intervenes

ENS Stockus was assigned to join a flight of F6F's on Tuesday, September 12, 1944, in Hellcat Bureau (Serial) Number 42800 for high-altitude oxygen training. They took off from Westerly Field at 1:50 PM, heading north for Massachusetts, and continually climbing toward an altitude of 30,000 ft.

An hour after take-off at about 28,000 ft, ENS Stockus' Hellcat suddenly broke from formation. His aircraft went into a slow roll and into a cloud bank. His colleagues attempted to raise him by radio, but he failed to respond.

The Hellcat fell to Earth, crashed, and exploded in a wooded area approximately two miles west of the town of Douglas, Massachusetts. ENS Arthur Stockus was killed in the crash.

Later, investigators theorized that his oxygen system had failed. At an altitude of over 10,000 ft, supplemental oxygen is essential for mental fitness and survival. Without it, a pilot would become severely disoriented, confused, and eventually unconscious.

His family was informed the following day that their son had been lost.

Arthur J. Stockus, Remembered

A military escort accompanied the body of ENS Arthur Stockus from Rhode Island to Monessen the following week, where he was interred at the city's Grandview Cemetery with full military honors on September 18, 1944.

The name of Arthur J. Stockus is inscribed on the Charlestown Naval Auxiliary Landing Field Memorial in Ninigret Park, Charleston, RI.

✯ ✯ ✯

PFC JOSEPH M. FIORILLO

Service Number 33413559
133rd Military Police Platoon, South Pacific, US Army
Killed at sea off New Caledonia, September 26, 1944

The captain of the transport ship carrying PFC Joseph Fiorillo and his colleagues in the 133rd Military Police Platoon did not realize that he had entered waters that hid underwater explosive mines.

The result would be the single largest loss of life for the platoon. The loss included Joseph Fiorillo.

The Fiorillo Family

Joseph Michael Fiorillo was born on August 15, 1913, to John Sr. and Assunta (née Giannotta) Fiorillo in the Hazelwood neighborhood of Pittsburgh, Pennsylvania. John and Assunta married in 1912. John was employed in boiler work at a Monessen factory while Assunta managed the Fiorillo family household.

Joseph's father John was born Giovanni Fiorillo in the village of Montagane, province of Campobasso, in the Molise region of Italy and immigrated to the United States in 1903 aboard the SS Germania. Joseph's mother Assunta was born in the village of Sparanise, province of Caserta, in the Campania

region of Italy, and immigrated to the US in 1906. Each eventually settled in Pittsburgh where they met, married, and started their family together. John became a naturalized US citizen in December 1923.

"Joe Michael" was the first of four siblings born to John and Assunta. His sister Vittoria "Victoria" was born next (b1916), followed by John Francis (1918) and Philomena (1927). The family lived most of their lives in rented homes on Third Street in Monessen. In 1920, they were in a 4-unit apartment at 104 Third St., moving to another 4-unit apartment at 312 Third St. by 1930, and to a two-family home at 221 Third St. by 1940. During that time, their father went from working as a laborer at the American Tin and Plate Company in Monessen in 1920, to a laborer at the local steel mill in 1930, to a welder at a Page Steel and Wire in Monessen in 1940.

Joe Michael completed his schooling after the eighth grade and went to work as a helper in a soda shop by 1930. In 1936, Joe was bowling for Monessen's Trianon team. By the end of 1940, he was working as a laborer at Pittsburgh Steel while living with his parents and siblings.

On October 16, 1940, Joe Michael joined millions of other young American men and registered for the US armed forces draft in Monessen on the first day it went into effect under the newly enacted Selective Service Act. He was a 5'9", 160 lb 27-yr-old with black hair and brown eyes. That same day, his younger brother John also registered. But John decided to enlist early and entered the US Army in July 1941. John would end up fighting in the Southwest Pacific theater and on the Solomon Island of Guadalcanal in 1942.

Joe fell in love and married Rosaline Mary Thomas of Pittsburgh on June 16, 1941. Rosaline was a salesperson in a retail clothing store. They settled into a home at 109 Renova Street in Hazelwood.

War Begins

The surprise attack by Japanese armed forces on the US military bases at Pearl Harbor, Hawaii, in December 1941 changed the world for Joe and his brother John. John, having already enlisted in the Army, was deployed overseas in March 1942. But until the draft called him to military service, Joe and

Rosaline tried to live a normal life and start a family. The following year, the happy couple was graced by the birth of a son, Joseph, Jr., on October 16, 1942.

On December 23, 1942, Joe was drafted into the US Army. He enlisted in Greensburg, Pennsylvania, and reported for boot camp. The Fiorillo's were now a two-Blue-Star Family.

Private Joseph Michael Fiorillo trained stateside at Fort Eustis, Virginia, and Shenango Personnel Receiving Center at Greenville, Pennsylvania. PVT Fiorillo was promoted to Private First Class (PFC) and was assigned to serve in the Army's Military Police as an "MP". In April 1943, he was deployed overseas to the Pacific theater of the war and landed in Australia.

PFC Fiorillo Arrives in the Southwest Pacific

In August 1943 at Port Vila on the island of Efate in the New Hebrides, the 133rd Military Police Platoon was formed, to which PFC Fiorillo was assigned. By September, the Platoon consisted of two officers and 81 enlisted men. Efate was the site of three US air bases and a seaplane base. While away, PFC Fiorillo often wrote home, mentioning his buddies in his MP outfit, "Milton, Jumbo, Pisano, Zombesh, and Buscimi". His last letter home was dated September 22, 1944.

On September 25, 1944, PFC Fiorillo and the entire 133rd Military Police Platoon boarded a transport ship, the SS Elihu Thomson MCE-427 for a 1 ½ day journey to Noumea, New Caledonia. The SS Elihu Thomson was a merchant marine Liberty Ship built in 1942 to support the war effort.

The SS Elihu Thomson was carrying cargo, explosives, and 211 US Army troops, including PFC Fiorillo and the 133rd, in a convoy of allied ships. After an overnight journey at sea in light rain, the Thomson rounded the southern end of the island of New Caledonia. At 0830 hrs on September 26 traveling at 11 knots and about 8 miles from the harbor at Noumea, the ship struck two undetected, underwater explosive mines. The mines hit the ship just behind its bow, blowing holes in its port side and bringing the Thomspon to a dead stop. The crew immediately attended to the damage and to the injured. The deck of the SS Elihu Thomson had ruptured, and the ship suffered extensive structural damage, but it remained afloat and was towed to Noumea.

SS Elihu Thomson War Casualty Report Sept 26, 1944, Page 1 (US Maritime Administration)

Of the 211 soldiers on board, 32 died when the explosions rocked the ship. PFC Joseph Michael Fiorillo suffered a fatal laceration of his liver and was one of the 20 men of the 133rd Military Police Platoon who died that day aboard the SS Elihu Thomson. It was the single largest tragedy of the war for the 133rd.

Joseph Fiorillo, Remembered

PFC Joseph Michael Fiorillo was initially buried at the US Military Cemetery #1 at Noumea, New Caledonia. He was relocated and reinterred at the US Military Cemetery, Schofield Barracks, Oahu, Hawaii in early 1947. At the request of his family under the Return of the War Dead program, he was brought to the US mainland aboard the US Army Transport ship Honda Knot, and reinterred at Calvary Cemetery in Pittsburgh, Pennsylvania, in October 1947.

Two years later in 1946, PFC Joseph Fiorillo's only son Joseph Jr. lost his life at the age of 3 to a rare form of children's kidney cancer. PFC Fiorillo's wife Rosaline would never remarry.

PFC. JOSEPH M. FIORILLO
Pfc. Joseph M. Fiorillo, husband of Mrs. Rosealine Fiorillo and son of Mr. and Mrs. John Fiorillo of 222 Third St., Monessen, was killed in the South Pacific on September 26, 1944.

Monongahela Valley Labor News April 6, 1945

★★★

T/5 NICHOLAS RAVENCHAK

Service Number 33292584
Company B HQ, 841st Engineer Aviation Battalion, US Army Corps of Engineers, USAAF
Died from wounds, Hollandia, October 8, 1944

Nicholas "Nick" Ravenchak was born on July 18, 1920, to Matthew and Frances (née Muskovac) Ravenchak in Konjarić Vrh, Croatia. Matthew and Frances had married in Croatia in 1907.

The Ravenchak Family

Matthew, born as Mato Ravenscak in Croatia, left his wife behind and immigrated to the United States in 1910 aboard the SS New York to find work, which he found with Pittsburgh Steel in Monessen, Pennsylvania. Frances, born as Franca or Franjica Vrbos Muskovac, followed in 1913 aboard the SS La Touraine.

Nick was the last of five children born to Matthew and Frances. Johan "John" was first born (1914) but died the following year. A daughter Frances was born in 1915. Another son named Nick was born in 1916 but died from cholera in 1918. Joe was born in 1919 but passed away in 1920. When Frances became pregnant with Nick, she may have been concerned that she had already lost three young children born in the US. She returned to her parents' home in Konjarić, Croatia with her daughter, where Nick was born.

Nick, his sister Frances, and his mother stayed in Konjarić where the children attended school. In 1929, they returned to the US aboard the SS President Harding, and rejoined Matthew in Monessen. The family was now renting a home on 1462 Schoonmaker Avenue.

By 1940, Nick had left high school after one year. At the age of 19, he was employed as a truck driver for a local grocery store. The family was now renting a home at 251 Morgan Ave in Monessen.

The surprise attack by Japanese armed forces upon the US military base at Pearl Harbor on December 7, 1941, changed the world for millions of Americans as it did for Nick. On February 16, 1942, Nick registered for the US military draft as a 5'11" 156 lb 21-yr-old with brown hair and hazel eyes. He had taken a job with Pittsburgh Steel in Monessen. The family had moved once more, and they were now living at 1045 Highland Avenue in Monessen.

Drafted!

Six months later, Nick received his draft notice, and he enlisted on August 28, 1942, in Greensburg, Pennsylvania. He was assigned to the US Army. After basic training, he was transferred to the 841st Engineer Aviation Battalion of the US Army's Corps of Engineers.

The 841st Engineer Aviation Battalion (EAB) was activated in September 1942 at Hunter Field, Savannah, Georgia. EAB's had the mission of constructing forward air bases for US Army Air Corps aircraft. EAB's were equipped with all of the equipment and supplies necessary to construct, expand, and repair air bases. They were staffed with engineers, general laborers, as well as experienced construction workers who learned their trade prior to enlistment. EAB's were also charged with helping to defend their airfields in the event of attack.

Private Nick Ravenchak transferred from Hunter Field on November 23, 1942, to Leesburg, Florida. He was eventually promoted to the rank of Technician 5th Grade (T/5), which was the equivalent rank of Corporal. T/5's were often referred to as Corporals by others. T/5 Ravenchak was assigned to Company B HQ of the 841st.

By the end of December 1942, the entire 841st EAB with 950 men was training at the Air Service Center in Leesburg, Florida. During the first half of 1943, the group was split up among the US Army air bases in Leesburg, Orlando, and Pinecastle, Florida, leaving a core group in Leesburg at about 800 men.

While in training, Nick's mother passed away on April 7, 1943, at the age of 54.

In April, the 841st was again transferred with orders to construct a new airdrome at Bushnell, Florida. The project was to be a training exercise, hints of their future. In May, the 841st made headlines in the Army Air Forces Training School newspaper when, having lived in tents and not eating in a mess hall for 5.5 months with only two days off, they constructed a 4,000 ft runway in 35.5 hours under simulated combat conditions in Bushnell, Florida, their new base. The group was commended for their performance.

In August 1943, the 841st passed its combat readiness inspection and was recommended for overseas deployment. In September, the group was transported across the country to the staging area at Camp Stoneman in Pittsburg, California, in preparation for deployment to the South Pacific theater of the war. On September 26, they left for Sydney, Australia. T/5 Nick Ravenchak was rostered with a military occupation specialty (MOS) of 345, or "Truck Driver, Light", one of 107 of that specialty in his unit.

Arrival on New Guinea

By October 1943, the Allied armies had landed on the island of New Guinea and were fighting the Japanese occupiers. They were successfully seizing Japanese airfields along its coast, which were desperately needed for offensive Allied fighters and bombers. But these airfields required repair from

Allied bombing raids and artillery craters, and upgrades to accommodate Allied air forces.

In October, the 841st went by rail to Brisbane, Australia. There, they prepared for the battle zone and were ordered to be equipped for extended tropical service. The group of 800 men staged their 743 tons of equipment and 200 vehicles for deployment. They sailed to their new station at Goodenough Island, codenamed Amoeba, just east of New Guinea. Amoeba was established as a staging point, supply base, and hospital base for operations in New Guinea and New Britain. The 841st EAB was now reporting to the US Sixth Army, code named Alamo Force, as part of Operation Cartwheel, the Allied campaign to island-hop from the central and southwest Pacific towards the Philippines and eventually, Japan.

Building Airfields During War

By December, the 841st EAB was in the thick of the war. The 841st was split and Company B was sent to Finschhafen on Cape Cretin, New Guinea, while the rest of the battalion went to Cape Gloucester, New Britain, to repair and upgrade airfields that were taken from the Japanese. At Finschhafen on an unimproved jungle coast with insufficient construction materials, Company B was to construct a supply and transshipment base with a staging area for 40,000 troops and facilities for headquarters of the Sixth Army. They completed the construction in April 1944, and the company later received a commendation for their accomplishment.

Company B was rejoined by the rest of the 841st EAB at Finschhafen, and the group departed for Hollandia on the north coast of New Guinea. The Allies had invaded and eventually overtaken the Japanese installation and airbase during the Battle of Hollandia. The 841st was needed to rebuild the Japanese base and convert it for use by Allied air forces. They reconstructed both the Sentani and Cyclops airdromes at Hollandia and made them operational in short order. The 475th Fighter Group with P-38 Lightning fighters moved in, while the 841st continued improving the air base.

While in Hollandia in September 1944, T/5 Nick Ravenchak was traveling in a vehicle when he received a severe penetrating abdominal wound. He was admitted to the Fifth Field Hospital in Hollandia, where he eventually died from his wounds on October 8, 1944. Initial reports stated that the wound was caused by an exploding hand grenade, but the reports were eventually revised to state the cause of the wound was an automobile accident.

T/5 Nicholas Ravenchak was initially buried in the US Army Air Force Cemetery #1 at Hollandia. In May 1945, he and others from Hollandia were reburied at the USAF Cemetery #2 at Finschhafen. In 1947, due to additional consolidation of American cemeteries, Nicholas Ravenchak's remains were removed and reburied at the Manila American Cemetery and Memorial, Manila, Philippines.

★★★

PFC ANTHONY SARIDAKIS

Service Number 33430282
Cannon Company, 155th Infantry Regiment, 31st Infantry Division, US Army
Died of wounds, Morotai, October 8, 1944

Anthony "Tony" Saridakis was born on August 14, 1921, to Komianos and Anastasia (née Zarpas) Saridakis in Monessen, Pennsylvania. Komianos and Anastasia married in 1917. Komianos worked in a Monessen steel mill while Anastasia managed the Saridakis family household.

The Saridakis Family

Komianos, born in Constantinople, Turkey, immigrated to the United States in 1905. Anastasia was born on the island of Chios in Greece and immigrated to the US in 1914. They met and married in Monessen.

Tony was the last of three children born to Komianos and Anastasia. Gustave "Gust" or "August" was born in 1919, and Katherine "Katie" arrived in 1920. Sister Katie died in 1930. In 1920, the family was living in a rented home at 1225 Morgan Avenue in Monessen, and by 1930 had moved into a rented apartment at 511 Schoonmaker Avenue. Ten years later they had moved a few doors down to 502 Schoonmaker.

Tony graduated from Monessen High School in the first semester of his senior year, in 1941. On December 7, 1941, Japanese forces attacked the US military bases at Pearl Harbor, Hawaii, bringing the United States into war with Japan, Germany, and Italy. Tony registered for the US armed forces draft on February 16, 1942, as a 5'9" 150 lb 20-yr-old with black hair and brown eyes. That year he attended welding school in Cleveland, Ohio.

On February 24, 1943, after attending one year of college and working as a welder, he was drafted into the US Army. He was off to Army boot camp.

Private Saridakis was assigned to the 31st Infantry Division, which was training in the southeastern US from 1940 onward. He proceeded to specialize in artillery sup-port and was placed in the Can-non Company of the 31st's 155th Infantry Regi-ment. As of July 1943, Cannon Companies were formed to provide indirect fire sup-

105mm Howitzer being towed (Library of Congress)

port for their regiments. They were typically equipped with six 105mm towed howitzers and 118 men.

PVT Saridakis Off to the Pacific

The 31st Division left for the southwest Pacific in 1944, landing at Oro Bay, New Guinea in April. After amphibious landing training, they moved to Aitape, New Guinea, in June, where they helped build bridges, roads, and docks, patrolled the area, and engaged small units of the Japanese Army. They awaited their next major operation. Along the way, he was promoted to Private First Class (PFC).

In July 1944, the Allied invasion of Mindanao in the Philippines planned for November required air bases and naval facilities for support. It was decided to invade the island of Morotai south of Mindanao, called Operation Tradewind.

Operation Tradewind would land the invasion force close to the planned airfield sites near the town of Doroeba. Two beaches, designated Red Beach and White Beach, were selected for the landings. On September 15, 1944, all three infantry regiments of the 31st Division landed across these beaches and began their drive inland to secure a perimeter for the planned airfields.

There was little opposition from the approximately 500 Japanese defenders. However, Japanese air bases in nearby Halmahera Island launched aircraft sorties that harassed the infantrymen of the 31st.

While the Cannon Company of the 155th Regiment was on White Beach, PFC Saridakis was struck in the left leg and hip by shrapnel from a nearby exploding aerial bomb. He died from his wounds on October 8, 1944.

PFC Anthony Saridakis was initially buried at the US military cemetery at Doroeba, Morotai. In January 1946, his remains were relocated to the US Armed Forces Cemetery No. 5 at Finschhafen, New Guinea. Later, the American military cemeteries on Pacific islands were consolidated, and PFC Saridakis' remains were finally interred at the Manila American Cemetery in the Philippines in September 1947.

★ ★ ★

T/5 JAMES WOODS

Service Number 33167317
Service Company, 15th Tank Battalion, 6th Armored Division, US Army
Killed in action, France, October 8, 1944

James Woods was born on May 5, 1917, to Michael and Margaret (née Lynch) Woods in Glasgow, Scotland. Michael and Margaret had married there in 1914. Michael was an assistant steward aboard the ship SS Columbia while Margaret managed the Woods family household.

The Woods Family

Michael, born in Scotland, immigrated to the United States aboard the Columbia in 1923, and came to Charleroi, Pennsylvania seeking work. Margaret was also born in Scotland and immigrated to the US the following year with James and the rest of their children aboard the SS Columbia.

James was the second of four children born to Michael and Margaret. Anne Patricia was first born (1914). After James, Margaret Marie (1918) and Thomas Joseph (1920) arrived. All of the children were born in Scotland.

By 1930, the family had moved into a rented home at 1172 Graham Avenue in Monessen, Pennsylvania. Michael had been hired as a laborer at Pittsburgh Steel in Monessen. All of the children were attending school that year. Margaret's brothers and a nephew were also living with them at the Graham Avenue home. By 1938, the family moved into a home at 47 Reed Avenue in Monessen.

In January of 1938, Margaret was diagnosed with heart disease. The family was devastated when she passed away ten months later at the age of 54.

James, now fondly called "Scotty", left high school after his junior year to help support the household by working at the steel mill. By 1939, James was working as a tester in the laboratory of the mill. The family moved once again to 118 Third Street in Monessen. Michael was now working as a switchboard operator at the Pittsburgh Steel mill. Anne had completed high school and was now working as a stenographer. Margaret Marie left to study at the Mercy Hospital School of Nursing in Pittsburgh.

With the rumblings of war heard in Europe and the Pacific, the US Congress passed the Selective Service and Training Act in September 1940, including the first peacetime draft for the US military. On October 16, 1940, James joined millions of fellow American young men and registered for the draft on its first day. According to his draft registration, James was a 23-yr-old young man standing 5' 6", 145 lb with blonde hair and blue eyes, with a scar on his chin.

The US Enters WWII

Japanese forces launched a surprise attack on the US military bases in Pearl Harbor, Hawaii, on December 7, 1941. The US declared war on Japan, and as an ally of the Japanese Empire, Germany declared war on the US. War was about to disrupt the Woods family.

James was drafted into the US Army, and he reported for duty on March 28, 1942, in New Cumberland, Pennsylvania. His application for US citizenship had just been processed a month earlier. He left for training immediately, and headed to Camp Chaffee, Arkansas. Camp Chaffee had just been activated.

Two months later, Private James Woods returned to Monessen where he married his sweetheart, Rita Jean DeStefano also of Monessen, on May 30, 1942. After a brief honeymoon, they left for Camp Chaffee where they would reside during training.

PVT Woods was assigned to train on armored vehicles for the US Army while at Camp Chaffee. Chaffee was the home training base for the 6th, 14th, and 16th Armored Divisions. The camp provided 67 training areas and 153 artillery and mortar positions and was well-suited for intensive armor training. PVT Woods was assigned to the Service Company of the 15th Tank Battalion in the 6th Armored Division, which would become known as the "Super Sixth". A Service Company was responsible for repair and replacement of equipment.

The 6th Armored Division participated in the VIII Corps Louisiana Maneuvers in August 1942, returning to Camp Chaffee in September. The Division then moved to Camp Young at the Desert Training Center in October 1942 and participated in the first California Maneuvers. The 6th AD then moved to Camp Cooke, California, to continue its training. But it was now time for PVT Woods and the 6th Armored Division to head overseas and into war. They staged at Camp Shanks, New York on February 3, 1944, and departed for Europe on February 11, 1944. The Division arrived in England on February 23, 1944.

But before he left the states, Rita became pregnant. She returned to Monessen where she would have their child with the support of her family. On September 11,1943, Rita gave birth to their daughter, Rita Marsha Woods.

James was eventually promoted to the rank of Technician 5th Grade (T/5), normally addressed as "Corporal".

T/5 James Woods with the Super Sixth

The 15th Tank Battalion of the 6th Armored Division trained heavily in England in preparation for supporting the Allied invasion of the European continent. T/5 Woods had the fortunate opportunity for a brief furlough and visited relatives in Scotland. He returned in time for the start of the invasion, which began on D-Day, June 6, 1944, and the 15th Tank Battalion arrived in Normandy on July 22, 1944.

The Division pushed into France, first moving westward into combat, and then east across the country. By September 1944, they entered Nancy, France, and were in the heat of battle with the German occupying forces.

On October 8, the Division was clearing the enemy from the banks of the Seille River when T/5 James Woods was struck in the chest by enemy gunfire. He did not survive the day. His family was informed of his loss by the War Department two weeks later.

James Woods would never again see his wife and daughter.

James "Scotty" Woods, Remembered

James Woods was initially buried in the US Military Cemetery in Andilles, France. He was eventually reinterred at the Lorraine American Cemetery and Memorial, Saint-Avold, Département de la Moselle, Lorraine, France.

★ ★ ★

PFC PACIFICO SACCHINI

Service Number 33396422
Company E, 135th Infantry Regiment, 34th Infantry Division, US Army
Killed in action, Italy, October 9, 1944

W hen Nicola and Rosa Sacchini emigrated from Italy to the United States in the early 1900's, they could not have expected that one of their sons would return to Italy to fight as a soldier in the US Army decades later.

That son, Pacifico, would eventually lose his life less than 150 miles from his parents' home town.

The Sacchini Family

Pacifico Sacchini was born on November 14, 1913, to Nicola "Nick" and Rosa "Rose" (née Evangelisti) Sacchini, in Monessen, Pennsylvania. Nick and Rose had married in 1911 in nearby Greensburg. Nick was a shoemaker and had a shop in Monessen,

PFC. P. 'PUGGIE" SACCHINI
Another of Monessen's casualties was Pfc. Pacifico "Puggie" Sacchini, son of Mr. and Mrs. Nicholas Sacchini, 301 Lenawee Ave. He was killed in action in Italy on Oct. 9, 1944.

Monongahela Valley Labor News April 6, 1945

while Rose managed the Sacchini family household.

Nick was born in Campofilone, in the Province of Ferno, Italy, and immigrated to the United States aboard the SS Sannio in 1907. Rose, also from Campofilone, was betrothed to Nick prior to coming to the US in 1910 aboard the SS Berlin. They married three weeks after her arrival.

Pacifico was named after his paternal grandfather and was fondly called "Pudgie" or "Puggie". He was the second of six children born to Nick and Rose. His brother Columbus "Slim" (b1911) was the first born, and Pacifico's younger siblings arrived next: Orlando Joseph "Arnold" (1916), Rainer "Reno" (1918), Madeline (1924), and Esther (1928). By 1920, the family was living in a rented apartment at 104 Lenawee Avenue in Monessen. Nick's brother Giuseppe "Joseph" had arrived in 1915 and was rooming with Nick and their family while working at their shoe repair shop. Their shop was now located at 406 Fourth St in Monessen.

By 1930, the success of their business had allowed them to purchase a home at 224 Delaware Street for their burgeoning family. Pacifico left school after the eighth grade and was working at the family shop at the age of 16. By 1940, the family sold their home on Delaware Street and bought a home on their old street at 301 Lenawee Ave. Pacifico and Reno were both working at the shoe shop. Columbus had left for college, earned a degree in mechanical engineering, married and moved to Cleveland Ohio by 1940. He eventually developed a number of patented inventions.

October 16, 1940, was the first day of the US armed forces draft under the newly passed Selective Service and Training Act. Pacifico joined millions of other young men that day and signed up for the draft. He registered as a 5' 10" 143 lb 26-yr-old with brown hair and brown eyes. His brother Orlando had already volunteered and joined the US Army in April 1941.

Over a year later, on December 7, 1941, the United States came under surprise attack at Pearl Harbor, Hawaii, and the US entered the war against Japan, Germany, and Italy. In November of the following year, Pacifico was drafted into the US military. He reported to the registration office in Greensburg and enlisted into the US Army on November 29, 1942. Private Sacchini left for basic training a week later. Reno had been drafted two weeks before Pacifico. The Sacchini's were now a three-blue-star family.

PVT Sacchini Heads to War

PVT Sacchini trained stateside at Camp Phillips, Kansas, and was shipped overseas to the European theater of the war in September 1943 as replacement infantry. He was assigned to Company E of the 135th Infantry Regiment in the 34th Infantry Division, known as the "Red Bull" Division.

The 34th Infantry Division had deployed to North Africa in November 1942 and fought in Algeria and Tunisia before heading to the invasion of Italy in September 1943. Pacifico Sacchini, now a Private First Class (PFC), arrived this month to join the war. He was now fighting in the homeland of his Italian ancestors.

PFC Sacchini in the 135th Regiment participated in the battles at the Volturno River crossing (Sept-Oct 1943), Cassino (Jan-Feb 1944), Anzio (March 1944), and Rome (June 1944). By September, they had pushed northward and were about 25 miles north of Florence near the town of Bruscoli.

On October 9, 1944, while in combat near Monzuno, Italy, PFC Sacchini was struck in the back by enemy fire. He did not survive. His family was informed by the War Department the following month.

PFC Pacifico Sacchini's remains were initially interred at the US Military Cemetery at Castelfiorentino, Italy. In 1948, at the request of his family, he was transported to the United States aboard the SS Lawrence Victory and was finally buried at Grandview Cemetery in Monessen in December 1948.

★★★

PVT ALEXANDER KOSZYKOWSKI

Service Number 33430307
349th Infantry Regiment, 88th Infantry Division, US Army
Killed in action, Italy, October 10, 1944

Alexander "Alex" Koszykowski was born on January 9, 1920, in Monessen, Pennsylvania, to Joseph and Mary (née Koszykowska) Koszykowski. Joseph and Mary had married in Greensburg, Pennsylvania, in 1910. Joseph was a grocery merchant while Mary managed the Koszykowski family household.

The Koszykowski Family

Joseph, born "Jozef" in the village of Rozanka, in the Galicia region of Poland, immigrated to the United States in 1909 aboard the SS Rhein. He arrived in Baltimore, Maryland, before moving to Monessen. Mary, born Maryia in the village of Konstantowka, also in Galicia, Poland, arriving in Baltimore aboard the SS Brandenberg in 1909 and heading to Monessen. Joseph applied for US citizenship and was naturalized in 1922.

349th Infantry Regiment Insignia (US Army)

Alex was the fifth of nine children born to Joseph and Mary. Stephania "Stella" was born in 1911, followed by Eugenia "Jenny" (b1913), Anthony "Tony" (1914), and Karol "Carl" (1917). Twin brothers "Joe" were born in 1922, but both died as infants, one at 1 month and the other at 3 months of age. Sister Marie was born in 1924. Another child was born and died sometime before 1929, according to Jenny's birth certificate.

In 1920, the family was living in an apartment at 97 East Schoonmaker Avenue in Monessen. By 1930, Joseph and Mary purchased a home at 625 Delaware Avenue in Monessen. It was a crowded, 1 bedroom home, but the family made do. Joseph was now a butcher in a local meat market.

By 1940, Joseph was employed as a carpenter on public works projects for the Work Progress Administration, a program funded by President Roosevelt's New Deal to grow employment and stimulate the US economy. Stella, Jenny, and Carl had moved out to start their own adult lives. Alex had left school after the eighth grade and was now, at age 20, working as a laborer on a reforestation project while living at his parents' home.

The following year of 1941 was an eventful year for Alex. He took a job as a laborer at the local Page Steel and Wire Company in Monessen and moved into his own residence at 210 Shawnee Avenue in town. Alex also met and fell in love with Mildred Dorothy Sabolek, and they married on April 21, 1941. Mildred was born in nearby Belle Vernon, Pennsylvania, but was working as a private nursemaid in New York state the prior year before returning and marrying Alex. On July 1, 1941, Alex registered for the US armed forces draft as a 5'10" 175 lb 21-yr-old with blonde hair and blue eyes.

The surprise attack by Japanese armed forces on the US military bases at Pearl Harbor, Hawaii, in December 1941 changed the world for millions of Americans, as it soon would for Alex and his brothers.

But first, Alex and Mildred enjoyed the blessing of the birth of their child, a son Ronald "Ronnie", born on December 22, 1942. However, even with Ronnie being only three months old, Alex was drafted into the US Army on February 24, 1943. He reported for duty on March 3 in Greensburg, Pennsylvania, and was off to US Army training camp.

Private Alex Koszykowski trained stateside and was eventually assigned to the 349th Infantry Regiment as a replacement. He left the US on July 28, 1944, to join the 349th Regiment already in combat in Italy.

PVT Koszykowski with the Blue Devils

The 349th Regiment had been called into active duty in July 1942. The 349th was attached to the 88th Infantry Division, nicknamed the "Blue Devils", and sent to French Morocco in December 1943. The 88th was the first Division composed almost entirely of drafted (vs volunteering) citizens. The 349th first saw combat when it landed in Naples, Italy at the end of February 1944. It aggressively fought its way into Italy and was soon nicknamed the "Kraut Killers".

In September 1944, the 349th Regiment was ordered to drive north toward Bologna, Italy. By October 5, the Regiment had taken Cuviolo south of Bologna and would engage in a hill-by-hill struggle against embedded German troops in its drive north.

On October 9, the Regiment was maneuvering around the hills near the village of Falchetto and received a directive from 88th Division headquarters to *"...continue to secure and hold hill-mass extending from HILL 543 to HILL 587 to HILL 565 with a minimum of one Bn {Battalion}."* followed by *"Not more than one Bn 349 Inf. may be moved to an assembly area south of the above mentioned hill-mass for showers and clothing issue. With approval of this Hq, Bns of the Regt. may be rotated."*

As fate would have it, PVT Koszykowski's battalion was not one of the first to rotate and retire to the assembly area. On October 10, 1944, after only three months in Italy, Alex Koszykowski was killed in action when he was struck in the chest by an enemy bullet.

Three weeks later, the War Department informed his wife Mildred that Alex had died in combat in Italy. Sadly, Ronnie's father did not live to see his only son's second birthday.

PVT Alex Koszykowski was buried at the Florence American Cemetery and Memorial in Florence, Città Metropolitana di Firenze, Toscana, Italy. He was posthumously awarded the Purple Heart.

★ ★ ★

PVT WILLIAM K. OLIPHANT

Service Number 33704039
Company G, 338th Infantry Regiment, 85th Infantry Division, US Army
Killed in action, Italy, October 13, 1944

William Kane Oliphant was born on August 25, 1925, to Chistopher "Chris" or "Christ" and Mary Agnes "Agnes" (née Kane) Oliphant in Charleroi, Pennsylvania. Chris and Agnes had married three years earlier. Chris was a lineman for the local electric utility while Agnes managed the Oliphant family household.

The Oliphant Family

The Oliphant family heritage traces to Scotland, England, and Germany, and their ancestors immigrated to the United States in the mid-to-late 1800's. The Kane family, originally "O'Kane", was from Ireland and immigrated to the US in the late 1800's. Both families settled in Western Pennsylvania.

William was the second of three children born to Chris and Agnes. First to be born was Margaret (b1922), and sister Edna Rose arrived in 1928. By 1930, the family and Agnes' parents were living in a rented home in Speers, Pennsylvania. In

September 1930, Chris had a run-in with the law and was incarcerated at Western State Penitentiary for 18-36 months.

Between 1935 and 1940, Agnes divorced Chris and married Ernest Jackson. Agnes and her children moved in with Ernest and his two daughters from a previous marriage, Florence and Myrtle. They were living in his rented home at 217 First Street in Monessen, Pennsylvania. Agnes subsequently gave birth to William's half-brother, Ernest, Jr., in 1940.

The surprise attack by Japanese armed forces on the US military base at Pearl Harbor, Hawaii, in December 1941 changed the world for William. He was working as a salesclerk at S. Monick Wholesale Tobacco and General Merchandise at 300 Schoonmaker Avenue in Monessen when he registered for the US armed forces draft on August 27, 1943. He was a 5'9" 126 lb 18-yr-old with brown hair and brown eyes.

William is Drafted

A month later, on September 30 , 1943, William was drafted into the US Army, and he reported for enlistment in Greensburg, Pennsylvania, entering service on October 21, 1943. Private William Oliphant was off to boot camp.

PVT Oliphant was assigned to Company G of the 338th "March On" Infantry Regiment in 85th Infantry Division of the US Army. The 85th, known as the Custer Division, arrived at Casablanca, Morocco, in January 1944, and then participated in the invasion of Italy by landing at Naples in March. They engaged in fierce fighting as they made their way northward up the boot of Italy and took Rome in June. By September, they were 200 miles north of Rome and cracking the German's defensive "Gothic Line" in fierce fighting.

In October the 338th Regiment was fighting the Germans on the hill of Monterenzio in Bologna. On the night of October 12, the Regiment cut off the German's supply and escape routes and converged on the defending German troops on the 13th. On that day, the German defenders of Monterenzio surrendered. But not before PVT Oliphant could escape the battle with his life.

PVT Kane Killed in Italy

On October 13, PVT William Kane Oliphant suffered a fatal wound to the head. He died that day.

The family of PVT Oliphant was informed that he was missing in action in October 1944. The following month, they were informed that he had been killed in action.

PVT Oliphant was initially buried in a temporary American military cemetery at Castelfiorentino, Italy. In 1949, PVT William Kane Oliphant was reinterred at the Florence American Cemetery and Memorial, Florence, Città Metropolitana di Firenze, Toscana, Italy. His family's place of worship, the First Methodist Church, held a memorial service in his honor in January 1945.

PVT William K. Oliphant was posthumously awarded the Purple Heart.

FIRST METHODIST CHURCH
MEMORIAL
Candlelight Communion Service
In Memory of
Private William Oliphant
7:45 P. M.
SUNDAY, JANUARY 14

✦   ✦   ✦

CHURCH SCHOOL at 9:30 A. M.

✦   ✦   ✦

Methodist Youth Fellowship
At 6:45 P. M.

✦   ✦   ✦

Sanctuary Service
10:45 A. M.
"The Kingdom Come"

✦   ✦   ✦

The visitor in town, and those of our town without church connection are cordially invited to this

Monessen Daily Independent, January 13, 1945

★ ★ ★

PFC MICHAEL REDISH

Service Number 3396234
Company F, 351st Infantry Regiment, 88th Infantry Division, US Army
Killed in action, Italy, October 25, 1944

Michael "Mike" Redish was born on April 29, 1920, to John and Dorothy "Fannie" (née Bobick) Redish in Jeannette, Pennsylvania. John was a laborer in a glass manufacturing plant.

The Redish Family

John and Fannie had married in the late 1890's in the Galicia region of Poland. They immigrated to the United States in 1908. John and Fannie had seven children: Katy (b1908), John (1911), Anna Marie (1913), Stephen (1915), Frank (1919), Mike, and Nick (1923). By 1930, the family was living in their home at 222 Penn Road in the Lincoln Heights neighborhood of Jeannette.

In February 1931, their father John suffered a heart attack and passed away. Over the next nine years, the older children grew to adulthood and moved away, leaving Mike and Nick at home with their widowed mother in 1940. They downsized and moved into a rented home at 139 Pitcairn Road in Jeanette. Mike had left school after the eighth grade and was

now working at the Hockensmith Wheel and Mine Car Company in Penn Station, Pennsylvania.

Mike registered for the US military draft on July 1, 1941, as a 5'8", 160 lb 21-yr-old with blue eyes and blonde hair. The surprise attack by Japanese armed forces upon the US military base at Pearl Harbor on December 7, 1941, changed the world for Mike.

The following year, Mike Redish was drafted into the US Army, and he enlisted in Greensburg, Pennsylvania on November 24, 1942. Before leaving for basic training, Mike married his sweetheart Helen Gettko (Gagatko) of Monessen, Pennsylvania, on November 26, 1942. Helen was fondly called Dolly. He left for training, leaving Dolly as an expectant mother.

Private Mike Redish went off to US Army training camp. While at training, Dolly gave birth to their son, Michael Stephen Redish Jr., on February 9, 1943. She eventually moved with Michael Jr., to live with her parents at 421 Ontario Street in Monessen.

PVT Redish trained stateside and was eventually assigned as a replacement to Company F of the 351st Infantry Regiment, which was fighting the war in Italy at the time. He was promoted to Private First Class (PFC) and was shipped overseas to join his company in May 1944.

The 351st Infantry Regiment had entered active service in July 1942 at Camp Gruber, Oklahoma as part of the 88th Infantry Division. The regiment was formed entirely from "citizen soldiers", or all-draftees, and were the first all-draftee regiment to enter combat during WWII. The 351st landed in North Africa in November 1943, where they continued their training. In February 1944, the regiment landed at Naples, Italy, to participate in combat operations in the Italian Campaign.

PFC Redish Heads to Italy

When PFC Redish joined the 351st, the regiment was in Carinola, Italy, north of Naples, and making their way toward Rome against stiff resistance courtesy of the occupying German ground forces along their defense Gustav

Line. Italy had already surrendered to the Allies in September 1943, and its forces had joined the Allies in opposing the Germans.

In June, the 351st participated in the liberation of Rome and received a joyous reception by its citizens. Then followed the battles for Lake Albano, Tarquinia, Pomorance, Volterra, Laiatico, and in July the battle for the Arno River crossing. By September, the 351st had now confronted the Germans' next defensive position, the Gothic Line, about 20 miles north of Florence. PFC Redish was receiving his share of combat experience.

On September 28, PFC Redish was struck by a bullet from a machine gun. He was admitted to the hospital and recovered quickly, rejoining his unit on October 16.But nine days later, his luck ran out. While advancing toward the regimental objective of Monte Calderaro Italy on the night of October 25, PFC Mike Redish went missing. The 351st was taking over 50% combat casualties amidst heavy night fighting and was forced to pull back to regroup. He was left behind.

Dolly and Michael Jr. would never see him again.

In November, his wife was informed about his September wound. But no further word was received until Dolly learned by January 1945 that her husband was missing in action. Six months later, in July 1945, the remains of PFC Mike Redish were found in the vicinity of Monte Calderaro, positively identified by his dog tags. It was concluded that he had been killed in action.

Mike Redish, Remembered

PFC Mike Redish was initially buried at the US Military Cemetery at Pietramala, Italy. He was eventually reinterred at the Florence American Cemetery at Florence Italy. PFC Redish was posthumously awarded the Purple Heart medal.

This IN MEMORIAM was published in the Monessen newspaper from Dolly and Michael Jr. on the one-year anniversary of his death, October 25, 1945:

> *"He has gone across the river, To the shores of ever green*
> *How we'd love to see his smiling face, But the rivers flow between*

And our aching hearts are calling, To the shadows dark and grey
For the dear one that has left us, One year ago today.
His life is a beautiful memory, His death is a silent grief
He sleeps in God's beautiful garden, In sunshine of perfect peace".

★ ★ ★

SM2C JOHN E. VARGA

Service Number 6534871
7th Fleet, US Naval Reserve
Life lost, Southwest Pacific Ocean, November 10, 1944

Life as an active-duty military service member far from home can place tremendous stresses on a 20-year-old. Adjusting to strange living conditions, difficult co-workers, demanding officers, and changing assignments can keep a young man off balance.

SM2c John Edward Varga had the added stress of the responsibilities of a US Navy shipboard signalman: staying up-to-date on ever-changing secret code systems and ensuring rapid receipt, transcription, and delivery of critical messages aboard ship.

The stress was more than he could bear.

The Varga Family

John Edward Varga was born on June 14, 1924, to Michael and Mary (née Svagraszki) Varga in Monessen, Pennsylvania. Michael worked at Pittsburgh Steel in Monessen while Mary managed the Varga family household.

Michael was born Mihály György Varga in the town of Tušice, Slovakia, and Mary was born Maria in Slavkovce, Slovakia when the country was a part of the Austro-Hungarian Empire. Michael immigrated to the United States in 1911 aboard the SS Prinz Adalbert. Mary had arrived in 1914 aboard the SS Rotterdam, destined to join her brother in Monessen. Michael and Mary met there and married in 1915.

John was the fifth of ten children born to Michael and Mary. Their first child, Michael Jr. (b 1916), fell victim to cholera as an infant. Anna Bernice arrived next (1916), followed by Mary Clara (1919), and Stephen Emil (1922). After John came Emil (1926), Joseph Michael (1929), and Frank Stephen (1931). Emil passed away in 1932 from congenital heart disease before his sixth birthday. Irene (1934) and Emil Stephen (1936) were the last children born to the family. In 1921, Michael and Mary adopted two of Michael's nieces, Mary and Helen Trusza, whose parents were tragically lost in a house fire. The children attended Holy Names Elementary School.

By 1930, Michael was working as a trucker in the steel mill and had purchased a home for the large family at 928 Graham Avenue in Monessen. Tragedy again struck the family when their mother Mary contracted tuberculosis and cancer and passed away from heart failure the day after cancer surgery in 1938. John had certainly witnessed his share of family tragedies.

Anna and the adopted sisters left the household to start their own lives by 1940, leaving behind Michael and the oldest daughter Mary to manage the 8-member household. Later that year, Michael married widow Maria Kovach Matty, also a native of Slovakia. Maria's husband had passed away four years earlier after having their own children.

With the rumblings of war heard in Europe and the Pacific, the US Congress passed the Selective Service and Training Act in September 1940, including the first peacetime draft for the US military. On October 16, 1940, Victor, Ralph, William, and James joined millions of fellow American young men and registered for the draft on its first day. According to his draft registration, Victor was a 23-yr-old young man standing 5' 6", 139 lb, with brown hair and brown eyes.

The US Enters WWII

Japanese forces launched a surprise attack on the US military bases in Pearl Harbor, Hawaii, on December 7, 1941. The US declared war on Japan, and as an ally of the Japanese Empire, Germany declared war on the US. The Varga family moved to a home at 929 Leeds Avenue in Monessen about that time.

John Varga was attending Monessen High School at the time, and he graduated the following year. The school yearbook described him: "If you see blonde hair and blue eyes mixed with a nice personality near a skating rink, it's John." After graduating, he took a job as a butcher at Fred Vincent's Food Store in town, and later, at the Monessen Coke and Chemical plant. A few weeks later, John registered for the US armed forces draft as a 5'8", 150 lb 18-yr-old.

John decided not to wait for the draft, so he joined the US Navy and enlisted on December 9, 1942. His brother Stephen had been drafted into the US Army in October. He reported for training and was assigned to the Naval Station Great Lakes in Illinois. While there, he demonstrated strong competencies for the role of Signalman (SM). Signalmen were responsible for transmitting, receiving, encoding, decoding, and distributing messages obtained via the visual transmission systems of flag semaphore, visual Morse code, and flag hoist signaling. After studying at Great Lakes, he took additional training at the University of Illinois. He completed his training with the rank of Signalman 3rd Class (SM3c).

In May 1943, John and his brother Stephen, now a Private in the Army, arranged to enjoy leave to visit home. The reunion was covered by the local newspaper in its "Our Boys in Uniform" feature.

John Varga to the Pacific

The following August, SM3c John Varga left the US and deployed to the Pacific theater of the war. On August 19, 1943, SM2c Varga stepped aboard his first station, the newly launched USS Amycus ARL-2 (Auxiliary Repair, Light), in San Francisco, California.

Our Boys in Uniform

BROTHERS WERE HOME ON RECENT LEAVE

Home on leave recently were Second Class Seaman John Varga, left, and Pvt. Stephen Varga, sons of Mr. and Mrs. Michael Varga of Leeds avenue. Seaman John graduated from Monessen High school in 1942, and enlisted in the Navy in January. Upon completion of his boot training at Great Lakes, Ill., he was assigned to the University of Illinois for specialist training. Pvt. Stephen graduated in 1940, and was inducted into the army in October. He is stationed at Camp Atterbury, Ind. He graduated recently from Radio School.

Monessen Daily Independent, May 25, 1943

The USS Amycus was one of 39 "Achelous-class" landing craft repair ships built for the US Navy during World War II. As the United States gained experience in amphibious operations, it was realized that a mobile repair facility was needed to repair the damage that frequently occurred to smaller amphibious vessels. The Auxiliary Repair Light (ARL) ship was designed to meet this need. ARL's were converted from Landing Ship, Tank (LST) vessels with low draught that could maneuver into shallow waters of small harbors, beaches, and rivers to recover amphibious vessels and boats needing repair. It had a crew of 22 officers and 233 enlisted men.

The Amycus conducted shakedown training along the California coast before departing San Diego on September 20, 1943. They were destined for the South Pacific to join the Service Forces of the US 7th Fleet. The Amycus stopped at Pago Pago, American Samoa; Nouméa, New Caledonia; Brisbane and Port of Townsville, Australia; and Milne Bay, New Guinea. On November

USS Amycus ARL-2 (Auxiliary Repair, Light) (NavSource)

29, they arrived at Buna, Papua New Guinea where she joined Task Force 76. She remained at Buna, servicing and repairing small escort vessels and landing boats.

On February 3, 1944, SM3c Varga was transferred to the USS Blue Ridge AGC-2. The Blue Ridge was one of four US Navy Appalachian-class command ships converted from cargo ships. The Blue Ridge was the flagship of Rear Admiral Daniel E. Barbey, Commander Seventh Amphibious Force (COM7thPHIB). Barbey's force was charged with creating an amphibious squadron, training the crews, and training the US Army troops on amphibious landings. The Blue Ridge was much larger than SM3c Varga's previous ship, carrying 739 men: a crew of 36 officers and 442 enlisted men, and a flag staff of 138 officers and 123 enlisted men.

The Blue Ridge was a busy ship. The 7th Amphibious Command oversaw the reconnaissance landings in the Admiralty Islands off New Guinea and Negros in The Philippines on February 29, 1944. It then supported multiple landings at the Battle of Hollandia on April 22 and then at the Battle of Wakde Island from May 17-21, 1944.

But as with any assignment in the US Navy, SM3c Varga's tour with the Blue Ridge was brief. On May 25, 1944, he was transferred along with several others to the destroyer USS Sampson DD-394 for temporary duty.

The Sampson had served in the Atlantic and patrolled near the Panama Canal Zone since the start of the war and was deployed to the Southwest Pacific in 1943. She escorted troop convoys throughout the area. Upon joining the 7th Fleet at Cape Sudest, New Guinea, she became the flagship of Task Force 77 for the upcoming raid on the island of Biak. SM3c Varga had just come aboard, and they set off for Biak. They began the attack with naval bombardment of the island on May 27. That afternoon, the Sampson was engaged in a stressful attack by four Japanese aircraft but survived intact after downing two of them. After returning to New Guinea at Cape Sudest, SM3c Varga was transferred back to the 7th Amphibious Command on June 1, 1944. He was eventually promoted to the rank of Signalman 2nd Class (SM2c).

By September, John Varga was suffering severe psychological stress and was admitted to the US Naval Base Hospital at Milne Bay, New Guinea. On October 4, 1944, he was transferred via the British troop transport ship HMS Glenearn to the ship Special Medical Unit LST-464 for further treatment.

However, 20-yr-old John Varga took his own life on November 10, 1944. He was buried at sea at 1015 hrs the next day with full military honors. His family was informed of his loss weeks later.

John Edward Varga, Remembered

The name of SM2c John Edward Varga is memorialized on the Courts of the Missing in the National Memorial Cemetery of the Pacific in Honolulu, Hawaii.

On the third anniversary of his loss, the local newspaper published a memoriam to him from the Varga family:

"In loving memory of our dear son and brother, S2c John E. Varga, who was buried at sea three years ago today, November 10, 1944:
He little thought when leaving home,
He would no more return,
That he in death so soon would sleep,
And leave us here to mourn.
We do not know what pain he bore,
We did not see him die,
We only know he passed away,
And never said goodbye,
But God is good; he gave us strength
To bear our heavy cross;
He is the only one who knows
How bitter is our loss".

★ ★ ★

SECOND CLASS SIGNALMAN JOHN EDWARD VARGA, 20, of 920 Leeds avenue, for whom a memorial requiem solemn high Mass will be sung tomorrow morning at 9 o'clock in the Holy Name Church. The pastor, Father John Liska, will officiate assisted by Father Nunzio Pirulli, of St. Gajetan's Church, and Father Valentine Sedlak of the Sts. Cyril and Methodius Church, Charleroi. Signalman Varga met his death in the Southwest Pacific area on Nov. 10 and was buried at sea with full military honors.

Monessen Daily Independent, December 5, 1944

CPL CYRIL M. LISCIK

Service Number 33278028
603rd Tank Destroyer Battalion, 6th Armored Division, US Army
Killed in action, France, November 12, 1944

The characteristics that made battle tanks effective all-purpose offensive weapons during WWII had the unintended consequence of reducing the effectiveness against other tanks.

Battle tanks were often thickly armored, heavily constructed, and equipped with a general purpose main gun and ammunition to attack enemy troop emplacements and structures. The US Army realized that they needed a weapon that could out-match battle tanks: a faster, lighter-weight armored vehicle equipped with armor-piercing gun and ammunition: the Tank Destroyer.

Monessen's Cyril Liscik trained as a tank gunner and was assigned to become a "Tank Hunter". It would prove to be a dangerous job indeed.

Monongahela Valley Labor News,
April 6, 1945

The Liscik Family

Cyril M. Liscik was born on July 27, 1921, to Michael and Mary (née Cekovska) Liscik in Monessen, Pennsylvania. Michael and Mary had married in about 1901. Michael was a laborer at Pittsburgh Steel while Mary managed the Liscik family household.

Michael, whose native given name was Majk, was born in the village of Varahely in a region of Slovakia within the Austro-Hungarian Empire. He immigrated to the United States in 1901 at the age of 19 aboard the SS Zeplim from Bremen Germany to Baltimore Maryland, settling in Braddock, Pennsylvania. Mary was born in the village of Laskovce, also within Slovakia under Austro-Hungarian rule. She also immigrated to the US in 1901 at the age of 20. Her surname was spelled several different ways in public records, including Ceskovsky, Cejkovsky, and Seykoski.

Cyril was the tenth of eleven children born to Michael and Mary. The eldest brother Michael John arrived in 1903, followed by John (1905), twins Andrew Joseph and Mary (1907), Paul Carl (1908), George Andrew (1911), Stephen Emil (1915), Ann Elizabeth (1917), Joe (1920), and Emil Frances (1923). Sons Michael, John, and George were born in Braddock, Andrew and Mary were born in Austria-Hungary, and the rest of the children were born in Monessen. The records are unclear regarding Andrew and Mary's birthplace of Austria-Hungary at the time when Michael and Mary were residing in Pennsylvania. Joe died as an infant.

In 1920 the family was living in their own house at 620 Ninth Street in Monessen. By 1930, the family had sold their home and moved to a rented home at 1305 Patton Avenue in Monessen. Mike, John, Andrew, George, and Paul were all working as laborers at the local factories of Pittsburgh Steel, Page Steel and Wire, and American Tin Plate. Ten years later, the family had purchased their home on Patton Avenue, and John, Mary, Paul, and Steven had moved out to start their own independent lives. Cyril was in his last year of schooling at Monessen Vocational High where he played and lettered in football. He graduated in 1940 and was hired by Pittsburgh Steel.

The surprise attack by Japanese armed forces on the US military base at Pearl Harbor, Hawaii, in December 1941 changed the world for Cyril and his brothers. On February 16, 1942, Cyril registered for the first US armed forces draft as a 5'11" 168 lb 20-yr-old with black hair and brown eyes.

Cyril was drafted four months later, in June 1942. He reported to Greensburg, Pennsylvania where he enlisted in the US Army on June 30th and reported for duty on July 14th. The draft would eventually ensnare Cyril's brothers Michael and George in 1942, Andy and Emil in 1943, and Steven in 1945, all into the US Army. By war's end, the Lisciks would have the unsettling distinction of being a six-blue-star family. Unfortunately, one of their sons would not return home.

Private Cyril Liscik was off to US Army training camp. He was soon designated to train as a gunner in armored vehicles and was assigned to the 603rd Tank Destroyer (TD) Battalion. PVT Liscik trained at Fort Bragg, North Carolina, Camp Pickett, Virginia, Camp Hood, Texas, Camp Shelby, Mississippi, and Camp Maxey, Texas.

Tank Destroyers

Recognizing the threat imposed by enemy tanks to Allied troops and positions, the US Army had requisitioned the development of armored vehicles specifically designed to hunt and destroy enemy tanks. These vehicles, called Tank Destroyers, looked like tanks, used tank chassis and engines, but carried armor-piercing guns with less heavy armor. The design was intended to enable faster, more maneuverable vehicles to counter the offensive firepower of heavy tanks. The US Army created special armored units composed of Tank Destroyers and deployed these units within armored divisions.

The 603rd TD Battalion was activated in December 1941, went into training in Washington, and was issued the new M18 Hellcat Tank Destroyer in October 1943 to elevate its combat force. PVT Cyril Liscik and the 603rd arrived at Cannock, England, in April 1944 in preparation for Operation Overlord, the Allied invasion of the European continent commencing June 6, 1944.

M18 Hellcat Tank Destroyer (The Tank Museum)

The 603rd was attached to General George Patton's Third Army and the 6th Armored Division. They landed at Utah Beach, Normandy, France on July 21-22, and entered battle on July 28 as part of Operation Cobra for the Allied breakout from Normandy. The battalion advanced through Brittany to Brest and then Lorient in August when PVT Liscik was admitted to the Army hospital for an undefined reason. He soon resumed his duties as the 603rd raced east to the Moselle River sector in September. They fought east of Nancy, France, in October and supported the push to the Saar River in November. Along the way, Cyril Liscik was promoted to the rank of Corporal.

But CPL Liscik's luck soon ran out. According to the unit history of the 603rd TD Battalion:

During the month of November, the Sixth Armored Division saw its hardest fighting to date. The Division battered its way across the Seille River, the Nied Francaise, and up to the Saar River. Tanks, AT {Anti-Tank} guns, minefields, AT ditches, heavy artillery, large mortar concentrations, and the rainiest season in 29 years were used to maximum advantage in the enemy's strong delaying action.

On November 12, 1944, CPL Cyril Liscik met his fate. He was killed in action when an artillery shell struck near his position, inflicting mortal wounds to his torso. His parents were informed by the War Department of his death three weeks later. A week prior, the family had received word that the brother-in-law of their son George had lost his life in the Southwest Pacific: SM2c John Edward Varga.

CPL Cyril Liscik was buried at the Lorraine American Cemetery in St. Avold, France, and was posthumously awarded the Purple Heart.

★ ★ ★

ENS ELMER A. HARKEMA

Service Number 414103
US Navy
Killed in training, Off coast of Florida, November 27, 1944

Elmer Albert Harkema was born on January 1, 1923, in Munster, Indiana, to Joseph G. and Sybrigje "Sadie" (née Jongsma) Harkema. Joseph and Sadie had married ten years earlier in 1913. Joseph was working in an auto shop while Sadie managed the Harkema family household.

The Harkema Family

Joseph was born Johannes Gerardus Harkema in Utrecht, (Holland) Netherlands, and immigrated to the United States in 1909 aboard the SS Noordam. Sadie was born in Sloten, (Holland) Netherlands and immigrated with her family to the US in 1907 aboard the SS Noordam. Joseph became a naturalized US citizen in 1918.

Elmer was the last of six children born to Joseph and Sadie. His oldest sister Marie Agnes arrived in 1914, followed by William (1916), Catherine "Kay" (1918), Emma (1920), and Pearson (1920). Emma passed away as a young child. Marie and William were born in Illinois, while the rest of the children were born in Munster, Indiana. In 1929, Sadie's father died, and her mother remarried to Klaas Jacob "Nicholas" Bouwhuis, also from the Netherlands, later that year.

By 1930, the family had moved into a rented home on East Fifth Street in Beardstown, Illinois, where their father had taken a job as an air brake mechanic for the steam railroad. Sadie's mother and step-father had moved to Monessen, Pennsylvania, for work, where Nicholas had been hired in the local steel mill. Between 1935 and 1940, Sadie and Joseph divorced, and Sadie, Marie, and Elmer moved from Beardstown to Monessen. By that time, Catherine had married, Pearson had stayed behind to work and moved in with his father, and William had moved to Chicago, Illinois. In 1937, Sadie's mother passed away, and Sadie married Nicholas Bouwhuis. Elmer was active in the US Boy Scouts and was promoted to First Class Scout in 1938.

By 1940, Elmer was living in Monessen with his mother, his step-father Nicholas, and his sister Marie at their rented home on 938 Knox Avenue. Elmer's brother Pearson moved to Monessen to be with his family. Elmer was attending Monessen High School and was enrolled in the vocational curriculum. Elmer was on the Vocational Student Council and Patrol and was on the staff of the Monessen High Greyhound Yearbook. His brother Pearson had enlisted in September 1940 with the US Navy and was stationed aboard the battleship USS Oklahoma that year.

The surprise attack by Japanese armed forces on the US military bases at Pearl Harbor, Hawaii, in December 1941 changed the world for millions of Americans, as it did for Elmer and his brothers. Seaman Pearson Harkema was aboard the USS Oklahoma when it was attacked on December 7, jumped into the water and swam to safety although 429 fellow crewmen lost their lives.

After graduating from Monessen Vocational High School in 1942, Elmer went to work for the Page Steel and Wire Company at their factory in Monessen. Elmer registered for the US armed forces draft on June 30, 1942, in Monessen. He was a 5'10", 162 lb 19-yr-old single man with black hair and gray eyes. Elmer was living with his parents, who had recently moved to a home at 521 Donner Avenue in Monessen.

Harkema Heads to Naval Flight Training

Elmer had his eyes set skyward and applied for flight training with the US Navy. He was accepted into the Naval Aviation Cadet program and enlisted on September 22, 1942. He was off to training. His brother William had already enlisted in June 1941 and was with the US Army Air Corps. With two sons in the US Navy and a son in the US Army Air Corps, the Harkema's were now a 3-Blue-Star family.

Cadet Elmer Harkema completed his flight training at the Naval Air Training Center in Pensacola, Florida, and was promoted to Ensign on September 26, 1944. ENS Harkema went on to advanced fighter training at the Naval Air Station Daytona Beach, Florida.

While flying the US Navy's new, advanced Grumman F6F Hellcat fighter during a routine gunnery exercise off the coast on November 27, 1944, ENS Harkema encountered difficulties of an unknown origin, and his Hellcat fell into the sea. The time of death is recorded at 3:28 PM. Although a rescue crew arrived at the presumed site of the crash 25 miles off the coast, neither ENS Harkema nor the wreckage could be found. The only evidence of the crash was a wheel from the landing gear floating on the ocean.

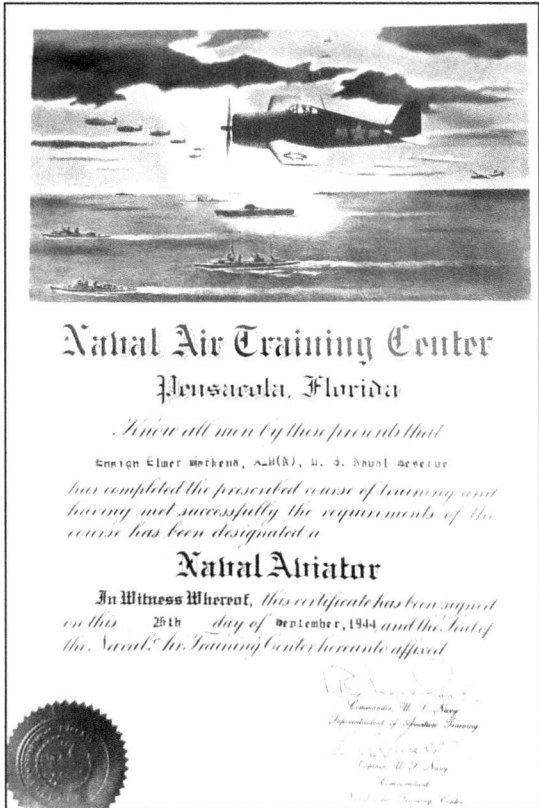

Harkema's Naval Aviator Certificate, Harkema Family

On December 3, 1944, a memorial service for ENS Harkema was held at the Station Chapel. His squadron mates attended the service seated together. The station officers and men presented a memorial wreath on behalf of ENS

Letter from Chaplain, Harkema Family

Harkema. On December 6, the station chaplain boarded a Navy plane with the wreath, flew to the site of the crash, and dropped the wreath into the ocean at precisely 12 noon. His squadron mates followed the chaplain, each in their own aircraft and circled the crash site in tribute to their fallen comrade.

From the prayer read at the chapel memorial service: "Thou, O God, know not the resting place of the body, for which we have searched in vain, and will keep it in vain until the day of resurrection."

His brother Pearson remarked at the 2010 Memorial Day Service in Memorial Park, Monessen, "I always remember him saying, 'I want to be in a plane where I'm by myself, so that if something happens, I'm not responsible for someone else's death.' He got his wish."

The author is grateful to Elmer Harkema, the nephew of Ensign Elmer Harkema, for the additional information and photos contained in this memorial story.

★ ★ ★

PFC WALTER ZAJACZKOWSKI

Service Number 33702968
Company F, 38th Infantry Regiment, 2nd Infantry Division, US Army
Died of combat wounds, Germany, December 16, 1944

Walter Zajaczkowski was Monessen's first combat infantryman to lose his life on the soil of the enemy's homeland.

Zajaczkowski landed at Normandy, France, on D-Day plus 1 (June 7, 1944) and fought across France and Belgium before advancing into Germany in October.

After being wounded in battle near Dreiborn, Germany, he would not live to see the year 1945.

The Zajaczkowski Family

Walter Zajaczkowski was born on December 22, 1908, to Martin and Lara (née Pavlovski) Zajaczkowski in Pittsburgh, Pennsylvania. Martin was a laborer in a tin mill in Monessen, Pennsylvania while Lara managed the Zajaczkowski family household.

Martin, born in Poland, immigrated to the United States in 1902. Lara, born Vladislava in Poland, immigrated to the US in 1900. Walter, originally named Vladislav, was the first child born to the couple. He was followed by Andrew Henry (1912), Stephen Anthony (1915), and Stanley Martin (1922). Family members altered their surname in public records over time, as Zajai, Zackowski, and Zajac.

By 1920, the family was living in a 3-family rented house at 266 Linden Avenue in Monessen. During the 1920's, their mother Lara passed away. Martin and the boys moved into a 6-family rented house at 241 Reed Avenue in Monessen. Walter left school after completing the eighth grade. In January 1930, their father Martin also died, leaving 21-yr-old Walter as the head of the household.

Walter met Mary Luczkowski from Cleveland, Ohio, and they married there on November 23, 1939. The couple settled in Monessen where Walter was working as a weighman at Pittsburgh Steel. They moved into a home at 709 Rostraver Street in Monessen. Walter also served as Vice President of the Monessen Polish National Alliance society.

With the rumblings of war heard in Europe and the Pacific, the US Congress passed the Selective Service and Training Act in September 1940, including the first peacetime draft for the US military. On October 16, 1940, Walter joined millions of fellow American men and registered for the draft on its first day. According to his draft registration, Walter was a 31-yr-old young man standing 5' 7", 173 lb, with brown hair and gray eyes.

The US Enters WWII

Japanese forces launched a surprise attack on the US military bases in Pearl Harbor, Hawaii, on December 7, 1941. The US declared war on Japan, and as an ally of the Japanese Empire, Germany declared war on the US.

Mary gave birth to a son, Robert, on October 22, 1942, and they moved into another Monessen home at 209 Knox Avenue. But war was about to interrupt the young family. Walter was drafted into the US Army on August 23, 1943, in Greensburg, Pennsylvania. He left for training on September 18.

Private Walter Zajaczkowski trained stateside until March 30, 1944, when he was shipped overseas into the European theater of the war. He was assigned to the 38th Infantry Regiment of the 2nd Infantry "Indianhead" Division and was placed in Company F. The 38th Infantry Regiment was known as the "Rock of the Marne" for its efforts during WWI along the Marne River, France.

During his time in service, Mary and their son Robert moved to Cleveland, Ohio to be near her mother.

PVT Zajaczkowski off to Europe

The 2nd Division was training in Northern Ireland and Wales when PVT Zajaczkowski arrived. The Division had landed in the United Kingdom in October 1943, and was training for the planned Operation Overlord, the Allied invasion of the German-occupied continent of Europe. PVT Zajaczkowski joined the Division just in time to participate in their landing at Normandy, France on D-Day plus 1, June 7, 1944.

The Division fought in the Normandy Campaign through the end of July, fighting westward across the Brittany Peninsula and ending with their support of the Battle of Brest, France. They advanced across Northern France through September of 1944. The Division began the campaign across Belgium and into Germany, with its first unit crossing the German border on October 4th. The fighting was fierce along the way. While on the campaign, Walter Zajaczkowski was promoted to the Private First Class (PFC).

On December 11, 1944, the 2nd Division was ordered to attack and seize the Roer River dams, if possible, or to force the enemy to blow the dams and eliminate the threat of the floodwaters, stopping the Allies from crossing the river. In the midst of a driving snowstorm, the Division started north to attack a German defensive stronghold at Wehlerscheid in the Monschau Forest. On December 13, the Wehlerscheid Offensive began. The Offensive became known as the Battle of Heartbreak Crossroads. It would be a savage, costly four-day battle in freezing weather.

On the morning of December 16, the 38th Infantry Regiment attacked towards its objective, Dreiborn, Germany. PFC Zajaczkowski and the 38th pushed against 1,500 yards of stubborn German resistance. But he would not see the end of the day unscathed.

During combat on December 16, PFC Walter Zajaczkowski was struck by a bullet in the forehead. He survived the initial wound, but it was a serious wound indeed. He was immediately transported from the front lines to the rear and to the 67th Evacuation Hospital.

But that day, PFC Zajaczkowski lost the battle for his life. Walter Zajaczkowski would never again see his wife and son.

Walter Zajaczkowski, Remembered

PFC Walter Zajaczkowski was buried in the Henri-Chapelle American Cemetery and Memorial, Henri-Chapelle, Arrondissement de Verviers, Liège, Belgium. PFC Zajaczkowski was posthumously awarded the Purple Heart.

☆ ☆ ☆

S/SGT GEORGE T. STANISH

Service Number 33393939
Company B, 27th Armored Infantry Battalion, 9th Armored Division, US Army
Killed in action, Germany, December 17, 1944

On December 17, 1944, S/SGT George Stanish and his unit were on the border between Belgium and Germany. They probably did not know that they were about to face the initial onslaught of a major surprise German engagement, the "Ardennes Offensive".

The bloody confrontation would become known as the Battle of the Bulge and called "the greatest American battle of the war" by Great Britain's wartime Prime Minister Winston Churchill.

Sadly, Monessen's George Stanish would not live to see the end of the day.

The Stanish Family

George Thomas Stanish was born on March 21, 1914, to Thomas George and Dora (née Sostar) Stanish in Monessen, Pennsylvania. Thomas was a wire drawer at Pittsburgh Steel Company while Dora managed the Stanish family household.

Thomas was born in Gornji Oštrc, Zagreb, Croatia, with the surname of Stanišić, and immigrated to the United States in 1895. Thomas and Dora had married in 1895 in Croatia prior to coming to the United States. Dora, also from Gornji Oštrc, arrived in the US in 1901.

George was the eighth of nine children born to Thomas and Dora. First to arrive was Michael (b1903), followed by Mary (1904), Charles (1905), Barbara (1907), Rose (1908), Mildred (Milka, 1909), Anna (1912), and Helen (1920). In 1910, the family lived in a rented home at 1003 Highland Avenue in Monessen. By 1920, they purchased a home in Monessen at the corner of Sixth and Chestnut Streets, and later, moved to a home at Ninth and Chestnut.

George played junior baseball with the local Yannigans' team, and he graduated from Monessen High School in the mid 1930's. By the late 1930's he was working as a steel rod trimmer at Pittsburgh Steel.

On October 20, 1939, while driving his Plymouth automobile into Monessen, George hit a pedestrian who had stepped out from between two parked cars. George put the man into his car and transported him to the hospital, where he recovered quickly, much to George's relief.

By 1940, the Stanish daughters married and moved from home to begin their own families. Mike, Charles, and George were young adults and worked with their father at Pittsburgh Steel.

The Rumblings of War

October 16, 1940, was the first day of the US armed forces draft under the newly passed Selective Service and Training Act. George joined millions of other young men that day and registered for the draft. He registered as a 5' 11" 150 lb 26-yr-old with brown hair and brown eyes. George also had a large scar on his right leg.

On December 7, 1941, the US entered the war against the Axis nations when Japanese forces attacked the US military bases at Pearl Harbor, Hawaii. It was only a matter of time before George and his friends in Monessen would get the call to serve their country.

The call came by way of a draft notice on October 30, 1942, and on November 14, 1942, George enlisted in nearby Greensburg, Pennsylvania, in the US Army. He was immediately off to Army boot camp.

Private George Stanish was eventually assigned to train as an armored infantryman and was placed with Company B of the 27th Armored Infantry Battalion (AIB). Company B of the 27th AIB had been formed from Company E of the 52nd Infantry of the Regular Army, known as Ready Rifles, which had been assigned to the 9th Armored Division in 1942 in Fort Riley, Kansas.

The 9th Armored Division

The 9th Armored Division trained at Camp Polk, Louisiana, for much of 1943, and drilled at various locations in Louisiana. At the start of 1944, they began preparations for overseas deployment. They were soon equipped with the M4A3 Sherman Tank, the newest model of what would become the ubiquitous US Army armored vehicle of the war.

On June 6, 1944, Operation Overlord, the Allied invasion of the European continent, began with D-Day. The men of the 9th knew that the door was being opened for their entry into the war.

In August 1944, the Division moved by rail to Camp Kilmer, New Jersey, their staging area for shipping out. Almost 11,000 men and their equipment and supplies were about to board ships for their journey across the Atlantic. They departed at the end of August and arrived at their receiving camps in England days later. The Division and George Stanish began final preparations for landing in France.

In October, the 9th boarded ships and sailed to the Cherbourg peninsula in Normandy, now fully under Allied control. The Allies had pushed the German east out of most of France and by November had moved into the German defensive "Siegfried Line". Hitler was not going to allow their penetration across the border of Germany and had planned a major offensive. The offensive and ensuing engagement would become known as the "Battle of the Bulge".

By November 1944, George Stanish had been promoted to the rank of Staff Sergeant (S/SGT).

The Battle of the Bulge Begins

The US Army had reformed its order of battle, and the 27th AIB was now in Combat Command B (CCB) of the 9th Armored Division along with other armored and regular infantry battalions. CCB was stationed in the area northeast of the Belgian town of Bastogne and was preparing an offensive march eastward to the river dams to prevent Germans from opening the dams and flooding the areas to be taken by US ground forces. After all US troops were deployed by the evening of December 15, nearly 70,000 men were stretched across an 88-mile-long front. Little did they realize that Hitler had moved 200,000 troops with their tanks and guns to their front. He was to unleash his largest western offensive of the war.

The Germans began the offensive with a massive cannonade against US troop positions on December 16. Failing to appreciate the scale of the attack, US commanders were slow to respond.

S/SGT Stanish and Company B of the 27th AIB were positioned on a line between Ambleve and Bullingen, Belgium. On the night of the 17th, the 27th was ordered to pull back and redeploy toward the town of St. Vith. They were then ordered to reconnoiter 4,000 yards south past Elcherath, Germany. The 27th, spearheading the column of CCB forces, sent Company A and C clear the hills around the town, while Company B continued along the main road.

There at Elcherath, they ran headfirst into the enemy. At the tip of the spear, S/SGT Stanish and Company B felt the full impact of the enemy encounter.

On December 17, 1944, the 30-yr old S/SGT George Stanish took his last breath when he received a fatal wound to his head and neck. He lost his life near Elcherath during combat on the second day of the Battle of the Bulge.

George Stanish, Remembered

His family was informed that their son was missing in action on January 23, 1945. Two months later in early March, they were informed that George had, in fact, been killed in action on December 17, 1944.

S/SGT George T. Stanish was initially buried at the US Military Cemetery in Foy, Belgium. He was eventually reinterred at the Henri-Chapelle American Cemetery and Memorial at the Arrondissement de Verviers, Liège, Belgium, with 7,986 of his fellow American service members. He was posthumously awarded the Purple Heart.

On the one year anniversary of his loss, the Monessen Daily Independent published an In Memorium from his family:

> *" 'Twas just one year ago today,*
> *Our hearts were made to weep*
> *When our loved one passed away*
> *Into that quiet sleep,*
> *Beautiful memories of you so dear,*
> *We cherish still with lover sincere,*
> *A day that comes with sad regret*
> *And one that we will never forget".*

★ ★ ★

PFC STEPHEN MALINCHAK

**Service Number 33705393
310th Infantry Regiment, 78th Infantry Division, US Army
Killed in action, Germany, December 21, 1944**

S tephen "Steve" Malinchak was born on October 5, 1925, to Martin and Anna (née Onvfrock) Malinchak in Monessen, Pennsylvania. Martin and Anna had married in 1906 in Susquehanna, Pennsylvania. Martin worked at the tin mill in Monessen while Anna managed the Malinchak family household.

The Malinchak Family

Martin immigrated from Poland to the United States in 1900 and initially settled in the town of Throop, Pennsylvania, where he worked as a coal miner. Anna was born in a village located in what was the Austro-Hungarian Empire, and she immigrated to the US in 1905. The couple lived in Throop and began raising their young family before moving to western Pennsylvania in 1920.

Steve was the last of seven children born to Martin and Anna. Michael, the oldest child, was born in 1907 in Throop. He was followed by Mary (b1909), Anna (1914), Helen (1916), Veronica "Vera" (1919), all born in Throop. John Paul (1921) and Steve were born in Monessen after the family relocated.

There was great demand by the heavy industrial factories of Monessen for employees that attracted immigrants from Eastern Europe. There were other Malinchak families in Monessen who may have been Martin's family members. With a burgeoning family, Martin and Anna were motivated to seek a better life outside of coal-mining country.

By 1930, the family was living in a rented home at 1014 Rostraver Street in Monessen. The oldest son Michael was now working as a crane operator at the tin mill with his father while the other children attended school.

In 1934, Martin passed away from respiratory and heart disease at the age of 53. The following year, the family moved to another rented home at 3 Aliquippa Avenue in Monessen. By 1940, Michael, Mary, and Anna had moved out to begin their own lives as adults. The following year, a cardiac arrest took Michael's life.

The surprise attack by Japanese armed forces on the US military base at Pearl Harbor, Hawaii, in December 1941 changed the world for Steve and his brother John. John was drafted into the US Army in December 1942.

On Steve's 18th birthday, October 5, 1943, he registered for the first US armed forces draft as a 6' 158 lb young man with brown hair and brown eyes. Nearly three months later Steve was drafted into the US Army, and he enlisted in Greensburg, Pennsylvania on December 30, 1943. Before departing for training, their mother Anna died of influenza and pneumonia on January 4, 1944, at the age of 56 years.

Malinchak Reports for Duty

Private Steve Malinchak reported for training on January 27, 1944, in Greensburg. He entered the service before completing his senior year of high school but would be awarded his diploma in absentia while away at infantry training. PVT Malinchak was assigned to the 310th Infantry Regiment.

The 310th Infantry had fought in WWI and was reactivated for WWII in August 1942. Attached to the 78th Infantry Division, it would initially serve as a replacement pool for overseas units. PVT Malinchak joined the 310th Regiment in Tennessee for the "Tennessee Maneuvers", then on to Camp Pickett, Virginia, in April. While at Camp Pickett, PVT Malinchak contracted cellulitis of the foot but recovered in an Army hospital during May.

In October 1944, PVT Malinchak and the 78th Division moved to Camp Kilmer, New Jersey, for staging ahead of overseas deployment. The Division departed the states and arrived in England later that month. After further training they deployed to France in November. The 78th entered combat in early December 1944 as US forces crossed into Germany. By then, PVT Steve Malinchak had been promoted to Private First Class (PFC).

In mid-December, the green troops of the 310th Regiment smashed into Simmerath, Witzerath, and Bickerath, Germany and were fighting in the bloody Battle for Kesternich when the Germans launched a counteroffensive in the Monschau area on December 18. The 78th Infantry Division lost over 1,500 dead, wounded, and missing in the engagement. PFC Malinchak had survived, but his luck would not hold out.

On December 21, 1944, the 310th Regiment was holding a 3,000-yard line which ran from a dam 600 yards north of Rollesbroich, Germany, through Rollesbroich to a point just north of Simmerath, Germany. PFC Steve Malinchak was driving a jeep when an enemy artillery shell exploded nearby. He was struck by shrapnel and mortally wounded. He died that day.

On January 4, 1945, exactly one year after the death of their mother, Stephen's siblings were informed that he had been killed in action in Germany.

PFC Stephen Malinchak was first buried in Europe. In November 1947, his remains were returned to the US aboard the transport ship Robert Burns under the Return of the War Dead program. He was the first Monessen war dead to be returned to the city, and the mayor ordered all flags to be flown at half-staff on the day of his church service. He was laid to rest at Saint Mary's Byzantine Catholic Cemetery in Monessen next to his father and mother.

✶ ✶ ✶

S/SGT WALLACE MARCINKIEWICZ

Service Number 33167736
Company A, 10th Armored Infantry Battalion, 4th Armored Division, US Army
Killed in action, Belgium, December 23, 1944

Company A of the 10th Armored Infantry Battalion was outgunned, out-numbered, and under attack by the advancing German troops. As they pulled back, Sergeant Wallace Marcinkiewicz set up his machine gun and fired desperately at the enemy to cover the withdrawal of his men.

A determined German bazooka team trained their weapon on Marcinkiewicz. In a flash, he was gone.

The Marcinkiewicz Family

Wallace Marcinkiewicz was born on July 16, 1914, to Peter and Tekla "Tillie" (née Urbanowicz) Marcinkiewicz in East Charleroi, Pennsylvania. Peter and Tillie had married in about 1908. Peter was a coal miner while Tillie managed the Marcinkiewicz family household.

Peter was born in Poland and immigrated to the United States in 1906. Tillie was also born in Poland and came to the US in 1904.

Wallace was given a traditional Polish name when he was born, Waclav. His name also appeared in public records as another Polish first name, Wetzel. He was the third of four children born to Peter and Tille. Alfred was first to arrive (b1909) who would later go by Albert. Frank was born in 1910, and their sister Apolonia Sofia "Pearl" arrived in 1919.

In 1920, the family was living in their own home on Essen Road in the LaGrange area of Rostraver Township, Pennsylvania. By 1935, the family purchased and moved into a home at 216 Coolidge Avenue in Monessen, but Peter was now unable to work. In 1940, the children, now ages 20-30 yrs, had all left formal schooling after the seventh grade and were living at home with their parents. Albert and Wallace were working to support the family. Wallace was a welder in the Pittsburgh Steel mill in Monessen.

On October 16, 1940, Wallace and his brothers joined millions of other American men and registered for the US armed forces draft on its first day after the passage of the US Selective Service Act. Wallace registered as a 6'2" 183 lb 26-yr-old with brown hair and gray eyes.

The surprise attack by Japanese armed forces on the US military base at Pearl Harbor, Hawaii, in December 1941 changed the world for Wallace and his brothers. He was drafted into the US Army and entered service on March 28, 1942. Frank was drafted into the Army four months later, and Albert was drafted in December that year. The Marcinkiewicz were now a three-blue-star family.

Marcinkiewicz Heads to Europe

Private Wallace Marcinkiewicz trained stateside at Fort Knox, Kentucky, and Pine Camp, New York, and participated in maneuvers in California through the rest of 1942 and most of 1943. He was recognized for his technical skills, assigned to train in armored tanks, and was promoted to Sergeant and then Staff Sergeant (S/SGT). S/SGT Wallace Marcinkiewicz shipped overseas

Sherman Tank of the 4th Armored Division (National Archives)

on November 22, 1943, and was eventually attached to Company A of the 10th Armored Infantry Battalion, 4th Armored Division.

The 4th Armored Division landed at Utah Beach on July 13, 1944, a month after the D-Day invasion on June 6, 1944, at the French Normandy coast. The 4th Armored Division spearheaded General George Patton's 3rd Army as it chased German forces eastward across France. In December 1944, the 4th Armored Division had crossed into Belgium and entered the fray against the German Ardennes Offensive, which became known as the Battle of the Bulge. S/SGT Marcinkiewicz was undoubtedly seeing his share of combat. Unfortunately, his luck would soon run out.

On December 23, 1944, the Germans attacked the American line at Chaumont, Belgium. The Sherman tanks of the 4th Division were sitting ducks against the larger, more powerful tanks of the German attackers. According to one written record, Patton's Vanguard:

"Company A of the 10th AIB was catching a hell. They were outgunned and outnumbered, and knew they had to get out. In a desperate effort to leave no one behind, many men risked their lives to pull out the wounded... Acts of

courage became epidemic as the Americans struggled to find a safe way out of the town. Staff Sergeant Wallace Marcinkierwicz [sp] *set up his light .30 caliber machine gun in a position that would cover A/10's withdrawal. His machine gun chattered away at the approaching Germans, until a round from a panzerfaust* [German bazooka] *killed him at his position."*

S/SGT Wallace Marcinkiewicz was reported missing in action on December 23, 1944, but four days later was determined as having been killed in action. A month later, his family was informed by the War Department of his death in combat in Belgium.

S/SGT Wallace Marcinkiewicz was initially buried in Europe. His remains were eventually brought back to the US under the Return of the War Dead program and laid to rest at St. Hyacinth Cemetery in Monessen.

★ ★ ★

PVT NICHOLAS BECK

Service Number 33427536
1403rd Anti-Aircraft Artillery Battalion, Coast Artillery Corps, US Army
Died of wounds, France, December 24, 1944

Nicholas Beck was born on January 7, 1923, to Jack and Roza "Rose" (née Ribic) Beck in Monessen, Pennsylvania. Jack and Rose married 12 years earlier in 1911 in Rankin, Pennsylvania. Jack was a machine operator for a fence manufacturer while Rose managed the Beck family household.

The Beck Family

Jack, born Yocob Beg in Selo Begovo, Brdo, Croatia, had immigrated to the United States in December 1905 aboard the SS La Bretagne, and became a naturalized citizen in 1936. Rose was also born in Begovo and had immigrated to the United States in 1911 aboard the SS Kronprinz Wilhelm.

Nicholas, known as Nick, was the seventh of nine children born to Jack and Rose. Drozo "Charles" was first (b1912), followed by Robert (1914), Matthew (1916), Helen Rose (1917), Jack Thomas (1919), and John (1921). Vilma

(1924) and Emil (1928) completed the family. After Charles' birth, Jack and Rose moved to Monessen where Jack had taken a job as a fence maker in the local steel mill. They would bear their remaining children in Monessen where they would attend school and grow to adulthood. In 1930, the family was living in a rented home at 1212 Maple Avenue. By 1940, they would move two blocks away to another rented home at 1115 Reservoir Avenue.

Nick grew into a stout teenager who loved to play sports. He was on the Monessen High School football team during all three years where he played halfback and was known as "one of the hardest drivers in the backfield". He also occasionally stepped in as quarterback and kicker. Nick was named to the Monongahela Valley Big Five Conference football team and the All-Westmoreland County team his senior year. Nick was also on the school's wrestling team but had other interests besides athletics as he was on the Glee Club and was President of his homeroom.

The surprise attack by Japanese forces upon the US military bases at Pearl Harbor, Hawaii on December 7, 1941, would intervene in the lives of millions of American youth. Nick's brothers Matthew, Jack, and John would soon enter service in the US armed forces. On June 30, 1942, Nick registered for the US armed forces draft as a 5' 11" 175 lb single 19-yr-old with brown hair and blue eyes. After his high school graduation in 1942, Nick went to work as a laborer at the Pittsburgh Steel Company mill in Monessen. But he had applied to Case Western Reserve University in Cleveland, Ohio, and was accepted and enrolled as a pre-medical student. During his first year there, he made the varsity football team.

On January 23, 1943, Nick was drafted into the US Army, and he formally enlisted in Greensburg, Pennsylvania. He was off to boot camp at Fort George Meade, Maryland on February 5, 1943, as a Private. Along with six other boys from Monessen, he entered further training at the Medical Replacement Training Center at Camp Pickett, Virginia. Upon graduating, he was promoted to medical specialist Technician Fifth Grade (T/5) to be an unarmed battlefield soldier assigned to field hospitals. The T/5 grade was equivalent to the rank of

Corporal, and T/5 specialists were addressed as Corporal. The Beck's were now a four-Blue-Star family.

T/5 Nick Beck was sent overseas to Europe on April 20, 1944, and was eventually assigned to the 1403rd Anti-Aircraft Artillery Battalion of the Coastal Artillery. On August 22, 1944, his rank was reduced to Private (PVT) for unknown reasons. (Subsequent records and news articles continued to erroneously report his rank as T/5).

While in the field in December 1944, he received a non-combat gunshot wound to his upper chest that penetrated his cervical spinal cord. He was transferred to the US Army's 48th General Hospital in Paris, France, where he died on December 24, 1944, at the age of 21.

The Beck family were informed of Nick's death in January 1945. His Blue star had turned Gold. Nick's three brothers would survive the war and return home from their military service.

Tributes to Nick Beck were later made during local school sporting events, honoring his life and his service. Nicholas Beck was initially buried at the US Military Cemetery in Solers, France. He was brought to the US under the Return of the Dead program transported by the ship USAT Carroll Victory and was interred at the Grandview Cemetery in Monessen on November 17, 1948. His brother Matthew would later be buried by his side in 1998.

On the one year anniversary of his loss, the Monessen Daily Independent published an In Memorium from his family:

"He has gone across the river
To the shores of ever green
How we'd love to see his smiling face
But the rivers flow between
And out aching hearts are calling
To the shadows dark and grey
For the dear one that has left us
One year ago today".

Nick Beck, Popular High School Gridder Killed in Action

One of the most popular athletes to have ever represented the Monessen High School on the gridiron, T/5 Nick Beck, 21, paid the supreme sacrifice while in the service of his country. He was killed in action in France on December 22.

The accompanying picture was sent to his parents, Mr. and Mrs. Jack Beck, Summit avenue, by a Scottish War Correspondent, Walker Tomkins. Mr. Tomkins said that he had taken the picture to use with an interview while Technician Beck was in Scotland but the young soldier was sent to France before the picture was published. Technician Beck was with the Medical Corps and in this picture is shown doing laboratory work. He was in service a year and a half and overseas for nine months.

While at Monessen High school Technician Beck played on the High school football team during his sophomore, junior and senior years. In the last season he was named to both the Monongahela Valley Big Five Conference football team and the All-Westmoreland County team. After being graduated from the local high school Technician Beck attended Western Reserve in Cleveland, O., where he was a pre-medical student. During his first year at college he made the varsity football team. One of his ambitions was to attend Notre Dame University after the war ended.

Besides playing football at the local school, Technician Beck also participated in the wrestling program.

He is survived by his parents, two sisters, Velma and Helen, and seven brothers, Pvt. John, at Fort McClellan, Ala.; Sgt. Jack, at Fort Meade, Md.; Staff Sgt. Matt, at Camp Ellis, Ill.; Charles, Emil, Bob and Steve, at home.

Sergeant Jack Beck also made a name for himself in high school

T/5 Nick Beck

football and was placed on the Monongahela Valley Big Five Conference team during his senior year. Emil was on the basketball team during the past season and Bob played on the local junior high basketball and football teams.

Monessen Daily Independent,
April 12, 1945

✷✷✷

1945

"See you in Monessen after the war"

PVT Stanley "Tash" Zazac to fellow Monessenite, Sailor Mike Matush,
aboard ship in the Southwest Pacific.

PVT Zazac was killed in action in The Philippines
less than two months later.

As Allied forces knocked on the doorsteps of Germany and Japan, the fighting by enemy forces became more fierce in defense of their homelands. Allied leaders knew that the Axis nations would not give up unless they were resoundingly defeated. The Allies committed their forces to doing just that.

In Europe, the Allies survived the costly Battle of the Bulge and pushed their forces across the German borders to the river Rhine against stiff resistance. Battles along the way, like the Colmar Pocket, proved costly to US forces. With troops of the Soviet Union advancing through eastern Germany upon Berlin and the troops of the US and UK closing in from the west, Adolph Hitler committed suicide in his Berlin bunker on April 30, 1945. The Third Reich finally gave in and unconditionally surrendered on May 8, 1945.

The Japanese proved to be just as committed to the defense of their territory. The battle for American repossession of the Philippine Islands continued at great cost but was ultimately successful by March. The brutal battle for the volcanic island of Iwo Jima was waged during February and March. The costliest battles of the war to both American and Japanese forces happened with the invasion of Okinawa from April through June. Japanese leaders sent suicide aircraft, or Kamikazes, to dive their explosive-laden planes

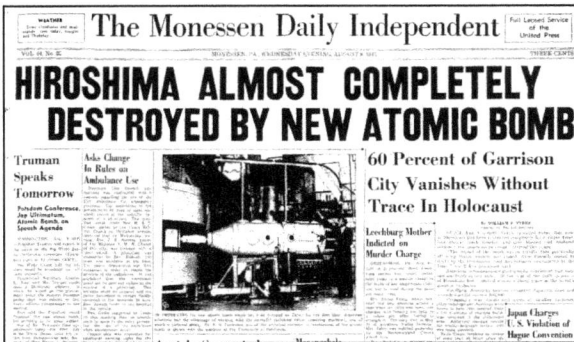

into ships of the US Navy in a desperate but unsuccessful attempt to halt the US advance.

The US Army Air Force escalated its bombing of the Japanese home islands from bases in the Mariana islands and continued the devastation. While Allied leaders planned for the ultimate amphibious invasion of the Japanese home islands, the top secret Manhattan Project put its finishing touches on the ultimate weapon, the atomic bomb. The final campaign against Japan culminated in the dropping of the atomic bombs on Hiroshima and Nagasaki in August. Japan surrendered on August 15, 1945. The war was over.

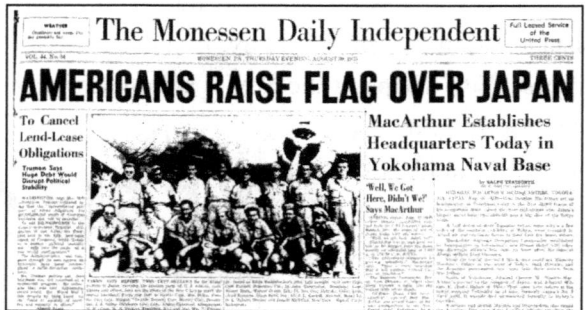

Twenty Monessen men lost their lives in the war's final combat as it wound down. The end of the war did not come soon enough for these soldiers. The last man from Monessen to lose his life during the war did not die in combat, but while on guard duty in Guam just two days before the surrender of Japan.

★ ★ ★

2LT Bernard F. Quinlan

Service Numbers O-825492 / 13133539
522nd Squadron, 27th Fighter-Bomber Group, 22nd Tactical Air Command, 12th Air Force
Killed in action, Italy, January 4, 1945

By January 1945, Monessen's LT Bernard Quinlan had already earned the US Army Air Force Air Medal, been hit by enemy flak, and completed thirty missions as a pilot of a P-47 Thunderbolt fighter. Certainly, he had earned his return ticket home from Italy's WWII battlefront.

But LT Quinlan would not live to see the end of the war. His return ticket home would never be used.

The Quinlan Family

Bernard Francis Quinlan was born on March 23, 1923, to Cyril Francis and Sara (née Monaghan) Quinlan in Monessen, Pennsylvania. Cyril and Sara had married in 1919. Cyril worked in a Monessen steel mill while Sara managed the Quinlan family household.

Monongahela Valley Labor News, April 6, 1945

The Quinlan family heritage traces back to Ireland, Northern Ireland, Germany, and France in the 1700's with ancestors who served in the American Revolutionary War. The Monaghan's were from Ireland and England, and Sara's parents immigrated to the United States in the late 1800's. Both families settled in Pennsylvania where Cyril and Sara met. Prior to marrying, Cyril served as a Private First Class with the US Army in France during WWI.

Bernard was the second of four boys born to Cyril and Sara. Firstborn was Donald Vincent (b1920). Eugene Leonard (1925) and Owen (1930) followed Bernard. In 1930, the family was living in a rented home at 941 Athalia Avenue in Monessen. In 1930, Bernard had more than his share of health issues as a seven-year-old when he was stricken with diphtheria and had a tonsillectomy and an adenoidectomy. Fortunately, he recovered and was on his way towards becoming a successful teenager.

By 1940, the family had moved to a home at 961 Donner Avenue. At Monessen High School, Bernard was in the school orchestra where he served as its secretary. He was a gifted orator and was in the National Forensic League, the school's debate club, and the science club. Bernard graduated from Monessen High School in 1941 in the college preparatory curriculum and received a merit award at commencement

Quinlan Brothers Off to War

The surprise attack by Japanese armed forces upon the US military base at Pearl Harbor on December 7, 1941, **changed** the world for Bernard and his brothers Donald and Eugene when America entered WWII. Donald joined the US Coast Guard a month after the US entered the war. On June 30, 1942, Bernard registered for the US military draft as a 5'9" 143 lb 19-yr-old with brown hair and blue eyes. He had taken a job in the metallurgy laboratory with Pittsburgh Steel in Monessen.

Bernard had his eyes set skyward, and while in Miami Beach, Florida, on February 1, 1943, he enlisted with the US Army Air Corps. He was assigned service number 13133539 and applied for the Aviation Cadet program in hopes of becoming a pilot. A month earlier, his brother Eugene also enlisted with the US Army Air Corps. The Quinlan's were now a 3-Blue-Star family.

Three months later, Bernard was accepted into the Aviation Cadet program and reported for training at the Nashville Army Air Center in May 1943. He was subsequently routed to Xavier University in Cincinnati, Ohio, for a five month course of instruction on mathematics, physics, navigation, English, geography, and ten hours of actual flight instruction. He then went to Jackson Army Air Base in Mississippi for Specialized Flying School. Cadet Quinlan demonstrated the competencies necessary to qualify as a fighter pilot. By January 1944, he had graduated with his wings at Maxwell Field, Alabama, was commissioned to the rank of Second Lieutenant (2LT), and was assigned service number O-825492. His brother Eugene had also qualified as a pilot with the US Army Air Force and was eventually sent overseas.

Life as a P-47 Fighter Pilot

By May 1944, 2LT Quinlan was transferred to train with the Pilots Replacement Section J at the 120th Army Air Force Base Unit (Fighter) at Richmond, Virginia. That month, he completed his high-altitude indoctrination in the Republic P-47 Thunderbolt fighter.

The P-47 was affectionately known as "The Jug" due to its large round radial engine. It was equipped with eight 50 caliber machine guns and could carry rockets and bombs to support ground troops. Fully loaded, it was 8 tons and among the heaviest Allied fighters. It was a formidable war machine, and this Monessen son was fortunate for the privilege to fly it.

In August 1944, 2LT Quinlan was shipped to the Mediterranean Theater of the war in Europe where he was assigned to the 522nd Fighter Squadron, 27th Fighter Group, XXII Tactical Air Command. The 27th Fighter Group was initially a Fighter/Bomber group equipped with A-36 Apache dive bombers when it arrived in North Africa in November 1942. The group converted to P-40 Warhawk fighters in January 1944 and then to P-47 Thunderbolt fighters that June. By July they were operating from the island of Corsica and then moved to southern France in August.

Republic P-47 Thunderbolt of the 27th Fighter Group (American Air Museum)

The 27th moved once again to Italy on October 4th to place their aircraft nearer to the US Army infantry fighting forces pushing the Germans northward out of Italy. The 27th base was placed at Tarquinio, just north of Rome. They began intensive tactical bombing and strafing missions in support of the Allied ground advance.

LT Quinlan in Combat

LT Quinlan arrived with the 27th during August-September, and began combat orientation. He flew his first mission on October 15 from Tarquinio in a group of eight P-47s and bombed a bridge southeast of Bologna. On his fourth mission, October 20, his aircraft was struck by flak but returned safely.

During his sixteenth mission, on November 18, 1944, LT Quinlan partici-pated in an 8-aircraft attack against enemy-occupied buildings near Modena, Italy, for which he would later be awarded the Air Medal. The medal's citation stated:

"Displaying great skill and aggressiveness as he maneuvered through a complete overcast to reach the target area, LT Quinlan in a precision bomb run scored direct hits on the enemy buildings. His outstanding proficiency in

combat and cool courage has reflected great credit upon himself and the Armed Forces of the United States."

At the end of November, the 27th FG relocated northward to Pontedera, Italy. LT Quinlan continued flying through December, and by the end of the day January 3, 1945, he had flown his 30th mission. Unfortunately, his good fortune ran out on his 31st mission.

Quinlan's Final Flight

On January 4, 1945, LT Quinlan joined three other P-47s as "Red Four" on an armed reconnaissance mission to Italy's east coast. Near the town of German-occupied Vicenza, LT Quinlan's P-47 was struck by flak. His aircraft fell to Earth near the village of Sarego southwest of Vicenza, exploding upon impact. LT Quinlan did not survive.

German troops buried LT Quinlan in a military cemetery near Vicenza. Three weeks later, his family was informed that he had been killed in action.

```
January 4, 1945

    Four missions were flown today. The weather is unbeatable. The group was kept
busy getting planes into the air. On the second mission Lieutenant Quinlan failed
to return as he was seen to go in south east of Verona. The pilots on that part-
icular mission were unable to figure out the cause for it. Another movie was shown
at the group theatre. Coffee and doughnuts were given out at Club Two Seven.
```

Excerpt from 27th Fighter Group War Diary

After the surrender of Germany, the remains of LT Bernard Quinlan were recovered and reinterred at the US Military Cemetery at Mirandola, Italy, in June 1945. On March 7, 1949, 2LT Bernard F. Quinlan was returned to the US, where he was finally buried in his hometown of Monessen in Grandview Cemetery. 2LT Bernard F. Quinlan was posthumously awarded the Air Medal two days after his death.

27th Fighter Group Mission Intelligence Report Jan 4, 1945

★★★

PVT ANGELO L. IMBURGIA

Service Number 36981329
Company A, 274th Infantry Regiment, 70th Infantry Division, US Army
Killed in action, France, January 5, 1945

A ngelo Imburgia was born on December 19, 1920, in Monessen, Pennsylvania, to Frank and Josephine (née DiLeonardo) Imburgia. Frank and Josephine had married in 1911 in Palermo, Sicily, Italy. Frank was a repairman for the railroad, while Josephine managed the Imburgia family household.

The Imburgia Family

Frank, born Francesco, immigrated to the United States in 1899 from the village of Campofelice di Roccella on the island of Sicily. Two years earlier, he had married his first wife Maria Ciminello and came to the US alone to find work. Maria gave birth to three children in Sicily: Giuseppi (Joseph, 1898), Cosimo (Thomas, 1900), and Lorenzo (Lawrence, 1902). Maria and their sons immigrated to the US in 1905 and settled with Frank in Mt. Pleasant, Pennsylvania. Another son, Charles, was born in 1905

while the family was living in Mt. Pleasant. A daughter, Rosa, was stillborn in 1907. The family moved to Monessen shortly thereafter.

However, Maria died suddenly from peritonitis at the age of 32 in 1909. Unable to raise the boys on his own, Frank placed them at St. Paul's Roman Catholic Orphanage in Chartiers Township, Pennsylvania. He returned to Sicily where he married his second wife, Giuseppa "Josephine" DiLeonardo in Campofelice di Roccella in 1911. They returned to western Pennsylvania later that year. Frank was reunited with his four sons who met their new mother Josephine, and they resettled in Monessen.

Angelo was the fourth child born to Frank and Josephine. His sister Rose arrived in 1914, followed by Samuel Frank (1916) and Ignatius Joseph (1918). By 1920, the Imburgia's crowded household was home to Angelo, his three siblings, and his four half-siblings. The family was living in a rented home at 132 Third Street in Monessen. A few years later, the family moved to a home that they had purchased at 454 McKee Avenue in Monessen.

In 1929, Angelo's mother Josephine passed away at the age of 50 from heart failure following gallbladder surgery. By 1930, Angelo's half-brothers Joseph and Lawrence had moved out to start their own families, Thomas and Charles were working at the Monessen tin mill, and the rest of the children were attending school. In 1933 Angelo played little league baseball for the Trojan Juniors team as left fielder, and he also pitched for the Pioneer's team. By 1938, Angelo was pitching and playing infield for the Cardinals in the Monessen City Junior League. Angelo then attended Monessen Vocational High School where he sang in the school chorus.

By 1940, Angelo's father had retired from the railroad and Thomas, Samuel, Ignatius, and Angelo were adults living with their father. Angelo graduated from Monessen High School in 1939.

The surprise attack by Japanese armed forces on the US military bases at Pearl Harbor, Hawaii, in December 1941 changed the world for Angelo and his brothers Thomas and Ignatius. Angelo had moved to Chicago, Illinois to work for Pioneer-General Motors, and was living with his half-brother Joseph and his family. On February 16, 1942, he registered in Chicago for the US armed forces draft as a 5' 6 ", 133 lb 21-yr-old single man with black hair and brown eyes.

On September 9, 1942, while driving a car in Chicago, Angelo struck and fatally injured a man. He was arraigned on charges of manslaughter. His acquittal is assumed as there are no public records of a trial or a conviction.

Angelo's brother Ignatius had already been drafted into the US Army in December 1941 and Thomas would be drafted into the Army in September 1942. It was Angelo's turn when he was drafted into the US Army on May 25, 1944, and immediately left for training. The Imburgia's were now a 3-Blue-Star family.

Private Angelo Imburgia was assigned to Company A, 274th Infantry Regiment of the 70th Infantry Division. The 70th Division, named "Trailblazers", was activated as a component of the Army on June 15th, 1943, with headquarters at Camp Adair, Oregon. The Division had one change of station to Fort Leonard Wood, Missouri, before embarking for the European Theater in December 1944.

Private Imburgia Heads to France

The three infantry regiments of the 70th Division began arriving in Marseilles, France, on December 10th. PVT Imburgia's 274th Regiment, now identified as "Task Force Fox" arrived at Brumath, France on Christmas Eve. They were immediately organized into Task Force Herren and assigned to the Seventh Army. Reaching the front on December 28th near Bischwiller, Germany on the west bank of the Rhine River, the task force engaged German units attempting to drive south from Bitche as part of an attack to cut off Seventh Army forces west of Severne Pass. This was Germany's last winter offensive, "Operation Nordwind".

The Seventh Army held the thinly-spread, 84-mile line from Saarbrucken, southeastward to Strasbourg, inside the German border. The objective of the German's three divisions was to cut off the lines of supply for the Seventh Army.

The Germans picked New Year's Eve for the offensive, believing that the holiday spirit would lower the Americans' guard. After months on the offensive, the Americans now found themselves on the defensive. American intelligence information was explicit. The enemy attack would come on New Year's Eve. All along the line, soldiers huddled down for that long, lonely, frightening wait for something to happen. The waiting ended with a trip flare, exactly 10 minutes before the start of 1945.

The flare revealed a fearful sight. Operation Nordwind had begun. The strength and ferocity of the attack had not been expected. The white-clad enemy, laying down heavy machine gun and small arms fire, were advancing relentlessly.

The battle roared for days on end. This baptism into combat was by total immersion. The Americans were using every weapon in their arsenal. As darkness fell on January 4th, the Trailblazers wrapped themselves in blankets and slept in the deep snow.

The following day, January 5, 1945, PVT Angelo Imburgia and six of his compatriots met their fate after only three weeks in Europe. A German artillery shell exploded near their position, with shrapnel mortally wounding PVT Imburgia and his fellow soldiers. He died that day in the vicinity of Niederbronn, France.

The Imburgia family was notified six weeks later by the War Department that their son, Angelo, had been killed in action.

PVT Angelo Imburgia was buried at the Lorraine American Cemetery in Saint-Avold, France with 10,480 other fallen American service members. He was posthumously awarded the Purple Heart.

★ ★ ★

PVT STANLEY ZAZAC

Service Number 33290271
Company I, 169th Infantry Regiment, 43rd Infantry Division, US Army
Killed in action, Philippine Islands, January 25, 1945

W hen Monessen's Private Stanley Zazac awoke on January 25, 1945, he probably shook his head, refusing to believe that he was still so far from home.

Two years after enlisting, "Tash" Zazac was with his fellow GI's halfway around the world. Instead of enjoying a beer inside a Monessen bar with a snowy winter blowing outside, he was in the hot, steamy climate of the tropics, slashing through a jungle on the Philippine island of Luzon.

Back in Pennsylvania, no one would have been trying to kill Infantryman Tash Zazac. But in Luzon, the enemy saw things differently…

The Zazac Family

Stanley Zazac was born on October 8, 1921, to Andrew and Felicia (née Vaydonosky or Waydonoski) Zazac in Monessen, Pennsylvania. Andrew was a laborer at the Page Steel and Wire in Monessen, Pennsylvania. Felicia, called Fannie, managed the Zazac family household.

Andrew was born in Poland and immigrated to the United States sometime prior to 1912. Fanny was also from Poland and immigrated to the US in 1912. Stanley was the sixth and last child born to the couple. He was preceded by Steve (b1912), Boleslaw "Robert Anthony" (1913), Walter (1914), Mary Ann (1916), and Carl (1917).

Tragedy struck early in the Zazac family. Steve succumbed to diphtheria in 1919 at the age of 7. The following year, Walter lost his life after being accidentally struck by a motorcycle in 1920 at the age of 5. And before Stanley was born, their father Andrew lost his life to the Spanish Flu, leaving Fanny to raise the young children on her own.

The Zazac's adapted to adversity as many Monessen families did. The next-oldest son Robert left school and was hired as a laborer at the Monessen tin mill to help pay the family's expenses while the other children attended school. In 1930, they were living in a rented apartment with another family at 304 Third Street in Monessen.

As recalled by his nephew David Zazac from a memory shared by his father Carl, "Stanley got into the usual mischief as a kid, painting his initials on the side of their apartment building with his best friend Billy Kuzma." Both boys' fathers had died when they were very young, and Stanley and Billy bonded over these losses.

By 1940, Stanley was the last of the Zazac family still attending school. Mary had married and moved out to start her own family. Robert and Carl were both working in Monessen factories. The three brothers were living with their mother at the home on Third Street. Stanley became known as "Tash" among his friends.

The US Enters WWII

Japanese forces launched a surprise attack on the US military bases in Pearl Harbor, Hawaii, on December 7, 1941. The US declared war on Japan, and as an ally of the Japanese Empire, Germany declared war on the US. Germany had invaded Poland two years before, so for the Polish Zazac family, the war was now personal.

Stanley registered for the US armed forces draft on February 16, 1942. He was a 5'9", 157 lb single 20-yr-old with brown hair and blue eyes. Stanley was working at the Star Theatre in Monessen. He graduated from Monessen High School mid-semester in 1942 and went to work for Pittsburgh Steel in Monessen. On July 31, 1942, Stanley was drafted into the US Army, and he immediately reported for duty. His brothers Robert and Carl would also enter the US Army, and the Zazac's became a three-Blue-Star family.

PVT Stanley Zazac left for Army boot camp, and he was soon sent to Fort Bragg, North Carolina to join the Field Artillery. He was an excellent marksman and decided that the fastest way to see action was to transfer to the infantry, so he did. Stanley continued to train stateside through most of 1943.

David Zazac relates a memory shared by his father Carl, "On leave before shipping out to the West Coast and the Pacific Theater, Stanley and some friends had a little too much alcohol to drink and were causing a ruckus at Johnson's Restaurant in downtown Monessen. According to his Navy friend Pat Santoro, they had pulled a potted Christmas tree out of its planter on the street and propped it up in a chair inside. They started singing 'O Christmas Tree' very loudly and with gusto. When other restaurant patrons voiced their disapproval, the restaurant staff said, 'These guys are going to fight for us. They can do what they want!' "

According to David's father, Stanley was a quiet guy who took in everyone's conversations and then would say something profound. He resumed his training at Fort Ord, California before shipping out.

PVT Zazac off to the Pacific

On December 8, 1943, PVT Zazac boarded a troopship and departed the US as a replacement infantryman in the 169th Infantry Regiment. The 169th deployed to the Pacific in September 1942 and were a part of the US Army's 43rd Infantry Division. The Regiment arrived at Guadalcanal in February 1943 after US forces defeated the Japanese occupiers and participated in the campaigns on the Solomon Islands of Pavuvu and New Georgia during the rest of the year. PVT Zazac joined the 169th at Munda Point, New Georgia.

In March 1944, the 43rd Division was sent to New Zealand for rest, rehabilitation, and additional training in preparation for its next combat deployment. While billeted in the town of Warwick, Stan was stunned by the pastoral beauty of New Zealand. The locals opened their doors and hearts to the Yanks. They were not rich but shared what they had with their visitors. Stan wrote to his sister Mary: "Please pick up a doll for the little girl whose family I'm staying with. These kids don't have anything." Mary did not hesitate to comply.

The unit was then sent into battle at Aitape, New Guinea, where it fought against the Japanese through the end of August until securing the area. They remained in Aitape for additional training in amphibious landings and jungle warfare for the upcoming invasion of the Philippine Islands. On December 10, 1944, the Division boarded ships destined for the Philippine island of Luzon.

Aboard their transport ship, Stan had the company of a fellow Monessenite, 19-year-old coxswain Mike Matush. Mr. Matush later recalled to the Zazac family, "On this long voyage from New Zealand, they treated the Army guys like animals. Just K-rations and cold saltwater showers. My brother palled around with Stan, and I considered him my brother, too. I got him hot food from the Navy mess and hot freshwater showers from the ship. When we arrived at our destination, Stan turned to me and said, 'See you in Monessen after the war.' "

The Allied invasion of Luzon was planned for January 9, 1945, codenamed "S-Day". The island was occupied by over 250,000 Japanese troops, and a major offensive would be necessary to dislodge the opposition. Over 800 Allied warships were on their way to Luzon.

At 700 hrs on S-Day, 70 warships bombarded Japanese defensive positions for an hour until landing forces assaulted the beach. PVT Zazac and the 169th Regiment came ashore as the central force in the first wave, just north of San Fabian. The regiment was relatively unopposed but faced artillery fire and small groups of enemy combatants which they quickly overran.

The regiment was used as a blocking force to allow a series of small quick mobile units known as "flying columns", of U.S. and Filipino troops to liberate allied prisoners of war camps in the south, closer to Manila.

Fate on Luzon

For the next sixteen days, the 169th moved inland and continued the attack with a hill-by-hill offensive operation to root out the defenders. They were often held up by intense artillery, mortar, machine gun, and rifle fire from Japanese counterattacks. The battle was not for the faint of heart.

Scene from the Battle of Luzon (32nd Infantry Division)

Then, on January 25, 1945, the 169th was subjected to an intense and continuous barrage of enemy artillery fire. According to Stanley's nephew David, "Company I was pinned down by snipers in the northern hills near San Fabian. A wounded GI, separated from the company, was pleading for help between the two lines. Stanley rushed out to save him and, as he turned to safely place him in the U.S. trench, was hit with bullets from three sides. He was dead before he hit the ground."

Three weeks later, PVT Stanley Zazac's family was notified that his life had been lost on Luzon. His loss was announced in a front-page story in the Monessen Daily Independent newspaper, which noted that his mother was severely ill and had not yet been informed. David recalls that the family made sure that Stanley's mother never saw the front-page story of his death. She was home-bound by then. Only later, did they break the news to her as best they could.

Tash Zazac had been highly regarded by his combat squad, so much so that they collected more than 300 Filipino dollars and sent it to his family.

Stanley "Tash" Zazac, Remembered

PVT Stanley Zazac was initially buried at the US Armed Forces Cemetery in San Fabian, Luzon, Philippines. He was later reinterred at the US Cemetery at Santa Barbara, Luzon, Philippines. PVT Zazac was eventually transported to the US under the Return of the War Dead program aboard the US Army transport ship SGT Morris E. Crain and finally buried at the Grandview Cemetery in Monessen in 1948.

"A few years after the war," David remembers, "my aunt Mary received a phone call from the soldier who Stan saved. He was distraught with guilt and asked if there was anything he could do to help out his sister, her son, and mother still at home. Aunt Mary graciously said, 'No, just live your life as best you can.' Mollified, the man agreed this would be the best course of action to honor Stanley and ended this conversation with hope in his voice. He continued to write letters to our family for at least the next seven years."

PVT Stanley Zazac was posthumously awarded the Bronze Star for valor, and the Purple Heart for his fatal wounds. His name is inscribed on the WWII Veterans Memorial Tablet, located at the intersection of Grand Boulevard and Euclid Drive in Monessen City Park.

The Monessen Daily Independent published an In Memorium from his family on the one year anniversary of his death:

"Today recalls sad memories,
Of a loved one gone to rest,
Ant those who think of him today,
Are the ones who loved him best.
The blow was hard, the shock severe,
We little knew that death was near,
But only those who have lost can tell,
The pain of parting without farewell".

The author is sincerely grateful to David Zazac for his generous contributions to this story.

✬ ✬ ✬

PVT MICHAEL DEMKO

Service Number 33705394
Company F, 254th Infantry Regiment, 63rd Infantry Division, US Army
Killed in action, France, January 28, 1945

M ichael Demko was born on October 25, 1925, in Monessen, Pennsylvania, to John and Mary (née Gazdik) Demko. John and Mary had married two years earlier, in 1923. John was a laborer in the local steel mill while Mary managed the Demko family household.

The Demko Family

John's family had immigrated to the United States from the Austrian-Hungarian Empire in eastern Europe around the turn of the century, as had Mary's family. John and Mary settled in Monessen, a community of transplants from Europe and other regions of the US, seeking work in Monessen's burgeoning industrial factories.

Michael was the second child born to John and Mary. His brother John Jr. was born in

Insignia of the 63rd Infantry Division (US Army)

Monessen in 1924. By 1930, the family was living in a rented apartment at 1264 Morgan Avenue in Monessen, up the hill from the factories along the Monongahela River. In May 1936, Michael had surgery for the removal of his

tonsils. By 1940, the family had relocated two blocks up the hill into a rented single-family home at 1245 McMahon Avenue. Michael and his brother John ended their public-school education after grammar school.

The surprise attack by Japanese armed forces on the US military bases at Pearl Harbor, Hawaii, in December 1941 changed the world for Michael. On October 25, 1943, he registered for the US military draft as a 6' 155 lb 18-yr-old with brown hair and blue eyes. Michael was single, working at Pittsburgh Steel, and living in the home of his parents at the time. His brother John was also employed by Pittsburgh Steel, living with the family, and had registered for the draft the previous year.

Two months later, on December 30, 1943, Michael was drafted into the US Army, and he reported to the draft office in Greensburg, Pennsylvania to complete his enlistment. Private Michael Demko was off to boot camp on January 20, 1944.

PVT Demko was eventually assigned to Company F, 254th Infantry Regiment of the 63rd Infantry Division. The 63rd Infantry Division, known as "Blood and Fire", had been activated on June 15, 1943, at Camp Blanding Florida. Shortly thereafter, the division moved to Camp Van Dorn, Mississippi. After 17 months of training the Division made its way to Europe. By war's end, the 63rd Infantry Division served for 119 days in combat in the European Theater including in the campaigns of Rhineland, Ardennes-Alsace, and Central Europe.

Private Demko Heads to France

PVT Demko left for Europe with the 254th Regiment on November 19, 1944. They arrived in the harbor of Marseilles in the south of France on December 8th, and advanced northward. On December 28th, the 254th was attached to the 3rd Infantry Division of the First French Army and was headed to the front line in German-occupied French territory for their first combat engagement with enemy forces. Their destination was the Colmar Pocket in central Alsace near the border of France and Germany by January 22, 1945.

The fighting in the Colmar Pocket was cold, tough, and fierce. The operation encountered the difficult Battle for Jebsheim on January 26-29th.

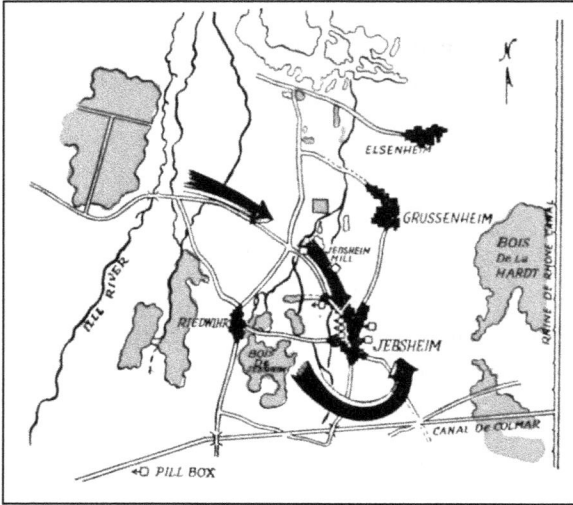

254th Regiment attacks Jebsheim Jan 26-29, 1945 (Unit History)

During the fight at Jebsheim, PVT Michael Demko was struck by fragments of an artillery shell near the town of Kunheim, France. He died on the battlefield on January 28, 1945, at the age of 19, but was reported as missing in action. PVT Demko remains were ultimately found and positively identified in April. His family would not learn of his death until later that month.

PVT Michael Demko was buried at Epinal American Cemetery, at the Département des Vosges, Lorraine, France, along with 5,251 other American military dead. The 254th Infantry Regiment would earn a Presidential Unit Citation for its accomplishments at Colmar.

The Monessen Daily Independent published an In Memorium from his family on the one year anniversary of his death:

> *"He has gone across the river, to the shores of ever green.*
> *How we'd love to see his smiling face.*
> *But the river flows between,*
> *And our aching hearts are calling*
> *To the shadows dark and gray*
> *For the dear one who has left us*
> *Just one year ago today".*

★ ★ ★

2LT STEPHEN G. MONICK, JR.

Service Numbers 13133418 / O-783450
350th Bomb Squadron, 100th Bomb Group, 8th Air Force, US Army Air Force
Killed in action over Germany, February 3, 1945

For one Monessen son, his first WWII combat experience was a bombing run to Berlin, Germany aboard a B-17 Flying Fortress bomber. Unfortunately for Stephen Monick, it was also his last.

Second LT Stephen G. Monick Jr. was a bombardier in the famed "Bloody Hundredth"... the 100th Bomb Group of the US Army Air Force based in the English village of Thorpe Abbotts. He had just arrived there in January 1945.

The Monick Family

Twenty-five years earlier, Stephen Sr. and Louise (née Urben) Monick welcomed their son Stephen Jr. on July 11, 1919. Louise was born in Pittsburgh to parents from Switzerland and Bavaria. Stephen Sr. had immigrated to the US from the Greek island of Chios in 1903 as Stephanos Alimonakis. Like many immigrants from southern and eastern Europe, he was

drawn to Monessen to escape the rumblings of what would become the Great War and by the promise of economic opportunity.

Stephen Jr's sister Louise was the first child born to the family, in 1913. Their father operated a billiard hall in Monessen before opening S. Monick Wholesale Tobacco and General Merchandise at 300 Schoonmaker Avenue. The family would eventually purchase a home at 422 Park Way in Monessen, just a block from their business. Stephen Sr. was very involved in the business community and elected director in the Monessen Kiwanis' Club. Daughter Louise became the company's bookkeeper after graduating from Monessen High School.

Young Stephen Monick

Young Stephen Jr.

Ever the adventurer, Stephen Jr. became active in the Boy Scouts when he joined in 1931. He attended scout camp in Westmoreland County, where he

became regular staff at Camp Wesco. Stephen earned a Life Saving award from the American Red Cross at Camp Wesco in 1933 and earned Eagle Scout in 1936 at the age of sixteen. Stephen graduated from Monessen High School and went to the College of Wooster, Ohio, where he played intramural basketball and graduated with a degree in economics in 1940. Stephen returned to Monessen and went to work in his father's business. As a new entrepreneur, he joined the Kiwanis Club to network with his fellow businessmen.

Hearing the drumbeats of war rumbling in Europe and the Pacific, the United States Congress passed the Selective Training and Service Act of 1940, creating the first peacetime conscription for young men. Stephen joined millions of his peers and registered on the first day of the draft, October 16, 1940. His draft card shows that he was a 5'9" 200 lb 21-year-old with brown eyes and black hair.

WWII Ensnares Stephen Monick

The following year on December 7, 1941, the surprise attack by Japanese armed forces on the US military base at Pearl Harbor, Hawaii, changed the world for Stephen and his family. World War II had begun.

Stephen watched as his friends left Monessen to fight the war in the trenches and on the seas. But he had set his eyes skyward, so he volunteered for the US Army Air Corps and enlisted in Pittsburgh on October 17, 1942. He was off to Air Corps training and attended pre-flight training at the 309th College Training Detachment at Dagley Field in Lubbock, Texas.

Although Stephen wanted to become a pilot, the Air Corps needed bombardiers. After attending further training at Keesler Field, Mississippi, the Air Corps redirected him to bombardier school. Located at Demming Army Airfield, New Mexico, Stephen learned the skills of the bombardier trade, including how to operate the highly sophisticated M-Series bombsight, commonly called the Norden Sight after its inventor.

Training a Bombardier

Dropping a bomb accurately from an aircraft traveling hundreds of miles per hour at an altitude of tens of thousands of feet in the air was exceedingly difficult. A bomb's path from the aircraft to the ground is determined by the bomb's type and weight, the speed of the aircraft, wind direction and speed, weather, and other factors. Designed before the digital age of microchips, the Norden bombsight was a mechanical computer with a gyroscope, designed to factor-in these variables and place the bomb on target. It took a highly competent bombardier with steady hands to adjust and trigger the device as his air-craft was bounced around by bursts of exploding anti-aircraft shells. The mission of everyone else in the aircraft was to deliver him safely over the target.

B-17 Bombardier's Station, Norden Bombsight, center (By Ducatipierre - Own work, CC BY-SA 4.0, https://commons.wikimedia.org/w/index.php?curid=97468602)

Bombardiers were also responsible for manning the guns installed in the nose of their aircraft, and Stephen attended Gunnery School at Las Vegas Army Airfield, Nevada in March 1944. Back at bombardiers' school, Stephen was quite nervous about meeting the required accuracy for bomb drops. In a letter home in April 1944, he shared that his practice bombing scores were not good: "494, 506, and 404, and the passing for bombing is 230." He had another week-and-a-half for practice before his final performance tests.

Stephen passed. He demonstrated strong competence and was awarded his wings with the Aviation Cadet Squadron 44-10, receiving his officers' commission as Second Lieutenant (2LT) in August 1944 at Deming. His parents traveled from Monessen to attend the graduation ceremony. LT Monick was then sent to the Army Air Base in Alexandria, Louisiana, where he was assigned to a B-17 bomber crew of nine men commanded by 2LT Orville H. Cotner of Lincoln, Nebraska.

Cotner Crew, LT Stephen Monick kneeling at right (100th Bomb Group)

In September 1944, he wrote home expressing concern about a rumor: bombardiers may be removed from some crews and those aircraft would drop their bombs when the lead aircraft dropped theirs. He was quite fond of his crew and did not want to leave them. Fortunately for LT Monick, his crew was not affected. In December 1944, they were sent to England with a layover in Labrador and Christmas dinner in Iceland. In a letter home dated December 25, he said about the Germans, "when they hear we are coming, they'll give up in a hurry." They arrived in England on December 28, 1944, and joined the Bloody Hundredth's 350th Bomb Squadron on January 8, 1945.

The 100th Bomb Group (BG) had earned their nickname after incurring devastating losses while bombing targets in Germany during 1943. By the time

Cotner's team arrived at Thorpe Abbotts as a replacement crew, the 100th BG had already flown over 230 combat missions.

One Tragic Mission

On February 3, 1945, 2LT Cotner and his crew were set to fly B-17 #44-6500 in their first combat mission, the 100th BG's 255th mission. The target was Berlin, Germany, and it was the eighteenth time the group was sent to drop bombs at Adolph Hitler's doorstep. Allied intelligence had received word that the German Sixth Panzer Army was moving by rail through Berlin toward the Russian Front, which, at this late stage of the war, was now only 35 miles east of Berlin. The group was to bomb the railroad marshaling yards in Tempelhof to disrupt this German troop redeployment.

The B-17s of the Bloody Hundredth departed Thorpe Abbotts between 7:15-7:45 AM. The group would be leading an armada of 536 bombers to Berlin. The residents of the city would soon look at a sky filled with American bombers taking aim at their heavily-defended city.

At 11:15 AM, the group arrived at its Initial Point (IP), where they began their bombing run. Suddenly, the skies were filled with anti-aircraft 'flak' whose gunners were trying their best to knock down as many bombers as they could. LT Cotner's B-17 was positioned within the 350th Bomb Squadron as the High squadron in the large formation of bombers. However, they were not out of reach of the German's 88 mm anti-aircraft guns and ground rockets.

2LT Stephen Monick was crouched over his Norden bombsight in the glass nose of Cotner's B-17. By this late time in the war, bombardiers were told to release their bomb load when they saw the lead aircraft drop its bombs. LT Monick kept a steady eye on that lead ship.

The moment came. LT Monick saw the bombs emerge from the bomb bay of the lead B-17. He pulled the lever and released the bombs from Cotner's B-17. It was the last task he would ever do.

Minutes later, at 11:25 AM, Cotner's B-17 was struck by deadly flak, believed to be from a ground rocket, at the root of the right wing. The wing folded up against the fuselage and the B-17 flipped over on its back. The wing's gasoline tank detonated, and the entire aircraft began to burn. It exploded in mid-air.

LT Cotner's B-17 fell to Earth on Hobrecht Street in the suburb of Neukoelln, Berlin. There were no survivors.

The families of the nine crew were informed that they were missing in action by the War Department three weeks later. A year later, on January 24, 1946, the family was informed that he was, in fact, killed in action.

LT Monick Remembered

On June 21, 1946, the Monicks received a personal letter from Carl Spaatz, Commanding General, Army Air Forces. He stated that LT Monick "had a reputation for energy and earnestness of purpose… and that he justified the trust which had been placed in him....The many friends he had are cognizant of the initiative and proficiency which marked him, and they share with you a deep feeling of bereavement. May your sorrow be alleviated by the memory of the high regard which comrades had for your son."

2LT Stephen G. Monick, Jr, and his crewmates were initially interred in a cemetery at Doeberitz, Germany. At the end of the war, their remains were moved to the Ardennes American Cemetery in Neuville-en-Condroz, Belgium. In 1949, LT Monick was transported to the US under the Return of the War Dead program aboard the US Army Transport Haiti Victory with 5,327 other American fallen service members and was buried in Grandview Cemetery in Monessen on June 24, 1949. He was posthumously awarded the Purple Heart.

★★★

T/4 ORLO JUNK

Service Number 33672151
Company F, 9th Infantry Regiment, 2nd Infantry Division, US Army
Killed in action, Germany, February 4, 1945

O rlo Junk was born on February 20, 1915, in Brownsville, Pennsylvania to Harry Clark and Sibbie Ellen (née Davis) Junk. Harry and Sibbie had married in 1904. Harry was an agent with the Prudential Insurance Company while Sibbie managed the Junk family household.

The Junk Family

The heritage of the Junk family traces back to the British colonies of Pennsylvania, New Jersey, and Massachusetts prior to the American Revolutionary War, and to Ireland and Scotland. The Davis family traces back to the colony of Pennsylvania and to Ireland and Germany. Ancestors in both families settled in southwestern Pennsylvania where Harry and Sibbie met.

Orlo was the fourth of ten children born to Harry and Sibbie. Paul Holmes (b1905) was first born, followed by George Hazelett (1909), Joseph Everett

(1913), Beatrice Evelyn (1917), John (1919), Richard Daves (1921), Olive Jane (1924), Harry Jr. (1926), and Beverly Ann (1932). Olive died of pneumonia in 1925 before her first birthday, George died in an automobile accident in 1931, and Paul succumbed to tuberculosis in 1939.

By 1917, the family moved to a rented home on Prospect Avenue in Charleroi, Pennsylvania. Harry had left the insurance business and was now working as a ruler in the local steel mill. In 1926, Orlo was admitted to the hospital after being injured when a large exhibition tent fell on him (for which his father sued and was awarded a settlement for his injuries). By 1930, the family had moved to a rented home at 349 Fourth Street in North Charleroi where the children attended school, and the three oldest boys were now working. That year, they attended a large Junk family of 260 members in Fayette County, Pennsylvania. The family held a reunion every three years, and this was the largest to date, with relatives traveling from as far as Iowa and Kentucky to join the event. Orlo attended Charleroi Junior High School where he played football.

Orlo graduated from high school around 1933. In 1934, Orlo was driving a delivery truck when another vehicle collided with him head-on, but fortunately he escaped with minor injuries. Orlo met and fell in love with Thelma Mary Morgan, also of Charleroi, and they married on June 20, 1936. In 1937, they moved from a home on Donner Avenue to 402 McKee Avenue in Monessen. By 1940, they were living in the rented home of her parents at 228 Clarendon Avenue in Monessen. Orlo and Thelma were members of the First Presbyterian Church.

On October 16,1940, Orlo joined millions of other young American men and registered for the US armed forces draft on its first day under the recently passed Selective Training and Service Act of 1940. He signed up in Monessen at 6'3" 198 lb 26-yr-old with blue eyes. Orlo was now living at 241 Reed Avenue in Monessen and working as an automobile mechanic at the JL Gibson garage.

Drafted!

The surprise attack by Japanese armed forces on the US military bases at Pearl Harbor, Hawaii, and the Philippines in December 1941 changed the world for Orlo. He was drafted into the US Army and enlisted on April 28, 1943, in Greensburg, Pennsylvania. Private Orlo Junk reported for duty in Pittsburgh, on May 5 and was off to war. His brother Joseph had joined the US Army Air Corps five months earlier.

PVT Orlo Junk remained stateside for Army training and was soon transferred for training on armored vehicles and tanks. In 1944, he was promoted to the rank of Technician 4th Grade (T/4) as an armor specialist. The rank of T/4 was typically addressed as Sergeant. He was serving as an instructor at Camp Hood, Texas. Starting in September 1944, T/4 Junk participated in an 8-week US Army experiment at Camp Carson, Colorado, to determine how soldiers fared on an exclusive diet of emergency rations. The Army claimed that the men were in excellent health at the start of the experiment and were in even better health at its conclusion.

Junk continued to train in the US until December 20, 1944, when his unit was transferred overseas to Europe. T/4 Junk was assigned to Company F of the 9th Infantry regiment, which was attached to the 2nd Infantry Division.

On January 28, 1945, T/4 Orlo Junk's unit was fighting in Belgium according to his letter home of that date. However, it was to be his last message home.

Killed in Action, Germany

T/4 Orlo Junk met his fate on February 4, 1945, when his unit, having crossed the border into Germany encountered their enemy in combat near Dreiborn, Germany. He was killed in action when he was struck in the right side by shrapnel from an exploding artillery shell. Junk was only in action for one week before he lost his life.

T/4 Orlo Junk was initially buried at the Henri-Chapelle American Military Cemetery in Belgium. His remains were recovered under the Return of the War Dead program and returned to the US in November 1947 aboard the transport ship USAT Robert F. Burns. He was buried at the Belle Vernon Cemetery in North Belle Vernon, Pennsylvania.

T/4 Orlo Junk was posthumously awarded the Purple Heart.

☆ ☆ ☆

2LT JOHN MATOLA, JR.

Service Numbers 06896670 / 0-890330
102nd Infantry Regiment, 101st Philippine Division, US Army
Died as POW, Japan, February 6, 1945

Three years, three prisoner of war camps, three hell ships. But no ticket home.

When John Matola Jr. joined the US Army in 1937, he may have been seeking adventure beyond his hometown of Monessen. Instead, he was heading into a 3-year nightmare.

Most Americans know that the US entered WWII when the US military base at Pearl Harbor, Hawaii, was attacked by surprise by the Japanese Imperial Navy on December 7, 1941. On the same day, the Japanese attacked the Philippines, Guam, Hong Kong, Singapore, Malaysia, and Thailand in a massive pan-Asian military operation.

Monessen's John Matola was a US Army Second Lieutenant (2LT) stationed in the Philippine Islands that day. He would spend the next five months
fighting the Japanese invaders, followed by 33 months fighting for survival as
a prisoner of war. It was a battle that he would not win.

The Matola Family

John Matola Jr. was the son of John Sr. and Anna (née Siskaninec) Matola,
who had married in their Eastern European homeland prior to 1907. In search
of a better life, John Sr. immigrated to the United States in 1910 aboard the SS
Amerika, leaving Anna behind while he sought work. He found it in Ford City,
Pennsylvania and sent for Anna, who arrived in 1912. They moved to Monessen in 1918.

The Matola's had six children. Sophia was born in Europe in 1907 and
came to the US with her mother in 1912. Born in Ford City were Frank, (1912),
Mary (1914), and John Jr. (September 21, 1916). Their father found a better
job at Monessen's Page Steel and Wire, and they moved there in 1918, where
daughters Anna (1919) and Irene (1921) were born. By 1930, the family was
living at 401 Third Street in Monessen. Unfortunately, John Sr. succumbed to
cancer three years later at the age of 52, and the widow Anna was faced with
raising the family on her own. The oldest children went to work to support the
household.

In 1931, John Jr. participated in the Monessen Junior High School operetta, singing in the chorus. In 1936, he portrayed a character in the play "The
Happy Maiden" at the Russian Orthodox Church.

John Volunteers for the US Army

In 1937, John Jr. left his job in a bakery and volunteered for the US Army
at the age of 21. Private Matola was assigned to the 12th Infantry Regiment
and transferred to Fort Myer, Virginia by 1939. In February 1940, he requested
a deployment to the Army's Hawaiian Department with the 102nd Infantry
Regiment (Pennsylvania). John Matola demonstrated keen military skills and
leadership, and he rose to the rank of Second Lieutenant.

Off to the South Pacific

By 1940, the Japanese Empire had aggressively seized territory in Korea, China, and French Indochina, with an appetite for more. The US saw the imminent threat to the Philippine Islands, then a US territory, and increased its military presence by deploying the 102nd Regiment and 2LT John Matola there in 1941. The 102nd was attached to the 101st Philippine Division of the US Army.

The surprise attacks on December 7, 1941, by Japanese armed forces put American troops in peril. The 101st Philippine Division immediately found itself on the defensive. The Japanese were overrunning the Philippines.

The 101st Division and LT John Matola were charged with repelling the Japanese invasion of the Philippine island of Mindanao. However, after the Japanese overcame the Allied troops who had escaped to the Bataan Peninsula and the island of Corregidor, the Allied command surrendered. The 101st Division on Mindanao was then ordered to surrender on May 9,1942.

Captured: The Fight For Survival Begins.

2LT John Matola and his troops were taken captive by the Japanese and imprisoned in Bilibid Prison in Manila, Philippines. For them, the fighting war was over but their fight for survival was just beginning. He was soon transferred to the notorious Japanese prisoner of war camp at Cabanatuan on the Philippine island of Luzon. Life as a POW at Cabanatuan was difficult in the extreme. Many lost their lives to disease, malnutrition, and physical abuse by their captors. John Matola desperately survived Cabanatuan for the next 2 1/2 years. His family had been informed that he was missing in mid-1942 but heard nothing more until 1943 when informed that he had been taken prisoner by the Japanese.

The Japanese began relocating Allied POWs closer to the Japanese homeland as hostages and potential bargaining assets. Thousands were boarded on "hell ships" for transport to camps in the Japanese homeland. Hell ships were merchant vessels requisitioned by the Japanese military. They became known for their inhumane conditions and cruelty by their crew. POWs were crammed inside cargo holds far below deck, with no furnishings, little or no ventilation, and a few buckets to share as latrines between hundreds of men. Men sat side-by-side in their own excrement with little food or water. Hell ships were un-marked and thus became fair play for attack by unwitting Allied aircraft and submarines.

Bombed Aboard the Hell Ship Oryoku Maru

In December 1944, John Matola was one of 1,619 Allied POWs in the Philippines destined for POW camps in Japan, Taiwan, and Manchuria. Now weak and malnourished after at least two years of imprisonment, they were ordered aboard the hell ship Oryoku Maru, a former luxury liner, on December 13. The ship departed Manila early on December 14, 1944, along with 1,900 Japanese civilian and military passengers in the luxury cabins above. John, crammed into the ship's rear cargo hold with hundreds of his compatriots, would now face his next test of survival.

SS Oryoku Maru, before WWII (Source Unknown)

As the Oryoku Maru and its convoy neared the Phil-ippine naval base at Olon-gapo in Subic Bay, they were spotted by US Navy F6F Hell-cat fighters from USS Hornet (CV12) on the morning of December 14. Dive bombers from the Hornet and the USS Cabot (CVL-22) attacked the unmarked ship throughout the day as its escorting convoy ships fled the scene. The POWs in the hold would have to endure the sounds of gunfire, explosions, and the screams of the Japanese passengers above them. The damaged Oryoku Maru remained afloat until bombers from the Hornet and Cabot returned at dawn on December 15 to finish the job. As explosions ripped open the ship, John and his fellow POWs escaped and swam to shore.

Imprisoned Again

SS Oryoku Maru on fire after attack, December 15, 1944 (US Navy)

LT Matola and about 1,300 POWs survived the sinking but were recaptured and sequestered on an uncovered tennis court on the naval base without sanitary facilities awaiting what would come next. They were forced to sit lengthwise in rows of 52 prisoners with their legs intertwined in the stifling tropical heat. LT Matola and his fellow officers took roll calls and compiled death lists from a referee's chair placed in the center of the court. On December 20, they were moved to a prison camp at San Fernando, Pampanga, and then sent by train to another

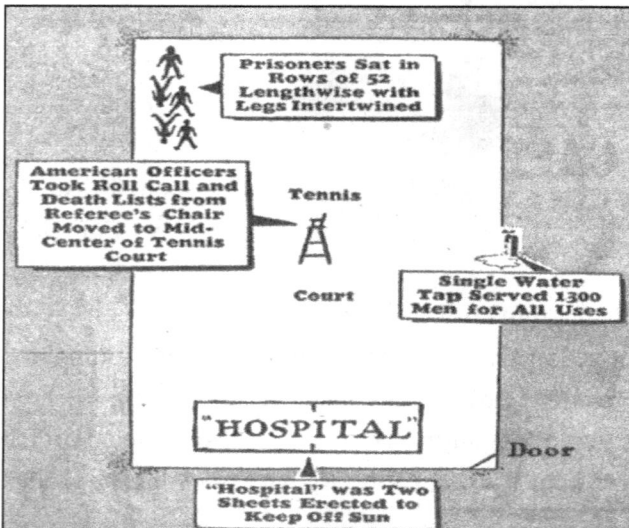

Staging of 1,300 POWs at naval base tennis court. (DPAA Dr.G.Kupsky)

camp at San Fernando, La Union on December 27. They would now begin the next leg of their fateful journey.

Escaping Death aboard Hell Ship Enoura Maru

John and his fellow POWs boarded the hell ships Enoura Maru and Brazil Maru, departing the Philippines for Formosa (now Taiwan) on December 27. Both ships reached Formosa on January 1, 1945. All of the POWs were then shuffled aboard the Enoura Maru awaiting transport to its next destination when, on January 9, the Enoura Maru came under attack by Allied aircraft. An explosion aboard the ship killed 300 POWs, but LT Matola lived to see another day.

The End of the Road: Hell Ship Brazil Maru and Japan

The Enoura Maru survivors were packed aboard the Brazil Maru on January 14, 1945, bound for Japan. They arrived at Moji, Japan on January 29, 1945. Of the 1,619 POWs that originally boarded the Oryoku Maru, only 500 had survived and disembarked from the Brazil Maru at Moji. LT John Matola was one of them.

LT John Matola was sent to the POW camp Fukuoka 4 (3-B) in Tobata on the Japanese island of Honshu. He had become seriously ill with colitis, but being in poor overall health and severely malnourished, he could not withstand the effects of the illness. He succumbed at the Kokura Military Hospital on February 6, 1945, at the age of 28.

Kokura Military Hospital, Honshu, Japan (National Archives)

On September 18, 1945, sixteen days after the surrender of the Japanese Empire, his mother was informed by the War Department that John had died in February. It had been at least five years since she last saw him, and two years since she last received any word about her son.

2LT John Matola's cremated remains were eventually recovered in 1946 and finally interred at the Manila American Cemetery and Memorial in Taguig City, Philippines in 1948.

Route of LT Matola from Philippines to Japan (DPAA, Dr.G.Kupsky)

★ ★ ★

PFC JOSEPH P. PLATKO

Service Number 33396409
Company E, 301st Infantry Regiment, 94th Infantry Division, US Army
Killed in action, Germany, February 7, 1945

Joseph Peter Platko was born on June 28, 1914, to Pawell "Paul" and Magdalena "Margaret" (née Kusner) Platko in Monessen, Pennsylvania. Paul and Margaret had married in Poland prior to immigrating to the United States. Paul was a laborer in the galvanizing department of Monessen's Page Steel and Wire mill while Margaret managed the family household and worked as a housekeeper.

The Platko Family

The native language of Paul and Margaret was Ruthenian, and they

Insignia of the 94th Infantry Division (US Army)

were born in the Galicia region of Poland. Paul immigrated to the US in 1911 aboard the SS Hanover, settling in Monessen to find employment. He then sent for Margaret and their two daughters, who arrived in the US in 1913 aboard the SS Neckar. The young family moved into a home at 282 East Donner Avenue.

Joseph, initially called Osyp by his parents (Yosef, or Joseph, in their homeland), was the family's third of nine children, and their first to be born in the US. Sisters Marya "Mary K" (b1906) and Antonia "Nancy" (1910) were born in Poland. Following Joseph were Michael (1916), Anna Margaret (1918), Helen (1919), Paul Jr. (1921), Olga (1923), and Marjorie Katheryna (1925). By 1930, the family had purchased a home at 235 East Schoonmaker Avenue in Monessen. Before 1940, Paul and Margaret separated, and he moved to an apartment. They would later divorce.

Joseph left school after his junior year and took a job at Page Steel and Wire in the Galvanizing Department. He was living with his mother and supporting the family in 1940. Antonia had married and moved out to start her own family, while Mary, Michael, Helen, and Paul all worked to contribute to their household. Joseph joined Monessen's Raven Athletic Club.

On October 16, 1940, Joseph joined millions of his fellow countrymen and registered for the US armed forces draft on its first day under the recently passed Selective Service Act. He was a 5'10" 141 lb single man with brown hair and gray eyes.

The surprise attack by Japanese armed forces on the US military base at Pearl Harbor, Hawaii, in December 1941 changed the world for Joseph and his brothers Michael and Paul. Paul volunteered for the US Army and entered the service in February 1942, eventually stationed with the 15th Air Force in Italy. Michael was drafted into the US Army in March 1942, and he eventually rose to the rank of Major in the Army Air Force. Joseph was also drafted, and he entered the US Army on December 9, 1942. With three sons in the war, the Platko's were now a 3-Blue-Star Family.

Private Joseph Platko was soon off to US Army boot camp. After boot camp, he was assigned to the 301st Infantry Regiments of the 94th Infantry Division. The 94th trained at three camps, Camp Phillips, Kansas (November 1942 - November 1943), Camp McCain, Mississippi (to July 1944), and Camp Shanks, New York (to August 1944). He was eventually promoted to the Private First Class (PFC).

The 94th Division was shipped overseas to England aboard the SS Queen Elizabeth, landing on August 12, 1944, for a brief period of training before heading into battle on the European continent. On September 6, 1944, the 94th landed at Allied-held Utah Beach in Normandy, France, viewing the debris-laden beach resulting from the massive D-Day invasion in June. They moved into Brittany and were immediately charged with containing 60,000 German troops besieged in the ports of Lorient and St. Nazaire on the coast of western France. PFC Platko's 301st Regiment was the first unit of the 94th Division to enter combat.

Killed in Action, Germany

PFC Joseph Platko and the 94th Division were relieved on New Years Day 1945 and were quickly shuffled east to support the penetration of the German defenses at the Saar-Moselle Triangle on the Siegfried Line. They battled under wintry conditions into Germany at Tettingen, Butzdorf, Nennig, Berg, Wies, and Orscholz through January.

On February 7, the 301st Regiment was attacking enemy positions near Besch, Germany, when, in the heat of

94th Infantry Division soldiers carrying ammunition to the front lines at Nennig, Germany, Jan 1945 (US Army)

battle PFC Platko was struck in the torso by enemy machine gun fire. He died that day. The Platko family was informed that their son was killed in action three weeks later.

PFC Joseph Peter Platko was buried at the Luxembourg American Cemetery and Memorial at Hamm, Canton de Luxembourg, Luxembourg.

✫ ✫ ✫

PFC ANTHONY F. LASZEWSKI

Service Number 13131681
Company A, 32nd Infantry Regiment, 7th Infantry Division, US Army
Died of combat wounds, Philippines, February 9, 1945

In the early 1900's, Tony and Katy Laszewski left Poland for America to seek a better way of life, and landed in Monessen, Pennsylvania. Unfortunately, they would encounter more than their fair share of tragedy.

Their son Private First Class Anthony Frank Laszewski would survive combat during World War II in the Aleutian Islands off Alaska and the Marshall Islands in the Pacific. The Philippine Islands were his last stop. The desperate enemy combatants would see to it that Anthony Laszewski would never make it home to Monessen.

The Laszewski Family

Anthony's father Tony was born in the Galicia region of Poland and immigrated to the United States in 1900 at the age of ten. After arriving, his last name was spelled in public records several different ways, including Laszewska, Larzsycki, and on his grave marker, Luszcwske. Katy, also called

Katherine but was born Katarzyna Habyak, also immigrated to the US from Galicia in 1913, where she met and married Tony. They both settled in Monessen and married in 1913. Tony was a crane operator at a Monessen tube mill while Katy managed the Laszewski family household.

Anthony Frank Laszewski was born into the family on June 11, 1917, in Monessen. Anthony was the third of their five children. First born was Anna (b1914), followed by Carl Anthony (1915), and then by Mary/Marie (1920) and Stella (1923). The family had been living in a rented home on Oak Terrace Avenue in Monessen. By 1925, they purchased their first home a block away at 37 East Luce Avenue.

In 1925, the first tragedy befell the family when Tony contracted influenza in February and died from the resulting acute pulmonary phthisis (tuberculosis) in April at the age of 36.

In 1930, widow Katy was now living with her five children in the home that Tony had provided for them on East Luce while the children attended school. However, two years later the youngest child Stella died of typhoid fever at the age of 9. The following year, 1933, the eldest child Anna was stricken with tuberculosis and died at the age of 18. In 1937, Katy lost her last daughter to illness when Marie died with tuberculosis at the age of 17. Over a span of twelve years, Katy lost her husband and three daughters to fatal diseases.

Both Carl and Anthony played sports in their youth. Anthony played guard in basketball for the "Sun-Tele" team in 1931 and the PNA Juniors from 1932 through 1934. The boys left school after the seventh grade to support their mother. By 1940, the boys, ages 24 and 22 respectively, were both working as laborers at Pittsburgh Steel while living with their mother on East Luce Avenue. Katy was renting out the rear of their home to another family to supplement her income. Later that year, Carl married and moved to his own residence in Fayette City, Pennsylvania.

The sons joined millions of their fellow American young men and registered for the first US armed forces draft on its first day, October 16, 1940, in accordance with the recently passed Selective Service and Training Act. Anthony registered as a 5'7" 165 lb 23-yr-old with brown hair and gray eyes. He had already joined the Pennsylvania National Guard.

The surprise attack by Japanese armed forces on the US military base at Pearl Harbor, Hawaii, in December 1941 changed the world for Anthony and his brother. Anthony was drafted into the US Army on October 19, 1942. His brother Carl was drafted the following year, in June 1943.

Anthony Heads to Training and to War

Anthony was off for US Army training, and by April 1943, he was ready to serve overseas with the Army Infantry. Private Anthony Laszewski was assigned to the 32nd Infantry Regiment in Company A, in the 7th Infantry Division. They trained in the deserts of California in anticipation of joining the Allied effort against German occupiers in North Africa. Their first surprise came when the 7th Division received orders to retrain for tropical amphibious landings in the Pacific. The second surprise came when they were ordered not to the tropics, but to the cold climate of the North Pacific.

In April 1943, PVT Laszewski, the 32nd Regiment, and the 7th Division were rushed to the Aleutian Islands off the far southwest coast of Alaska. Japanese forces had landed on American soil on the island of Attu. The 7th Division was sent to evict them. Fierce fighting by the American forces finally ejected the Japanese in May. They remained in the Aleutians through August that year.

PVT Laszewski was eventually promoted to Private First Class (PFC), and the 7th Division was sent to Hawaii for additional training on amphibious landings. In January 1944, the Division joined with the US Marines in landings at Kwajalein in the Marshall Islands. They opposed the entrenched Japanese there and on the islands of Roy, Namur, and Eniwetok, and secured the Marshalls for the US in February 1944. The Division returned to Hawaii for further training.

In September 1944, the 7th Division joined General Douglas MacArthur's forces for his promised return to the Philippine Islands. In October, the 32nd

Regiment spearheaded the first landings on Leyte Island, Philippines. Fighting in swamps, tropical jungles, and over rugged mountains, they battled over 37 miles in 60 days of bitter combat. But the Battle of Leyte had just begun.

In the eighteen months since PFC Anthony Laszewski arrived in the Pacific, he endured combat in the Aleutian Islands, the Marshall Islands, and now the Philippines. He was certainly earning

7th Infantry Division on Leyte November 1944 (National WWII Museum)

his wages, but his luck was about to run out.

PFC Anthony Laszewski's 32nd Regiment in the 7th Division continued to press its case against the entrenched Japanese forces on Leyte. They had swept across the island and were about to close the book on their success over the Japanese on Leyte. Word began to spread that they would soon be heading to their next major encounter, this time on the Japanese home island of Okinawa.

But before they left for Okinawa, fate would intervene. In January 1945, while in combat PFC Anthony F. Laszewski was struck by a bullet to his chest, hitting an artery and his spleen, sending him into shock. He was rushed to the Army hospital, but despite multiple blood transfusions and a splenectomy, he died of his wounds on February 9, 1945. His mother was informed by the War Department of his death in March 1945.

Anthony Laszewski Laid to Rest

PFC Anthony F. Laszewski was initially buried at a temporary American cemetery in the Philippines. He was eventually recovered under the Return of the war Dead Program and returned to the US. On September 4, 1948, PFC Anthony Laszewski was buried at St. Hyacinth Cemetery in Monessen, and was posthumously awarded the Purple Heart.

Anthony's brother Carl Laszewski would survive the war. Their mother Katy would eventually be buried alongside her son.

★ ★ ★

PFC ERNEST J. KACHURSKY

Service Number 33704931
Company E, 5th Ranger Battalion, US Army
Killed in action, Luxembourg, February 19, 1945

E rnest John Kachursky was born on February 5, 1923, in Monessen, Pennsylvania to John and Marie (née Horvath) Kachursky. John and Mary had married a year earlier in Donora, Pennsylvania. John was a motorman at the steel mill in Monessen while Marie managed the Kachursky family household.

The Kachursky Family

John Kachursky, also spelled Kacsurszky, was born in Bishop, Pennsylvania to parents who immigrated to the United States from villages in the Austro-Hungarian Empire in the 1800's. Marie was born in the village of Jarmy Elemer-Tanya in Hungary in 1902 and immigrated with her parents to the US in 1911, settling in New Jersey, before she moved to western Pennsylvania where she met and married John.

Ernest was the first of three sons born to John and Marie. His brother Edward was born in 1925, followed by Elmer Julius in 1927. In 1930, the family was living in a rented home at 725 Rostraver Street in Monessen, and their father was working as a tractor operator at Page Steel and Wire in Monessen. By 1935, the family had purchased a home at 425 East Schoonmaker Avenue in Monessen.

In 1942, Ernest graduated from Monessen High School where he had taken the vocational curriculum and participated in the Follies and football. The high school yearbook noted his interest "Since autos fascinate Ernie, he is going to be a skilled mechanic".

The surprise attack by Japanese armed forces on the US military bases at Pearl Harbor, Hawaii, in December 1941 changed the world for Ernest. On June 30, 1942, after graduating from high school, he registered for the US armed forces draft in Monessen. At the time he was a 5'9" 200 lb young single man with brown hair and brown eyes, and he had obtained work as a laborer at the Pittsburgh Steel Company mill in town.

Drafted!

Seventeen months later, Ernest was drafted into the US Army, and he enlisted on November 29, 1943, in Greensburg, Pennsylvania. He reported for duty at Fort George Meade, Maryland on December 20, 1943. His younger brother Edward had just been drafted into the US Army in October. The Kachursky's were now a two-blue-star family.

Private Ernest Kachursky remained stateside for Army training and was soon accepted into the US Army Rangers. The Rangers were voluntarily formed as an elite unit of the US Army to engage in special operations. The 1st Ranger Battalion landed with allied forces in North Africa under Operation Torch in November

1942, and soon after the 3rd and 4th Ranger Battalions were created and joined the fighting as the Allies advanced into Italy.

The 5th Ranger Battalion was formed at Camp Forrest, Tennessee, in November 1943. PVT Kachursky was assigned to the 5th Ranger Battalion and trained with them through April 1944. The 5th Rangers were shipped overseas to the UK in early 1944, where they prepared to join Operation Overlord, the D-Day invasion of continental Europe against German forces. The 5th Battalion landed at Normandy on June 6 and engaged in combat with Allied forces as they pushed the defending Germans back. Kachursky, now Private First Class (PFC), joined the fight with Company E of the 5th Rangers.

A month after the start of the invasion in July 1944, PFC Kachursky was struck by a bullet in the hand causing a fracture, which kept him hospitalized through October. He rejoined his unit while in respite in Belgium and Luxembourg. The 5th Rangers were defending St. Avold, France, while the Battle of the Bulge was occurring to their north.

Killed in Action, Luxembourg

On February 19, 1945, PFC Ernest Kachursky met his fate when he was killed in action in Luxembourg.

PFC Ernest John Kachursky was initially buried in a temporary cemetery in Belgium or France. His remains were recovered under the Return of the War Dead program and returned to the US in July 1948 aboard the transport ship SS Oglethorpe Victory. He was buried at the Grandview Cemetery in Monessen, Pennsylvania. His mother and father would eventually be buried alongside their son.

★ ★ ★

1LT ANTHONY R. RIZZUTO

Service Numbers 13171393 / O-723858
587th Bomb Squadron, 394th Bomb Group, Medium, 9th Air Force, US Army Air Corps
Killed in action, France, February 25, 1945

The pilot was flying the twin-engine B-26 bomber up into its place in the bomber formation. The bombers were to proceed from its base in France on a bombing raid to their target in Germany.

As the bomber's navigator, 1st Lieutenant Anthony Rizzuto's job was to tell the pilot the way to go, identify and communicate course corrections along the way, and plot the course back to home base after the raid. It was not Rizzuto's job to check what was above them.

For B-26 pilots, seeing directly above, below, or behind their aircraft was not always easy. As his aircraft ascended, the pilot of Rizzuto's B-26 did not spot the B-26 bomber directly above them. At 6,300 ft high, they collided.

The Rizzuto Family

Anthony Robert Rizzuto was born on January 22, 1923, to Domenic and Olympia (née Fazzi) Rizzuto in Monessen, Pennsylvania. Domenic and Olympia had married three years earlier in Wellsburg, West Virginia. Domenick was a laborer in a Monessen steel mill while Olympia managed the Rizzuto family household.

Domenic's parents were from Cosenza in the province of Calabria, Italy, and immigrated to the United States in 1900. Olympia's parents were also from Italy and came to the US in 1900. Domenic and Olympia were born in the US after their parents' arrival. Both families settled in the Monongahela River Valley where Domenic and Olympia met.

Anthony was the second of four children born to Domenic and Olympia. James Edward (b1921) was first to arrive. Brothers Louis Carl (1926) and Edmund (1931) completed the family. In 1930, the Rizzuto's were renting an apartment at 415 Reed Avenue in Monessen, and they moved to 415 Fourth Street by 1940.

While growing up, Anthony became skilled at the game of marbles, and he was a runner up in a grade school competition at the age of nine. An avid movie-goer as a teenager, he was asked by the local newspaper to name his top ten films of 1935 and he cited David Copperfield, Here's to Romance, Les Misérables, Lives of a Bengal Lancer, Shipmates Forever, Top Hat, Broadway Gondolier, She, Dante's Inferno, and Last Days of Pompeii. Anthony graduated from Monessen High School in 1940 and went to work in the stainless-steel department at Pittsburgh Steel in Monessen. On June 16, 1942, he registered for the US armed forces draft at the age of 19. Anthony was a 5'7", 180 lb young man with black hair and brown eyes.

Anthony Heads to the Air Corps

Anthony took great interest in aviation, and in December 1942, he volunteered to enlist with the US Army Air Corps. He was immediately sent off for training. Like many his age, he may have been hoping to become a pilot. However, the Air Corps needed navigators, and Aviation Cadet Rizzuto was diverted to the 839th Navigator Training School at Hondo Army Airfield, Texas.

By March 1944, Aviation Cadet Rizzuto passed his competency tests and medical examination and was deemed a fully qualified navigator. He won his wings and became a Second Lieutenant (2LT) in the US Army Air Force.

2LT Rizzuto was assigned to train as a crewmember on the B-26 Martin Marauder twin-engine bomber. He also trained as a bombardier, as B-26 navigators also served as a combination bombardier/navigator on their missions. In June 1944 LT Rizzuto shipped overseas to join the 394th Bomb Group (BG), Medium, now stationed at Boreham, England.

B-26 Bombers of the 394th BG over France (US Air Force)

The 394th BG had been formed in March 1943 at McDill Airfield in Florida. After training, they arrived at Boreham in March 1944, beginning combat operations that month. In the months leading up to June of that year, the unit's B-26 bombers helped to 'soften' the German defenses in France in lead up to the upcoming Operation Overlord, the Allied invasion of the European continent.

2LT Rizzuto joined the 394th BG as a replacement crew in the 587th Bomb Squadron (BS), where he began flying bombing missions over enemy held territory in France. They attacked German defenses and airfields in support of the advancing Allied armies as they made their way cross country and toward Germany.

As the Allies gained ground in continental Europe, the 394th BG moved its bases forward to support the effort. The moved to Holmsley, England in July 1944, from where LT Rizzuto flew his first mission on July 18. He joined several other missions out of Holmsley, and the group relocated across the English Channel in August to the temporary airfield at Tour-en-Bessin, France, built by the Allies after D-Day. In September, they once again moved forward, this time to Bricy, France, and then on to Cambrai/Niergnies, France in October.

LT Rizzuto flew in different roles, as the crew's navigator, bombardier, combination bombardier/navigator, and the "Gee" navigator. The Gee radio-navigation system, developed by the British, measured the time delay between two radio signals to produce a fix, with accuracy of a few hundred yards at ranges up to about 350 miles, and required a dedicated navigator to operate. Between July 1944 and February 1945, LT Rizzuto was promoted to 1st Lieutenant (1LT) and earned an Air Medal for flying over 20 combat missions.

On February 25, 1945, 1LT Rizzuto was in the navigator position piloted by 1LT Reuben E. Corbin, Jr, aboard B-26G #43-34228, on a bombing raid to Colbe, Germany, in a crew totaling nine. The B-26's of the 394th BG took off from Cambrai at about 1100 hours.

As the group formed up, at about 6,300 ft of altitude due west of the airfield, LT Corbin's B-26 rose up, colliding with the aircraft above it, B-26B #42-96044 piloted by 2LT Russell H. Clevenger. Both aircraft fell to Earth near Marcoing, Nord, France.

Fourteen crew members from the two bombers, including 1stLT Anthony Rizzuto, perished in the accident. In March, 1LT Anthony Rizzuto's family was informed by the War Department that he had been killed in action.

Anthony Rizzuto Remembered

1LT Rizzuto was initially buried at the temporary American military cemetery in Champigneul, Marne, France. Under the Return of the War Dead program, his remains were subsequently returned to the United States in 1948. 1LT Anthony Rizzuto was buried at Grandview Cemetery in Monessen on January 29, 1949, with full military honors.

★ ★ ★

SGT CARL RAMSEY

Service Number 426292
20th and 4th Combat Engineers, 4th Marine Division, US Marine Corps
Killed in action, Iwo Jima, March 13, 1945

The Pacific island of Iwo Jima offered nothing of interest to the average WWII soldier. It was 12 square miles of black sand beaches, and volcanic rock.

But to American military planners, the island was vital. Iwo Jima provided a site for a key air field between its air bases in the Marianna Islands and the Japanese home islands. For long range B-29 Superfortress bombers stationed in the Marianna's on 15 hour, 3,000 mile roundtrip missions to Japan and back, Iwo Jima could provide an emergency landing respite along the way. It was also an ideal station for their P-51 Mustang fighter escorts.

Insignia of the 4th Marine Division (USMC)

American forces were tasked with taking the island from the Japanese at all costs. The Japanese defenders would defend their possession, at all costs. Monessen's Carl Ramsey found out the hard way just how costly the battle would be.

The Ramsey Family

Carl Ramsey was born on April 2, 1921, to Reuben Augustus and Mary Edna (née Burkett) Ramsey in Stonerstown, Pennsylvania. Reuben and Mary had married ten years earlier in Everett, Pennsylvania. Reuben was an engineer for the railroad while Mary managed the Ramsey family household.

The Ramsey family had resided in Pennsylvania since it was a British colony prior to the American Revolutionary War. The Burket family heritage traces back to the British colonies of Pennsylvania and Maryland, as well as to Germany. Both families had settled in Bedford County, Pennsylvania by the mid 1800's.

Carl was the third of four children born to Reuben and Mary. Mildred (b1913) was firstborn, followed by Ethel (1915). Paul was their last child to arrive (1936). By 1930, the family had moved into a rented home at 252 Donner Avenue in Monessen, Pennsylvania, where Reuben had taken a job in a Monessen steel mill. By 1940, the family had moved into another rented home at 222 Fourth Street in Monessen. That year, Carl had left high school after his second year and was now working 72 hours a week as a delivery man for a local grocery store.

The surprise attack by Japanese armed forces upon the US military base at Pearl Harbor on December 7, 1941, changed the world for Carl. On February 16, 1942, Carl registered for the US military draft as a 6' 166 lb 20-year-old with brown hair and brown eyes. He had taken a job with Page Steel and Wire in Monessen.

Carl Ramsey Volunteers with the Marine Corps

Carl decided not to wait to be drafted into military service and volunteered to fight in the war alongside his peers. He enlisted with the US Marine Corps on July 22, 1942, and left for training at Parris Island, South Carolina.

A year after enlisting, Carl returned to Monessen where he married his sweetheart, Julia Sabol, also of Monessen, on July 23, 1943. After a seven-day furlough, he left for Camp LeJeune to resume Marine Corps training.

During training, Carl was recognized for his technical skills and assigned to Company C of the 19th Marines (Engineers, Training Center) at New River, North Carolina, to train as a Combat Engineer. Combat engineers perform a variety of military engineering, tunnel and mine warfare tasks, as well as construction and demolition duties in and out of combat zones. Combat engineers facilitate the mobility of friendly forces while impeding that of the enemy. They also work to assure the survivability of friendly forces, building fighting positions, fortifications, and roads. They conduct demolition missions and clear minefields manually or through use of specialized vehicles. Common combat engineer missions include construction and breaching of trenches, tank traps and other obstacles and fortifications; obstacle emplacement and bunker construction; route clearance and reconnaissance; bridge and road construction or destruction; emplacement and clearance of land mines; and combined arms breaching. Typically, combat engineers are also trained in infantry tactics and, when required, serve as provisional infantry.

Now Private First Class (PFC), Carl Ramsey was assigned to the 20th Marines (Engineer) of the 4th Marine Division, which was activated in August 1943 at Camp Pendleton, San Diego, California. The Division trained in preparation for deployment to the Pacific Theater of the war. In January 1944, he was promoted once more, this time to the rank of Corporal (CPL), and they headed to war.

To the Pacific

The 4th Marine Division arrived in Hawaii on January 26, 1944, and immediately entered its first combat engagement on the island of Roi-Namur at the Battle of Kwajalein in the Marshall Islands from January 31 to February 3, 1944. The Japanese put up stiff resistance, but its forces were overcome by the Marines. They returned to the Hawaiian island of Maui for rest and further training. By May, it was clear that they were going to battle once more.

On June 15, 1944, Operation Forager kicked off. Forager was a massive assault against entrenched Japanese forces in the Mariana and Palau Islands. Taking the Mariana Islands of Saipan, Tinian, and Guam would provide island air bases within range of Japan for the new, long-range B-29 Superfortress heavy bombers. The 4th Marines arrived at Saipan who helped secure the island within 24 days. In the heat of battle during June, CPL Ramsey was wounded but eventually returned to the 20th Engineers. He was awarded the Purple Heart for his wounds. The 4th Marines immediately entered the Battle for Tinian on July 24, but CPL Ramsey may have missed the Tinian offensive while hospitalized for his wounds received on Saipan. Tinian was secured by August 1.

In August 1944, the 4th Marines returned to Maui for rest, resupply, and continued training. The 20th Engineers were merged into the 4th Engineers of the 4th Marine Division. They were preparing for their next major offensive, and full fighting capacity and readiness was essential for success. CPL Carl Ramsey was promoted to the rank of Sergeant (SGT) and was appointed Construction Chief in Company C of the 4th Engineers.

The next offensive for the 4th Marines was coming: The Battle of Iwo Jima. The island of Iwo Jima was midway between the Marianas and Japan and could provide a critical stopping point for B-29 bombers returning from bombing missions over Japan. The Japanese were building up defensive capa-

US Marines on the beach during the Battle of Iwo Jima (National Archives)

bilities on the island in hopes of deterring Allied offensives against the Japanese home islands. They had garrisoned over 21,000 troops on the island and had built a wide network of hardened defensive emplacements linked by tunnels through the island's volcanic rock. The US would commit 110,000 men to the battle.

SGT Ramsey on Iwo Jima

The 4th Marines landed on February 19 and entered the thick of battle. SGT Carl Ramsey, with Company C of the 4th Engineers, landed with the 23rd Regimental Combat Team. For days, they fought under difficult circumstances and moved inland from the beaches. The 4th Engineers were tasked with constructing roads from the beaches to facilitate the movement of equipment inland, as well as to set up and operationalize distillation equipment to provide fresh water for the troops. They also began constructing revetments along the existing airfield to house US aircraft. The presence of land mines made the process exceedingly difficult.

During late February, SGT Ramsey met four other Marines from Monessen on Iwo Jima: Richard Danser, Jack Snyder, George Kopko, and Morris Gluhank. CPL Danser wrote a note home on February 27 telling of their chance encounter. Unfortunately, it would be the last mention of anyone seeing SGT Carl Ramsey alive.

On March 4-5, after days of hard work under fire from the enemy, Company C was given a brief respite. On March 6, they immediately returned to duty in demolitions, removing land mines, and road construction.

During the work of the 4th Engineers on March 13, 1945, SGT Carl Ramsey was mortally wounded. He died that day. Three weeks later, his family was informed that he had been killed in action on Iwo Jima.

Carl Ramsey, Laid to Rest

SGT Carl Ramsey was initially buried in the 4th Marine Division Cemetery on Iwo Jima. In January 1949, his remains were returned to the US aboard

the US Army Transport Ship Dalton Victory.
He was finally buried in the cemetery at Everett, Pennsylvania on Sunday, January 30, 1949,
in a solemn service. His Marine Iwo-Jima colleagues from Monessen served as pallbearers.

* * *

Sgt. Carl Ramsey

Monessen Marine Killed in Action In Iwo Invasion

Sgt. Carl Ramsey, who served
with the Marine Corps for more
than two years, was killed in action during the invasion of Iwo
Island, according to work received
by his wife, Mrs. Julia Sabol Ramsey, 1114 Miller avenue, and his
parents, Mr. and Mrs. Ruben Ramsey, 222 Fourth street. He was
slain on March 13.

In December, 1944, Sergeant
Ramsey was awarded the Purple
Heart for wounds received dur-
ing the battle of Saipan in June.
The award was made by Major
General Clifton B. Cates, com-
manding General of the Fourth
Marine Division.

The 24-year-old Marine was a
member of an Engineer Battalion.
Before joining the military service he was employed at the Page
Steel and Wire Division here.

Besides his parents and his wi-
dow, he is survived by two sisters,
Mrs. Mildred Dowlin and Mrs.
Ethel Degg, of Monessen.

Monessen Daily Independent,
April 4, 1945

PFC ANDREW EVANICH, JR.

Service Number 33440893
Company E, 7th Infantry Regiment, 3rd Infantry Division, US Army
Killed in action, Germany, March 15, 1945

Andy Evanich was serving with the US Army in the Mediterranean The-ater of WWII in the summer of 1944 when he received the news: his oldest brother, George, was killed in action on the Pacific Island of Saipan.

Grieving with his fellow infantry-men was the only thing that he could do. Returning to Monessen to console his widowed father wasn't a choice for a soldier preparing for his unit's next combat action.

In nine months, his father would have one more son to mourn.

The Evanich Family

Andrew Evanich, Jr., was born on August 8, 1924, to Andrew Sr. and Anna "Annie" (née Marin) Evanich in Monessen, Pennsylvania. Andrew and Annie met in Glassport, Pennsylvania, down the Monongahela River from Monessen, and they married in Glassport

in 1921. Andrew was a laborer in a Monessen steel mill while Annie managed the Evanich family household.

Andrew Sr. was born Andraj Ivanis II in Zavosyna, Hungary, and immigrated with his father to the United States in 1912 aboard the SS Bremen. Annie was born in Velke Berezne, a village 6 miles away from Zavosyna, and immigrated to the US in 1920 aboard the SS Rochambeau. Both villages are in the region of Carpathian Ruthenia, in the present-day area of far western Ukraine. Little did they realize that they would travel more than 4,500 miles to meet their future spouse who once lived but 6 miles away from where they grew up.

Andrew Jr, "Andy", was the second of three children born to Andrew Sr. and Annie. His brother George arrived first (b1923), followed by his brother John (1927). By 1930, the family was living in their home at 929 Grant Street in Monessen. They continued living there through 1940 while the boys attended school. The family were members of St John the Divine Church. Andy was active in the Boy Scouts.

Andy attended Monessen High School where he played the violin in the high school orchestra. In May 1941, his mother Annie was stricken with myocarditis associated with hepatitis, and she passed away while at St. Francis Hospital in Pittsburgh at the age of 37 yrs.

Andy graduated from high school in 1941-42 and went to work at the Corning Glass Works in nearby Charleroi while living at home with his father and brothers.

Drafted!

The surprise attack by Japanese armed forces on the US military bases at Pearl Harbor, Hawaii, in December 1941 changed the world for millions of Americans, as it did for Andrew. On December 7, 1942, his brother George enlisted with the US Marine Corps. Five days later, at the age of 18 yrs, Andrew registered for the US armed forces draft in Monessen. He was a 5'4" 160 lb young single man with brown hair and brown eyes. Four months later he was drafted into the US Army, and he enlisted at Greensburg, Pennsylvania on

March 20, 1943. Private Andrew Evanich was off to Army boot camp a week later. With George in the Marines and Andy in the Army, the Evanich's were now a two-Blue-Star family.

PVT Evanich trained stateside until April 1944. He was deployed overseas to the 7th Infantry Regiment, known as the "Cottonbalers" of the 3rd Infantry Division as a replacement, and was promoted to Private First Class (PFC).

The 3rd Infantry Division was nicknamed "Rock of the Marne" for its heroic defensive efforts during WWI. The 3rd Division is the only division of the U.S. Army during World War II that fought the Axis on all European fronts and was among the first American combat units to engage in offensive ground combat operations. The Division had been fighting in the European theater since landing with the Allied invasion of North Africa in November 1942 during Operation Torch. The unit saw combat in North Africa, Sicily, Italy, France, Germany and Austria for 531 consecutive days. During the war, the 3rd Infantry Division consisted of the 7th, 15th, and 30th Infantry Regiments, together with supporting units.

In April 1944, PFC Evanich joined Company E of the 7th Regiment. That month, the 3rd Division was breaking out of combat in the Battle of Anzio in Italy and were fighting their way inland and northward during a period of the 3rd Division known as the "Big War of Little Battles" from March to May. The 3rd Division pushed forward and eventually participated in the liberation of Rome. The Division was removed from the front line and went into training for Operation Dragoon, the Allied invasion of the south of France planned for August 1944.

Learns of Brother's Loss

Before Operation Rangoon, PFC Andrew Evanich was informed that his brother, PFC George Evanich, was killed in action on June 19 during the invasion of Saipan, Mariana Islands, in the Pacific.

But Andy had to focus on his responsibilities to his unit. The 3rd Division landed in France during Operation Dragoon and advanced from St. Tropez,

France, up the Rhone Valley, through France's Vosges Mountains, approaching near the Rhine River at Strasbourg in November 1944. After maintaining defensive positions in the brutal winter weather they took part in clearing the Colmar Pocket in January-February 1945.

During battle in France in January 1945, PFC Evanich was struck in the face by shrapnel from an exploding German hand grenade. Fortunately, he recovered from his wounds in the hospital and returned to his unit in February. It was a lucky brush with death. However, PVT Evanich's luck would not hold out.

By March, the 3rd Division was now poised at the France-German border, preparing to cross into the heavily defended homeland of the Third Reich. The crossing was set: March 15 at 0100 hrs. The commander announced to his troops, "Within one hour after the jump off, you will be in Germany". Within 31 minutes, the first troops crossed the border.

On March 15, the Division struck against German Siegfried Line positions south of Zweibrücken and entered Germany against stiff resistance. The German 17th SS Panzer Division stood in their way, as did minefields, trenches, and other obstacles.

Killed in Action

That day during battle, PFC Andrew Evanich Jr. was fatally struck in the abdomen, back, and arm by shell fragments from an artillery round, and died in battle in the vicinity of Utweiler, Germany. His family would be informed three weeks later that he had been killed in action. In less than one year, their second blue star had turned gold. The Germans would surrender less than two months later, ending the war in Europe.

PFC Andrew Evanich, Jr. was buried at the Lorraine American Cemetery at St. Avold, Lorraine, France along with 10,480 other American military dead. He was posthumously awarded the Purple Heart with Oak Leaf Cluster.

★ ★ ★

AOM3C PAUL GRATA

Service Number 8963752
USS Franklin, CV-13, US Navy
Killed in action, Off Coast of Japan, March 19, 1945

B y March 1945, Paul Grata had already witnessed multiple scenes of destruction aboard the US Navy's aircraft carrier USS Franklin. On the 19th of that month, he would experience the worst yet.

Paul Grata was in the ship's hangar deck that morning, preparing TBF Avenger torpedo bombers for an air strike upon the Japanese home islands. He could not have witnessed the Japanese dive bomber releasing its bombs upon the flight deck overhead. Paul Grata would only have heard and felt the concussion of the surrounding explosions.

The Grata Family

Paul Grata was born on January 16, 1918, to William Grata and Marcyanna Surowiec in Portage, Pennsylvania. William and Marcyanna had married in 1910 in Portage. William was a coal miner while Marcyanna managed the Grata family household.

William was born Wincenty Grata in the Galicia region of Poland and immigrated to the United States in 1906. Marcyanna was also born in Galicia and immigrated to the US in 1910. They both settled in Portage where they met and married.

Paul was the fourth of eight children born to William and Marcyanna. Joseph Frank (b1911) arrived first, followed by Mary (1914), Helen (1915), Stanley (1920), Lucy (1923), and Mildred (1925). The last child born to the family, Pegy (1928), passed away at the age of four. All of the children were born while the family was living in Portage.

In 1930, William went to live in Fayette, West Virginia, to work as a coal miner. The rest of the family remained in Portage, where Paul's older siblings were working to support the household and the school-age children attended school. By 1940, William had moved back to Portage where he resumed work as a miner. Joseph, Mary, Helen, and Lucy had married and moved away to start their own families. Paul had ended formal schooling after the eighth grade and was now working as coal miner with his father and his brother Stanley.

Later in 1940, Paul left Portage to live with a cousin in Detroit, Michigan. While living there, Paul joined millions of other young American men and registered for the US armed forces draft in Monessen on the first day it went into effect, October 16, 1940, under the newly enacted Selective Service Act. Paul was a 5'10", 158 lb 22 yr old adult with brown hair and brown eyes.

Paul returned to the Monongahela River Valley where he went to work for the Page Steel and Wire Company factory in Monessen, Pennsylvania. While there, Paul met and fell in love with Joan Mary Netspoon of nearby Belle Vernon, and they married.

The US Enters WWII

The surprise attack by Japanese armed forces on the US military bases at Pearl Harbor, Hawaii, in December 1941 changed the world for millions of Americans, as it did for Paul and his brothers. Paul decided to join the US Naval Reserves, which he did on October 29, 1943, in Greensburg, Pennsylvania. His brothers John and Stanley would enlist in the US Army and head to

Europe. With three sons serving in the US military, the Grata's would display in their front windows a service banner with three blue stars. The hope was that none of the stars would be exchanged for a gold one, the symbol of a family's loss.

Seaman Paul Grata was off to US Navy training, but by the end of 1943, Joan was already eight months pregnant. Before Seaman Grata was deployed overseas, he was introduced to his newborn son, Paul Joseph Grata.

By early 1944, Paul Grata became Seaman 1st Class (S1c), and was assigned to Headquarters Squadron, Fleet Air Wing 14, at the Naval Air Station in San Diego, California. He began his overseas service that March, and on May 21, 1944, S1c Grata was transferred to the USS Franklin CV-13 Aircraft Carrier at Pearl Harbor, Hawaii.

The USS Franklin CV-13 was one of 24 Essex-class aircraft carriers built during World War II for the United States Navy. Commissioned in January 1944, she eventually served in several campaigns in the Pacific War, earning four battle stars.

By the end of June, S1c Paul Grata had become an Aviation Machinist's Mate (AMM), a technical rating specializing in aircraft engines and propellers. By the end of September, AMM Grata was a specialist Aviation Ordnanceman (AOM), responsible for managing aviation ordnance equipment, such as guns, bombs, torpedoes, rockets, and missiles. In November, his rating was formally changed to Aviation Ordnanceman 3rd Class, Turrets (AOM3c (T)), specializing as an aircraft turret mechanic. The Franklin carried eighteen Grumman TBF Avenger torpedo bombers, each equipped with a gun turret, thus the need for this technical expertise aboard ship.

1944: The Franklin Goes on Offense

The months of June through October 1944 proved to be busy and dangerous for the USS Franklin. In June 1944, the Franklin's aircraft flew their first

TBF Avenger Torpedo Bomber with AOM3c Grata's specialty, its gun turret (National Archives)

air strikes upon Japanese military installations. These were directed at the Bonin Islands such as Iwo Jima to impair the ability of the Japanese to defend the planned July amphibious assault upon the Mariana Islands of Guam, Saipan, and Tinian. Then in July, the Franklin sent its fighters and bombers to support the US troops invading Guam. In September, Franklin's fighters and bombers took part in the attack against Yap Island and provided air support for the devastating US invasion of Peleliu.

October proved to be a critical and deadly month for the ship. On the 13th while launching air attacks against the island of Formosa, one of five attacking Japanese G4M "Betty" bombers crashed across its flight deck. Although sustaining relatively minor damage, one crewman was killed and 10 were wounded. Their vulnerability to attack was now plainly apparent and it certainly had a psychological impact upon the crew. Their sense of vulnerability was reinforced when Franklin was bombed two days later by a Japanese Yokosuka D4Y "Judy" dive bomber, killing 3 and wounding 22 men, yet again with minor damage to the ship.

But on the last day of October, while providing air support for the US invasion of the Philippine island of Leyte, catastrophe occurred when Franklin's task group was attacked by Japanese bombers. Although most of the enemy aircraft were shot down, one Japanese kamikaze, either a Judy bomber or a Zero fighter, penetrated the Franklin's defensive anti-aircraft barrage and slammed into the Franklin's flight deck. The attack killed 56 men and wounded 60. Although the ship could still sail under its own power, the 30 by 40 foot hole in its deck meant that it could no longer launch and land aircraft, its primary function. The Franklin was sent back to the naval shipyard at Puget Sound, Washington, for proper repairs.

AOM3c Paul Grata and his crewmates were experiencing a lifetime of peril at sea jammed into four months. They would have four months in port to reflect before being subjected to the peril once again.

Back in the Fight, then Disaster

After repairs were completed, the Franklin returned to Pearl Harbor Hawaii in February 1945. By this time, the Japanese Navy had suffered irrecoverable losses, and the boundaries of their empire were shrinking. The Franklin was again sent on offense. On March 18, 1945, Franklin sailed to Okinawa within 100 miles of Japan to execute the first carrier strike of the war against the Japanese home islands of Kyushu and Honshu.

The next day the Franklin was to launch additional air strikes. By 0700 hrs, 45 of its planes were already airborne, 31 fueled and armed aircraft were on the flight deck preparing to launch, and 22 were in the hangar below to be fueled and armed.

At 0708 hrs, a single Judy dive bomber approached the Franklin undetected by radar, evaded defensive fire from the Franklin's gunners, and dropped two armor-piercing bombs. The massive explosions ignited fires through the second and third decks, and over two dozen armed and fueled aircraft warming up on her flight deck caught fire almost immediately. As heat from the fires "cooked-off" ammunition, bombs, and rockets, secondary explosions rocked the ship while damage control parties attempted to fight the fires.

Nearby, men aboard the Franklin's sister ships watched the carnage in horror. With a nearly 15 degree list to starboard, it took six hours to bring the fires under control. The ship was eventually sailed to New York harbor for repairs by April 1945, since shipyards on the US west coast were at capacity repairing other damaged US Navy ships.

USS Franklin after attack of March 19, 1945 (National Archives)

Out of a crew of 2,600 officers and enlisted men aboard the Franklin on March 19, 1945, 807 were killed and more than 487 wounded. It was one of the deadliest disasters for the US Navy during WWII.

AOM3c Paul Grata lost his life in the attack that day. He was buried at sea with his fallen shipmates and was posthumously awarded the Purple Heart.

Paul Grata, Remembered

AOM3c Paul Grata is memorialized on markers at the Belle Vernon Cemetery, North Belle Vernon, Pennsylvania and the Honolulu Memorial, Honolulu, Hawaii. His name is inscribed on the WWII Veterans Memorial Tablet, at the intersection of Grand Boulevard and Euclid Drive in Monessen City Park.

His son, Paul Joseph "Joe" Grata, would go on to become a community leader and longtime, award-winning journalist. He was one of the nation's premier transportation reporters with a career spanning fifty years and more than 10,000 articles. He passed away in 2022.

★ ★ ★

PVT ANDREW ZRENCHAK

Service Number 33430440
Company F, 187th Glider Infantry Regiment, 11th Airborne Division, US Army
Killed in action, The Philippines, March 26, 1945

W hen Monessen's Andrew Zrenchak enlisted into the US Army in February 1943 to fight in WWII, he probably did not imagine that he would eventually ride engine-less gliders into battle. Yet here he was, serving with the 187th Glider Infantry Regiment heading into combat on the Philippine Island of Luzon.

Two years after enlisting, Private Andrew Zrenchak was with his fellow paratroopers halfway around the world. They were fighting against the entrenched Japanese defenders to dislodge the enemy from a mountain stronghold.

The glider infantryman from Monessen found himself fighting on Mount Maculot on March 26, 1945. But he would never see his hometown again.

The Zrenchak Family

Andrew Zrenchak was born on September 6, 1923, to Adam and Josephine (née Domjanicic) Zrenchak in Monessen, Pennsylvania. Adam was a mill laborer at Pittsburgh Steel, while Josephine managed the Zrenchak family household.

Adam and Josephine were born in Slovakia and immigrated to the United States, with Adam arriving in 1899 and Josephine in 1909. They met and married in Pennsylvania, settling in Monessen. Andrew was the seventh and last child born to the couple. He was preceded by Steve (b1911), Michael (1912), Mary (1914), Josephine (1917), Catherine (1918), and Anna (1921). The family's surname was occasionally spelled Zrinchak, Zrincak, and Zrinschak.

Tragedy struck early in the Zrenchak family. Steve died as an infant before the end of 1912, and Michael lost his life in 1914 before Mary was born.

Early in the family's life, they lived in the Wireton neighborhood of Monessen. By 1930, they were renting a Monessen home at 230 Third Street, and all of the children were attending school. Adam's niece from Connecticut, Mildred, was living with them.

By 1940, the older children had left home to start their own adult lives while Anna and Andrew remained to complete their education at Monessen High. They were now living in a rented apartment at 1157 Schoonmaker Avenue.

The US Enters WWII

Japanese forces launched a surprise attack on the US military bases in Pearl Harbor, Hawaii, on December 7, 1941. The US declared war on Japan, and as an ally of the Japanese Empire, Germany declared war on the US.

Andrew graduated from Monessen High in 1942. His yearbook entry notes that "Andy" was a member of the school's Sportsmen club, participated in the tumbling team, and was an expert hunter.

After graduating, Andy registered for the US armed forces draft on June 30, 1942. He was a 5' 10", 130 lb, single 18-yr-old with brown hair and brown eyes. Andy was now working at Pittsburgh Steel.

The following year, on February 25, 1943, Andy was drafted into the US Army. He enlisted and reported for duty on March 5, 1943.

PVT Andrew Zrenchak left for Army boot camp, and he was soon sent to Camp Mackall, North Carolina. Camp Mackall was a new, specialized training facility for US Army paratroopers and glider infantrymen. Historian Stephen Ambrose described the camp as a "marvel of wartime construction", having been converted from 62,000 acres of wilderness to a camp "with 65 miles of paved roads, a 1,200-bed hospital, five movie theaters, six huge beer gardens, a complete all-weather air-

Parachutists in training at Camp Mackall, NC (Journal of Army Special Operations History, 2005)

field with three 5,000-foot runways, and 1,750 buildings" in just four months.

PVT Zrenchak was training to drop from the sky behind enemy lines, either alone in a parachute or as a passenger on a glider. Training included lengthy forced marches, simulated parachute landings from 34-and-250-foot towers, and practice jumps from transport aircraft. It would be dangerous work, indeed. He was soon assigned to Company F of the 187th Glider Infantry Regiment in the 11th Airborne Division.

Waco CG-4A Glider (National Museum of the USAF)

PVT Zrenchak off to the Pacific

The 187th Glider Infantry Regiment moved to Camp Polk in January 1944 for glider training. They staged at Camp Stoneman, California in April 1944 in preparation for deployment to the Pacific Theater of the war. The regiment departed from San Francisco May 6, 1944, and into the heat of battle. They arrived at Milne Bay, Papua New Guinea on May 29, 1944, and continued their training while acclimatizing to the jungle environs.

The regiment left New Guinea on 11 November 11, 1944, to participate in the invasion of the Philippine Island of Leyte. The 11th Airborne Division operated in the role of regular infantry and assisted in the attack against the Japanese occupiers. The 187th saw heavy fighting and suffered heavy casualties taking Leyte's Purple Heart Hill. They fought through their holiday season on Leyte.

On to Luzon, Philippines

On January 27, 1945, the regiment was sent from Leyte to the island of Luzon, where it would support the invasion of the island. The invasion began on January 9 and was well underway. The Army's objective was the capture of the Philippine capital city, Manila. On January 31, the 187th performed a para-amphibious assault at Nasugbu Bay on Luzon and fought their way into the jungle toward Tagaytay Ridge.

Around March 23, the 187th was sent south to attack the Japanese defensive stronghold on Mount Maculot (aka Macolod). According to the Division's Major Edward M. Flanagan:

"The 187th was preparing for the bloodiest and toughest battle of its military history... The third ridge was heavily wooded and was actually a saddle connecting Mount Macolod with Bukel Hill, a lesser eminence some five hundred yards due east of Macolod. In this area, the Japanese had constructed a formidable defensive position. They had employed impressed Filipino laborers to construct the underground positions and had slain the laborers when the job was complete to insure secrecy. Only dummy positions were visible from

the air, and the mountain bristled with artillery and automatic weapons care-fully laid to cover all approaches with interlocking bands of fire."

Then, on March 26, 1945, while fighting on Mt Maculot, PVT Andrew Zrenchak was mortally struck multiple times by enemy gunfire. He died that day.

Three weeks later, PVT Andrew Zrenchak's family was notified that his life had been lost on Luzon. His loss was announced in a front-page story in the Monessen Daily Independent newspaper.

Andrew Zrenchak, Remembered

PVT Andrew Zrenchak was initially buried at the US Armed Forces Cemetery in Batangas, Luzon, Philippines. He was later reinterred at the Manila American Cemetery and Memorial, Manila, Philippines.

★ ★ ★

PFC LOUIS G. KATSULERIS

Service Number 33950468

Company K, 104th Infantry Regiment, 26th Infantry Division, Third Infantry, US Army

Killed in action, Germany, April 2, 1945

Louis George Katsuleris was born on October 8, 1917, in Monessen, Pennsylvania to George Emanuel and Marigo "Mary" (née Horates) Katsuleris. George and Mary had married in 1910. George was a painter at the Pittsburgh Steel Company in Monessen while Mary managed the Katsuleris family household.

The Katsuleris Family

George and Mary were born on the island of Ikaria in the Aegean Sea. At the time of their birth, Ikaria was under the control of the Ottoman Empire, or Turkey, but it came under the control of Greece in 1912. George immigrated to the United States in 1902, and Mary arrived in 1910. They settled in Monessen to raise a family.

Louis, born Elias, was the second child born to George and Mary. His older sister Dimitria George was born in 1912, followed by Emanuel "Mike" George in 1914. The youngest sister Lena was born in 1923. The family lived

in a rented home at 1047 Schoonmaker Avenue in Monessen, and by 1930, they had purchased a multi-family home at 806 Schoonmaker Avenue. Dimitria had married and moved to a home on Schoonmaker to start her family. In 1931, Louis sang in the boys chorus in the Monessen Junior High School operetta. He was also active in sports, playing junior football with the Jones' Terraplanes in 1932, shortstop for the GAPA baseball team in 1933 and basketball for the Greek All Stars. He graduated from Monessen High in 1936.

In 1939, Louis met and married Clara Henrietta Krofcheck. Clara, from Jerome, Pennsylvania, had been engaged to marry another fellow the prior year before breaking up and marrying Louis. Their first child, George, was born January 11, 1940, and they were living with Louis' parents and his sister Lena in their parents' home at 806 Schoonmaker Avenue. Louis' brother Mike was in his second marriage and was living next door with his wife and daughter.

On October 16, 1940, Louis joined his fellow countrymen and registered for the US armed forces draft on its first day under the recently passed Selective Service Act. He was working as a craneman at the Pittsburgh Steel mill in Monessen as a 5'8" 153 lb married man with brown hair and brown eyes.

The surprise attack by Japanese armed forces on the US military bases at Pearl Harbor, Hawaii, in December 1941 changed the world for Louis. But that did not stop Louis and Clara from growing their family. On March 24, 1942, their second son, Anthony, was born, and on November 6, 1943, their daughter Joan Maria was born.

Drafted!

On June 24, 1944, Louis was drafted into the US Army. Since he was supporting a wife and three young children, he could have sought a deferment under the Selective Service Act Class IIID (Deferred by reason of extreme hardship and privation to wife, child, or parent), but he sensed his call to duty. Louis immediately entered active service and headed out for training. The Allied Invasion of continental Europe had just begun with Operation Overlord and D-Day earlier in June, and fierce combat was now occurring in France and continuing in northern Italy.

After boot camp and more specialized infantry training, Private Louis Katsuleris was assigned as a replacement infantryman and would be attached to Company K, 104th Infantry Regiment, of the 26th Infantry Division. The 26th Division had sailed from the US and landed directly in Normandy, France in September 1944. A month later the Division was in combat and was battling its way across France.

Louis Katsuleris, now Private First Class (PFC), joined the 104th Regiment in January 1945, when it was in the final phase of the Battle of the Ardenne. The Division then maintained defensive positions in the Saarlautern area in southwest Germany from the end of January until early March 1945. The division then drove to the Rhine River and across it at Oppenheim, Germany toward the end of March. The 26th took part in the house-to-house reduction of Hanau and broke out of the Main River bridgehead, heading through to Fulda, Germany on April 1. PFC Katsuleris had been informed that he was to be promoted to the rank of Sergeant shortly.

The following day, April 2, 1945, PFC Louis Katsuleris met his fate. PFC Katsuleris was in combat when he was fatally struck in the abdomen by a bullet. He died that day. Three weeks later, Clara was informed by the War Department that her husband had been killed in action. Two weeks later, Germany surrendered, ending the war in Europe. Clara mourned as others celebrated.

Louis Katsuleris, Remembered

PFC Louis George Katsuleris was initially buried in a temporary cemetery in Europe. His remains were recovered under the Return of the War Dead program and returned to the US in November 1948 aboard the transport ship SS Carol Victory. He was buried at the Grandview Cemetery in Monessen, Pennsylvania, on January 8, 1949.

✫ ✫ ✫

S/SGT CARL A. KRONANDER

Service Number 33159294
35th Infantry Regiment, 25th Infantry Division, US Army
Killed in action, The Philippines, May 3, 1945

Carl Albert Kronander was born on January 10, 1920, in Monessen, Pennsylvania to Albert and Olga (née Wallin) Kronander. Albert and Olga had married about 1915. Albert was a laborer in the barbed wire department of the Pittsburgh Steel Company in Monessen, while Olga managed the Kronander family household.

Insignia of the 35th Infantry Regiment (US Army)

The Kronander Family

Albert was born Albert Walter Augustsson Kronander in Åhult, Sjötofta, Västra Götaland, Sweden and immigrated to the United States in 1900 aboard the SS St. Louis. Albert became a naturalized US citizen in 1910. Olga was born Olga Kristina Wallin in Galve, Sweden, and immigrated to the US in 1913 on the SS Adriatic. Albert and Olga ended up in Monessen in search of employment, where they met, fell in love, and married.

Carl was the fourth of eleven children born to Albert and Olga. His eldest sister Dagny Erika Gustava arrived first (b1915), followed by Agnes Margaret (1917), and then Arthur (1918). After Carl's birth came Knute Enar (1922),

Wilhelmina Barbara (1923), Rober Walter (1925), Dorothy Mae (1927), Lars Arnold (1929), Martin Oliver (1930), and Anders Hubert (1932).

In 1920, the family was living in a rented home at 463 Clarendon Avenue in Monessen. By 1930, they had moved two blocks away to another rented home at 413 Motheral Avenue. The family moved to another rented home at 406 Second Street by 1940. Dagny had left for work in Pittsburgh, but the rest of the children were living together in the small home. A Second Street neighbor[14] recalled the older Kronander boys as tough kids.

In 1940, Carl was working as a truck driver after graduating from Monessen High School. The following year, he took a job at the Kuosman Hardware store on Sixth Street. On July 1, 1941, Carl registered for the US armed forces draft as a 5'9" 165 lb single man with blonde hair and blue eyes.

Hearing the drumbeat of war in Japan and Europe, Carl's brother Knute joined the US Army Infantry in January 1941. His oldest brother Arthur enlisted in the US Army Air Corps in August 1941. Then the surprise attack by Japanese armed forces on the US military bases at Pearl Harbor, Hawaii, in December 1941 changed the world for Carl and his brothers.

On February 25, 1942, Carl was drafted into the US Army and reported for duty in Pittsburgh. Later that year, his brother Robert joined the US Navy in August 1942. The Kronanders were now a four-blue-star family.

Off to the Pacific

Private Carl Kronander remained stateside for Army training and left to join the US Army 35th Infantry Regiment and the 25th Infantry Division by June 1942. During his tenure with the 35th Regiment, he was promoted to Staff Sergeant (S/SGT).

The 25th Division had been activated in October 1941 and stationed at Schofield Barracks, Honolulu Hawaii. The Division had a front row seat when the Japanese attacked Pearl Harbor. The 35th was sent to Guadalcanal in November 1942 to relieve Marines near Henderson Field. They entered combat in January 1943 in some of the most bitter fighting of the Pacific campaign.

---

[14] Michael Turanin (1931-2024), the author's uncle.

The 35th Regiment took part in the capture of Vella Lavella from August through September 1943.

After further training in New Caledonia, the Division landed on the island of Luzon in January 1945 to enter the struggle for the liberation of the Philippines in the Battle of Luzon. In February, the Division began operations in the Caraballo Mountains and fought its way against fierce enemy counterattacks. At the beginning of May, the 35th Regiments encountered stiff Japanese resistance at the Balete Pass. The Japanese commander had given the order to stand ground at all costs.

On May 3, 1945, S/SGT Carl Kronander met his fate when he was killed in action during the Battle of Balete Pass. Three weeks later, the War Department informed

155mm Artillery Firing during Battle of Balete Pass (National WWII Museum)

his family that he had been killed in action on Luzon. He was 25 yrs old.

S/SGT Carl Albert Kronander was buried at the Manila American Cemetery and Memorial, Manila, Philippines with 16,858 other American service members. He was posthumously awarded the Purple Heart. His three brothers returned home alive by the end of the war.

★ ★ ★

2LT CARL G. CEKOLA

Service Numbers 13038286 / O-1999680
305th Squadron, 442nd Troop Carrier Group, Ninth Air Force, US Army Air Force
Killed during training, France, May 7, 1945

By May 1945 the war in Europe was coming to an end. Soviet forces were battling the desperate defending German troops on the Eastern outskirts of Berlin, Germany. American and British armies were just miles away approaching Berlin from the west.

In France, pilot Second Lieutenant Carl Cekola had every reason to be optimistic about going home. But rumors spread that American forces in Europe might be transferred to the Pacific to fight the Japanese once Europe was won. All he could do was go about his normal routine in France, which included training of his fellow pilots.

On May 7, 1945, the day before Germany surrendered, Lt Cekola's training flight ended tragically. He was the last man from Monessen to lose his life in Europe before the end of the war with Germany.

The Cekola Family

Carl George Cekola was born on March 6, 1918, to John and Louise (née Schedor or Chedor) Cekola in Monessen, Pennsylvania. John and Louise had married four six years earlier in Germany before immigrating to the United States. John was a laborer in a tube factory while Louise managed the Cekola family household. John Cekola was born Severin Czekala in Pozen, Poland, and Louise was born in Gelsenkirchen, Germany, where they married in 1912. They immigrated to the United States the same year aboard the SS Caronia, arriving at the home of Louise's father in Rillton, Pennsylvania. Their first son, Adolf, was born in 1912 in Germany but died as an infant after his arrival in the US.

Carl was the last of three children born to John and Louise after their arrival in Pennsylvania. John Joseph was the first born (b1913) in Rillton. The family then moved to Monessen, where Elsa (Elsie) was born in 1917. By 1920, the Cekola's were living in a rented home at 538 Linden Avenue. Ten years later, the family had moved to a rented home several blocks up the hill at 1024 Rostraver Street.

Carl enjoyed baseball and played first base for the Luce All Stars in 1934 at 16 yrs of age. By 1940, Carl's siblings John and Elsie had married and left home to begin their own families. Carl left school after completing seventh grade and worked with his father at Pittsburgh Steel Mill in Monessen while living at home with his parents.

On October 16, 1940, Carl joined millions of other young American men and registered for the US armed forces draft on the first day it went into effect under the newly enacted Selective Service Act. He was a 5'11" 165 lb young single man with brown hair and gray eyes, living at 1515 Rostraver, down the street from the home of his parents.

Hearing the growing drumbeat of war in Europe and the Pacific, Carl decided to enlist with the US Army Air Corps, which he did on September 25, 1941, in Donora, Pennsylvania. He was assigned service number 13038286. By December, the US would enter the war after the surprise attack by Japanese armed forces on the US military bases at Pearl Harbor, Hawaii.

Private Carl Cekola initially served in the US Army Military Police and was stationed in Bakersfield, California. He was eventually promoted to Sergeant and then Staff Sergeant (S/SGT). S/SGT Cekola elected to apply to train as a glider pilot when the opportunity became available to non-commissioned officers. S/SGT Cekola attended and graduated from Basic Glider Training School, operated by the Arizona Glider Academy, at Echeverria Field, Wickenburg, Arizona, by March 1943. Afterwards he proceeded to Big Glider School in Albuquerque, New Mexico. S/SGT Cekola transitioned to South Plains Army Airfield, the "Home of the Winged Commandos", at Lubbock Texas, that May. South Plains was the Army Air Corps' largest glider school in the nation.

Being a Glider Pilot

Glider pilots were required to master the skills of taking-off while in tow by a large propeller-driven towing aircraft, such as the C-47 Skytrain, maintaining flight while in tow, and guiding his aircraft after release to a safe landing on unimproved terrain. It was not an easy assignment, but one that S/SGT Cekola would eventually conquer.

S/SGT Cekola, now 25, met and fell in love with Stella Alta Wolf, a student nurse, age 21, of Clovis, New Mexico. They married on July 25, 1943, in Lubbock where he was stationed.

On July 28, 1943, S/SGT Cekola met training requirements demonstrating the required competencies for piloting gliders and was made Flight Officer (FL O). He was off for additional training in Kentucky. FL O Cekola was eventually assigned to the 305th Troop Carrier Squadron (TCS) of the 442nd Troop Carrier Group (TCG) in the US Army Airborne Infantry.

The 305th TCS had been constituted in May 1943 and was activated that September. The unit flew C-47 Skytrains both as troop carriers and for towing glider aircraft. The unit was equipped with the CG-4A "Haig" Glider, made by the Weaver Aircraft Company (WACO). The CG-4A was constructed of fabric-covered wood and metal and was crewed by a pilot and copilot. It could carry 13 troops and their equipment, or a 1/4-ton truck (i.e. a Jeep), a 75 mm howitzer, or a 1/4-ton trailer, loaded through the upward-hinged nose section.

With Carl in training, Stella stayed behind to complete nursing school and went to work at Clovis Memorial Hospital. By March 1944, she accepted a nursing position at a hospital in the Monongahela Valley and moved to Carl's parents' home in Monessen.

Waco Gliders being towed by a C-47 Skytrain (US Air Force)

In March 1944, FL O Carl Cekola was sent overseas to Europe with the 305th TCS, and settled into their base at Fulbeck, Lincolnshire, England. Their deployment was in anticipation of the upcoming D-Day invasion of occupied Europe.

The massive invasion was launched on June 6, 1944. The 305th arrived over France on D-Day plus 2, June 8. Piloting his CG-4A glider that day, FL O Carl Cekola delivered additional airborne troops into the fray. After D-Day, the group moved to RAF Weston Zoyland, England, and supported the invasion from there. In mid-July, the 305th was sent to Follonica airfield in Italy where they took part in air drops supporting the invasion of southern France in August. In September 1944, the group supported the ill-fated Operation Market Garden attack across the Netherlands. The 442nd TCG would earn a Presidential Unit Citation for its work in Europe.

By November 1944, the 305th had moved to France, first to Peray, and then to the former German Luftwaffe airfield at St-Andre-de-L'Eure. Carl

Cekola, now 2nd Lieutenant (2LT) would participate in all 305th TCS operations over the European continent through Spring of 1945. German forces were on their heels as the Allied advanced into the German homeland. On April 30, 1945, the dictator Adolf Hitler committed suicide which was announced the next day. The surrender of Germany was days away.

No Celebrating for the Cekola Family

While US troops in Europe celebrated the demise of Adolph Hitler, they and their families pondered their return home. Word was that American forces may be redeployed to the Pacific to fight the stubborn Japanese aggressors. Regardless, soldiers were ordered to continue to fight the Germans until the end. For those stationed at the rear like Lt Cekola, normal routines were still the orders of the day.

On May 7, 1945, at 1215 hrs, 2LT Carl George Cekola and FL O Willie M. Jones (service number T-138508) departed St-Andre-de-L'Eure airfield on a routine training mission. FL O Jones was to be 'checked-out' on an L-4 Grasshopper (a USAAF Piper J-3) liaison aircraft, an aircraft he had not flown before. While LT Cekola was flying the aircraft in a tight turn at low altitude over the nearby village of Pacy-sur-Eure, the aircraft lost its lift, spinning twice in a descent, and fell to the village's cobblestone street at 1240 hrs. FL O Jones sur-

L-4 Grasshopper Reconnaissance Aircraft (US Army)

vived the crash, but 2LT Carl Geoge Cekola did not.

Carl Cekola's family was likely celebrating the end of the war in Europe and awaiting word on when he might return home. Glee turned to grief when they learned of his loss two weeks later. He was the last Monessen man to lose his life in the European theater during the war.

2LT Carl George Cekola was initially buried locally in France. Under the Return of the War Dead program, he was brought to the United States and buried at Grandview Cemetery in his hometown of Monessen on June 29, 1949. He was awarded the Air Medal for his performance in Europe with the 305th TCS.

★ ★ ★

SGT JACK W. SWANEY

Service Number 329660
Company C, 1st Battalion, 1st Marines, 1st Marine Division, USMC Reserves
Killed in action, Okinawa, June 9, 1945

U S Marine Corps SGT Jack W. Swaney had just arrived as the critical Battle of Okinawa was underway in April 1945. Having been stationed in the virtual safety of the Panama Canal Zone since the beginning of WWII, he was undoubtedly prepared to experience real combat.

After 32 months in Panama, it would only take 8 weeks in Okinawa to end his tour of duty. As his company viciously fought the entrenched Japanese forces defending Kunishi Ridge, he caught a bullet in his gut.

Jack Swaney would never see his wife and family again.

The Swaney Family

Jack Wilbur Swaney was born on April 26, 1916, to Robert James and Pearl Emma (née McKee) Swaney in Monessen, Pennsylvania. Robert and Pearl had married in 1913. Robert was an assistant roller at Pittsburgh Steel in Monessen, while Pearl managed the Swaney family household.

The Swaney and McKee families' trace back to Western Pennsylvania in the early 1800's. The Swaney's also have ancestry from the Alsace-Lorraine region of France in the late 1700's, while the McKee family has some of its roots in England from the early 1800's.

Jack was the second of five children born to Robert and Pearl. Robert Jr. was firstborn (1913). A daughter, Grace Elizabeth, (1918) followed Jack. Brothers William Delmont (1921) and Thomas Edward (1926) completed the family. In 1920, they were living in their home at 207 Chestnut Street in Monessen. By 1930, the family moved to a larger Monessen home at 1122 Graham Avenue, as their father was now a foreman in the steel mill.

A student at Monessen High School, Jack was a leader and participated in several scholastic activities. He was elected vice president of the ICS Engineers, and in 1933 as a member of the football team, was groomed to become its co-captain. According to the local newspaper, Jack carried his weight at 224 lbs as a "giant tackle" for the team. The coach molded his team around Jack and two other players. He was an aggressive player, slacking through the line and blocking a punt against the team from McKeesport in September 1935. His teammate, guard August Restaino, would later join the US Army Air Corps where he lost his life in combat over France. By the end of 1935, Jack was named to the second team of their league's Big Six All Stars. He went on to graduate the following year.

As did many graduating students, Jack took a job as a laborer at Pittsburgh Steel in Monessen. With the rumblings of war heard from Europe and the Pacific, the United States Congress passed the Selective Service and Training Act in 1940. The act established the first peacetime draft for the US military and created a path for building the armed forces. On October 16, 1940, Jack joined millions of other young men and registered for the military draft on its first day. He was a 6', 210 lb 24-yr-old with brown hair and brown eyes, living at the home of his parents at 1336 Summit Avenue in Monessen.

Jack had been an active member of the Methodist Church, the Knights of Pythias, and the Elks Lodge in Monessen.

The US Enters WWII

Japanese forces launched a surprise attack on the US military bases in Pearl Harbor, Hawaii, on December 7, 1941. The US declared war on Japan, and as an ally of the Japanese Empire, Germany declared war on the US. Jack decided to help defend his country and immediately enlisted with the US Marine Corps on December 8. He left for training three days later to Marine boot camp at Parris Island, South Carolina, where he celebrated his first Christmas away from home. When Jack joined the Marines, the local paper noted his past prowess on the Monessen football team, commenting "Let's throw a flying tackle at those Japs...".

Before long, Jack's brother William enlisted in the US Army Air Force, and Thomas joined the US Army. The Swaney's became a 3-Blue-Star Family.

It was not long before Private Jack Swaney was deployed. The US had to ensure that the critical passageway between the Atlantic and Pacific Oceans, the Panama Canal, was secured. In January 1942, he was sent to the Marine garrison at the Panama Canal Zone aboard the USS President Hayes. It was his first trip to the tropics. By April, he was assigned to the Marine Guard at the Marine Barracks in Balboa, Canal Zone, and was promoted to Private First Class (PFC) by July.

In January 1943, PFC Swaney was admitted to the US Naval Hospital for three days and recovered quickly. By July of that year, he was promoted to the rank of Corporal, and then to Sergeant by January 1944. That month, he was reassigned to the Tank Farm at Gatun, Canal Zone. The Gatun Tank Farm was a major fuel storage facility used to supply ships traversing between the two oceans. He served as a police sergeant during his Gatun detachment.

In July 1944, SGT Jack Swaney left the Canal Zone for the Marine Barracks at the Norfolk Navy Yard, Portsmouth, Virginia. He had been in the Canal Zone for 32 months and was certainly happy to return to the continental US.

SGT Swaney was sent to US Marine training at Camp Lejeune, North Carolina, by October 1944, and was placed in the Headquarters and Service Company, Infantry Schools Battalion, Schools Regiment. He was granted furlough to return to Monessen in December 1944, where he married Betty Virginia Menefee on December 22. Betty was also a native of Monessen and worked as a receptionist in a dental office.

But Marines were needed in the Pacific, and SGT Swaney had to prepare for combat. He was included in the Marines' 54th Replacement Draft and transferred to Camp Pendleton, California, in preparation for deployment in the Pacific. While at training, he learned that his cousin, PVT John F. Swaney, had been killed in action in the Battle of Iwo Jima on March 2, 1945. The Swaney family mourned. Jack's younger brothers William and Thomas had also joined the service, and the Swaney's were now a 3-Blue-Star Family. It was a serious time, indeed.

Jack Swaney left US soil for the last time on April 14, 1945.

SGT Jack Swaney was assigned to Company C, 1st Battalion, 1st Marines, of the 1st Marine Division. He was about to be inserted into one of the bloodiest battles of the war. Jack would never see Betty again.

Battle of Okinawa

1st Marines on Okinawa (US Marine Corps)

The 1st Marines had already landed with Operation Iceberg, the US invasion of the Japanese home island of Okinawa on April 4, 1945, as part of the III Amphibious Corps. They had landed on the western shore of the northern part of the island. Upon landing on Okinawa, SGT Swaney was quickly transported to their location to join the fight.

The battle in April and May saw ferocious fighting. By June 5, the 1st Marine Division was progressing southwest to seal off Japanese forces on the Oroku peninsula. They then turned southward toward Iwa in the central southern part of the island on June 6. The Japanese had placed their final defensive line in the area of the Kunishi Ridge. Kunishi Ridge was a steep, coral escarpment which totally dominated the surrounding grasslands and rice paddies. Kunishi was high and long and honeycombed with enemy caves and tunnels. The Japanese were firmly established for their final stand on Okinawa.

As SGT Swaney's company fought along Kunishi Ridge, he was struck by a bullet in his abdomen. The date was June 9, 1945. SGT Jack Swaney was killed in action that day at the age of 29. Two weeks later, his family was informed that his life had been lost in combat.

Jack Swaney, Remembered

SGT Jack W. Swaney was initially buried at the First Marine Division Cemetery #1 in Okinawa. He was eventually transported to Monessen, where he was finally interred at Grandview Cemetery in 1949.

★ ★ ★

2LT HUGH B. SMYTH

Service Numbers 13130597 / O-715044
333rd Fighter Squadron, 318th Fighter Group, 7th Air Force, US Army Air Force
Killed in action, Japan, July 8, 1945

From the cockpit of his P-47 Thunderbolt fighter, Monessen's LT Bud Smyth watched his friend's flaming aircraft crash into the sea.

As he circled the downed airman off the coast of Japan, Bud suddenly felt the rapid staccato of bullets punching into the aluminum skin of his P-47. The swarm of Japanese fighters came out of nowhere, and it was too late to evade them. His damaged aircraft was now engulfed in flames.

Unable to control or escape the P-47, LT Smyth and his fatally-stricken aircraft plummeted into the sea seconds later. His fellow American pilots circled where his Thunderbolt went down, but Bud and his fighter were gone.

The Smyth Family

Hugh Bernard "Bud" Smyth was born on May 10, 1921, to Hugh Alexander and Alice Margaret (neé Murphy) Smyth in Monessen, Pennsylvania. Hugh and Alice married in Monessen in 1919. Hugh was an office clerk in a Monessen steel mill while Alice managed the Smyth family household.

Hugh Sr. was born in Monongahela, Pennsylvania to parents who had immigrated to the United States in the mid 1800's from Scotland and England. Alice was born in Scottdale, Pennsylvania to parents who came to the US in the late 1800's from Ireland and England. Both families settled in Western Pennsylvania where they raised their families.

Their son Hugh was fondly called "Buddy" or "Bud". He was the second of six children born to the Smyths. The first, daughter Nell Margaret, was born in 1920. After Hugh came Vincent James (1922), Margaret Alice (1924), Patricia Marie (1926), and Rita Elaine (1927). Buddy suffered a bout of diphtheria at the age of five, and contracted childhood illnesses of measles, chickenpox, and whooping cough, not atypical for a child during the 1920's.

By 1930, the family was living with Hugh Sr's parents in a large Monessen home at 169 Schoonmaker Avenue. Hugh Sr. was active in the community and served as the Grand Knight of the Monessen chapter of Knights of Columbus.

In 1940, the family was living in a rented Monessen home at 842 Donner Avenue. Their father was now out of work, but Alice was employed as a time-keeper, and Nell, Buddy, and Vincent were all working to support the family. Buddy was driving a truck for the Civilian Conservation Corps (CCC), a public works organization created during President Roosevelt's New Deal during the Great Depression. The CCC put citizens to work on national development projects.

On December 7, 1941, the US suffered a surprise attack by Japanese forces at Pearl Harbor, Hawaii, and the US entered the war against Japan, Germany, and Italy. It was only a matter of time before Bud would step up to do his patriotic duty.

On February 16, 1942, Bud joined millions of others and registered for the military draft. He was a 5'9" 150 lb 20-yr-old with brown hair and hazel eyes.

By that time, he had been hired by the Koppers Construction Company and working in Monessen. Eight months later, on October 8, 1942, Bud volunteered to serve in the US Army and was assigned service number 13130597.

But Bud quickly learned that Army infantry was not his calling... flying was. He applied for Aviation Cadet training in the US Army Air Corps and was accepted in June 1943. Bud was eager to give it a go, and was off to San Antonio Aviation Cadet Center, Texas.

Bud Smyth earns his Wings as a Fighter Pilot

By the end of 1943 the war was raging. Bud was now in flight training at Aloe Army Airfield in Victoria, Texas, in the Aviation Cadet Class "44-C". Cadet Hugh Smyth successfully completed basic, primary, and advanced flying training and in January 1944, he qualified as an Army Air Corp pilot. He was commissioned as Second Lieutenant (2LT) and received his officer's service number O-715044.

Most aviation cadets aspired to fly single engine fighters, the sports cars of the sky. Many, at the sole discretion of the Army Air Corps, were instead sent to train for large bombers or transport aircraft. To his delight, Bud was determined by the Air Corps to have the aptitude to fly fighters, and 2LT Hugh "Bud" Smyth was sent off to fighter school.

Bud's first stop for fighter school was the Army Airfield at Miami Beach, Florida in Feb 1944, and then on to the Technical Training School at Seymour Johnson Field, North Carolina in May. After a short stay at Johnson Field, Bud transferred to Bluethenthal Field, NC from May to June 1944 with the 124th Army Air Force Base Unit. He was checked out with the Pilot Replacement Section J, 120th Army Air Force Base Unit (Fighter), in Richmond Virginia where he passed his medical exam.

While at Bluethenthal, Bud received intensive indoctrination on the US Army Air Corps' Republic P-47 Thunderbolt fighter. The P-47 was affectionately known as "The Jug" due to its large round radial engine followed by its barrel-shaped fuselage. It was equipped with eight 50 caliber machine guns and could carry rockets and bombs to support ground troops. Fully loaded at 8 tons, the P-47 was among the heaviest of Allied fighters. It was a formidable war machine, a flying beast, and this Monessen son had the privilege to fly it. When he completed his training at Bluethenthal, LT Bud Smyth was a qualified P-47 pilot.

In September 1944, Bud departed stateside and headed to his new assignment: the 318th Fighter Group (FG), now stationed in the Pacific's Mariana Islands. He was headed to war.

The 318th Fighter Group in the Pacific

The 318th FG had formed and trained on the Hawaiian island of Oahu after the entry of the US into WWII. They expected to be deployed further west in the Pacific Ocean as the war progressed.

The US had a strategic objective to construct airfields within range of the Japanese home islands. A new, long-range bomber, the Boeing B-29 Superfortress, was just being delivered to the Army Air Force, and the Mariana Islands of Saipan, Tinian, and Guam were within the B-29's range of Japan. But first, the islands had to be wrestled from the Japanese.

While the eyes of the world focused on Operation Overlord, the Allies' D-Day invasion of France in June 1944, another strategic invasion was underway. Operation Forager, the amphibious invasion of the Mariana Islands, was launched.

Forager began with the Invasion of Saipan on June 15. Once taken at great cost, the 318th FG flew in from Oahu early July to set up its air base at East Field. The 318th quickly joined the fighting by protecting ground troops and attacking Japanese defenses during the invasion of the neighboring islands of Guam and Tinian. By the end of July, all three islands were firmly in the hands of US forces.

Bud flies air combat over Saipan

Upon his arrival on Sept 27, 1944, LT Bud Smyth was assigned to the 318th's 333rd Fighter Squadron. By then, the 318th consisted of 84 P-47D Thunderbolts, six P-61 Black Widow night fighters, and five F-5 Lightning photo reconnaissance aircraft. With a modest contingent of about 30 officers and 70 enlisted men, they were in dire need of manpower. Bud arrived just in time.

LT Smyth soon flew with the 318th in combat air patrol, or CAP, flying in predetermined flight patterns to defend the conquered islands. But by November, the group's mission had changed from tactical support of the Marianas to strategic, including long range bomber escort and fighter interdiction. A squadron of longer-range P-38 Lightning fighters was added to the 318th to protect the newly arriving B-29's.

In November, the B-29's based at Saipan and Tinian began bombing the home islands of Japan. This drew additional Japanese bomber and fighter attacks at those bases, and the 318th was pressed into additional CAP flights over the islands.

By January 1945, the group had grown to over 260 officers and 200 enlisted men. The P-47s flew constant daylight combat air patrol over Saipan and Tinian, while the radar-equipped P-61s did so at night. LT Bud Smyth was undoubtedly busy rotating with his fellow pilots between CAP flights.

Bud's first non-CAP mission was on January 26, 1945, in a 2-hour flight of four P-47s to strafe the non-operational Japanese air base on Pagan Island, about 100 miles north. Still occupied by Japanese stragglers, these missions kept this enemy airfield out of the war.

But the P-47D Thunderbolts of the 318th had become war-weary and required significant maintenance. It was time to retire them… and to move westward.

New P-47s and Ie Shima

With the Mariana Islands now securely in the hands of US forces, the fighters of the 318th were needed at the new front lines of the Pacific war… the Ryukyu islands. In March, the group was informed that they would be relocating their base, and in April, they began the move. While the ground crews boarded transport ships, the pilots stayed behind to receive new fighters and fly them to their new base.

Republic P-47N Thunderbolt Fighter, loaded with rockets and bombs (National Museum of the USAF)

Their new aircraft was the "N" version of the P-47. The P-47N was developed for the longer range necessary for the Pacific and could fly over 2,000 miles. The most notable visual difference was its bubble canopy, versus the razorback canopy of the P-47D, which gave the pilot an unobstructed view of enemy fighters approaching from behind.

LT Smyth's first mission in the P-47N was to experience the aircraft in combat. On May 6, 1945, a flight of 20 P-47Ns went west from Saipan to the Japanese-held island of Truk on a fighter sweep seeking targets of opportunity. It was a 6 ½ hour round trip mission which hit three Japanese planes and three ships. It was Bud's final mission from the Saipan base.

In May 318th conducted the largest, longest aircraft ferrying project of the war. The group flew their 111 new P-47Ns over 5,500 miles, with stops at six island air bases to their final destination: the Ryukyu island of Ie Shima. The island had just been secured from occupying Japanese forces in April, and Ie Shima was a strategic location for the 318th.

The Battle of Okinawa, the larger Japanese island just three miles east of Ie Shima, was underway. Heavy fighting by US Marines and Army infantry required close air support. Armed with guns, rockets, and bombs, the P-47Ns were just the aircraft to provide it.

The Japanese had also introduced a menacing weapon, suicide Kamikaze aircraft, whose pilots purposely intended to crash their bomb-laden aircraft into ships of the US Navy surrounding Okinawa. The Navy needed protection in the air, and the P-47s were on the job.

Because Ie Shima was within range of enemy airfields in Japan and along the coast of China, the 318th was also to attack these bases in preemptive strikes. The Japanese recognized the threat imposed by US aircraft on Ie Shima and began aerial strikes on the 318th three times a day. It was a dangerous and busy place, indeed.

LT Smyth's first combat mission from Ie Shima was May 28, 1945. He joined a flight of twelve P-47Ns to the Japanese home island of Kyushu. The flight, termed a "heckling mission", was to surprise and harass the Japanese in their homeland. They traveled three hours to Kyushu and "heckled" the Japanese defenses by strafing with their machine guns for an hour. The group shot down four defending Japanese Zero fighters.

On June 7, 1945, LT Smyth flew a mission with 42 P-47Ns to escort two USN PB4Y Privateer bombers and two F-5 Lightning reconnaissance planes to southern Kyushu. The highly successful seven-hour flight resulted in the downing of 24 enemy aircraft after fighting for 1 1/2 hours in the sky over Kyushu. Unfortunately for LT Smyth, the turbocharger of his P-47 malfunctioned, and he was forced to return to Ie Shima before completing the mission.

LT Bud Smyth joined a flight of 38 P-47s to dive bomb enemy airfields on Kyushu on June 20. Smyth was now flying wingman to his flight leader, providing cover from attacking enemy aircraft. The four-hour flight damaged the Kikai airfield and took out a radar installation. LT Smyth's squadron alone fired over 1,000 rounds of ammunition.

He again flew missions to Kyushu on June 25 and 27, and July 1 and 3, successfully returning from all. Bud had survived the gauntlet of defenses over one of Japan's home islands. The Japanese pilots, however, were not about to give up.

Bud Smyth's luck runs out

LT Bud Smyth was assigned to fly P-47N #44-88059 on July 8, 1945, as one of eight P-47N Thunderbolts to dive-bomb enemy targets of opportunity in the Chusan (Zhoushan) archipelago off the coast of China. The group took off from Ie Shima at 1323 hrs and headed northeast.

En route, the flight rendezvoused with their navigating escort, a US Navy PB4Y Privateer. The pilot of the Privateer informed them that their mission had been diverted to the Sasebo/Nagasaki area in northwest Kyushu to attack targets of opportunity. While the pilots of the 318th had been repeatedly warned of a concentration of enemy power in that area, there were no specific intelligence briefings about this target prior to their mission. They had only been briefed on the original target of Chusan and could not be certain of what might await them over Kyushu that day.

Flying at 10,000 ft, the P-47s arrived over the Kyushu area at 1545 hrs. They located and dive-bombed an enemy radar station at Kabashima island and a boat. Proceeding northwest to Ukushima island, they bombed a dock, trucks, and structures, then aimed their aircraft east toward Hirado Shima, and attacked a lighthouse and two boats. LT Smyth bombed an enemy ship and sent it to the bottom of the sea.

Then the skies over Kyushu became complicated.

One of Bud's fellow fliers, 2LT Billie D. Holt (O-714923), attempted to skip-bomb a boat from a height of 150 ft. When the bomb hit the water, it exploded, sending bomb fragments forward into his plane, which immediately caught fire. LT Holt pulled up sharply and bailed out. The Privateer immediately dropped a life raft to him while the other P-47s circled his location.

Without warning, eight or nine Japanese fighters arrived and pounced upon the unsuspecting American fliers. The fighters were thought to be Nakajima Ki-44 "Tojo"s or Kawanishi N1K "George"s, two of the best Japanese aircraft. The Japanese pilots aggressively attacked the outnumbered P-47s.

LT Smyth's aircraft was hit almost immediately. Flying at only a few hundred feet over water, he did not have time to escape the burning aircraft. His P-47 fell into the sea in flames, about a mile northwest of Hirado Shima's southern peninsula. A search of the area by his fellow fliers failed to reveal any sign of the plane or LT Smyth. Bud Smyth was never seen again.

Bud mourned by family and fellow airmen

On August 1, 1945, his family received a telegram from the US War Department notifying them that their son had been killed in action over Kyushu. Days later, they received a letter from Bud's commanding officer, which read:

"The superior airmanship and bravery displayed by Hugh during several combat missions deep into the Japanese homeland were a source of inspiration to the younger pilots in our organization. On the ground, Hugh was the highest type of gentleman. His likable personality and his gentle manner endeared him to the hearts of all of us. Believe me, Mrs. Smyth, your son's loss is a severe blow to our squadron."

Just a month after Bud's loss, atomic bombs were dropped on Hiroshima (August 6) and Nagasaki (August 9), compelling the Japanese to surrender on August 15. The war was over.

Three years later, after failing to find any evidence of his wreck, imprisonment as a POW, or interment, LT Hugh "Bud" Smyth was formally declared non-recoverable by the War Department. His downed colleague LT Billie Holt was rescued by Japanese civilians, spent the remainder of the war in a prison camp, and returned to the US after the war.

The name of Hugh Bernard Smyth is inscribed on the Courts of the Missing at the National Memorial Cemetery of the Pacific in Honolulu, Hawaii. He was posthumously awarded the Air Medal and the Purple Heart.

★ ★ ★

PVT HOSEY DAWKINS

Service Number 33430433
Company A, 1864th Engineers Battalion Aviation, Corps of Engineers, US Army
Killed during Guard Duty, Guam, August 13, 1945

The Pacific Island of Guam had been retaken from the Japanese a year earlier. Two major US Army Airfields had since been constructed, and their Boeing B-29 Superfortress bombers were now releasing bombs upon the Japanese home islands. Although enemy stragglers were known to be hiding in the mountain jungle, Americans troops felt relatively safe.

News had spread that the US had dropped two devastating bombs upon Hiroshima and Nagasaki Japan on Aug 6th and 9th. The surrender of the Japanese Empire was sure to follow. On August 13, 1945, there was every reason for the men stationed on Guam to be optimistic, including PVT Hosey Dawkins. That day, he was assigned guard duty. He took up his rifle and reported to his station. It would be his final assignment.

The Dawkins Family

Hosey Dawkins was born on May 6, 1921, in Henry County, Alabama, to Edward "Ed" and Ida (née McAllister) Dawkins. Ed and Ida had married in 1910 in Eufaula, Alabama. Ed was a farmer while Ida managed the Dawkins family household.

The Dawkins and McAllister family roots were primarily from Alabama and South Carolina. The McAllister family includes Native American heritage.

Hosey was the seventh of thirteen children born to Ed and Ida. A daughter Johnie was the first child (born ~1910), followed by Eddie "Roy" (1911), Clare Lue (1913), Rosella (1914), George Onslow (1918), Joseph (1920), Mark (1923), and Martha (1923), all while the family was living in Alabama. Ed then relocated the family to a rented home at 114 Ninth Street in Monessen, Pennsylvania, for work, where their remaining children were born: Elizabeth (1926), Paul Edward (1927), Mary Lee (1931), and Ida Jane (1933). Ed had been hired as a laborer in the local steel mill, as was Roy.

Monessen was a community of transplants who sought work in the local factories. They immigrated from European countries or relocated from regions within the US, as had the Dawkins family from Alabama. By 1940, the family had moved to 1259 Morgan Avenue in Monessen in an area called Bouquet Flats, where many Black families had concentrated.

Boxer Hosey Dawkins, "Knock-out Artist"

Hosey left public school after the seventh grade. He and a few friends stepped over the law and had been arrested. Hosey was subsequently remanded to the Pennsylvania Industrial Training School in Cecil Township in nearby Washington County, Pennsylvania. He became a skilled boxer, a "knock-out artist", and competed in the Diamond Belt Tournament in Pittsburgh in January 1938 at the age of sixteen as a 135 lb novice. Hosey advanced to the semi-final round of the Golden Gloves tournament. The following year, Hosey competed in the Golden Gloves tournament in Pittsburgh, in the 135 lb class. The local newspaper described Hosey as "...one of the smoothest fighters at the {Pennsylvania Industrial Training} school...He has a nice set of hooks and moves around nicely. Dawkins is in good condition and will keep up a fast pace as long as his opponents require it." He was also described as "a well-built youngster with a mule-kick punch," who, in his fight, gave "such a bad beating that Boyd refused to return for a third round". Hosey advanced to the finals in a highly anticipated match against "knock-out artist" Pete "Kid" Spotti. Unfortunately for Hosey, he was knocked out in the second round after "an exhibition of slugging that threatened to send one of them into the 14th row".

Hosey Dawkins Drafted

By 1940 at the age of 18, Hosey was living at the home of his parents and five of his siblings while working as a gas station attendant. The surprise attack by Japanese armed forces on the US military bases at Pearl Harbor, Hawaii, in December 1941 changed the world for Hosey. Three months later, on February 16, 1942, Hosey registered for the US military draft as a 5'10" 160 lb 20-yr-old with black hair and black eyes. Hosey was single, unemployed, and living in the home of his parents at the time. The following year, on February 25, 1943, Hosey Dawkins was drafted into the US Army, and he enlisted in Greensburg, Pennsylvania. At the time he was employed in construction. Private Hosey Dawkins was off to training.

PVT Dawkins was in training and duty stateside through June 1945. During that time, he was assigned to the 703rd Chemical Maintenance Company at Columbia Airfield, South Carolina, where he was a noted boxing athlete in 1944. Later that year, while stationed at Barksdale Airfield, Louisiana, he was another boxing winner. In February 1945, now at the Dale Mabry Field in Tallahassee, Florida, he had taken ill and was temporarily admitted to the station hospital where he recovered.

PVT Dawkins was eventually assigned to Company A of the 1864th Engineers Aviation Battalion (EAB). EAB's had been formed by the US Army to establish, construct, and maintain airfields for the US Army Air Corps. As it was an unfortunate but common practice in the US armed forces during WWII, some EABs were created as segregated units primarily consisting of

Engineer Aviation Battalion constructing an airfield
(National Museum of the USAF)

Black Americans. The 1864th EAB was formed in December 1944 at Drew Field, Florida.

After US forces captured Guam in the Mariana Islands from the Japanese in July 1944, three airfields were constructed: Depot, North, and Northwest. PVT Dawkins and the 1864th EAB departed the US on July 1, 1945, and arrived on Guam on July 10, 1945.

The 1864th EAB was put to work improving Northwest Field. In July and August, PVT Dawkins and Company A were assigned construction projects that included the construction camp and facilities, water system and wells, and the generator house.

Engineer Aviation Battalion constructing an airfield
(National Museum of the USAF)

PVT Dawkins' Loses his Life on Guam

On August 13, 1945, the 1864th EAB suffered its first fatality: PVT Hosey Dawkins. The Battalion's Historical Report of September 4, 1945, described the unfortunate event.

On 13 August 1945 we had our first fatality. While on guard duty Pvt
Dawkins accidently shot and killed himself. There was a complete investigation
made and the findings forwarded. Pvt Dawkins was buried with full military
honor at cemetery #2Guam on 15 August 1945 with the Battalion Chaplain
performing the service.

Excerpt from 1864th EAB Historical Report August 1945

The day after PVT Dawkins' death, President Harry Truman announced the surrender of the Japanese Empire. On September 2, 1945, Japan signed the surrender documents aboard the battleship USS Missouri in Tokyo Bay.

PVT Hosey Dawkins was initially buried in Guam. His remains were then brought to United States territory under the Return of the War Dead program and finally buried at the National Memorial Cemetery of the Pacific in Honolulu, Hawaii, on February 16, 1949.

PVT Hosey Dawkins was Monessen's only Black American to lose his life during the war. He was also the last man from Monessen to die during WWII.

Author's Note: The "U.S., World War II Hospital Admission Card Files, 1942-1954" record for PVT Hosey Dawkins states "Diagnosis: Wound(s), perforating (points of entrance and exit) with artery involvement only; Location: Heart, generally; Causative Agent: Bullet, Rifle". The author has been unable to locate records of the "complete investigation" cited in the 1864th EAB Historical Report. It remains unclear how PVT Dawkins was able to accidentally inflict upon himself a mortal wound to the heart with a rifle.

★ ★ ★

AFTER THE WAR

"There is nothing we can do to ease their pain but to go on hoping and praying that somehow and soon civilization will right itself and men will find a way to live together in the world without shooting each other."

Editor, Monessen Daily Independent, August 28, 1946

After Victory-in-Europe Day, May 8, 1945, and Victory-in-Japan Day, September 2, 1945, the US Government pulled out all of the stops to bring its soldiers home. At the end of the war, the US had more than 12 million men and women in the armed forces, with 7.6 million stationed overseas.

US Troops returning home (National WWII Museum)

Operation Magic Carpet was launched to bring them home. Hundreds of ships began transporting soldiers from Europe to the United States in June 1945. In October 1945, nearly 400 US Navy ships were engaged to ferry soldiers from the Pacific Theater. The European phase of Operation Magic Carpet concluded in February 1946 while the Pacific phase continued until September 1946. For soldiers and their families, it could not happen fast enough.

But some US soldiers were ordered to remain behind to help secure the peace. Many new recruits were sent overseas so that the war-weary troops could be brought home.

In 1946 two Monessen soldiers stationed in Europe, PFC Walter Leonard Kujawa and CPL Matthew Comko, died in the defense of victory. Their losses placed an unwanted capstone upon the grief of the city.

★★★

PFC WALTER L. KUJAWA, JR.

Service Number 33969075
Company M, 351st Infantry Regiment, 88th Infantry Division, US Army
Killed on patrol, Italy, July 16, 1946

W alter Leonard Kujawa, Jr., was born on January 12, 1927, to Walter and Josephine (née Zajac) Kujawa in Monessen, Pennsylvania. Walter Sr. was a truck driver at Pittsburgh Steel while Josephine managed the Kujawa family household.

The Kujawa Family

Walter Sr. was born in Pecena, Poland and immigrated to the United States in 1910. Josephine was also born in Poland and came to the US in 1902. Walter Sr. served in France with the US Army as a Private First Class during World War I. He was wounded in the arm and leg during battles at St. Mihiel and Meuse Argonne before being discharged honorably in 1919.

Josephine first married Stanley Bialousz and had four children together: Stella (1909), Chester (1911), John (1914), and Henry (1917). Stanley passed away sometime before 1921, and Josephine married Walter Kujawa, Sr. They settled in Monessen. Josephine and Walter Sr. gave birth to Anthony (1921), Edward (1923), and Walter Jr. By 1934, the combined family was living at 924 Summit Avenue in Monessen. Son Henry had long suffered an intestinal disorder and died during surgery in June 1934 at the age of 17.

By 1940, Stella and Chester Bialousz had married and moved away to start their own families. The teenage boys were at Monessen High School while John Bialousz worked at the steel mill with their father. In 1941, John enlisted with the US Army and left to serve. After the US entered World War II in December 1941, Anthony (Tony) joined the Army Air Corps after two years of college in 1942.

In 1942, Walter Jr. was playing baseball for a local Monessen team, the Blue Streaks, when he batted 6 for 6, hitting two home runs and 4 singles. He played guard for the Monessen Junior High School basketball team. At Monessen High School, Walter was popular and a drum major with the high school band. In 1944, he was pitching for the Cherry Alley baseball team.

Walter Jr's brother Tony would become a Staff Sergeant and flight engineer/top turret Gunner in B-17 Flying Fortress bombers with the 303rd Bomb Group in England. He was shot down twice, the last time in 1943 over Holland. S/SGT Kujawa was taken prisoner and served the remainder of the war in the POW camp Stalag Luft 3 in Sagan-Silesia Bavaria. Their brother Edward was drafted into the Army in February 1943 where he eventually served with the 188th Parachute Infantry Regiment of the 11th Airborne Division in the Southwest Pacific Theater.

Walter Kujawa Joins the US Army

On January 12, 1945, Walter Jr. registered for the US armed forces draft as a 5'4" 129 lb single man with brown hair and blue eyes. He had completed his studies at Monessen High School after two years and was working at the Corning Glass Works in nearby Charleroi. On March 18, he was drafted and enlisted into the service in Pittsburgh on April 30.

The war in Europe was winding down, and Germany surrendered on May 8, 1945. The war in the Pacific Theater was still raging, and so PVT Walter Kujawa continued to train, anticipating a potential deployment overseas.

Fortunately, Japan surrendered on August 14, 1945 (US time), thus relieving the anxiety of facing combat. However, US soldiers were still needed to secure the peace, and after completing training in October 1945, he shipped overseas to Italy to become what was known as a "Victory Soldier".

Kujawa, now a Private First Class (PFC), was stationed in Italy near the Yugoslavian border. Yugoslavia was in turmoil after WWII, with disparate partisan groups vying for control in the aftermath. Anyone traveling near the border was at risk as the partisans fought amongst themselves and with the forces of the dictator Marshal Josip Broz Tito.

Struck by Sniper Fire

On July 16, 1946, while traveling in a jeep on patrol in riot-torn Trieste, Italy, with other American soldiers, his unit was ambushed. PFC Walter Kujawa was stricken by a sniper's bullet to the head. He died instantly. He was 19 years old.

On August 17, 1946, PFC Walter Kujawa was returned to Monessen for burial. He was laid to rest at St. Hyacinth Cemetery on August 18, with full military honors attended by approximately 100 active and former service members.

'We Regret to Inform You—'
Victory Soldiers Also Die

Monessen Youth Gives His Life Guarding Peace Which His Three Brothers Helped to Win

MONESSEN, Pa., July 25 (UP) — Nineteen-year-old Walter L. Kujawa led the enthusiastic celebrations when his three older brothers returned unharmed from the war—Edward from the Engineers, and Jonn from the Paratroops, Anthony from the Air Force.

Now, he told them, he could go, too. At least to guard the victory. So they held another and even better celebration at the Kujawa home. And when they went over to the Veterans Hospital in Aspinwall where the father of the boys remains a casualty of the first World War, they promised "the kid" the biggest homecoming of all.

Walter sailed for Italy last September after four months' training in the Army. And since that time his family has thrilled to the stories of his travels.

But all that is ended now. The War Department's telegram to Mrs. Kujawa arrived yesterday.

It disclosed that Walter was the soldier who was fatally wounded last week when shots from ambush blasted an American jeep patrol of four men as they rode along the highway near troubled Trieste at the head of the Adriatic.

"The kid" died—guarding the victory.

The Pittsburgh Press. July 25, 1946

★ ★ ★

CPL MATTHEW M. COMKO

Service Number 13192184
910th Air Engineering Squadron, 492nd Air Service Group US Army Air Force
Killed in unprovoked air attack, Yugoslavia, August 19, 1946

Matthew Michael Comko was born on October 1, 1926, to Michael "Mike" and Matilda "Tillie" (née Bialschek or Blycak) Comko in Monessen, Pennsylvania. Mike and Tillie married about 1916. Mike was a laborer at the Pittsburgh Steel plant in Monessen, while Tillie managed the Comko family household.

The Comko Family

Mike Comko was born of Ruthenian descent in the village of Sanok in the Galicia region of Eastern Europe when it was under the rule of the Austro-Hungarian Empire. He immigrated to the United States about 1912. Tillie was also from Galicia and arrived in the US the same year. They settled in Monessen after marrying.

Matthew was the fourth of five children born to the couple. Ann (b1918) was first to arrive, followed by Julia (1921), and then Charles "Chookie"

(1924). Alice, the youngest, was born in 1929. Mike made a good wage at the steel mill and by 1930 the family was living in their own house at 533 Delaware Street in Monessen.

By 1940, Ann and Julia had graduated from Monessen High School. Ann became a stewardess on a steam ship and Julia was a salesclerk in a dress shop. Chookie, in his first year at Monessen High, was becoming a popular athlete on the high school sports teams. Matt and Alice were attending middle and elementary schools respectively.

The US entered WWII in December 1941 when the Japanese bombed its bases in Hawaii, Guam, and the Philippines. Like most Monessenites, the Comkos followed news of the war daily as it progressed.

Matt graduated from Monessen Vocational High School in 1945 with plans to become a machinist. His senior yearbook caption addressed his dreams: "To sleep and dream of summer weather, owning his own trucking business, steak, and polkas are all super to Matt. Gas rationing, sports, and mill work result in nightmares."

Charles enlisted with the US Navy in June 1944 and became an Aviation Radioman. He served with Bombing Squadron 12 aboard the USS Randolph Essex Class aircraft carrier and saw action in the Pacific Theater at the battles of Iwo Jima and Okinawa. Ann enlisted with the Women's Army Corps in December 1944, became a Staff Sergeant, and served in Europe.

Matt Comko Joins the Air Force

Matt decided to volunteer to serve in the Reserves of the US armed forces, and he enlisted on March 7, 1945, in New Cumberland, Pennsylvania. He entered the US Army Air Force, and was training stateside when Germany surrendered on May 8, 1945, followed by the surrender of Japan on August 15, 1945. While he would not see combat in WWII, he would be part of the US military charged with ensuring the peace and was sent overseas to Europe in November 1945. Matt trained as a flight engineer and was eventually promoted to the rank of Corporal (CPL).

CPL Comko was assigned to the 910th Air Engineering Squadron, which had been constituted in April 1945 and activated in June. The unit was part of the 492nd Air Service Group, which, working with the 2nd Air Disarmament Wing, participated in the dismantling and documenting of the defeated German Luftwaffe. The 492nd was initially stationed in Munich, Germany, then moved to Furth, Germany in October where CPL Comko joined them in November. In January 1946, the unit relocated to Capodichino Air Base outside of Naples, Italy.

CPL Comko routinely joined flights of Douglas C-47 Dakota transport planes as they ferried men and materials from Naples to other air bases. The work might have seemed safe and routine, but in neighboring Yugoslavia, political disarray and internal partisan conflicts could spill over to neighboring countries. Yugoslavian dictator Marshal Josep Broz Tito was working hard to cement his power over the warring factions. On August 9, 1946, Yugoslavian fighters forced down a USAF C-47 and captured the ten crew and passengers, which they claimed had flown into Yugoslavian airspace.

CPL Comko Caught in International Incident

On August 19, 1946, CPL Comko boarded C-47A serial number 42-24374 in Wein Airbase in Vienna, Austria, for a short flight to northeast Italy at Udine Airbase at Campoformido. While crossing near the Yugoslavian border, their aircraft was attacked by Russian-made Yak-3 fighter aircraft of the Yugoslavian Air Force, whose pilots claimed that the C-47 had encroached upon Yugoslavian airspace. The defenseless transport aircraft was mortally wounded and fell to Earth near the town of Bled, Yugoslavia (now Slovenia). All five crew members perished in the crash.

Days later, the Comko family was informed of the loss of their son. In addition to their son, the crewmen lost in the attack were Captains Richard H. Claeys (pilot), Blen H. Freestone and Harold F. Schreiber, and CPL Chester I. Lower. Their loss became front page news across the US, including in the Monessen Daily Independent.

Local Yugoslavian citizens temporarily buried the airmen in a shared grave near the village of Koprivnik, where villagers decorated the grave with flowers. The bodies of the airmen were eventually transported to the US, where they were buried in a shared grave at Arlington National Cemetery, Virginia, on September 25, 1946.

The event became an international incident between the US and Yugoslavia, with the Slavs offering to compensate the families of the victims $30,000 each. The families expressed bitterness and outrage at a monetary offer for the losses and insisted upon criminal penalties as retribution. It is not known if any such punishment was ever meted out by the Yugoslavian government.

FLAG-DRAPED CASKETS of five Army fliers, including that of Cpl. Matthew Comko, of Monessen, are shown yesterday (top photo) at Amphitheater Chapel of Arlington National Cemetery, Washington, after a flight from Rome to the U. S. The bugler sounding Taps is S/Sgt. George Myers. In the lower picture, the first of the bodies is being carried through an honor guard at the National Airport en route to Arlington. In background, the second casket is carried from the plane.

Monessen Daily Independent, September 13, 1946 ("Top photo" referenced above caption not shown)

✷ ✷ ✷

PAYING MORE THAN OUR SHARE

Reprinted Editorial, Monessen Daily Independent, August 28, 1946

> *Monessen, it would seem, is being called upon to pay rather more than her fair share for the failure of the Allied nations to establish peace in the world. Scarcely had we buried young Walter Kujawa, Jr., who was shot in the head, apparently by a gang of Balkan hoodlums, until we are told that Matthew Comko was one of the five Americans to be killed when the Yugoslavs deliberately shot down one of our unarmed transport planes. Either of these losses was cruel enough; together they are more than one little community can accept with anything like equanimity.*
>
> *Both of these boys were 19 years of age, never had a chance to get started in life. Both were snatched into military service, given a few months of hasty training and dispatched to Europe. Both were shot down by people who owe this country their very lives, are accepting its charity and insisting upon keeping the world in strife and turmoil. It is asking too much that we should not be bitter.*
>
> *The American people are finding the way of international cooperation exceedingly rough. It is not hard to make a case for the feeling that the people of Europe don't want a decent peace or don't want it enough to establish governments which will honestly seek peace. The people we used to call isolationists, who suggested that we could do no good in Europe and had better stay out of it as much as possible have not yet been proved entirely wrong. It will not take many more young American lives to convince us that they may actually have been right.*
>
> *The sympathies of this community go to this stricken home. The Comko family, like the Kujawa family, already had made more than its full contribution to what it is that the nations are striving for. This tragedy runs their measure over. There is nothing we can do to ease their pain but to go on hoping and praying that somehow and soon civilization will right itself and men will find a way to live together in the world without shooting each other.*

★★★

AFTERWORD

Nearly 3,500 men and women from Monessen served in the United States Armed Forces and Merchant Marine during World War II. Some returned with wounds, both physical and psychological, that would affect them for the rest of their lives. Eighty-two did not return.

Monessen's contributions to the war effort went much further than supplying manpower to the military. The city's factories of Pittsburgh Steel, Carnegie Steel, and American Cable and Wire were major suppliers to both the military and to finished goods suppliers to the military. During the war years the US government procured from these three Monessen factories over $16 million (nearly $300 million in 2025 dollars) combined for steel products, Marston mats (steel airfield runways), and welding materials[15]. Monessen laborers contributed their share to help fight the war.

None from Monessen sacrificed more for the war effort than the men whose lives were lost and the families who said their last goodbyes.

★ ★ ★

Who were these men? Most were lost during the prime of their early adulthood. The average age of Monessen Fallen was 25 yrs. The youngest man who lost his life was 18 yrs, 8 months. The oldest man was 60 yrs old. Of the 82 US service members from Monessen who did not return alive, 12 (15%) were

---

[15]"Alphabetic Listing of Major War Supply Contracts, Cumulative June 1940 Through September 1945, Volumes 1-2", 1946, United States Civilian Production Administration

younger than 21, 43 (52%) were between the ages of 21-25 yrs, 14 (17%) were age 26-29, 11 (13%) were ages 30-39, and two (2.4%) were over 40 yrs old.

Of the service branches, the majority of the Monessen Fallen (56 of 82) served in the US Army (infantry, artillery, armored units) and 13 served in the US Army Air Force. Six served with the US Navy, four with the US Marine Corps, and two served with the US Merchant Marine.

The majority (42) were enlisted men of the rank of Private (PVT, PFC, S2c, RM2c, SM2c, AOM3c, FM, WT). Of non-commissioned officers, 18 were the rank of Sergeant (S/SGT, SGT, TSGT, T-4) and nine were the rank of Corporal (CPL, T-5). Thirteen of the Monessen losses had attained the rank of Officer (1LT, 2LT, FL O, ENS).

Nine lost their lives while in the US and on the seas of the Atlantic Ocean, 21 were lost in the Pacific theater, and most (52) were lost in the European and Mediterranean theaters.

Monessen's war losses began slowly. In the two years from April 1942 through March 1944, less than one loss occurred per month, a total of 21 men.. But over the next 12 months, losses skyrocketed to an average of 4.3 per month, a total of 52 men. Six were lost during the remaining six months of the war, and two in 1946 while keeping the peace in Europe.

Sixty-three were killed-in-action (KIA), and four died of wounds (DOW) received in action. Thirteen were considered "Died Non Battle" (DNB)[16], and two lost their lives as POWs.

Perhaps the most remarkable characteristic shared by 76 (92.7%) of 82 whose lives were lost is this: *They were first generation Americans*. One or both of their parents were immigrants. These immigrants came to the US, found new lives and the promise of opportunity, and paid the price for a better future by sacrificing their sons. Forty-one of the families were from Central and Eastern Europe (Austria-Hungary, Croatia, Czechoslovakia, Poland, Russia, Lithuania, and Ukraine). Sixteen were of Italian ancestry. Twelve were from Scotland, Germany, Wales, Ireland and the Netherlands.

---

[16] KIA, DOW, DNB, are 3 "Casualty Codes" used by the US military in WWII.

Some sons spilled their last blood on the soil of their parents' homelands. Some still remain there. Thirty-seven of the 82 men were eventually interred in the USA (25 in Monessen, eight elsewhere in Pennsylvania, two in Hawaii, and two at Arlington National Cemetery, Virginia). Twenty were buried in France, Belgium, and Luxembourg. Six were laid to rest in The Philippines and five in Italy. Fourteen men rest beneath the waves.

✯ ✯ ✯

After the war, the city of Monessen continued to prosper as the American economy transitioned from producing war materials to peacetime goods. In the 1950's and 1960's, the Monessen story was one of hard work and success. However, the 1970's and 1980's brought economic hardship as global competition heated up and forced reductions in investment and manpower in the factories of Mon-

Monessen in 1954 (O'Neil Photo Service, Historical Society Western PA)

essen, Pittsburgh, and all around Western Pennsylvania.

Monessen never recovered. Businesses shuttered and families left. Its population was over 20,000 in 1940. By 2020, it was less than 7,000. Abandoned homes in the community only remind us of what Monessen once was.

✯ ✯ ✯

The children and grandchildren of Monessen still recall many memories of bustling life in the city: The hard work, the family reunions, the fabulous food, the crowded bars, the proud sports teams, and the busy schools.

We will always remember the sons of 82 families who gave their lives to defend the United States and democracy. Their stories are now told. Keep speaking their names and their memories will stay alive.

We die twice, once when we take our last breath, and the second time, when our name is last spoken.

★ ★ ★

Acknowledgements

My sincerest appreciation goes out to those who helped create Tin Men Steel Soldiers.

To family members of the Monessen Fallen (and those who networked to find them) who provided background documents, and images that helped tell the stories: Feyette Dawkins Holliday, David Zazac, Marian Monios Clevenstine, Patricia Nash, Nicole Holmes, Brian Filardi, Claudia Sawa, Vera Klein, Judith Kroll, Paula Shank, Brian Columbus, Andrew Pease, Kristine Samloff, Kathryn Mihalich, Argia Campagna, Gail Ogle, Elmer Harkema, Corinna Stonage, Candyce Holden, Bruce Weinrod, Ann Sweany, and Frank Bartosik.

To my wife Carol who supported my many hours of research and writing and proofread many versions of each story.

To Charles "Sandy" Hanson, whose editing, partnership and guidance were essential to producing this work.

To my friends at Stories Behind The Stars who have supported me along the way: Kathy Harmon, Chris Moyer, Linda Simpson, Tom Boyer, and Don Milne.

To Daniel T. Zyglowicz and the team at the Greater Monessen Historical Society for assisting with research and images used in this work.

To Stacy Wolford of the Mon Valley Independent for her support and access to Monessen Daily Independent archives.

And to Trevor Baldock for his assistance in restoring several images.

My apologies if I missed anyone, but I can assure you that I am grateful for your kind assistance.

BIBLIOGRAPHY

1941-1942

Louis C. Stephens

"Accident Vought OS2U-3 Kingfisher 5852, Tuesday 21 April 1942." Flightsafety.org. 2021. https://asn.flightsafety.org/wikibase/249957.

"Fighting U-Boats in American Waters." National Museum of the United States Air Force™. 2025. https://www.nationalmuseum.af.mil/Visit/Museum-Exhibits/Fact-Sheets/Display/Article/195991/AFmuseum/fighting-u-boats-in-american-waters/.

"Ens Arnold Lagraff (1919-1942) - Find a Grave..." Findagrave.com, 2025, www.findagrave.com/memorial/26583967/arnold-lagraff..

"Arnold W P Lagraff in US, American Battle Monuments Commission, 1914-1950." Fold3. 2025. https://www.fold3.com/record/530007891/arnold-w-p-lagraff-us-american-battle-monuments-commission-1914-1950.

Frank Bartosik

"Vincennes II (CA-44)." Public1.Nhhcaws.local. https://www.history.navy.mil/research/histories/ship-histories/danfs/v/vincennes-ii.html.

"Disaster at Savo Island, 1942." Public2.Nhhcaws.local. https://www.history.navy.mil/research/library/online-reading-room/title-list-alphabetically/d/disaster-savo-island-1942.html.

Lewis, Winston B. "The Battle of Savo Island, 9 August 1942" 1943, US Navy Department, Office of Naval Intelligence, Combat Narrative

Jack E. Jennings

"19th Bombardment Group - World War II - History." 5thaf.org. 2025. https://www.5thaf.org/19th-bomb-group.cfm.

Rickard, J (14 March 2013), 19th Bombardment Group, http://www.historyof-war.org/air/units/USAAF/19th_Bombardment_Group.html

"HyperWar: US Army in WWII: The Fall of the Philippines." Ibiblio.org, 2025, www.ibiblio.org/hyperwar/USA/USA-P-PI/.

Jacovos Monios

"Mary Luckenbach | the United States Navy Memorial." Navymemorial.org, 2025, navylog.navymemorial.org/mary-luckenbach.

Pocock, Michael. "MaritimeQuest - Daily Event for September 14, 2008 SS Mary Luckenbach." Maritimequest.com. 2025. https://www.maritimequest.com/daily_event_archive/2008/09_sept/14_ss_mary_luckenbach.htm.

"Royal Navy Pays Tribute to 80th Anniversary of WWII Arctic Convoy PQ18." The Maritime Executive. October 2, 2022. https://maritime-executive.com/article/royal-navy-pays-tribute-to-80th-anniversary-of-wwii-arctic-convoy-pq18.

Cherrett, Martin. "Churchill's Arctic Convoys." Ww2today.com. World War II Today. September 25, 2022. https://www.ww2today.com/p/churchills-arctic-convoys.

"Flagship to Murmansk : A Gunnery Officer in HMS 'Scylla', 1942-43 : Hughes, Robert, 1914- : Internet Archive." 2021. https://archive.org/details/flagshiptomurman0000hugh.

Edward R. Cipriani

Rickard, J (14 March 2013), 19th Bombardment Group, http://www.historyof-war.org/air/units/USAAF/19th_Bombardment_Group.html

"19th Bomb Group, USAAF in Australia during WW2." Ozatwar.com. 2020. https://www.ozatwar.com/19thbg.htm.

"Pacific Wrecks - 1st Lt John S. Hancock Crew with B-17E 'Spawn from Hell' 41-2662." Pacificwrecks.com. 2025. https://pacificwrecks.com/aircraft/b-17/41-2662/b17-spawn-of-hell-crew2.html.

"Pacific Wrecks - B-17E Flying Fortress Serial Number 41-2635." Pacific-wrecks.com. 2021. https://pacificwrecks.com/aircraft/b-17/41-2635.html.

"Pacific Wrecks - 30th Bombardment Squadron (30th BS)." Pacificwrecks.com. 2023. https://pacificwrecks.com/units/usaaf/19bg/30bs.html.

"South Atlantic Air Ferry Route in World War II." Military Wiki. Fandom, Inc. 2025. https://military-history.fandom.com/wiki/South_Atlan-tic_air_ferry_route_in_World_War_II.

"Project 'X' - Ferrying of B-17s and LB-30s to Java in Early 1942." Ozat-war.com. 2023. https://www.ozatwar.com/usaaf/projectx.htm.

Wolford, Stacy. "His Just Reward, Monessen's First WWII Hero, Missing in Action for Nearly 60 Years, to Get Military Funeral." The Valley Independent , 4 July 2001, pp. 1, 8.

"William G Kittiko." Fold3. 2025. https://www.fold3.com/memo-rial/83750307/william-g-kittiko/stories.

John W. Wargo

"John Woodrow Wargo (1918-1942) - Find a Grave..." Findagrave.com. 2022. https://www.findagrave.com/memorial/118684164/john-woodrow-wargo.

1943

Charles H. Stonage

"Units." Schistory.net. 2025. https://schistory.net/campcroft/units.html.

Hill, Chuck. "Convoy SG-19 and the Sinking of USAT Dorchester–When Things Went Terribly Wrong." Chuck Hill's CG Blog. February 5, 2017. https://chuckhillscgblog.net/2017/02/05/convoy-sg-19-and-the-sinking-of-usat-dor-chester-when-things-went-terribly-wrong/.

"Dorchester (American Troop Transport) - Ships Hit by German U-Boats during WWII - Uboat.net." Uboat.net. 2025. https://uboat.net/allies/mer-chants/ship/2616.html.

"No Greater Glory: The Four Chaplains and the Sinking of the USAT Dorchester." The Army Historical Foundation. January 26, 2017. https://armyhistory.org/no-greater-glory-the-four-chaplains-and-the-sinking-of-the-usat-dorchester/.

"Narsarsuaq Air Base." Wikipedia. Wikimedia Foundation.

Victor A. Trilli

Kurtz, Thomas. "History of the 17th Artillery Compiled from Different Sources and References, Edited." https://www.17thartilleryregiment.org/wp/wp-content/uploads/2020/06/History-of-the-17th-Artillery-Part-One-1917-1971.pdf.

"Battle Analysis of the Battle of Sidi Bou Zid, Tunisia, North Africa. Defensive, Encircled Forces, 14 February 1943" CSI BATITLEBOOK TSX BATTLEBOOK 4-D. n.d. https://apps.dtic.mil/sti/tr/pdf/ADA151626.pdf.

"Battle of Sidi Bou Zid." Wikipedia. Wikimedia Foundation.

"M114 155 Mm Howitzer." Wikipedia. Wikimedia Foundation.

John M. Hotovchin

"Merchant Marine Casualties during World War II, Names Begin with H." USMM.org. 2017. http://usmm.org/killed/h.html.

"CONVOY COMMUNICATIONS." https://www.globalsecurity.org/military/library/policy/navy/nrtc/14243_ch7.pdf.

"Convoys HX 229/SC 122." Wikipedia, Wikimedia Foundation.

"WRECKSITE - HARRY LUCKENBACH CARGO SHIP 1919-1943." Wrecksite.eu. Wrecksite. 2018. https://www.wrecksite.eu/wreck.aspx?141073.

"Crewlist from Harry Luckenbach (American Steam Merchant) - Ships Hit by German U-Boats during WWII - Uboat.net." Uboat.net. 2025. https://uboat.net/allies/merchants/crews/ship2791.html.

George Sholtis

"Page 4 - Unit History - US, 45th Infantry Division, 1918-1945." Fold3. 2020. https://www.fold3.com/image/689800617/1940-1945-ohc-history-summary-page-4-unit-history-us-45th-infantry-division-1918-1945.

Michael Gramatikos

"Five Servicemen Killed in Collision." Newspapers.com. July 6, 1943. https://www.newspapers.com/article/press-of-atlantic-city-five-servicemen-k/131517101/.

Joseph O. Scrip

"Sgt Scrip Dies of Sunstroke." Newspapers.com. July 22, 1943. https://www.newspapers.com/article/the-daily-herald-sgt-scrip-dies-of-sunst/145318273/.

John Kvaka, Jr.

Maurer, Maurer, ed. [1961]. Air Force Combat Units of World War II (PDF) (reprint ed.). Washington, DC: Office of Air Force History.

"Pacific Wrecks - C-47-DL 'Liliane' Serial Number 41-18682 Call Sign VH-CCI." https://pacificwrecks.com/aircraft/c-47/41-18682.html.

"Pacific Wrecks - Tsili Tsili Airfield (Tsile-Tsile, Fabua) Morobe Province, Papua New Guinea (PNG)." https://pacificwrecks.com/airfield/png/tsili-tsili/index.html.

August Restaino

"Page 6 - US, Missing Air Crew Reports (MACRs), WWII, 1942-1947." Fold3. 2024. https://www.fold3.com/image/38295075/41-31629-page-6-us-missing-air-crew-reports-macrs-wwii-1942-1947.

"387th Bombardment Group." 387bg.com. 2025. https://387bg.com/.

"Brief History of the 387th Bomb Group." B26.com. 2025. https://www.b26.com/page/387thbombgroup.briefhistoryof.htm.

John E. Zapora

"Dictionary of American Navy Fighting Ships: USS Savannah (CL-42)." *Ibiblio.org*, 2025, www.ibiblio.org/hyperwar/USN/ships/dafs/CL/cl42.html.

"USS Savannah (CL-42) at Salerno." https://www.history.navy.mil/browse-by-topic/wars-conflicts-and-operations/world-war-ii/1943/salerno-landings/savannah-salerno.html.

"U.S.S. SAVANNAH (CL42), Bomb Damage, Gulf of Salerno, Italy, 11 September 1943" US Navy, 1944.

Albert S. Wargo and Joseph Malena

"H-022-2 Loss of HMT Rohna." Navy.mil. 2025. https://www.history.navy.mil/about-us/leadership/director/directors-corner/h-grams/h-gram-022/h-022-2.html.

"Home - TRSMA." 2024. TRSMA. April 9, 2024. https://rohnasurvivors.org/.

Fleiss, Alex. 2021. "Worst Loss of U.S. Life at Sea : Sinking of HMT Rohna, 26 November 1943." Rebellion Research. August 11, 2021. https://www.rebellionresearch.com/worst-loss-of-u-s-life-at-sea-sinking-of-hmt-rohna-26-november-1943.

Thomas Irvine

"351st Bomb Group." 351st.org, 2023, www.351st.org/.

"Mission Report, 351st Bomb Group, Group Mission #66" 351st Bomb Group, https://www.351st.org/351stMissions/Mission066/Mission66.html

"Page 12 - US, Missing Air Crew Reports (MACRs), WWII, 1942-1947." Fold3, 2024, www.fold3.com/image/28719099/28719056.

Carville, Daniel. 2018. "Recherche de France-Crashes 39-45." Francecrashes39-45.net. 2018. https://francecrashes39-45.net/page_fiche_av.php?id=1953.

1944

Ross J. Naccarato

"83rd Chemical BN." Army.mil. 2025. https://home.army.mil/stewart/units/tenant-units/83rdChem.

"Rounds Away: History of the 83rd Chemical Mortar Bn." 4point2.org. 2025. https://www.4point2.org/hist-83.htm.

"Anzio Beachhead: The Anzio Landing (22-29 January)." History.army.mil. https://history.army.mil/books/wwii/anziobeach/anzio-landing.htm.

"WWII True Story: Sinking Ship, Leaky Life Vest, Two Men Hanging On!" Hibiscushouseblog.com. September 18, 2016. https://www.hibiscushouseblog.com/2016/09/wwii-true-story-sinking-ship-leaky-life.html.

Charles W. Lucas

"Pacific Wrecks - SBD-4 Dauntless Bureau Number 10350." Pacificwrecks.com. 2024. https://pacificwrecks.com/aircraft/sbd/10350.html.

"Page 7 - US, World War II War Diaries, 1941-1945." Fold3. 2023. https://www.fold3.com/image/277040652/war-diary-21-2944-mission-reports-page-7-us-world-war-ii-war-diaries-1941-1945.

3rd Defensive Battalion Unit History. Fandom.com. 2025. https://military-history.fandom.com/wiki/3rd_Littoral_Anti-Air_Battalion.

"1Lt Hobart Kemp (Unknown-1944)" Findagrave.com, www.findagrave.com/memorial/56761350/hobart-kemp.

Andrew Desack

"History of the Third Infantry Division in World War II : United States. Army. 3rd Division." 2015. Internet Archive. https://archive.org/details/HistoryOfTheThirdID.

Harry E. Boyer

"Home Page." 454th Bomb Group in Italy. 2024. http://www.454thbombgroup.it/.

"Page 5 - US, Missing Air Crew Reports (MACRs), WWII, 1942-1947." Fold3. 2024. https://www.fold3.com/image/29035574/29035582.

Paul F. Newman

"Page 12 - US, Missing Air Crew Reports (MACRs), WWII, 1942-1947." Fold3. 2024. https://www.fold3.com/image/28638311. Missing Air Crew Report 4854 B-17G-5-VE #42-39884

"42-39884 | B-17 Bomber Flying Fortress – the Queen of the Skies." B17flyingfortress.de. 2024. https://b17flyingfortress.de/en/b17/42-39884/.

"95th Bomb Group." 95thbgdb.com, 2025, 95thbgdb.com/aircraft/212.

"95th Bomb Group." 95thbgdb.com. 2025. https://95thbgdb.com/mission/129.

James Mazzer

"The 337th Infantry in Italy in WWII." 337thinfantry.net. 2025. https://www.337thinfantry.net/unit.php.

Leonard A. Mihalich

"Page 2 - US, Missing Air Crew Reports (MACRs), WWII, 1942-1947." Fold3. 2024. https://www.fold3.com/image/28633485/28633435.

"42-102647 | American Air Museum." Americanairmuseum.com. November 27, 2017. https://www.americanairmuseum.com/archive/aircraft/42-102647.

"Mihalich, Leonard A. - S/Sgt - 401st Bomb Group (H) Association." 401bg.org, 2024, 401bg.org/Main/History/Members/Details.aspx?ID=2280.

"Mission 376: Battle Over The Reich: 28 May 1944", Ivo De Jong, Google Books. www.google.com/books/edition/Mission_376/PoA-IUpvSAnEC?hl=en&gbpv=1&bsq=bto.

Thomas, Gary. "Monessen Veterans Story 'Wrapped' in History." TribLIVE.com. March 14, 2004. https://archive.triblive.com/news/monessen-veterans-story-wrapped-in-history/.

George Evanich

1st Lt John C. Chapin, USMCR "The 4th Marine Division in World War II", History and Museums Division, HQ, USMC.

Patsy S. Columbus

"History of the 313th Infantry in World War II", S. Wood, Et. Al. 1947

"79th Infantry Division (United States)." Wikipedia.

John Komlos

"83rd Infantry Division Documents - 330th Infantry Regiment."
83rdinfdivdocs.org. 2024. https://83rdinfdivdocs.org/units/330th-ir/.

"83rd Infantry Division Documents - Staff Sergeant John Komlos ASN
33391678." 83rdinfdivdocs.org. 2024. https://83rdinfdivdocs.org/heroes/se-
rial/33391678.

"After Action Report July 1944 330th Inf 83rd Div" Aug 9, 1944.
https://83rdinfdivdocs.org/documents/330th/AAR/AAR_330_JUL1944.pdf

Anthony Thiry

"Page 1 - Unit History - US, 115th Infantry Regiment, 1944-1945."
Fold3. 2019. https://www.fold3.com/image/676386616/1944-1945-history-
page-1-unit-history-us-115th-infantry-regiment-1944-1945.

"115th Infantry (1st Maryland) – 29th Division Association." 29thdivi-
sionassociation.com. 2025. https://29thdivisionassociation.com/29th-divi-
sion-115th-infantry/.

"115th Infantry Regiment - 29th (US) ID - after Action Reports." D-Day
Overlord. February 19, 2016. https://www.dday-overlord.com/en/battle-of-
normandy/after-action-reports/29th-infantry/115th-infantry-regiment/.

"World War II Unit Histories & Officers." Unithistories.com. 2025.
https://www.unithistories.com/units_index/in-
dex.php?file=/units/115th%20Inf.Reg.htm.

Ernest C. Renzetti

"83rd Infantry Division Documents - 331st Infantry Regiment."
83rdinfdivdocs.org. 2024. https://83rdinfdivdocs.org/units/331st-ir/.

"Brothers-In-Arms: 83rd Division, 331st Infantry." Kb8tt.net. 2016.
https://kb8tt.net/brothers/.

"After Action Report July 1944, 331st Infantry Regiment" 83rdinfdiv-docs.org. 2024

John Kalie
"Page 2 - US, Missing Air Crew Reports (MACRs), WWII, 1942-1947." Fold3. 2024. https://www.fold3.com/image/28690089.

"459th Bombardment Group." Historyofwar.org. 2025. http://www.his-toryofwar.org/air/units/USAAF/459th_Bombardment_Group.html.

"John Kalie - WWII Serviceman - 459th Bombardment Group - 758 Squadron - K-6376." 459bg.org, 2025, www.459bg.org/Ka-lie_John_K6376_459BG.cfm. Accessed 27 Mar. 2025.

"KALIE John - 758 BS 459 BG." Database-Memoire.eu. 2025. https://www.database-memoire.eu/prive/en-us/normandy-all-soldiers/46-colleville-k-us/3595-kalie-john-758-bs-459-bg.

William H. Hagerty
"US Army Divisions." US Army Divisions. 2025. https://www.armydivs.com/77th-infantry-division.

"World War II Divisional Combat Chronicles." History.army.mil. https://history.army.mil/html/forcestruc/cbtchron/cc/077id.htm.

"World War II Operational Documents." Oclc.org. 2019. https://cgsc.contentdm.oclc.org/digital/collection/p4013coll8/id/4341/rec/3.

William C. Caville and Joseph P. Leone
"World War II Unit Histories & Officers." Unithistories.com, 2025, www.unithistories.com/units_index/in-dex.php?file=/units/115th%20Inf.Reg.htm.

"Pennsylvania National Guard > Army National Guard > 28th Infantry Division." Www.pa.ng.mil, www.pa.ng.mil/Army-National-Guard/28th-In-fantry-Division/.

"'Operation COBRA and the Breakout at Normandy,' | Article | the United States Army." Www.army.mil. https://www.army.mil/article/42658/operation_cobra_and_the_breakout_at_normandy.

Wayne R. McVay, Paul Denitti, and James Woods
"Combat History of the 6th Armored Division." 2025. Bangor Community: Digital Commons@Bpl. 2025. https://digicom.bpl.lib.me.us/ww_reg_his/41/.

"Super Sixth: The American 6th Armored Division in WW II." Super6th.org. 2024. http://www.super6th.org/.

Super6th.org. 2025. http://www.super6th.org/campmap/sixer_campaign_map_1945.jpg.

"Roster." 6tharmoreddivision.com. 2025. https://www.6tharmoreddivision.com/roster.

Christopher Parnella
"Chapter 3 - Northern France." 35thinfantrydivision-Memory.com. 2025. https://35thinfantrydivision-memory.com/site/en/history-of-the-137th-infantry-regiment-chapter-3-northern-france-109.

"Record of PARNELLA, Christopher - 137th Infantry Regiment." 35thinfantrydivision-Memory.com. 2025. https://35thinfantrydivision-memory.com/site/en/record-of-Private-First-Class-Christopher-PARNELLA-33702960-137th-Infantry-Regiment-Company-C-6665.

Bernard J. Rosenson
The Official Site of the 4th Fighter Group - World War II. 2025. http://www.4thfightergroupassociation.org/.

"Missions." The Official Site of the 4th Fighter Group - World War II. 2025. http://www.4thfightergroupassociation.org/missions.html.

"Rosenson Bernard J." 2025. Uswarmemorials.org. 2025. https://www.uswarmemorials.org/html/people_details.php?PeopleID=28091.

Joseph J. Skruber

"Operation Dragoon: The Allied Invasion of France in the South." Warfare History Network. https://warfarehistorynetwork.com/article/operation-dragoon-the-allied-invasion-of-france-in-the-south/.

"Field Artillery History - United States Field Artillery Association." Www.fieldartillery.org. https://www.fieldartillery.org/field-artillery-history.

Arthur J. Stockus

"Ensign Arthur J. Stockus | New England Aviation History." Newenglandaviationhistory.com. 2015. https://newenglandaviationhistory.com/tag/ensign-arthur-j-stockus/.

"Photo: Memorial Detail: Names & Dates." Hmdb.org, 2018, www.hmdb.org/PhotoFullSize.asp?PhotoID=419077.

"Page 1 - US, World War II War Diaries, 1941-1945." Fold3. 2023. https://www.fold3.com/image/279829563/war-diary-824-3144-page-1-us-world-war-ii-war-diaries-1941-1945.

"The Development of Night Fighters in World War II." U.S. Naval Institute. January 1, 1989. https://www.usni.org/magazines/naval-history-magazine/1989/january/development-night-fighters-world-war-ii.

Joseph M. Fiorillo

"The 133D Military Police Platoon. - Free Online Library." Thefreelibrary.com. 2015. https://www.thefreelibrary.com/The+133D+military+police+platoon.-a0491576064.

"ELIHU THOMSON." Dot.gov. 2025. https://vesselhistory.marad.dot.gov/ShipHistory/Detail/1402.

"Liberty Ships Built by the United States Maritime Commission in World War II." USMM.org. 2024. http://www.usmm.org/libertyships.html#anchor435563.

Anthony Saridakis

"US Army Divisions." US Army Divisions. 2025. https://www.armydivs.com/31st-infantry-division.

"U.S. Army Infantry Cannon Company (1943-45)." Battle Order. 2019. https://www.battleorder.org/usa-1943-cannonco.

"Battle of Morotai." Wikipedia. Wikimedia Foundation.

Pacifico Sacchini

County, Hamilton, Doug Bailey, David Young, Wes Sweedler, Damian Col, and Donahoe. n.d. "RED BULL." https://cms2.revize.com/revize/hamiltonia/Red%20Bull%20monument.pdf.

"A Condensed History of the 135th Infantry Regiment From Gettysburg to the Po". Kreger. Vessey Collection, Minnesota Military Museum. Undated. https://www.34ida.org/images/Kreger,_A_Condensed_History_of_the_135th_Infantry_from_Gettysburg_to_the_Po.pdf

Alex Koszykowski

"349th Infantry Regiment - 88th Infantry Division Blue Devils - MtMestas.com World War II Research Website." Mtmestas.com. 2025. https://www.mtmestas.com/349th-infantryregiment.htm.

"DRAFTEE DIVISION." http://www.88thinfantrydivisionarchive.com/88th-infantrydivision/drafteedivision-254pgs.pdf.

William K. Oliphant

"World War II Operational Documents." Oclc.org. 2019. https://cgsc.contentdm.oclc.org/digital/collection/p4013coll8/id/3171/rec/1.

"The Operations of 2ndBn 338th Infantry in Taking Mt Della Forniche Italy 10-13 Oct 1944", Bloch, 1946. https://www.337thinfantry.net/reports/Battalion%20Reports/The%20Operations%20of%20the%202nd%20Battalion,%20338th%20Infantry%20Bloch.pdf

Michael Redish

Nardin, Ted. "History of the 351st Infantry Regiment." 351INF.com. February 12, 2022. https://www.351inf.com/post/history-of-the-351st-infantry-regiment.

John E. Varga

"Seventh Amphibious Force - Command History 1945." Navy.mil. 2024. https://www.history.navy.mil/research/library/online-reading-room/title-list-alphabetically/s/seventh-amphibious-force-command-history1945.html.

"USS Amycus." Wikipedia. Wikimedia Foundation.

"USS Blue Ridge (AGC-2)." Wikipedia. Wikimedia Foundation

"USS Sampson (DD-394)." Wikipedia. Wikimedia Foundation.

Cyril M. Liscik

"Super Sixth: The American 6th Armored Division in WW II." Super6th.org. 2024. http://www.super6th.org/6ad.htm.

"603rd Tank Destroyer Battalion – Tankdestroyer." Tankdestroyer.net. 2023. https://tankdestroyer.net/units/battalions600s/198-603rd-tank-destroyer-battalion/.

"Unit History 603 Tank Destroyer Battalion" 1944. https://tank-destroyer.net/images/stories/ArticlePDFs/603rd-UH_1944.pdf

Elmer A. Harkema

Buckley, Chris. 2010. "Monessen's Harkema Recalls Brother's World War II Death." TribLIVE.com. May 31, 2010. https://archive.triblive.com/news/monessens-harkema-recalls-brothers-world-war-ii-death/.

Walter Zajaczkowski

"Combat History of the Second Infantry Division", Google Books 2018. https://www.google.com/books/edition/Combat_History_of_the_Second_Infantry_Di/G8BsDwAAQBAJ?hl=en&gbpv=1.

"Second Indianhead Division Association Timeline." 2023. https://www.2ida.org/timeline.

"Battle of Heartbreak Crossroads." Military Wiki. Fandom, Inc. 2015. https://military-history.fandom.com/wiki/Battle_of_Heartbreak_Crossroads.

George T. Stanish

"The Battle of the Bulge & the Defense of St. Vith." Warfare History Network. June 30, 2023. https://warfarehistorynetwork.com/article/the-battle-of-the-bulge-the-defense-of-st-vith/.

"World War II Operational Documents." Oclc.org. 2025. https://cgsc.contentdm.oclc.org/digital/collection/p4013coll8/id/362/rec/2.

"Chapter 12-the ARDENNES: BATTLE of the BULGE." Army.mil. 2024. https://history.army.mil/books/wwii/7-8/7-8_12.HTM.

"C.C.B. 9th Armored Division, Battle of the Bulge." Battle of the Bulge Memories. November 2, 2010. https://www.battle-of-the-bulge-memories.be/index.php?option=com_content&view=article&id=551:ccb-9th-armored-division-battle-of-the-bulge&catid=70&Itemid=100120.

Steve Malinchak

"US Army Divisions." US Army Divisions. 2025. https://www.armydivs.com/78th-infantry-division.

"The Story of the 310th Infantry Regiment, 78th Infantry Division in the War against Germany, 1942-1945." Brubeck, William E, and Lewis S Hollins. Bangor Community: Digital Commons@Bpl. 2025. http://digicom.bpl.lib.me.us/ww_reg_his/36.

Wallace Marcinkiewicz

"Marcinkiewicz, Wallace – 4th Armored Division - Ardennes Breakthrough Association." Ardennes Breakthrough Association - Historical Research Page. November 11, 2021. https://ardennes-breakthrough-association.com/marcinkiewicz-wallace-4th-armored-division/.

"Patton's Vanguard: The United States Army Fourth Armored Division". Fox, Don M. 2007. McFarland. Google Books https://www.google.com/books/edition/Patton_s_Vanguard/H_NTCgAAQBAJ?hl=en&gbpv=1&dq=wallace+marcinkiewicz&pg=PA384&printsec=frontcover

1945

Bernard F. Quinlan

"27th Fighter Group." Historyofwar.org. 2025. https://www.historyofwar.org/air/units/USAAF/27th_Fighter_Group.html.

"Combat Squadrons of the Air Force in World War II : United States. USAF Historical Division: Internet Archive." 2015. https://archive.org/details/CombatSquadronsOfTheAirForceWWII/page/624/mode/2up.

"Pontedera Airfield." Wikipedia Wikimedia Foundation

Angelo Imburgia

"Trailblazer History." Trailblazersww2.org. 2025. https://www.trailblazersww2.org/history.htm.

"Abbreviated history of the 70th Infantry Division". 70th Infantry Division 50th Reunion. https://view.officeapps.live.com/op/view.aspx?src=https%3A%2F%2Fwww.trailblazersww2.org%2FDocs%2Fdivision_history.doc&wdOrigin=BROWSELINK

Rick Bruni. "Monessen Man Will Tell Uncle's Story at Veterans Day Program." TribLIVE.com. November 10, 2015. https://archive.triblive.com/news/monessen-man-will-tell-uncles-story-at-veterans-day-program/.

Stanley Zazac

"History of the 43rd Infantry Division, 1941-1945" WWII Operational Documents, Oclc.org. 2019. https://cgsc.contentdm.oclc.org/digital/collection/p4013coll8/id/3015/rec/2.

"Historical Report, Luzon Campaign, 43rd Infantry Division", WWII Operational Documents. Oclc.org, 2019, cgsc.contentdm.oclc.org/digital/collection/p4013coll8/id/4452/rec/5.

Michael Demko
"The Trail of 254 thru Blood & Fire." Peel, Harris. Bangor Community: Digital Commons@Bpl. 2025. https://digicom.bpl.lib.me.us/ww_reg_his/46/.
"63rd Infantry Division - 'Blood and Fire' - WorldWarTwoVeterans.com." Worldwartwoveterans.org. 2025. https://worldwartwoveterans.org/63rd-infantry-division-blood-and-fire/.
"F Company 254th Infantry Regiment 63rd Infantry Division – WorldWarTwoVeterans.com." Worldwartwoveterans.org. 2025. https://worldwartwoveterans.org/f-company-254th-infantry-regiment-63rd-infantry-division/.
"Jebsheim – a Town Turned into a Slaughterhouse." Standwheretheyfoughts Jimdo Page! 2018. https://standwheretheyfought.jimdofree.com/alsace-2011-the-battle-of-jebsheim-jan-24-feb-2-1945-then-and-now/.

Stephen G. Monick
"Page 2 in US, Missing Air Crew Reports (MACRs), WWII, 1942-1947." Fold3. 2025. https://www.fold3.com/document/28632568/.
"B-17 Bomber Flying Fortress – the Queen of the Skies." B17flyingfortress.de. 2022. http://b17flyingfortress.de.
"100th Bomb Group Home - 100th Bomb Group Foundation." 100th Bomb Group Foundation. 2025. http://100thbg.com.

John Matola
"The Enoura Maru Project", G. Kupsky, Historian, DPAA US Dept of Defense. https://www.dpaa.mil/Portals/85/WWII%20Hellship%20Losses.pdf

"The Japanese 'Hell Ships' of World War II." Navy.mil. 2020. https://www.history.navy.mil/browse-by-topic/wars-conflicts-and-operations/world-war-ii/1944/oryoku-maru.html.

Joseph P. Platko
"94th Infantry Division Historical Society Home Page, a WWII Army Division." 2017. 94thinfdiv.com. 2017. https://94thinfdiv.com/.
"US Army Divisions." US Army Divisions. 2025. https://www.armydivs.com/94th-infantry-divsion.
"History of the 94th Infantry Division in World War II : United States. Army. 94th Division : Internet Archive." Internet Archive. 2015. https://archive.org/details/HistoryOfThe94thInfantryWWII.

Anthony F. Laszewski
"7th Infantry Division (United States)." Wikipedia. 2024. https://en.wikipedia.org/wiki/7th_Infantry_Division_(United_States).
"32nd Infantry Regiment (United States)." Wikipedia, 2024. https://en.wikipedia.org/wiki/32nd_Infantry_Regiment_(United_States)

Ernest J. Kachursky
"5th Btn." 2024. Wwiirangers.org. 2024. https://wwiirangers.org/our-history/ranger-history/5th-btn/.
"Battalion History | 5th Rangers c Company." 5th Ranger c Company. 2025. https://www.5thrangerbncco.com/battalionhistory.

Anthony Rizzuto
"394th Bombardment Group (USAAF)." Historyofwar.org. 2025. https://www.historyofwar.org/air/units/USAAF/394th_Bombardment_Group.html.
"Mid-Air Collision Accident Martin B-26G Marauder 43-34228, Sunday 25 February 1945." Aviation-Safety.net. 2025. https://aviation-safety.net/wikibase/109844.

Carl Ramsey

"The 4th Marine Division in World War II : Chapin, John c : Internet Archive." Internet Archive. 2025. https://archive.org/details/The4thMarineDivisionInWorldWarII.

"History of the 4th Marine Division, 1943-2000 : United States. Marine Corps. Marine Division, 4th. Historical Detachment : Internet Archive." Internet Archive. 2025. https://archive.org/details/HistoryOfThe4thMarineDivision1943-2000/page/n23/mode/2up.

"Fourth Marine Division Operations Report, Iwo Jima, 19 February to 16 March, 1945 : Fourth Marine Division Cre : Free Download, Borrow, and Streaming : Internet Archive." Internet Archive. 2025. https://archive.org/details/OperationsReport4thMarineDivisionIwoJima/page/n1/mode/2up.

"US Marine Corps Casualties - Killed and Died, World War 2." Naval-History.net. 2025. https://www.naval-history.net/WW2UScasaaDB-US-MCbyNameR.htm.

"Combat Engineer" Wikipedia. https://en.wikipedia.org/wiki/Combat_engineer

Andy Evanich

"History of the Third Infantry Division in World War II : United States. Army. 3rd Division: Internet Archive." Internet Archive. 2015. https://archive.org/details/HistoryOfTheThirdID.

Paul Grata

"USS Franklin (CV 13) World War II Cruise Book 1944-45 - Chapter One - Big Ben Is Born." Navysite.de, 2025, www.navysite.de/cruise-books/cv13-45/011.htm.

"Aircraft Carrier Franklin." WW2DB, 2015, ww2db.com/ship_spec.php?ship_id=386.

"USS Franklin CV-13 War Damage Report No. 56." Public1.Nhhcaws.local, www.history.navy.mil/research/library/online-reading-room/title-list-alphabetically/w/war-damage-reports/uss-franklin-cv-13-war-damage-report-no-56.html.

Andrew Zrenchak

Buhay Batangas. "The 187th Regiment and How It Overcame the Japanese on Mt. Maculot in 1945." Batangas History, Culture and Folklore. July 27, 2018. https://www.batangashistory.date/2018/07/187th.html.

Buhay Batangas. "Photos of the Battle at Mt. Maculot 1945." Batangas History, Culture and Folklore. February 2018. https://www.batangashistory.date/2018/06/maculot.html.

"Pacific Paratrooper." Pacific Paratrooper. 2025. https://pacificparatrooper.wordpress.com/.

Louis G. Katsuleris

"US Army Divisions." US Army Divisions. 2025. https://www.armydivs.com/26th-infantry-division.

"26th Division, Summary of Operations in the World War" Prepared by the American Battle Monuments Commission, 1944. https://babel.hathitrust.org/cgi/pt?id=uc1.b3125042&seq=7

"104th Infantry Regiment (United States)." Wikipedia. https://en.wikipedia.org/wiki/104th_Infantry_Regiment_(United_States)

Carl A. Kronander

"35th Infantry Regiment." 25th Infantry Division Association. April 18, 2016. https://www.25thida.org/units/infantry/35th-infantry-regiment/.

"Dalton Pass." Wikipedia. Wikimedia Foundation. 2024. https://en.wikipedia.org/wiki/Dalton_Pass

Carl G. Cekola

"442nd Troop Carrier Group | American Air Museum." Americanairmuseum.com. February 10, 2017. https://www.americanairmuseum.com/archive/unit/442nd-troop-carrier-group.

"305th TROOP CARRIER SQUADRON (HEAVY)" https://ww38.usa-funithistory.com/PDF/0300/305%20TROOP%20CARRIER%20SQ.pdf

"Saint-André-De-l'Eure Airfield." Wikipedia. 2023. https://en.wikipedia.org/wiki/Saint-Andr%C3%A9-de-l%27Eure_Airfield

Jack W. Swaney

"THE FINAL CAMPAIGN: Marines in the Victory on Okinawa." Ibiblio.org. 2019. https://www.ibiblio.org/hyperwar/USMC/USMC-C-Okinawa/index.html.

"CMH Pub 11-1 Chronology: 1941-1945" M. Williams. 1960. https://archive.org/details/CMHPub11-1-nsia

Hugh B. Smyth

Jones, Wilbur D. "Remembering Bluethenthal Army Air Base: When the Skies Were Filled with Patrols, Training." Wilmington Star-News, Wilmington StarNews, 14 Nov. 2021, www.starnewsonline.com/story/news/2021/11/14/bluethenthal-army-air-base-during-world-war-ii-new-hanover/6384065001/.

"318th Fighter Group - WWII - World War II - Army Air Forces." Armyaircorpsmuseum.org. 2025. http://www.armyaircorpsmuseum.org/318th_Fighter_Group.cfm.

Microfilmed records at the Air Force Historical Research Agency at Maxwell AFB, Reel B0239.

Hosey Dawkins

"Engineer Aviation Battalions." National Museum of the United States Air Force™. 2025. https://www.nationalmuseum.af.mil/Visit/Museum-Exhibits/Fact-Sheets/Display/Article/196123/engineer-aviation-battalions/.

"Aviation Engineers on Guam." Brown, HE. 1945. "The Military Engineer 37 (240): 398–401. https://doi.org/10.2307/44606854.

"Corps of Engineers Units" Www.cbi-History.com. https://www.cbi-history.com/part_iv_eng.html#TOC.

1864th EAB Historical Report, September 4, 1945, AFHRA Reel A0284
P 616-679

1946

Matthew Comko
"Accident Douglas C-47A (DC-3) 42-24374, Monday 19 August 1946."
Flightsafety.org. 2025. https://asn.flightsafety.org/asndb/337234.
"910th AIRCRAFT MAINTENANCE SQUADRON - OCP." Flight-
lineinsignia.com, 2025, flightlineinsignia.com/product/910th-aircraft-mainte-
nance-squadron-ocp/.
"The Lusty Men." Eaglehorse.org. 2016. https://www.eagle-
horse.org/home_station/hidden_stories/40s/lusty_men/lusty_men.htm.

About Ancestry.com Family Trees and Profiles

For each US service member included in this book, a family tree and profile was created on Ancestry.com by John J. Turanin between 2022-2025. Each
was created solely for the purpose of researching public records for each Monessen WWII Fallen service member and establishing a repository for the evidence contained in their story. These family trees should not be regarded as
complete ancestral histories.

The Ancestry.com profile of each service member contains select images,
public documents, news articles, and links to public records related to the individual and their immediate family members. The author did his best to con-
firm any material information found in any family trees created by other
Ancestry members.

Research was limited to immediate family members and to ancestors who
could establish the heritage of the individual's paternal and maternal families
where possible. Diligence was focused upon the profiles of the individual and
their parents and if applicable, the spouse; Other than demographic information, the accuracy of information collected within the profiles of siblings
and other family members may require further examination by those inter-
ested.

"Public Member Trees," database, Ancestry.com (http://www.ancestry.com). All trees and Profiles were created by John J. Turanin 2022-2025 and entitled with the following surnames:

Bartosik	Komlos	Ravenchak
Beck	Koszykowski	Redish
Boyer	Kronander	Renzetti
Caville	Kujawa	Restaino
Cekola	Kvaka	Rizzuto
Cipriani	Laszewski	Rosenson
Columbus	Leavor	Sacchini
Comko	Leone	Saridakis
Dawkins	Liscik	Scrip
Demko	Lucas	Sholtis
Denitti	Malena	Skruber
Desack	Malinchak	Smyth
Evanich	Marcinkiewicz	Stanish
Fiorillo	Matola	Stephens
Gramatikos	Mazzer	Stockus
Grata	McVay	Stonage
Hagerty	Mihalich	Swaney
Harkema	Monick	Thiry
Hotovchin	Monios	Trilli
Imburgia	Naccarato	Varga
Irvine	Newman	Wargo
Jennings	Nicoden	Woods
Junk	Oliphant	Zajaczkowski
Kachursky	Parnella	Zapora
Kafkalas	Platko	Zazac
Kalie	Quinlan	Zrenchak
Katsuleris	Ramsey	

ABOUT THE AUTHOR

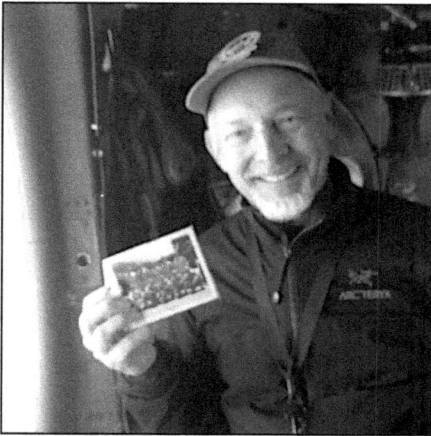

John J. Turanin, a native of Western Pennsylvania, is retired from a career in the life sciences industry. He has authored more than 200 memorial stories for Stories Behind The Stars, a non-profit organization whose volunteers are writing memorial stories for all US service members who lost their lives during WWII.

John is an amateur military historian who has served as a docent at aviation history museums. With a large library of military aircraft flight and maintenance manuals, he works with warbird restoration projects around the world to secure equipment essential for restoring aircraft to static display or to flight service (via AeroAntique.com). John has had the good fortune to fly as a passenger in restored WWII bombers Boeing B-17 Flying Fortress, Consolidated B-24 Liberator, and Boeing B-29 Superfortress.

John Turanin flying in his father's gunner position in the restored B-29 Superfortress bomber "Fifi". In his hand is a photo of his father's crew in 1945.

He is a resident of El Dorado Hills, California, and can be contacted at jjturanin@gmail.com.

★★★

www.ingramcontent.com/pod-product-compliance
Lightning Source LLC
Chambersburg PA
CBHW062355090426
42740CB00010B/1290